THREE PLAYS BY

GEORGE KELLY

THREE PLAYS BY

GEORGE KELLY

THE TORCH-BEARERS
THE SHOW-OFF
CRAIG'S WIFE

Biographical and Critical Essays
by William J. Lynch

FOREWORD BY WENDY WASSERSTEIN

LIMELIGHT EDITIONS
NEW YORK

PUBLISHED BY THE PRINCESS GRACE FOUNDATION-USA
Distributed by Limelight Editions, imprint of Proscenium Publishers Inc.,
118 East 30th Street, New York, New York 10016

George Kelly's plays, *The Torch-Bearers*, *The Show-Off*, and *Craig's Wife*, are
reprinted with the permission of the George Kelly Trust. All inquiries regarding
performance rights must be referred to Samuel French, Inc., 45 West 25th Street,
Dept. W, New York, NY 10010

Biographical and Critical Essays by William J. Lynch © William J. Lynch, 1999

Foreword by Wendy Wasserstein © Wendy Wasserstein, 1999

Library of Congress Cataloging-in-Publication Data

Kelly, George, 1887-1974
  [Plays. Selections]
  Three plays / by George Kelly: biographical and critical essays
  By William J. Lynch; foreword by Wendy Wasserstein. — 1st Limelight ed.
    p. cm.
  At head of title: A publication of the Princess Grace Foundation.
  Included biographical references.
  Contents: The torchbearers — The show-off — Craig's wife.
  ISBN 0-87910-282-9. — ISBN 0-87910-279-9 (pbk.)
  I. Lynch, William J. II. Princess Grace Foundation. III. Title. IV. Title: 3 plays
  by George Kelly.
  PS9521.E425AS 1999
  812'.52–dc21   99-19841
  CIP

Book design by Gloria Adelson/Lulu Graphics

First Edition, April 1999

CONTENTS

Princess Grace Awards

FOR ASPIRING YOUNG THEATER, DANCE AND FILM ARTISTS IN AMERICA

During Her lifetime, H.S.H. Princess Grace of Monaco was deeply committed to helping aspiring young artists realize their career goals. This, too, is the mission of the Foundation named in Her honor.

National in scope, the Princess Grace Awards are dedicated to identifying and assisting young talent in theater, dance, and film through grants in the form of scholarships, apprenticeships, and fellowships.

Awarded on an annual basis, the first grant recipients were named in 1984. Since then, it has become increasingly clear how vital a role the Foundation plays in encouraging new generations of artists.

The Foundation's trustees share Princess Grace's dedication to supporting the arts, and they believe, as She did, that cultivation and training of emerging young talent in America is a priority to ensure sustained excellence in the arts.

The Arts Advisory Board, composed of three panels, one for each area of grants awarded, reviews the nominations and makes recommendations to the Board of Trustees.

Incorporated in 1982, the Princess Grace Foundation-USA is a tax-exempt, non-profit, publicly supported organization. Contributions are welcome and are tax deductible by law.

ACKNOWLEDGMENTS

For financial and moral support, many thanks are due to the Princess Grace Foundation-USA, especially to John F. Lehman, chairman of the board. Much gratitude also goes to Gloria Adelson, the talented graphic designer, and to Carol Edwards, the eagle-eyed editor, for their exceptional work in bringing this book to final form.

Grateful acknowledgment is also made to The Free Library of Philadelphia for permission to use the photos included in this book and to Geraldine Duclow, head of the Library's Theatre Collection, whose expertise and generous assistance have been greatly appreciated.

FOREWORD BY
WENDY WASSERSTEIN

George Kelly's plays are not "edgy." They do not confront an audience with the author's riveting rage. The plays in this volume are not parables of social injustice nor hilarious indictments of the ruling elite. There is nothing politically incorrect or correct about these collected plays of George Kelly. They are just amazingly good.

Looking for some sweeping generalization to describe these very different works, I kept returning to "American Classics." These plays have grown with hindsight and now take their place beside the other American masters of the period: Philip Barry, S. N. Behrman, Maxwell Anderson. Like these mainstream writers in the Golden Age of American Theatre, George Kelly had an ear and eye for how we live. When theatre was still the popular American art form, George Kelly put the lives of his audience on the stage. Any matinee lady at a performance of *The Torch-Bearers* had surely dabbled in a bit of amateur theatre. Certainly someone's neighbor in the balcony of *The Show-Off* had a tendency to exaggerate just like Aubrey Piper. And, finally, what husband seeing *Craig's Wife* after a busy day at the office wouldn't ruminate that he was as much under the thumb of an overbearing mate as Walter Craig.

These plays endure because the craft and eye of the playwright endures. George Kelly's plays are character comedies. In other words, even the sharpest satire derives not from pratfalls or one-liners, but from the keenly observed obsessions and neuroses of personalities. Mrs. J. Duro Pampinelli, Aubrey Piper, and even Harriet Craig are the larger-than-life characters in all of our lives. The genius of George Kelly is that he took their innate theatricality out of the middle-class domestic drawing room and into the theatre.

Comedy, that ability to prick an audience into unified gasping submission, is a highly under-rated skill. Ask any playwright who dares to indulge in it, and he or she will tell you it's the hardest trick to pull off because it is immediately obvious when it isn't working. *The Torch-Bearers* is a deeply funny play. Loving satirists of their own craft from Shakespeare and George S. Kaufman to contemporaries such as Paul Rudnick and Christopher Guest have all sharpened their pens on amateur groups with pretensions of professionals. According to Gerald Gutierrez, the Tony Award-winning director of *The Heiress* and *A Delicate Balance*, "George Kelly created the amateur from hell with Mrs. J. Duro Pampinelli because he knew her cold. She is, for anyone who loves the theatre in any era, simply hilarious."

Mrs. Pampinelli is also the well-known first in the, shall we say, non-wallflower parts for women created by Mr. Kelly. Mrs. Pampinelli's opinions on theatre are about as sacred and profound to her as Mrs. Fisher's opinions on marriage in *The Show-Off*. Amazingly, Mr. Kelly has taken the traditional "character" roles, the stuff that supporting comic parts are made of, and transformed them into the female leads. A didactic ideologist could argue that George Kelly was wrong to portray these women as stubborn, illogical, or even silly. But I would make a case, as would many actresses over thirty-five, that what George Kelly did was in the the mainstream feminist tradition. He actually dared to make the character woman the lead. Looking back over American Drama it is in the social mores plays of George Kelly and Philip Barry that women found some of their juiciest leading roles.

Any comic writer, those of us who can't resist a turn of phrase or an out-of-left-field revelation, will say they also consider their work to be quite serious. The skill of the playwright is finding a balance between the comic and serious texture in each play. As George Kelly's plays evolve so do their serious proportions. *The Show-Off* is a comic masterpiece, an airtight manipulation of domestic values and the outside world's estimation of economic success. And just like any comic masterpiece there is something hauntingly sad about it. Somewhere Mrs. Fisher seems profoundly lonely and Aubrey Piper, the show-off to end all show-offs, is trapped in a narcissistic game of pretend. It is no wonder to me that a great clown like Red Skelton or the very masculine Spencer Tracy played Aubrey in the film versions. He is an American everyman; loving, devoted, lonely and lost.

In many ways the Pulitzer Prize-winning *Craig's Wife* seems to be the synthesis of these plays. Mrs. Craig's fanaticism in the domestic details of her life could be easily satirized. But here the playwright instead lets his character's determination and outrageous belief in her own rules of order destroy the very backbone of her life. Walter Craig shattering his wife's vase has the resonance of *The Heiress* demanding "Bolt the door, Maria" when Morris Townsend comes to call or Hedda Gabler tossing Lovborg's manuscript into the fireplace. There is no turning back from these acts. The die is cast and forever a life is changed.

Again in Harriet Craig we have a larger-than-life female lead with a powerful determination. Is she destructive to those around her? Yes. But, frankly, Phaedre or Medea weren't so great to be around in their domestic situations either. Furthermore, from a feminist point of view, Harriet is a direct descendant of her sexual class. There is nowhere else for Harriet to place substantial organizational skills than in the domestic details of her house. In a way *Craig's Wife* is a perfect feminist call to arms. Both Walter and Harriet, husband and wife, need a different domestic model—the one they live in is clearly suffocating them.

Styles in the theater inevitably change. No playwright will occupy his or her place similarly for every generation. The criteria change and even the playwright's body of work changes. But what is so stunning about this collection is that it further substantiates the American Theatre's claim to the tradition of the well-crafted play of social manners. It is a tradition in which we have always bowed to the British, be it Terrence Rattigan, Noel Coward, or currently Alan Ayckbourne. Ranging from the high comic satire of *The Torch-Bearers*, the character cavalcade of *The Show-Off* and the well-made tragedy of *Craig's Wife*, the plays of George Kelly encompass pure examples of a genre often ignored as our theatrical tradition.

When Walter Craig tells his wife that he will be going "where a lot like me are going out of fashion," he surely wasn't referring to a style of playwriting. But just in case he was, I am, for one, extremely grateful to have it brought back in this wonderfully inspiring collection. Reexamining George Kelly's plays could begin a refreshingly important reexploration in contemporary American Theatre.

THREE PLAYS BY

GEORGE KELLY

The Kelly Family circa, 1900

Standing (l. to r.) Walter, Charles, Kate (Mrs. Patrick Kelly), George, Patrick ("PH")

Seated (l. to r.) Mary (daughter), John B., John, Sr., John II (grandson), Mary, Grace, Anne

THE KELLY MEN

Standing (l. to r.): Charles Kelly, George Kelly,
John B. Kelly, Patrick ("P.H.") Kelly
Seated (l. to r.): John Kelly, Sr., Walter C. Kelly

GEORGE KELLY
THE MAN

The much-used adjective *conservative* describes George Kelly in almost every aspect of his person, his life, and his work. Although his early stage successes and his years of film work made him a wealthy man, his spending and investments were careful, his tastes simple, and his living habits almost Spartan. Unlike the legendary Algonquin crowd, he never became part of the fashionable New York literary and intellectual scene, and he was seldom photographed or interviewed, even in his glory years. He preferred an anonymous solitude, consecrating his entire life to his calling as a dramatist, which he deemed as sacred as that of a priest.

Kelly's passion for anonymity was a double-edged sword. It gave him time to pursue his work and whatever travel he wished to undertake, without the extensive social demands placed upon him as a distinguished theatrical personage. But his deliberate avoidance of publicity (there are precious few articles or photographs of him), along with his inability to repeat the continued successful output of his early years, helped to contribute to the image of a writer who was fading from theatrical existence both personally and artistically. Of all the major playwrights of his era, his name provokes the least recognition; yet his plays, once mentioned by name or described by plot, invariably elicit a favorable, even warm response.

Fastidious by nature, Kelly was conservative even in his dress. Tall (six foot one) and spare (never over 175 pounds), with long dark brown (later gray) hair and brown eyes, he favored sport jackets and flannel trousers, solid-colored shirts and ties, and dark shoes. He was soft-spoken, humorous, and, when among intimates, given to the role of raconteur. He had an amazing memory, not just for his own plays but also for the writing of others. He loved to quote from literary works, especially plays and poems. These ranged from Shakespearean excerpts to sentimental poetry of the nineteenth century—for example, John Greenleaf Whittier's "Maud Muller," Robert Bulwer-Lytton's "Aux Italiens," and Thomas Moore's "Paradise and the Peri." He was erect and theatrical in bearing, with a resonant but modulated voice, articulate and precise in his diction. He reminded one of a genteel nineteenth-century cleric—a theatrical Cardinal Newman.

Though Kelly's temperament was basically a gentle, reserved one, he could be firm, even single-minded in his convictions. He was scrupulously consistent in his refusal to discuss his private life, especially his youth, and was careful to destroy any personal material that would be of possible assistance to a biographer. He refused any suggested attempt at autobiography; he would always offer humility as his motive for declining such an undertaking, but the real reason was probably his almost fanatic desire for anonymity. He never abandoned his delightful, but a trifle forbidding, dramatic pose. He was always in control of his mind, of his emotions; one was permitted only as much a glimpse into him as he would allow.

Critics have described Kelly as reclusive, but he was merely selective of his company. He preferred dinner and postprandial conversation with a tiny group of intimates to a large gathering, formal or informal. He took particular care of his health; except for an occasional game of golf, he scorned sports, despite the athletic side of his family. He watched his diet carefully; he almost never used alcohol and gave up smoking after having suffered his only real illness, a bleeding ulcer, during his fifties. Yet he was an easy victim of fall and winter colds, a major reason for his attraction to the temperate climate of California. And even his travel to and from there was done conservatively—always by train, until his final trip to Philadelphia, by plane. His trips to Europe were by boat, and always in the first-class section.

Kelly seldom associated with his fellow playwrights. Philip Barry, the Harvard-educated author of comedies of manners, and Thornton Wilder, the prep school teacher turned playwright, came closest to him in temperament, but neither was ever a close friend. He would see them only occasionally, usually at meetings of the Dramatists Guild, founded to protect playwrights' financial and legal rights. He seldom attended the plays of others; he preferred to concentrate on the perfection of his own work, as author and director.

Edward Maisel, in a penetrating essay on Kelly's career, firmly establishes Kelly the playwright as a born moralist.[*] Certainly he was so in his private life, and his morality was essentially an old-fashioned and personal one, based on the ethos of hard work, clean living, honesty, and personal virtue. He was capable of acts of kindness and generosity, but he usually preferred his charitable donations to remain anonymous. Most of all, he despised vulgarity in every form: speech, dress, manners, and values. Its frequent presence in the modern theater contributed to his gradual withdrawal from his profession. Still, he recognized the essential literary worth of playwrights like O'Neill and later Tennessee Williams, both of whose plays were uninhibited in their use of frank sexual themes and language.

Kelly's sexual morality was a rigid one. As his plays (for example, *Behold the Bridegroom*, *The Deep Mrs. Sykes*, et al.) indi-

[*]Edward Maisel, "The Theater of George Kelly," *Theater Arts*, February 1947, 41.

cate, he believed in the sanctity of marriage, although in an impossible situation (for example, see *Craig's Wife, The Fatal Weakness*), he could understand a separation, even a divorce. He was less tolerant toward adultery and casual sex.

Arthur Lewis, a Kelly family biographer, asserts that Kelly was a homosexual, but he offers as speculative proof only a kind gesture performed by Kelly for a young hotel clerk (he loaned the lad money for his college tuition).* Certainly Kelly preferred bachelorhood to the married state, and he always had a live-in valet/cook, who occasionally served as a travel companion. But basically he was a loner, devoted to his work, and puritanical about sexual matters. There was a strong monastic side to him, which would indicate a bent toward celibacy rather than any sexual preference of a strong nature. All his emotions were channeled into his writing, to which he was as firmly devoted as a monk to his life of cloistered contemplation.

As one would expect, Kelly's politics were those of a right-wing Republican. He had made it to the top of his profession by a combination of talent and dedication. Consequently, he viewed the Democratic party's social legislation as nothing more than a senseless giveaway of his tax money to those who were unwilling to work as hard as he. He despised Franklin D. Roosevelt (frequently alluding to him as "the great knave"). He did not share the national adulation of John F. Kennedy, despite their common ties of religion and Irish ancestry. He was an admirer of Dwight D. Eisenhower and a staunch defender of Richard Nixon, even after Watergate. He generally disapproved of unions, but he was sympathetic to Actors' Equity because he had seen much managerial abuse in his early touring days as a performer. He was a rigid anti-Communist, and he deeply resented the influence of left-wing playwrights like Clifford Odets, who, he felt, were attempting to change the theater from a temple of morality to a raucous political arena.

Perhaps in an effort to overcome his limited formal education, Kelly became a voracious but selective reader. He read

*Arthur Lewis, *Those Philadelphia Kellys* (New York: William Morrow, 1977), 124.

heavily in classical and Elizabethan drama, but little of the work of modern playwrights except Ibsen and Strindberg. He preferred Longfellow and Whittier to Whitman, Frost, and Eliot. He enjoyed Victorian fiction, especially the novels of Dickens, Eliot, and Thackeray. He avoided the psychiatric/psychological writings of Freud and Jung, whom he contemptuously categorized as "the mentalists," and disclaimed any of their influence on his work.

Kelly was unusually interested in religious writing. Though born into a strict Irish-Catholic family, throughout most of his life he was only a casual observer of formal Roman Catholic worship, partly because his heavy acting and writing schedule made compulsory Mass attendance extremely difficult, if not impossible. In addition, his reclusive nature made private devotions preferable to public ones. He read heavily in the Scriptures, and such mystical writers as John of the Cross, Teresa of Avila, Thomas à Kempis, and Thomas Merton, and would attend religious or philosophical lectures, regardless of their denomination. He was outspoken in his criticism of Christian Science, though he could quote liberally from the works of Mary Baker Eddy. In the last two decades of his life, he became more faithful, even devout, in his observance of the rituals of pre–Vatican II Catholicism. He preferred the Latin Mass to the later vernacular rite with its guitars and "kiss of peace," both which he considered common and most unaesthetic.

For all his pose as a *laudator temporis acti*, Kelly was essentially a happy, well-adjusted individualist. Because of a frugal lifestyle and sound financial investments, he was able to live comfortably within his own world. He despised the ostentation and rudeness of the nouveau riche even more than what he considered the vulgar behavior of the lower classes; he avoided both whenever possible. Yet he admired kindness and graciousness in any human being, and he was always comfortable in the presence of such a person.

George Kelly (1887–1974)

GEORGE KELLY
THE PLAYWRIGHT

George Kelly was born on January 16, 1887, in the East Falls section of Philadelphia. He was the seventh of ten children of John Henry Kelly, an immigrant from County Mayo, Ireland, and his American wife, Mary (née Costello).

The Kelly family was a poor but exceptionally talented one, and its members would eventually enjoy success in the business, athletic, and artistic worlds. The oldest son, Patrick Henry ("P.H."), became an eminent Philadelphia building contractor. Another son, Walter C., achieved international fame as a monologist ("The Virginia Judge") whose specialty was dialectal humor. The youngest son, John B., owned a prosperous brick business. He was an Olympic gold medal oarsman and emerged an important figure in the Democratic party of Pennsylvania. He was also the father of the late Grace, Princess of Monaco, a distinguished film and stage actress.

George's education was limited to a few years in elementary

school and some evening courses in draftsmanship. His true interest, however, was always the theater; in his early twenties, he left his position in a local steel company and set out for New York to make his living as an actor.

When Kelly began his acting career in 1911, the theater was still the primary source of mass entertainment in the United States, and acting jobs in touring companies were not hard to come by. From 1911 to 1916, Kelly barnstormed the country in crudely constructed comedies and melodramas, such as the stage adaptation of Owen Wister's novel *The Virginian*, in which he played the leading role. These years served as Kelly's apprenticeship, not just as an actor but as a future playwright, for he was getting the feel of different audiences as well as an introduction to diverse dramatic forms.

In 1915, Kelly entered vaudeville, at the time a respectable form of variety show, which featured such performers as Sarah Bernhardt, Ethel Barrymore, Sir Harry Lauder—and Walter C. Kelly. George scored a major acting triumph as the male lead in *Woman Proposes*, a sketch by Paul Armstrong, author of slight but popular melodramas like *Alias Jimmy Valentine*. Armstrong praised Kelly's performance and suggested that he write sketches for himself, as vaudeville had a constant need for fresh material.

Such advice was encouraging to Kelly, who had been copyrighting plays as early as 1912. So from 1916 to 1922, with a brief time out for army duty during World War I, he wrote, directed, and frequently acted in a succession of successful vaudeville sketches. *Mrs. Ritter Appears* (1919), a spoof of amateur theater, was the genesis of his first full-length play, *The Torch-Bearers; Poor Aubrey* (1919) would be expanded into his most popular comedy, *The Show-Off*.

By the early 1920s, Kelly had left vaudeville for good. His skills as a playwright had matured beyond "two-a-day" sketches, and constant travel, along with his directing chores, was cutting into his writing time. Producer Rosalie Stewart urged him to write three-act plays, and in 1922, she produced *The*

Torch-Bearers, his hilarious satire of the Little Theatre. It became an immediate hit, thrusting the hitherto-unknown playwright into the talented new group of American dramatists headed by the future Nobel Prize winner Eugene O'Neill.

Kelly's next play, *The Show-Off* (1924), was a major triumph, a critical and popular success. This penetrating comedy of Philadelphia row-house life was the judges' solid choice for the 1924 Pulitzer Prize, but Columbia University, which officially awards the honor, rejected the judges' decision in favor of *Hell-Bent fer Heaven*, written by Hatcher Hughes, a Columbia faculty member. This unprecedented reversal of the jury's selection created a critical uproar, which was only partially quieted by the awarding of the 1926 Pulitzer to Kelly for his domestic tragedy, *Craig's Wife* (1925).

Kelly had reached eminent stature early in his career. He had attained financial and critical success both as a playwright and as a director. In the latter capacity, his reputation had become almost legendary. He had a precise sense of timing and knew every nuance of his characters; he also had an exceptional ear for dialogue and demanded that his players follow his instructions precisely. As far as Kelly was concerned, his was the only interpretation of his characters, and he would permit no deviation from it; he would even act out a male or female role himself during rehearsal in order to demonstrate exactly what he wanted in a performance. He was a martinet, but his casts respected his wishes because they knew that he was a perfectionist and that the result would be a first-class product, which critics would describe almost reverently as a distinctive creation: "the Kelly Play."

Although Kelly's first two plays were remarkable for their comic moments, he never considered himself anything but a serious dramatist, and the success of *Craig's Wife* proved his ability as such a playwright. He believed that the theater was a place for moral instruction as well as for entertainment, and underlying his amusing dialogue there was always a serious theme. His next play, *Daisy Mayme* (1926) was a study of greed within a middle-class family, and *Behold the Bridegroom* (1927), his personal favorite, was an incisive moral tragedy about a hedonistic upper-class woman. *Maggie the Magnificent* (1929) was a bitter play, centered on a turbulent mother-daughter relationship. But all three were commercial failures, and Kelly began to be disillusioned with the theater for the first time. The critics and public seemed to want him only as a comic dramatist, whom they could forgive for an occasional successful serious play such as *Craig's Wife*.

And then came a change in the entire tone of the American theater. During the Great Depression of the 1930s, audiences began to demand a type of drama centered on the common man and his struggle for economic survival. Strident dramas of social protest arose from young leftist organizations like the Group Theatre. The public turned away from Kelly's stylized studies of character to the crude but exciting protest dramas of Clifford Odets, the eccentric whimsies of William Saroyan, the shocking melodramas of Lillian Hellman, and the escapist comedies of Kaufman and Hart.

Kelly was not comfortable in such company. He dismissed proletariat drama as loud, chaotic, and, above all, vulgar. So when *Philip Goes Forth*, his 1931 satire of an aspiring but untalented playwright, failed, he retreated to Hollywood and a well-paid but unsatisfying job as a screenwriter for MGM. He returned to the Broadway stage only once during this decade—in 1936, when *Reflected Glory*, a study of backstage life, starring Tallulah Bankhead, had a short run.

By the time World War II was drawing to a close, the bleakness and anger of the thirties had been replaced by a certain stability, even euphoria, in the United States. Kelly chose this postwar period for his final offerings. *The Deep Mrs. Sykes*, a penetrating portrait of an egocentric, "intuitive" wife, was produced in 1945; this was followed by a charming high comedy, *The Fatal Weakness* (1946). The critics were glad to see Kelly back, but they gave his two plays only mixed notices, and the public once more failed to attend. A 1947 revival of *Craig's Wife*, directed by Kelly, received a similar reception.

Through it all, Kelly always preserved an admirable, if somewhat stubborn, sense of personal creative pride. He refused to write for mere commercial success; he would not pander to the shifting values and tastes of the American theatergoer, and he declined to turn out "more of the same," however successful his most recent play might have been.

Kelly was not an experimenter. Early in his career, he settled on his own particular brand of realistic-naturalistic drama and stayed doggedly within it. His was not the cosmic sense of tragic vision that marked the dramas of O'Neill. Kelly's scope was more narrow, more earthbound. He concentrated mostly on American middle-class characters in a domestic setting, and there attempted to reveal their foibles and weaknesses, usually with a touch of wry humor. He presented a world whose men and women were recognizable individuals, capable of free will and ultimately responsible for their actions. Not for him were the Freudian or Marxist trends of the twenties and thirties that explained away human behavior on the basis of the unconscious or of economics. Tragic or comic, his people were their own masters, and he rewarded or punished them according to his own conservative morality, usually tempered by his essential good humor.

The three plays in this volume show Kelly at his best. There is general critical agreement that he was one of the finest portrayers of women in the twentieth-century American theater. He had an instinctive understanding of the female personality, which he could project with uncanny dramatic accuracy. Thus, *The Torch-Bearers* features Mrs. J. Duro Pampanelli, the forceful but foolish directress of amateur theater; *The Show-Off* has Mrs. Fisher, the acidulous mother-in-law of the title character; and *Craig's Wife* exposes the conniving, cynical nature of its protagonist, Harriet Craig.

These plays also demonstrate Kelly's ability to reproduce dialogue with remarkable accuracy. He was a master at making the speech fit the character, to whatever station in life he or she belongs. Thus, he could move from the literate upper-middle-class talk of *The Torch-Bearers* and *Craig's Wife* to the frequently ungrammatical but always recognizable row-house dialect of the working and lower-middle classes that lends authenticity to *The Show-Off*.

The Torch-Bearers, *The Show-Off*, and *Craig's Wife* demonstrate Kelly's dramatic versatility. He was at ease with satirical farce, domestic comedy, and domestic tragedy. And the universality of their characters and themes preserve the plays from any sign of datedness. For there will always be an amateur theater and it will inevitably have its share of humorous but incompetent figures like Mrs. Pampanelli. The obnoxious but good-natured, loudmouthed dreamer Aubrey Piper will invariably find a natural antagonist like Mrs. Fisher, Piper's sharp-tongued, provincial mother-in-law. And marriages such as that of the cold, dominating Harriet Craig and her guileless, gentle Walter are always with us.

George Kelly died on June 18, 1974, in a hospital in Bryn Mawr, Pennsylvania, about fifteen miles from his birthplace. Just before he left Philadelphia in 1971 to take up permanent residence in Sun City, California, he destroyed what few personal documents he had chosen to keep. A lifelong bachelor, he was a modest, retiring man, with a virtual fetish for anonymity, and he firmly opposed any biography of himself. He always preferred that his plays speak for him; *The Torch-Bearers*, *The Show-Off*, and *Craig's Wife* fulfill his wish most eloquently.

THE
TORCH-BEARERS

THE TORCH-BEARERS

The *Torch-Bearers*, George Kelly's first full-length play, opened on Broadway in August 1922 and achieved instant critical success, as well as a respectable and profitable run of 130 performances. It is an expansion of *Mrs. Ritter Appears*, Kelly's 1919 vaudeville sketch, which basically constitutes the third act of the longer play. Both comedies are satires of the Little Theatre movement, which was enjoying an increase in popularity among the American middle class during the prosperous twenties.

The amateur theater has always been an essentially harmless pastime, which gives a personal satisfaction to its participants and a pleasant few hours to a small, often undiscriminating, but usually enthusiastic audience. Kelly sees the darker side of the Little Theatre. He concentrates his satire on its foolish egotists, who gravitate to the movement as actors and, worst of all, directors.

One of the latter is Mrs. J. Duro Pampanelli, the talentless matron of *The Torch-Bearers,* whose larger-than-life presence makes her the central satirical target of Kelly's play. She and her band of sincere but absolutely incompetent amateurs provide the bulk of the play's humor in their clumsy first-act rehearsal and disastrous second-act performance of a melodramatic sketch.

Mrs. Pampanelli is a dangerous influence both theatrically and personally. Talentless and untrained, she has dared to intrude upon a profession to which Kelly has devoted his life. Worse, she has misled others with her hilarious but foolish instructions, punctuating her tips on character interpretation with an insistence on sweeping gestures, grand entrances, and long, pointless dramatic pauses. (As Foster Hirsch notes, she is the very antithesis of Kelly the director, who insisted on low-keyed naturalistic performances from his casts.[*]) Finally she nearly breaks up the marriage of her ingenue, Paula Ritter, by urging her to leave her home and husband and go to New York to pursue an acting career.

Kelly pillories Pampanelli not just for professional incompetence but also for her overbearing vanity—two sins that rank high on his list of personal vices. Ironically, in doing so, he has created a memorable figure—one of the most colorful and funniest in all his plays.

The danger in satire is that it can emerge as mere caricature, even burlesque. Kelly has managed to avoid both in his masterful creation of Pampanelli, and he was particularly careful in his meticulous direction of Alison Skipworth, the talented comedienne who originated the role. In a letter to Margaret Anglin, whom he hoped to cast as Pampanelli in an 1938 revival of *The Torch-Bearers*, Kelly insisted that the part be played only by ". . . an absolutely legitimate actress . . . one that can play comedy—legitimately. For while she [Pampanelli] is a grand, damned fool, she doesn't know it. And most of the actresses that specialize in comedy roles find it difficult to keep within the limits of their characterization. And the result is caricature."[†]

Kelly is gentler with the rest of the amateurs, whom he depicts as an amusing group of bumblers taken in by Mrs. Pampanelli's formidable personality. There she is the multimarried, -divorced, -widowed Nelly Fell, the delightful gabby promptress who basks in the reflected glory of her colleagues. These include Huxley Hossefrosse, he of the booming voice and poor memory; Ralph

---

[*]Foster Hirsch, *George Kelly* (Boston: Twayne, 1975), 56.

[†]George Kelly, letter to Margaret Anglin, June 9, 1938; Theater Collection of the New York Public Library at Lincoln Center.

Twiller, ever late for his entrances and exits; and Teddy Spearing, given to fainting in mid-performance. Mr. Spindler, full of military precision gained from stateside World War I service, is Mrs. Pampanelli's fawning acolyte, ever ready with a quotation; bland Florence McCrickett has the title role in *The Doctor's Wife*, the group vehicle chosen for a one-time performance. Together, they constitute the most unintentionally hilarious troupe since Bully Bottom's gaggle of zanies in Shakespeare's *A Midsummer Night's Dream*. And quite the most inept performer of all is Paula Ritter, the "other woman" in the Pampanelli production.

Paula is a plump but attractive housewife whose dearth of dramatic talent is obvious to all but her cohorts and her gullible audience. Her ghastly first performance causes her husband, Fred, to faint twice in the play; the last unseen collapse occurs while he is witnessing Paula in action at Horticultural Hall ("Hutchy-Kutchy" to Mrs. Pampanelli). Fred Ritter's position in the play is an awkward one. He is certainly important as the spokesman for Kelly's views, but his position as an outsider in the midst of the rehearsal seems contrived. He is not present at all in the second act and is stiffly sententious in the third, prompting Percy Hammond to describe him as a "chill barbarian who kids the proceedings with a desperate venom."* To his credit, he obviously loves Paula and wants to protect her from further stage embarrassment; yet he also wants to keep her tied to her home, where both he and Kelly feel she really belongs. Hirsch observes that Ritter's last-act confrontations with Paula and Pampanelli constitute just another round in the battle of the sexes that would culminate in *Craig's Wife*.† In each case, Kelly's sympathy is with the male, and in *The Torch-Bearers* he allows Mr. Ritter to give the Kelly coup de grace to Mrs. Pampanelli and her ilk: "The theatre is a matter of qualifications— the same as any other profession; and it will be only through those qualifications that your Little Theatre will ever be brought about."

Both Hirsch‡ and Kenneth Macgowan (in his glowing preface

---

*Percy Hammond, review of *The Torch-Bearers*, *New York Herald Tribune*, August 3, 1922.
†Hirsch, *George Kelly*, 57.
‡Ibid., 55.

to the first edition of *The Torch-Bearers*)* observe that the comedy is not a "well-made play" in the Scribean sense. The three acts constitute the beginning, middle, and end of the play, but each is so different in tone and content that one can almost perceive the thin dramatic glue holding them together. The first act is purely expository, relatively low-key in its satire; Fred's fall on the staircase is its only incident of broad humor. The second act, the best of the play, alternates happily between farce and burlesque. However, it is united with the first act only on the flimsiest basis: the transition from a silly rehearsal to a hilarious performance. The serious, moralizing tone of the final act is too much of a contrast to the previous two. It is as if Kelly did not know how to end his comedy, but since he began his composition with the last act (*Mrs. Ritter Appears*), even this explanation is problematic.

There is no doubt that the final act seems more of an awkwardly added addition than the actual foundation of the play. Arthur Hobson Quinn, one of Kelly's earliest academic admirers, felt that the play built up to no real climax, and that its main significance was Kelly's development away from one-act sketches to "something more important."† Even Macgowan, while lauding Kelly's "strain of divine and devilish madness," found the act a "rather prosy" letdown.‡ There is also a question of the play's central conflict. Is it between Fred and Mrs. Pampanelli? If so, he may be the victor, but she dominates the play. Or does it focus on Ritter and his wife? There, Ritter wins again, but over a weak, rather silly opponent, and he must resort to the crude device of a fake phone call to carry the day.

Finally, there is the problem of the universality of Kelly's satirical theme. The Little Theatre has always had a genuine yet only limited appeal in the United States, but Robert A. Parker gave Kelly credit for making his audience believe that the movement was "no merely isolated symptom of American life."§ And a strong case

---

*Kenneth Macgowan, preface to George Kelly, *The Torch-Bearers* (New York: American Library Service, 1923), xv.

†Arthur Hobson Quinn, *A History of the American Drama from the Civil War to the Present Day*, rev. ed. (New York: Appleton-Century-Crofts, 1936), 225.

‡Macgowan, xv

§Robert A. Parker, "New Playwrights and New Producers," *The Independent*, December 3, 1922.

could be made that the major target of Kelly's satire is as much personal as theatrical—the foolish vanity that permeates Mrs. Pampanelli and her ridiculous cohorts. There is also Kelly's sense of amusement at the secret that he had revealed so cleverly in his vaudeville sketch *The Flattering Word*: that in our souls we are all born actors and thus potential prey to all the Pampanellis of the world.

As an added treat, Kelly has indulged in a bit of "inside," self-deprecating humor. The one-act play that the amateurs attempt is actually a combination of two of Kelly's earlier one-acters: *Dr. Arlington's Wife* (1913), which emerged in final form as *One of Those Things* (1918). The plot and the names of the characters come from the earlier, unpublished play; the lines spoken by Pampanelli's crew are from the later one. Both plays are melodramas of marital infidelity; neither is very good, and Kelly seems to be aware of this fact as he throws the two up for butchering at the hands of the "torch-bearers."

The Torch-Bearers is not George Kelly's most polished work, but its ebullient humor, its gallery of believable middle-class characters, its pointed satire, and the magnificent presence of Mrs. J. Duro Pampanelli make it a remarkable first play. It earned Kelly a prominent early position in the ranks of the most promising dramatists in what would prove a remarkably rich decade in the American theater. And if the test of time has anything at all to do with a play's merit, *The Torch-Bearers* has passed it with high grades indeed. It continues to be presented by the very group that it so wickedly spoofs—the Little Theatre.

CAST

"The Torch-Bearers," by George Kelly, was presented by Stewart and French for the first time on any stage at the Savoy Theatre, Asbury Park, New Jersey, on the night of Monday, August 14, 1922, with the following cast:

MR. FREDERICK RITTER	ARTHUR SHAW
MR. HUXLEY HOSSEFROSSE	DOUGLAS GARDEN
MR. SPINDLER	EDWARD REESE
MR. RALPH TWILLER	BOOTH HOWARD
TEDDY SPEARING	WILLIAM CASTLE
MR. STAGE MANAGER	J. A. CURTIS
MRS. PAULA RITTER	MARY BOLAND
MRS. J. DURO PAMPINELLI	ALISON SKIPWORTH
MRS. NELLY FELL	HELEN LOWELL
MISS FLORENCE MCCRICKETT	ROSE MARY KING
MRS. CLARA SHEPPARD	DAISY ATHERTON
JENNY	MARY GILDEA

Play staged by the Author.

Note—The form of the present manuscript is exactly that in which this play was presented during its run at the Vanderbilt Theatre, New York City, New York. —THE AUTHOR.

"There are a couple of little changes here on page twelve. I have them marked." Mrs. Pampinelli (Alison Skipworth) confers with her prompter, Nelly Fell (Helen Lowell). *The Torch-Bearers*

THE TORCH-BEARERS

✦ ACT I ✦

NOTE:—The drawing room at Ritter's, in which the first and last acts are laid, is a comfortable-looking room, suggestive of good circumstance. Toward the back there is a fancy wooden partition separating the hallway from the room proper. This partition begins rather high up on the side walls and curves deeply down to two ornamental columns, five feet high and set about five feet apart, forming the entrance from the hallway to the room. Straight out through this entrance, and paralleling the partition, is the staircase, running up to the left and through an arched doorway. The foot of the staircase is just to the right of the center door; and then the hallway continues on out to the front door. On the left, there is a passageway between the staircase and the partition, running through an arched doorway to the body of the house. In the proper room, breaking the angle of the right wall and the partition, is a door, opening out, and below this door, a casement window. Just inside the partition, is the mantelpiece, and below it a door, opening out. Just inside the partition, on either side of the center door, is a built-in seat.

The entire room and hallway is done in a scheme of silver and lighter shades of green. All of the woodwork and furniture, including the piano and mantelpiece, is finished in silver-green and the walls and ceilings are in blended tones of orchid, gray and green, decorated with tapestried panel-effects. The carpet is gray-green, and the vases and clock on the mantelpiece, as well as the little cuckoo-clock over the door at the left, are green. The drapes on the casement window and the doorways, at the head of the stairs and in the left hallway, are in rose-colored brocade satin; and the pads on the partition-seats are covered with the same materials. The piano-throw is a garishly subdued blend of old-rose, Nile green and canary-colored silk.

Right out between the little wooden columns of the center door, set flat against the staircase, is a small console-table, holding a most beautiful rose-colored vase filled with wisteria; and on the piano there is a similar vase filled with white and yellow blossoms. On either side of the console-table there is a tall torchiere with a rose-colored shade; and the shades on the wall-lights, and the one on the lovely rose-colored vase-lamp on the table down at the right below the casement window are all rose-colored.

There's a brilliant array of cushions about the room, all shapes and sizes and every color of the rainbow—and many books and magazines. The piano, up at the right, is littered with music, cigarettes, in a fancy container, flowers and candy—in a pretty box made of pink satin.

The two armchairs in the room, one just to the left of the table below the window, and the other at the left side of the table over at the left, are overstuffed in green-and-silver brocade.

There is a small table below the piano, with a light little chair beside it, the left side, and there is a similar chair over at the extreme left, below the door.

The keyboard of the piano parallels the right wall, with enough room, of course, between the piano stool and wall to permit easy use of the door. There must also be room enough above the piano for a passageway between it and the partition-seat.

The rights and lefts employed in the foregoing descriptions are, of course, the player's rights and lefts.

After a slight pause, a door out at the right is heard to close, and immediately Mr. Ritter comes along the hallway beyond the partition and into the room. He is a brisk, rather stocky type of man, in his early forties, wearing a brown suit and overcoat, a derby hat, and carrying a suitcase. He sets the suitcase down on the partition-seat at the right, and, with a glance around the room, at the unusual arrangement of the furniture, starts out into the hallway again, removing his gloves and overcoat. He glances along the hallway to the left and up the stairs as he goes. Jenny comes along the hallway from the left carrying a small, light chair. As she is about to come into the drawing room proper from the hallway, she becomes conscious of Mr. Ritter out at the hall rack at the right. She stops and peers in that direction. She is a pleasant little English person, plump and trim, dressed in the regulation parlormaid's black and white.

JENNY. Is that you, Mr. Ritter?

RITTER. That's who it is, Jenny! How are you?

JENNY. [*Bringing the little chair forward and placing it above the little table at the left*] Pretty well, thanks, Mr. Ritter, how are you?

RITTER. [*Coming along the hallway from the right*] I'm whatever you are, Jenny. [*Jenny gives a faint laugh and proceeds with her arrangements, and Ritter picks up several telegrams from the stand in the hallway, just to the left of the center entrance.*]

JENNY. Ain't you back a bit soon?

RITTER. [*Coming forward to the small table at the right, below the piano*] Yes, I thought I'd have to go down to Cincinnati for a week or two, but I didn't.

JENNY. Mrs. Ritter ain't expectin' you, is she?

RITTER. [*Glancing through the telegrams*] No, she isn't, Jenny.

JENNY. I thought I didn't remember hearin' her sayin' nothin'.

RITTER. Where is she?

JENNY. [*Starting for the hallway*] She's upstairs, sir, I'll call her.

RITTER. [*With a glance at the furniture*] What are you doing around here, Jenny, housecleaning?

JENNY. [*Turning and coming back*] No, sir, there's a rehearsal here tonight. [*Ritter stops reading and looks at her quizzically for a second.*]

RITTER. What kind of a rehearsal?

JENNY. Why, a rehearsal for a show that Mrs. Ritter's takin' part in tomorrow night. They done it at the Civic Club the week after you went away, and they liked it so well they're doin' it again tomorrow night.

RITTER. *Who* liked it?

JENNY. Sir?

RITTER. I say, who liked it so well that they're doing it again?

JENNY. Why, everybody seemed to like it, Mr. Ritter, from what the papers said.

RITTER. What kind of show is it?

JENNY. Why, I think it's a tragedy, from what I gather.

RITTER. Did you see it, Jenny?

JENNY. No, sir, *I* didn't get to see it, I'm sorry to say; but I heard everybody connected with it sayin' it was a *great success*. [*Ritter resumes his telegrams, then looks at Jenny suddenly.*]

RITTER. How did Mrs. Ritter get into it?

JENNY. Why, I think somebody died, Mr. Ritter, if I'm not mistaken.

RITTER. [*Shaking his head conclusively, and resuming his telegram*] I assumed it was an extremity of *some* kind.

MRS. RITTER. [*At the top of the stairs at the back*] Fred Ritter! Don't tell me that's you down there! [*Jenny turns quickly and goes to the foot of the stairs.*]

RITTER. No, I'm still out in Chicago!

MRS. RITTER. Is it, Jenny?

JENNY. Yes, ma'm, I was just comin' to tell you.

MRS. RITTER. [*Starting down the stairs*] I *thought* I heard his voice! [*Jenny laughs.*] I've been standing here for the last *five* minutes saying to myself, "Who can that *be* that has a voice so much like Fred's!" [*Coming into the room from the hallway*] Why, Fred, darling, what are you doing here! [*He has moved up towards the center door.*]

RITTER. [*Laughing a little*] How is the old kid! [*Kisses her*]

MRS. RITTER. I thought you wouldn't be back till the first! [*Jenny passes along the hallway to the left.*]

RITTER. Why, that Cincinnati thing's been postponed till after Thanksgiving.

MRS. RITTER. [*Turning away from him and stepping out into the hallway again*] Well, why didn't you wire or something?

RITTER. I was afraid of giving you a shock.

MRS. RITTER. Oh, Jenny!

RITTER. You're such a frail little flower.

MRS. RITTER. [*Turning back to him*] Now stop, Fred! I've really lost a lot since you went away.

RITTER. How do you know? [*Jenny comes along the hallway from the left.*]

MRS. RITTER. Why, my dear, I can tell by my clothes. [*She turns to Jenny*] Jenny, will you get me a glass of water, please?

JENNY. [*Starting out*] Yes, ma'm.

RITTER. You're not going to faint, are you?

MRS. RITTER. [*Turning back to him again with a flip of her hand at him*] No, I'm not.

RITTER. [*Slipping his arm around her waist and coming forward*] Any mail here for me?

MRS. RITTER. Not a single thing, Fred; I sent everything right on to Chicago as soon as it came: there must be several letters there for you now.

RITTER. [*Disengaging himself and taking her hands and looking at her*] I'll get them all right. How have you been treating yourself while I've been away?

MRS. RITTER. All right; only I'm glad to see you back.

RITTER. Kiss me.

MRS. RITTER. The house seemed awfully lonesome.

RITTER. Kiss me. [*She kisses him.*]

MRS. RITTER. [*Passing above him to the piano at the right*] Crazy thing. [*He moves over to the little table at the left, rummaging in his pocket for a cigar, and Mrs. Ritter commences to rummage in a sewing basket at the piano. This basket is Mrs. Ritter at a glance, all green and yellow satin, fraught with meaningless bows and weird looking knots. She undoubtedly made it herself, and it must have taken her months. But she's a practical woman; at least she thinks she is; and the sewing basket helps in a way to sustain the conviction. Poor Paula! As one looks at her and listens to her he appreciates the fortune of the circumstance that there is some sane and capable person between her and the world; and as he more closely observes the sewing basket, he rejoices in the blessing of the sane and capable person's ability to spare her the necessity of having to make her own clothes. Although, as a matter of fact, she would look lovely in anything; for Paula is pretty—charmingly so. And her hair is marvelous. So gold—and satiny. She is wearing a dress now of lime green silk with a standing collar edged with black fur, and gold colored slippers.*] Did you have anything to eat, Fred?

RITTER. Yes, I ate on the train. What's this Jenny was saying? Something about a show you're in?

MRS. RITTER. Oh—[*Looking at him*] did she tell you?

RITTER. I wondered what had happened to the furniture when I came in.

MRS. RITTER. [*Coming around and forward towards the little table below the piano*] Yes, there's a rehearsal here tonight. We have it every Tuesday and Thursday. Of course, it's just to run over the lines, because we've done it already at the Civic Club on the fourteenth. And, my dear, it was perfectly marvelous.

RITTER. What kind of show is it?

MRS. RITTER. [*Standing back of the table*] Oh, it's just a one-act play— in one act, you know. And it was really *quite* wonderful. [*She gives an inane laugh.*] I had no idea. [*She touches her hair and turns towards the back of the room again.*]

RITTER. So how did *you* happen to get into it? [*Jenny starts out again.*] Jenny, will you go to the top of the stairs and see if I left the lights burning in my room?

JENNY. [*Turning and starting towards the foot of the stairs in the right hallway; and setting the tray on the little stand as she goes*] Yes, ma'm.

MRS. RITTER. [*Coming forward holding the glass of water*] I think I did. [*She sips.*]

JENNY. [*As she crosses the center door*] Do you want that suitcase taken up, Mr. Ritter? [*Mrs. Ritter turns round to the right and watches Jenny.*]

RITTER. Yes, you can take it up if you will, Jenny, thanks. [*Jenny lifts the suitcase from the partition-seat and goes out and up the stairs.*]

MRS. RITTER. [*Turning to Ritter*] You know, I wrote you about poor Jimmy Sheppard—

RITTER. Yes, what was that, had he been sick?

MRS. RITTER. Why, not a day, my dear! that's the reason it was all so dreadful. Of course, he'd always had more or less of a weak heart; but nothing to threaten anything of that kind. And just three days before the performance, mind you—couldn't happen any other time. And *poor* Mrs. Sheppard playing one of the *leading* parts. [*She turns to her left and goes up to the center door, where she looks out toward the right hallway expectantly.*]

RITTER. [*Casually depositing the band from his cigar on the tray at his left*] Did he *know* she was to play one of the leading parts?

MRS. RITTER. [*Turning at the center door and looking at him*] Who—Mr. Sheppard?

RITTER. Yes.

MRS. RITTER. [*Coming forward again*] Why, of course he did—she'd just finished telling him when he fell over. [*Ritter appears to be unduly occupied with his cigar, and Mrs. Ritter takes advantage of the circumstance to refresh herself with another sip from the glass.*] My dear, poor Clara Sheppard is a *wreck*—you want to write her a note, Fred, when you get time. And he never spoke—not a solitary word. But, she says—just as he was dying—he gave her the funniest look. Oh, she says—if she lives to be a thousand, she'll *never* forget the way he looked at her. [*She goes up to the center door and sets the glass down on the tray.*]

RITTER. [*Still busy with his cigar*] Had he ever seen her act?

MRS. RITTER. [*Turning to him, thoughtfully*] I don't know—whether he ever had or not. [*Jenny comes down the stairs.*] Oh, yes he had, too! For I saw him myself at the Century Drawing Rooms last Easter Monday night, and she was in that play there that night, you remember. [*She moves to the piano and starts looking for something in the sewing basket; he moves to the mantelpiece, up at the left, apparently looking for a match.*]

RITTER. No, I wasn't there.

MRS. RITTER. Oh, weren't you! I thought you were.

RITTER. No. [*He feels in his pockets.*]

MRS. RITTER. There are matches there on that little table there, Fred. [*She indicates the table below the mantelpiece.*]

RITTER. [*Discovering some in his pocket*] I have some here. [*He moves to the armchair at the left of the table and sits down.*]

MRS. RITTER. [*As Jenny passes along the hallway towards on the left*] Oh, Jenny!

JENNY. Yes, ma'm?

MRS. RITTER. Jenny, will you ask Mrs. Brock if she'll make some of that drink she made the last time?

JENNY. I think she 'as made it already, Mrs. Ritter.

MRS. RITTER. Well, will you see, Jenny, please?

JENNY. [*Starting away*] Yes, ma'm.

MRS. RITTER. [*To Ritter*] The folks liked it so much the last time. [*She picks up her sewing basket.*]

JENNY. All right, Mrs. Ritter. [*She disappears at the left.*]

MRS. RITTER. [*Stepping out into the hallway*] Oh, and, Jenny!

JENNY. [*Out at the left*] Yes, ma'm?

MRS. RITTER. Tell her to put a little of that *gin* in it, the way she did before.

JENNY. All right, ma'm.

MRS. RITTER. Tell her she'll find some gin in the little buffet in the big dining room.

RITTER. She probably knows where it is.

MRS. RITTER. [*Coming forward carrying her sewing basket*] Well, anyway, that's how I happened to get into it. [*She sits on the chair at the left of the small table below the piano.*] Mrs. Pampinelli called me up first thing this morning, and she said—

RITTER. Is she in it, too?

MRS. RITTER. [*Looking up from the arrangement of a couple of strips of lace which she has taken from the sewing basket*] Who? Mrs. Pampinelli?

RITTER. Yes.

MRS. RITTER. No, she doesn't take any part; she's just in charge of everything.

RITTER. That suits her better.

MRS. RITTER. Kind of directress, I suppose you'd call her. [*He has some difficulty keeping his face straight.*] Tell us where to go, you know, on the stage—so we won't be running into each other. [*Ritter laughs.*] Really, Fred, you have no idea how easy it is to run into somebody on the stage. You've got to know where you're going every time you move. [*He laughs louder.*] Why, what are you laughing at?

RITTER. I was just thinking of a few of the things I've heard Mrs. Pampinelli called.

MRS. RITTER. [*Looking over at him reproachfully*] Oh—now, that isn't a bit nice of you, Fred Ritter. I know you don't like her.

RITTER. I like her all right.

MRS. RITTER. No, you do not, now, Fred—so *don't* say you do.

RITTER. I think she's marvelous.

MRS. RITTER. Well, she's tremendously clever at this stage business, I don't care what you say. You just ought to hear her talk about it sometime. Now, the last rehearsal we had—over at her house—she spoke on "Technique in Acting as Distinguished from Method;" and you've no idea how interesting it was. [*Ritter glances over at her as he deposits some ashes from his cigar on the little tabletray.*]

RITTER. You say you've given this show before?

MRS. RITTER. Oh yes! We gave it on the fourteenth at the Civic Club. And, my dear, that audience just loved it. And you'd be surprised too, for it's a terrifically serious thing. In fact, in a way, it's too serious—for the general public—that's the reason several of the people who saw it suggested that, if we give it again, we should give a dance right after it. [*She looks closely at her nee-*

dle and Ritter looks discreetly at the end of his cigar.] But, as Mrs. Pampinelli says, it's an absolute impossibility to give a dance at either the Civic Club or the Century Drawing Rooms, so that's how we're giving it this time down at Hutchy Kutchy. [*Ritter looks over at her with a quizzical squint.*]

RITTER. Where?

MRS. RITTER. [*Looking over at him*] Horticultural Hall—there at Broad and Spruce, you know.

RITTER. Yes, I know—what did *you* call it?

MRS. RITTER. Hutchy Kutchy. [*She laughs inanely.*] Mrs. Pampinelli always calls it that—I suppose I've gotten into the habit too, from hearing her. [*She gives another little laugh, then finishes with an amused sigh.*]

RITTER. What's the show for, a charity of some kind?

MRS. RITTER. [*Turning to him suddenly, and with a shade of practicality*] It's for the Seamen's Institute. Kind of a refuge for them, you know, while they're in port; so the sailors won't be wandering around the streets getting into bad company. [*Ritter disposes of more ashes, with an unusual precision, and Mrs. Ritter resumes her sewing. Then, suddenly, she glances towards the casement window at the right.*] It was Mrs. Pampinelli's idea, [*She gathers her things into the sewing basket and gets up, swinging round to her left and talking as she goes.*] so of course she *didn't* want anything to happen. [*She sets the sewing basket down on the piano, and, with another glance through the window at the right, crosses to the little table at the left where Ritter is sitting.*] So she called me up the first thing in the morning, and she said, "Paula darling, *have* you heard the news?" So, of course, I said "No;" because up to that time I *hadn't*, and, naturally, I *wasn't* going to say that I had.

RITTER. Certainly *not*.

MRS. RITTER. "Well," she said, "*poor* Jimmy Sheppard has *just* passed on." Well, luckily I was sitting down at the time, or I *positively* think I should have passed on myself.

RITTER. [*Raising his hand from the table as though distressed by the extremity of her remarks*] Don't say such things.

MRS. RITTER. [*Mistaking his attitude*] No, really, Fred, you've no idea the *feeling* that came over me when she said that. "Well," I said, "Betty, what on earth are we going to do!" Because the tickets were all sold, you know. "Well," she said, "Paula—the only thing *I* see to do, is to have *you* step right into Clara Sheppard's role." "Me!" I said. "Yes," she said; "you are the only person in *my* opinion who is qualified to play the part." "But, my dear," I said, "I've never stepped on a stage in my *life*!" "That is absolutely inconsequential," she said, "it is entirely a matter of dramatic instinct. And," she said [*She simpers a bit here and moves around from the right of the little table where she has been standing to the back of her husband's chair, at the left of the table.*] "you have *that*—to a far greater degree than you've *any* idea of." [*He makes a sound of dry amusement.*] No, really, Fred, everyone was saying it was a positive tragedy that you couldn't have been there to see me—I never forgot myself once. [*She rests her hand on his left shoulder, and he reaches up and takes her hand.*]

RITTER. What are you going to do now, become an actress?

MRS. RITTER. No, but it surprised me so, the way everybody enthused; because I didn't think I'd done anything so extraordinary—I just walked onto the stage, and said what I'd been told to say, and walked off again. [*She emphasizes this last phrase by an indefinite gesture of nonchalance in the direction of the door at her left.*] And yet everybody seemed to think it was wonderful. Why, Nelly Fell said she'd never seen even a *professional actress* so absolutely unconscious. [*He makes a sound of amusement.*] Really, Fred, you ought to have heard them. Why, they said if they didn't know, they never in the *world* would have believed that it was my first offense.

RITTER. You musn't believe everything these women tell you; they'll tell you anything to get their names in the paper.

MRS. RITTER. Well, it wasn't only they that said it—people that I didn't even *know* said it. Why Mrs. Pampinelli had a letter from a woman away out at Glenside that happened to see the performance, and she said that, at times, my repose was *positively* uncanny. And the papers simply raved; especially "The Evening Breeze." I have it upstairs, I must show it to you. It said that it didn't understand *how* I had escaped the public eye so long. [*She glances at the cuckoo clock over the door at the left, and, in doing so, notices a book that has been left lying on the chair below the door: she steps over and picks it up.*] I was awfully sorry you couldn't have been there, Fred. I was going to write you about it when Mrs. Pampinelli first spoke to me about going on, but there was so little time, you see. And then, I didn't think you'd mind; especially on account of its being for charity. [*He is very carefully putting ashes on the little tray. She stands holding the book, looking at him. And there is a slight pause.*] You *don't* mind my going on, do you, Fred?

RITTER. [*Rather slowly*] No—I don't mind, if you're able to get away with it.

MRS. RITTER. [*Trailing across back of his chair*] I didn't think you would.

RITTER. [*Raising his hand from the table quietly*] But a—[*She comes to a stop and regards him over her left shoulder.*] I don't want any of these women exploiting you for their own vanity. [*She doesn't quite encompass his meaning, and stands looking at him for a second. Then she abstractedly lays the book down on the table beside him. There is a very definite ring at the front doorbell.*] I guess that's some of the people. [*She starts towards the hallway.*]

RITTER. [*Preparing to rise*] Where do you do this thing, here?

MRS. RITTER. [*Turning to him and indicating the general arrangement*] Yes—just the way we have it fixed.

RITTER. [*Rising briskly and crossing to the table below the piano at the right, while Mrs. Ritter continues to the center door and stands looking toward the front door. Jenny appears in the left hallway.*] I think I'll beat it upstairs.

MRS. RITTER. [*Turning to Jenny*] I guess that's some of the people, Jenny. [*She comes forward towards Ritter again.*]

JENNY. Yes, ma'm. [*She passes back of Mrs. Ritter and along out into the right hallway to answer the door.*]

MRS. RITTER. Won't you wait and see the rehearsal, Fred? [*He is gathering up the telegrams from the table, where he left them earlier.*]

RITTER. [*Turning and going up towards the center door, thrusting the telegrams into his inside pocket*] No, I think I'd rather wait and see the show. [*He passes her, to her left.*]

MRS. RITTER. [*Turning and trailing up toward the center door after him*] It's really *very* interesting.

MRS. PAMPINELLI. [*Out at the front door*] You see how considerate I am of you, Jenny, letting myself in? [*Mr. and Mrs. Ritter stop in the center door and look toward the front door.*]

JENNY. [*At the front door*] Oh, that's all right, Mrs. Pampinelli.

MRS. RITTER. [*Turning quickly to Ritter at her left*] You can't go up now, Fred, she'll see you.

[*Mrs. Pampinelli and Ritter, together*]

MRS. PAMPINELLI. Well, I daresay you'll have to open this door quite often enough tonight without my troubling you.

RITTER. [*Coming back into the room with a slight gesture of annoyance*] I don't want to have to listen to her gab. [*He goes over to the mantelpiece at the left and takes up his position there, while Mrs. Ritter, with a movement to him to be silent, drifts down beside the piano at the right.*]

MRS. PAMPINELLI. [*Coming into view from the right hallway*] Well, I suppose I'm still the shining example of punctuality. [*She sweeps through the center door, carrying a large black bear muff, a fan of black ostrich plumes, and a notebook and pencil.*] How do you do, Mr. Ritter? [*She goes towards Mrs. Ritter.*]

RITTER. [*Nodding*] How do you do?

MRS. PAMPINELLI. I'm glad to see you.

MRS. RITTER. [*Moving towards Mrs. Pampinelli*] Hello, Betty.

MRS. PAMPINELLI. Hello, Paula Child—[*Kisses her*] how are you, dear? [*Mr. Spindler hurries in from the right hallway, carrying several books. Mrs. Pampinelli steps to the table below the piano.*] Will you give those things to Mrs. Ritter, Mr. Spindler; she'll set them down somewhere. [*She sets her own encumbrances down on the table, and Mrs. Ritter passes back of her to Spindler.*]

SPINDLER. [*Standing in the middle of the room, toward the back*] Certainly, certainly.

MRS. RITTER. Good evening, Mr. Spindler.

SPINDLER. Good evening, good evening. [*Jenny comes in from the right hallway, takes the tray and glass from the hall table, and goes out the left hallway.*]

MRS. RITTER. I'll just take these.

SPINDLER. [*Giving her the books and a manuscript*] If you please.

MRS. PAMPINELLI. [*Crossing directly to Ritter*] Florence McCrickett told me you were back; she saw you getting into a taxicab at the station. [*Giving him her hand*] I'm glad to see you.

RITTER. I just got in.

MRS. PAMPINELLI. And I suppose you already heard about the great event?

RITTER. Yes, she's just been telling me. [*They laugh together.*]

MRS. PAMPINELLI. Well, my dear, you may count that day lost that you missed it. [*She half turns to Mrs. Ritter, who is engaged in conversation with Spindler.*] Mayn't he, Paula? [*But Paula hasn't heard what she's been saying, so she just looks at her and gives an inane little laugh. Mrs. Pampinelli continues to Ritter.*] Although you'll have an opportunity tomorrow night; unless you're going to run away again before that.

RITTER. No, I'll be here now till after Thanksgiving. [*Mrs. Ritter leaves Spindler and goes over to a small table at the extreme right, below the casement window, where she sets the books and manuscript down.*]

MRS. PAMPINELLI. [*Turning from Ritter and crossing back again to the table at the right below the piano*] Wonderful! Did you hear that, Paula?

MRS. RITTER. What is it, dear?

MRS. PAMPINELLI. Mr. Ritter says he will be here for the performance tomorrow night.

MRS. RITTER. Yes.

MRS. PAMPINELLI. [*Unfastening her fur neckpiece*] So you will have an opportunity after all of revealing to him what gems of talent the unfathomed caves of matrimony bear. [*They both laugh.*]

MRS. RITTER. [*Picking up Mrs. Pampinelli's muff from the table and taking the neckpiece*] I'll just take these, Betty.

MRS. PAMPINELLI. [*Settling her beads*] Anywhere at all, dear. [*Mrs.*

Ritter. starts to the right.] Oh, and by the way, Paula—[*Mrs. Ritter stops and turns to her.*]

MRS. RITTER. Yes?

MRS. PAMPINELLI. [*Indicating the books on the table below the window*] There's a remarkable article in one of those books I brought, on a—gesture.

MRS. RITTER. [*Looking at the books*] Yes?

MRS. PAMPINELLI. The little grey book I think it is, if I'm not mistaken. [*She turns to her left and acknowledges Mr. Spindler with a touch of state.*] Mr. Spindler—[*He returns a smiling and very snappy little bow.*] brought it to my attention—[*She turns back again to Paula, who has gone up at the right of the piano and is putting the furs on the partition-seat, while Spindler, becoming suddenly conscious that Ritter is looking at him, stiffens abruptly, glances at Ritter, and turns back again to Mrs. Pampinelli.*] and it really is remarkable. So many of my own ideas—things that I have been advocating for years. I brought it especially for *you*, Paula—so you must read it when you have time. [*She picks up her lead pencil from the little table and, tapping it against her right temple, thinks profoundly.*] What is that wonderful line of Emerson's that I'm so fond of—something about our unexpressed thoughts coming back to accuse us— [*Turning to Spindler*] You know all those things, Mr. Spindler.

SPINDLER. [*Pedantically*] Coming back to us "with an alienated majesty."

MRS. PAMPINELLI. That is the one I mean. [*She turns back again to Paula, who has, by this time, come forward again at the right of the piano, while Mr. Spindler, again becoming conscious that Ritter is looking at him, gives him another glance, this time with a shade of resentment in it, and, coughing briefly, as an emphasis of his dignity, which Ritter's general attitude somehow suggests is not being sufficiently esteemed, turns back to Mrs. Pampinelli.*] Well, that is exactly what occurred to me when I read that article—my own thoughts returning to me from an alienated majesty. [*She finishes her version of the quotation to Spindler and Mr. Ritter.*] Oh, by the way—[*She gives a little mirthless laugh.*] I'm afraid I've neglected to introduce Mr. Spindler. [*Indicating Ritter with a very casual gesture of her left hand, and picking up her lead*

pencil from the little table] This is Mrs. Ritter's husband, Mr.
    Spindler. [*Spindler strides towards Ritter and extends his hand with that
    vigor which usually characterizes the greetings of unimportant persons.*]

SPINDLER. Glad!

RITTER. [*Tonelessly*] How are you?

MRS. PAMPINELLI. [*Addressing Ritter directly*] Mr. Spindler is a young
    man who has made quite an exhaustive study of the Little
    Theatre Movement throughout the country; [*Spindler moves back
    towards his former position, and Paula, over at the right, takes a piece
    of fudge from a box on the little table below the casement window.*]
    and is working very hard to bring about something of the same
    kind here. [*Ritter inclines his head, and Spindler listens to Mrs.
    Pampinelli, wreathed in smiles.*] And is going to succeed, too,
    aren't you, Mr. Spindler?

SPINDLER. [*With a kind of pert assurance*] Never fell down on a big job
    yet. [*He gives a self-conscious little laugh and glances at Ritter, under
    whose coldly-appraising eye the laugh freezes instantly into a short,
    hollow cough. Then he turns away.*]

MRS. PAMPINELLI. I'm sure he has all the qualifications.

SPINDLER. [*With a wooden smile, and saluting*] Thank you, thank you.

MRS. PAMPINELLI. Hasn't he, Paula?

MRS. RITTER. [*Nibbling at the fudge*] Yes indeed, Mr. Spindler's quite
    indispensable. [*Spindler gives her a little pert nod, by way of
    acknowledgement.*]

MRS. PAMPINELLI. [*To Mrs. Ritter*] I think that's what I shall have to
    call him hereafter—[*Turning to Spindler*] the indispensable Mr.
    Spindler. [*They all laugh—a trifle more than the brilliancy of the
    remark should reasonably occasion, and Mr. Spindler accounts it even
    worthy a salute.*]

SPINDLER. Bouquets were falling [*Here the front doorbell gives two
    sharp little staccato rings.*] thick and fast. [*He starts toward the cen-
    ter door.*]

MRS. PAMPINELLI. Well, it's true—

SPINDLER. [*Speaking directly to Mrs. Ritter*] I'll answer it. [*He hurries
    out into the right hallway.*]

[*Mrs. Pampinelli and Mrs. Ritter, speaking together*]

MRS. PAMPINELLI. I know I don't know what on earth I should do without him.

MRS. RITTER. [*Addressing Spindler as he hurries out the hallway*] All right, if you will, Mr. Spindler.

SPINDLER. [*Calling back*] Sure!

MRS. PAMPINELLI. He is one of those rare persons who never forsakes one in the hour of quotation. [*She turns to Mrs. Ritter, who is chewing fudge at her right.*] What are you eating, Paula?

MRS. RITTER. A bit of fudge. Would you like some, Betty?

MRS. PAMPINELLI. [*Very definitely*] No, thank you, dear.

MRS. RITTER. [*Indicating the table below the casement window*] There's some here.

MRS. PAMPINELLI. [*Raising her hand in a gesture of finality, and speaking with conviction*] I never eat immediately before using my voice. And you should not, either, Paula—particularly candy. [*She moves across to the left to Mr. Ritter. She is an imposing woman, in her late fifties, with a wealth of false hair, perfectly done, and a martial bearing. She is one of those matrons who is frequently referred to in the suburban weeklies as a "leading spirit"; and this particular description has always so flattered Mrs. Pampinelli's particular vanity, that she overlooks no opportunity of justifying it: an effort that has resulted in a certain grandeur of voice and manner; which, rather fortunately, becomes the distinction of her person. She is gowned in sapphire blue velvet, close-fitting, with an independent, triangular train, from the waist, probably four yards long. Her necklace, comb, the buckles on her black velvet slippers, and her rings, are all touched with sapphire.*]

MRS. RITTER. [*Looking vaguely at the fudge box*] There's so much of it here. [*Jenny appears from the left hallway.*]

[*Mrs. Pampinelli and Mrs. Ritter, speaking together*]

MRS. PAMPINELLI. [*Coming to Ritter's right*] Very tragic about poor Sheppard, wasn't it, Mr. Ritter?

MRS. RITTER. [*Going up to the center door, and speaking to Jenny as she goes*] Mr. Spindler is answering the door, Jenny, you needn't bother.

[*Ritter and Jenny, speaking together*]

RITTER. [*To Mrs. Pampinelli*] Yes, it *was*—too bad.

JENNY. [*To Mrs. Ritter*] Oh, all right, then. [*She withdraws, and Mrs. Ritter stands looking out into the right hallway.*]

MRS. PAMPINELLI. I suppose Paula wrote you.

RITTER. Yes.

MRS. PAMPINELLI. Dear me—I don't know when anything has so upset me. [*Ritter stands looking at the end of his cigar and Mrs. Pampinelli looks straight ahead.*] I don't believe I closed an eye the entire night—wondering where on earth I should find someone to play his wife's part. [*Ritter glances at her, as he places the cigar in his mouth, and Mrs. Pampinelli looks at him quickly.*] Because, of course, you know that Mrs. Sheppard was to have played the part that Paula plays.

RITTER. Yes, so she told me. [*Mrs. Ritter, still nibbling at the fudge, wanders down and stands in the middle of the room.*]

MRS. PAMPINELLI. But we only had three days to get someone; and it didn't seem possible to me that anyone could memorize that part in that length of time. [*Mrs. Ritter touches her hair and makes a little sound of amusement—a kind of modest acknowledgment of the brilliancy of her achievement.*] So I thought at first—of having Clara Sheppard go on anyway, and I should make an announcement; but, you see, Mr. Sheppard was buried on the fourteenth, and that was the night of the performance; and as I thought the matter over, it seemed to me that perhaps it was just the little too much to expect of her.—[*Ritter gives her another glance.*] Considering her experience as an actress, I mean.

RITTER. [*Taking his cigar from his mouth and speaking with a shade of deliberation*] Couldn't she have kept his death a secret—until after the performance?

MRS. PAMPINELLI. Well, I thought of that, too; [*Ritter looks at her steadily.*] but, you see, it was three days—[*He nods, understandingly.*] and he was so very well known. [*She moves back across the room towards the table below the piano, and Ritter stands looking after her. Simultaneously, there is a frantic giggle from the right hall-*

way. Mrs. Ritter goes up to the center door, looks in the direction of the laughter, and waves her handkerchief, while Mrs. Pampinelli, passing below the table, gathers up her notebook and pencil and continues to the table below the casement window, where she secures the manuscript. Ritter steps forward from his position before the mantelpiece, and disposes of some ashes on the little tabletray.]

MRS. FELL. [*Out in the right hallway*] Paula, that's a very dangerous young man you have on that door tonight.

MRS. RITTER. [*Calling to her*] I think it's very kind of Mr. Spindler. [*Mrs. Pampinelli comes around in front of the big armchair below the casement window.*]

MRS. FELL. [*Coming into view, with considerable flourish*] Kind! My dear, I haven't heard anything like it since I was twenty! [*She gives a little wave of her gorgeous, single white ostrich plume fan at Mrs. Pampinelli.*] Hello, Betty! [*Then to Mrs. Ritter*] How are you, darling?

MRS. RITTER. Hello, Nelly. [*Nelly kisses her.*]

MRS. PAMPINELLI. [*Enthroning herself in the armchair at the right*] Is it *really* possible!

MRS. FELL. [*Turning from Mrs. Ritter and hurrying through the center door*] You're a sweet child! [*Extending the fan towards Mrs. Pampinelli, and coming quickly forward to the table at the right below the piano*] Yes, and I should have been here every night at this hour if it weren't for that dreadful officer up at the parkway! [*She sets her fan and black velvet bag on the table. Spindler comes in from the right hallway and engages in conversation with Mrs. Ritter in the center door.*] He seems to take a fiendish delight in selecting *my* car, of all the *millions* that pass there at this hour, to do *this*! [*She extends her right arm and hand, after the fashion of traffic officers.*] So I told him yesterday afternoon, I said, "Look here, young man!" [*She points her forefinger as though reproving the officer.*] "You needn't expect any Christmas present from *me* next Christmas, for you just—won't—get it. Not till you change your tactics." So he says, after this, he's just going to let me go ahead and run into a trolley car—see how I like that. [*Mrs. Pampinelli, making marginal notes in the manuscript, laughs faintly.*] "Well," I said, "it'd be a change, anyway—from being stopped all the time." [*She abstractedly picks up her fan again.*] I don't think he likes my chauffeur. And I don't blame him; I don't like him myself. He drives too slow.—[*She starts for the center door.*] He's like an old woman. [*She sees Ritter, peering at her, and starts abruptly.*] Well, for Mercy's sake, Frederick Ritter, you don't mean to tell me that's you!

RITTER. I was here a minute ago.

MRS. FELL. [*Laughing flightily*] Well, I declare! I don't know what's happening to my eyes! [*Turning to Mrs. Pampinelli*] I saw him standing there, [*Turning back again and starting towards Ritter, with her hand extended*] but I thought it was one of the other gentlemen! How are you, dear boy? [*He takes her hand and stoops over as though to kiss her. She turns her head away quickly.*] Stop it! Frederick Ritter! [*Mrs. Pampinelli glances over, then resumes her notes. Mrs. Fell half-turns to Mrs. Ritter, who is still talking to Mr. Spindler out at the center door.*] Paula!—do you see what this bad boy of yours is doing? [*Paula just looks and laughs meaninglessly, and resumes her conversation with Spindler.*] What brought you back so soon?

RITTER. [*Assuming the attitude and tone of a lover*] I got thinking of you.

MRS. FELL. [*Touching her hair*] I thought you were out in Seattle or South Carolina or one of those funny places.

RITTER. [*Leaning a bit closer and speaking more softly*] I couldn't keep away from you any longer. [*Nelly darts a swift glance at him.*]

MRS. FELL. [*Starting towards the right*] Don't play with fire, Frederick— [*He laughs hard. She pauses in the middle of the room and turns and looks at him.*] You know what they say about widows, and I've been all kinds. [*She continues over towards Mrs. Pampinelli.*] Oh, Professor Pampinelli! [*Turning and addressing Ritter directly*] I call her Professor, she knows so much. [*Turning back to Mrs. Pampinelli*] Mrs. P.

MRS. PAMPINELLI. [*Looking up suddenly*] I beg your pardon, Nelly dear—I didn't know you were speaking to me.

MRS. FELL. I want to know if you can take me home in your car tonight?

MRS. PAMPINELLI. Why, certainly, dear.

MRS. FELL. My chauffeur has been deviling me for the past two days about some boxing bee—or wrestling match or something that he wants to see; and I told him he could go if there were someone here to take me home.

MRS. PAMPINELLI. I can take you, of course.

MRS. FELL. All right, then, I can chase him; [*She turns to the left.*] I won't hear anymore about that. Oh, Mr. Spindler!

SPINDLER. Yes, ma'm? [*Excuses himself to Mrs. Ritter, who steps into the left hallway and beckons with her finger for Jenny*]

MRS. FELL. Would you mind doing a favor for a very old lady?

SPINDLER. [*Who has hurried forward and is standing in the middle of the room, at attention*] You know what I told you out at the door? [*Nelly gives a shriek, and giggles.*]

MRS. FELL. [*Looking coyly over Spindler's shoulder at Ritter*] Oh, you hear that, Frederick Ritter? You have a rival on the premises. Mr. Spindler told me out at the door tonight—that *my* will was *his* pleasure.

RITTER. [*Looking at the tip of his cigar*] San Juan is never dead while Mr. Spindler lives. [*There is a general laugh.*]

SPINDLER. [*Turning to Ritter*] Say, that's pretty good!

MRS. FELL. Yes, I was afraid he was something of a gay deceiver.

SPINDLER. [*Speaking directly to Mrs. Fell*] Only one way to find out. [*Mrs. Fell laughs deprecatingly and sweeps the tip of her fan across his nose*].

MRS. FELL. Naughty boy. [*She giggles a little more, then becomes practical.*] Well then, I'll tell you what you may do for me, Mr. Spindler, if you don't mind. [*Jenny appears in the left hallway and Mrs. Ritter gives her an order of some sort, which appears to require a bit of explanation.*] Go out to my chauffeur, [*She turns him round by the shoulder and they move up towards the center door.*] you'll probably find him asleep in the car, and tell him I said it's all right—he can go along—that Mrs. Pampinelli will take me home in *her* car.

SPINDLER. [*Hurrying out the right hallway*] Righto! [*Jenny withdraws.*]

MRS. FELL. [*Standing in the center door and calling after him*] Like a good boy. [*She turns, to find Mrs. Ritter at her left in the center door. She takes her arm and they come forward.*] Come in here, Paula Ritter, and explain to me *why* [*They stop in the middle of the room, just above the line on which Ritter is standing.*] you didn't tell me my—lover [*She peers around in front of Paula's shoulder at Ritter.*] was coming back today?

MRS. RITTER. [*Laughing faintly*] My dear, I didn't know it myself until twenty minutes ago.

MRS. FELL. [*Becoming instantly rigid, and piercing Mrs. Ritter with a look*] You don't mean to tell me he returned unexpectedly?

MRS. RITTER. He never even sent a wire.

MRS. FELL. [*Moving over to the right, to the little table below the piano*] I'm surprised at you, Frederick. I consider that the supreme indiscretion in a husband—[*She lays her fan down on the table.*] to return unexpectedly. Isn't it, Paula? [*She commences to unfasten her cloak.*]

MRS. RITTER. [*Moving over to help her*] I never got such a surprise in my life.

MRS. FELL. It has probably wrecked more perfectly good homes than any other one thing in the calendar. [*She slips her cloak off her shoulders, and Mrs. Ritter, who has passed back of her, takes it. It is a flowing affair in black and silver, with voluminous kimona sleeves edged with black fur, and a deep circular collar of silver cloth and fur.*]

MRS. RITTER. I love your cape, Nelly.

MRS. FELL. [*Settling her ornaments*] Do you, really?

MRS. RITTER. [*Examining it*] Beautiful.

MRS. PAMPINELLI. [*Reaching for it*] Let me see it, Paula.

MRS. RITTER. [*Handing it to her*] Where's your seal, Nelly?

MRS. FELL. I thought I wouldn't take it out this winter; I got to so tired looking at it last year. I want to have that collar and cuffs taken off, anyway, before I've wear it again—there's too much skunk there.

MRS. PAMPINELLI. This is perfectly gorgeous, dear. [*To Mrs. Ritter*] Isn't it?

MRS. RITTER. [*Picking up Nelly's fan from the table*] Lovely. And isn't this sweet? [*Mrs. Pampinelli takes the fan from Mrs. Ritter and returns the wrap.*]

MRS. PAMPINELLI. Charming.

MRS. FELL. I'm so glad you like it—I was afraid at first perhaps it might make me look a little too much like a bride.

RITTER. [*With mock derision*] Ha! [*Nelly snaps her head toward him and pins him with a narrow glare.*]

MRS. FELL. Don't be peevish, Frederick—

MRS. RITTER. [*To Mrs. Pampinelli, as she takes the fan from her and replaces it on the table*] Isn't he terrible!

MRS. FELL. It isn't my fault that your wife is a great actress. [*She gives a comic nod and wink at Mrs. Ritter. Ritter laughs.*]

MRS. RITTER. [*Starting towards the door up above the casement window, at the right, with Mrs. Fell's cape*] Now, Fred Ritter, you just stop that!

MRS. PAMPINELLI. Never mind him, Paula—[*Paula goes out with the cape.*] He'll probably change his tune after tomorrow night. [*Mrs. Fell picks up her fan and commences to fan herself.*]

RITTER. [*Standing over above the table at the left, smoking*] I'm thinking of what happened to poor Jimmy Sheppard. [*Jenny comes in at the left hallway carrying a small punch bowl filled with claret, which she sets down carefully on the little stand in the hallway. Mrs. Ritter re-enters from the door on the right and crosses over to Jenny, whom she assists.*]

MRS. FELL. [*Strolling across towards Ritter, fanning herself*] Oh, I suppose it must be *very* difficult for the marvelous male, to suddenly find himself obliged to bask in the reflected glory of a mere wife. [*Mrs. Pampinelli laughs, over her notes.*] For I've never known one yet who was able to do it gracefully. [*She flips the tip of the fan at Ritter's nose. Mrs. Ritter gives Jenny a direction of some kind and Jenny goes out again at the left hallway.*]

MRS. PAMPINELLI. [*As Mrs. Fell saunters back again across the room*] Well, perhaps Mr. Ritter will show himself consistently *masculine* in this instance, and do the exceptional thing. [*Mrs. Ritter follows Jenny out.*]

RITTER. I suppose that's what you'd call *veiled* sarcasm, isn't it? [*Mrs. Pampinelli laughs and rises.*]

MRS. FELL. [*Standing in the middle of the room*] I shouldn't say it was veiled at *all*. [*Moving towards the table below the piano*] I don't think it's even *draped*.

MRS. PAMPINELLI. [*Laughing still, and coming to the little table*] Here's the manuscript, Nelly.

MRS. FELL. [*Stepping closer to the table*] Yes, dear.

RITTER. What are you going to do now, keep *on* giving this show?

MRS. PAMPINELLI. Well, not this particular one, Mr. Ritter, no; but we are going to continue giving shows.

RITTER. What's the idea?

MRS. FELL. They're to be for different charities.

MRS. PAMPINELLI. And then they will afford the boys and girls an opportunity of developing themselves as artists.

RITTER. What are they going to do, all go on the stage?

MRS. PAMPINELLI. Well, hardly all of them will go—but those that we feel have sufficient talent we will encourage to go on, by all means.

RITTER. Do you think Mrs. Ritter has sufficient talent?

MRS. FELL. She's wonderful, Fred, really.

MRS. PAMPINELLI. Yes, I should say that Paula had a very remarkable talent.

RITTER. Well, what will you do about *her*?

MRS. PAMPINELLI. How do you mean, Mr. Ritter, what will we *do* about her?

RITTER. Why, I mean—you'd hardly encourage *her* to go on the stage, would you?

MRS. PAMPINELLI. And why not?

RITTER. Why, what about her home? [*Nelly Fell touches her hair and gives Mrs. Pampinelli a look of amused impatience.*] She couldn't very well walk away and leave that, could she?

MRS. PAMPINELLI. Well, personally, Mr. Ritter, I have always felt that, where it is a question of talent, one should not allow himself to be deterred by purely personal considerations.

MRS. FELL. She's really awfully good, Fred! You wait till you see— you'll want her to go yourself.

RITTER. [*Stepping quietly to the table at the left and disposing of some cigar ashes*] She'll have to be pretty good.

MRS. FELL. Won't he, Betty?

MRS. PAMPINELLI. Well, as far as that is concerned, I think that the question of whether to be or not to be an actress, is one that every woman must, at sometime or another in her life, decide for herself. [*Spindler hurries in from the right hallway and down to Mrs. Fell's left, where he stands at attention, saluting, of course, as usual. Mr. Spindler is full of salutes. He was in the army—drafted ten weeks before the armistice; and subjected throughout the long term of his service to the dangers and exposure of a clerkship in the Personnel at Upton. And he's never gotten over it; being of that immature type of mind upon which the letter of the Military makes a profound impression. He's a peppy person, thin and stilted—in dinner clothes—with sleek hair and goggle glasses: one of that distressing student-order that is inevitably to be found in the retinue of some Mrs. Pampinelli—her social status and constant companionship of so-called artistic movements affording him a legitimate indulgence of his particular weaknesses. So he becomes a kind of lead pencil-bearer extraordinary to her ladyship; and her ladyship tolerates him—for a variety of reasons; not the least of which is his unfailing attitude of acquiescence in all her opinions. And she has so many opinions—and on so many different subjects, that this feature of Mr. Spindler's disposition is far from inconsiderable. Then, he has a most highly developed faculty for small correctnesses—an especially valuable asset, in view of the enormous amount of detail work incidental to Mrs. Pampinelli's vast activities. He reminds her of things, or, "brings them to her attention," as she puts it. For Mr. Spindler is one of those—fortunately few—people who remembers things—word for word—even the things he's read—and he appears to have read most everything. And he quotes incessantly. As Mrs. Pampinelli has already observed of him, "he is one of those rare persons who never forsakes one in the hour of quotation".*] Look here, Nelly.

MRS. FELL. Yes, dear. [*Mrs. Ritter comes in from the left hallway carrying several punch glasses, which she puts down on the hallway table.*]

MRS. PAMPINELLI. [*Indicating a certain line in the manuscript with her lead pencil*] There are a couple of little changes here on page twelve—[*Mrs. Fell opens her lorgnon and looks at the manuscript.*] I have them marked.

MRS. FELL. [*Becoming conscious of Spindler at her left*] Pardon me, Betty. [*Turning to Spindler*] Did you tell him, Mr. Spindler?

SPINDLER. Yes, ma'm; he's gone on his way rejoicing.

MRS. FELL. You're a sweet child.

SPINDLER. [*Snapping his salute*] Thank you. [*He does an about-face and goes up to Mrs. Ritter—Ritter watching him with an expression susceptible of indefinite interpretation.*]

MRS. FELL. The only man I've met in a long time that has made me wish I were—10 years younger.

RITTER. Ha!

MRS. FELL. [*Pertly*] Outside of you, of course.

MRS. PAMPINELLI. [*With a touch of wearied impatience*] Look here, dear.

MRS. FELL. [*Stepping quickly to the table again and readjusting her lorgnon*] Yes, I beg your pardon.

MRS. PAMPINELLI. You see, in this line here—the author has employed a defective verb in the perfect tense. [*Mrs. Fell looks suddenly at her and then right back to the manuscript again. Ritter is watching them closely.*] Will you come here for a moment, Mr. Spindler?

SPINDLER. Certainly, certainly. [*Excuses himself to Mrs. Ritter, with whom he has been chatting, and comes down briskly to Mrs. Fell's left*]

MRS. PAMPINELLI. If you please.

MRS. FELL. [*Appearing to have some difficulty locating the defective verb*] Where is that, now, that you were saying, Betty?

MRS. PAMPINELLI. [*Indicating with the point of the pencil*] Right there, dear. [*Nelly just looks at the spot, through her lorgnon.*] This is the point I was speaking to you about last night, Mr. Spindler.

SPINDLER. [*Securing his goggles*] Oh, yes, yes! [*Ritter draws Mrs. Ritter's attention to the group down at the table. She reproves him with a steady stare. He smiles and shakes his head hopelessly.*]

MRS. PAMPINELLI. You see, this author has employed a defective here, in the perfect tense.

SPINDLER. [*Looking closely*] Ah, yes, I see.

MRS. PAMPINELLI. [*Looking at him directly*] So I have changed it. [*He straightens up and looks at her, and Mrs. Ritter looks from one to the other.*]

SPINDLER. A very good change. [*He nods and crosses over to the left, passing below the table at the left. Ritter watches him until he takes up his position just below the mantelpiece, rather ill at ease under Ritter's gaze.*]

MRS. PAMPINELLI. I think so. So, if you'll just watch that, Nelly. [*She picks up the manuscript.*]

MRS. FELL. All right, I'll watch for it. [*She reaches for her bag and takes out a lipstick. Jenny appears from the left hallway with the tray of cakes, which Mrs. Ritter assists her in making room for on the hall table.*]

MRS. PAMPINELLI. [*Starting for the center door*] I must show it to Paula, it's her line. [*The doorbell rings.*] Paula child. [*Jenny passes back of Mrs. Ritter and goes out into the right hallway to answer the doorbell.*]

MRS. RITTER. [*Eating a cake*] Yes, dear? [*Mrs. Pampinelli calls her attention to the change in the manuscript. Mrs. Fell is making up her lips down at the table below the piano. Ritter is watching her, and Spindler is watching Ritter, and trying to assume his general deportment.*]

RITTER. Are *you* in the show, Nelly?

MRS. FELL. [*Without turning, and applying the lipstick, with the aid of the little mirror in her handbag*] Who, me?

RITTER. Yes.

MRS. FELL. [*Half-turning, and giving him a melting look*] Yes—I play a chicken. [*She returns to her mirror.*]

RITTER. [*Casually*] In the last act, I suppose. [*Nelly snaps her head around and pierces him with one of her looks.*]

MRS. FELL. No, and not in the last stages, either. [*She resumes her make-up. Nelly is forever making up. But, she does know how to do it. Of course, she should, considering the years of her experience in the*

*art. For Nelly Fell's age amounts to an achievement; one of those
attainments so absolutely undisputed that it is perfectly permissible to
refer to it in any gathering. She says she'll "soon be sixty"; but the
short and simple annals of society record flutterings of the lady as far
back as the first term of President Grant. And she's still fluttering—a
perennial ingenue, full of brittle moves and staccato vocalisms. She
looks like a little French marquise, so chic, and twittery—and rich.
For, of course, Nelly is wealthy—enormously so; it would be utterly
impossible to have her hair and not have money; the feature is financial in itself; so silver white, with a lovely bandau of small, pale pink
leaves, tipped with diamond dewdrops; all heightened tremendously
by the creation in black velvet she is wearing. This gown is heavily
trimmed with silver, and quite sleeveless, with two panels of the goods
fastened at the waist on either side and trailing at least a yard. She has
a preference for diamonds and pearls, obviously, for her earrings, dog
collar, bracelets and rings are all of those gems, and her long, triple-
string necklace is of pearls. Altogether, Nelly is a very gorgeous little
old lady—from the topmost ringlet of her aristocratic hair, to the pearl
buckles on her tiny black velvet slippers.]*

SPINDLER. Mrs. Fell is the official promptress.

MRS. FELL. *[Turning her head and looking at Ritter]* I *prompt* everybody.
   [She replaces her lipstick in the handbag.]

RITTER. Yes?

MRS. FELL. *[Putting the handbag down again on the table]* As well as
   lending my moral support.

RITTER. Yes? *[Spindler laughs.]*

MRS. FELL. *[To Ritter]* You bold thing!

HOSSEFROSSE. *[Coming into view from the right hallway]* Good evening,
   everybody!

MRS. PAMPINELLI. *[Turning to him, from Mrs. Ritter, with whom she has
   been discussing the change in the manuscript]* Oh, good evening
   Mr. Hossefrosse. *[They shake hands.]*

MRS. RITTER. Mr. Hossefrosse. *[Mrs. Pampinelli comes forward into the
   room again, bringing the manuscript with her.]*

HOSSEFROSSE. Mrs. Ritter—good evening. *[Mrs. Ritter asks him if he will have a glass of claret and he says yes, so she proceeds to fill him out one.*]

MRS. PAMPINELLI. I hope the rest of the people aren't far behind you.

HOSSEFROSSE. Are we late?

MRS. FELL. [*Waving to him*] Hello, Huxley.

MRS. PAMPINELLI. Not very.

HOSSEFROSSE. Hello, Nelly. How are you? [*Mrs. Ritter gives him the claret, and he stands up at the center door with her, drinking it. Teddy Spearing wanders in from the right hallway.*]

MRS. PAMPINELLI. [*Passing below the little table below the piano and laying the manuscript on it*] Here's the manuscript, Nelly. [*She continues to the armchair below the casement window, and, picking up her notebook from the little table at her right, sits down and commences to make notes.*]

MRS. FELL. [*Seeing Teddy Spearing, and starting towards the right partition*] Oh, Teddy Spearing!

TEDDY. Hello, Nelly.

MRS. FELL. [*Beckoning him with her fan*] Come here, dear, I've got something to tell you. [*Teddy leans over the partition at the right and Nelly kneels on the partition-seat and whispers something to him. Hossefrosse and Mrs. Ritter are conversing in the center door, Mrs. Pampinelli is making notes down at the right, Ritter is standing over in front of the mantelpiece, smoking, and Spindler is standing just below him, to his left, watching him.*]

SPINDLER. [*In a sudden surge of courage, and taking a rather nonchalant step towards Ritter*] Could you spare one of those cigars, please? [*Ritter looks at him keenly, then reaches in his vest pocket for a cigar.*]

RITTER. Do you smoke?

SPINDLER. Semi-occasionally, yes. [*Ritter hands him the cigar and he steps nonchalantly back to his former position, Ritter keeping one eye on him. He examines the cigar curiously, and, being apparently very near-sighted, seems to have considerable difficulty in deciphering the band inscription.*]

RITTER. You can light *either* end of it.

SPINDLER. [*Very self-conscious*] Yes—I was just looking at this label here: it's rather keen. [*He puts the cigar in his mouth, and attempts an attitude of careless detachment.*]

RITTER. Have you got a match?

SPINDLER. I don't—[*As he opens his mouth to speak the cigar falls on the floor, and he scrambles after it.*]

TEDDY. [*Laughing incredulously and turning away from Nelly*] Oh, Nelly!

MRS. FELL. Upon my word, dear! Come here till I tell you. [*Teddy returns to the partition and Nelly proceeds with her gossip.*]

SPINDLER. [*Straightening up, and attempting another man-of-the-world attitude*] I don't care to smoke just now, thank you. [*He holds the cigar in his fingers.*]

RITTER. [*As things settle again*] You've been in the army, haven't you?

SPINDLER. [*Turning to Ritter with a suggestion of military erectness*] Yes; I put in the better part of three months down at Upton, in the Personnel.

RITTER. I imagined from your salute you'd been around one of the camps.

SPINDLER. Yes—I was Third Lieutenant down there—[*Ritter looks at him sharply; then Spindler turns and meets the look.*] Regimental Sergeant Major.

RITTER. Rest.

MRS. FELL. [*Coming away from the partition*] So I'm going to ask him right out the very next time I meet him. [*She comes down to the little table below the piano again. Mr. Hossefrosse comes through the center door towards Ritter, rubbing his hands, and Teddy moves over towards Mrs. Ritter, who is still officiating at the punch bowl.*]

[*Teddy and Hossefrosse, speaking together*]

TEDDY. [*Speaking to Mrs. Fell*] Maybe he doesn't know it himself.

HOSSEFROSSE [*Addressing Ritter*] Ah, Mr. Ritter! How do you do, sir? [*They shake hands.*]

RITTER. How do you do?

[*Mrs. Fell and Hossefrosse, together*]

MRS. FELL. Well, I'm going to find out, whether he does or not.

HOSSEFROSSE [*To Ritter*] Decided there was no place like home, eh? [*He laughs, with a mirthless effusiveness.*]

RITTER. Are you in the show, too? [*Mrs. Ritter fills out a glass of claret for Teddy.*]

[*Mrs. Fell and Hossefrosse, together*]

MRS. FELL. I should say he is in it.

HOSSEFROSSE. We're all in it.

MRS. FELL. He's the leading man. [*Hossefrosse raises his right hand toward Nelly and laughs deprecatingly.*] Unfortunately, there isn't a place in the play where he can use that perfectly gorgeous singing voice of his. [*Hossefrosse is quite overcome, and crosses, with hand extended, to Spindler.*] It's true.

HOSSEFROSSE. Good evening, Mr. Spindler.

SPINDLER. Good evening, good evening. [*In shifting the cigar from his right hand to his left he drops it.*]

HOSSEFROSSE. Uh! I beg your pardon! [*Mrs. Ritter laughs at something Teddy has said to her, then hands him a glass of claret. Mr. Hossefrosse stoops to pick up Spindler's cigar.*]

SPINDLER. [*Stooping also, after the cigar*] That's all right.

[*Hossefrosse and Spindler, together*]

HOSSEFROSSE. I'll get it. [*He picks it up and hands it to Spindler.*]

SPINDLER. It isn't lit.

HOSSEFROSSE. There we are.

SPINDLER. Thank you very much.

HOSSEFROSSE. Don't mention it. [*He crosses down to Nelly, who is looking through the manuscript at table below the piano.*]

TEDDY. [*Coming through the center door and speaking to Ritter*] How do you do, Mr. Ritter?

RITTER. [*Shaking hands with him*] How are you?

TEDDY. [*Nodding to Spindler*] Good evening.

SPINDLER. Good evening, sir; good evening.

MRS. PAMPINELLI. Teddy!

TEDDY. [*Crossing towards the piano*] Yes?

[*Mrs. Ritter, Mrs. Pampinelli and Hossefrosse, together*]

MRS. RITTER. [*Waving her handkerchief toward the right hallway*] Hello, Florence!

MRS. PAMPINELLI. [*Addressing Teddy*] Did you telephone that man about those tickets?

HOSSEFROSSE. [*Standing at Mrs. Fell's left shoulder*] What are you doing, Nelly?

[*Florence, Mrs. Fell and Teddy, together*]

FLORENCE. [*Out in the right hallway*] Am I the last? [*She hurries into view and whispers something to Paula at the center door which sends Paula into a fit of laughing.*]

MRS. FELL. [*To Hossefrosse*] Making more changes. [*He crosses over to the right in front of Nelly and sits on the piano stool, back of Mrs. Pampinelli.*]

TEDDY. [*Answering Mrs. Pampinelli*] Yes, I did, Mrs. Pampinelli, he said he'd have them there all right.

MRS. PAMPINELLI. Thank you so much. [*Teddy goes up and crosses above the piano, where he engages Mr. Hossefrosse in conversation*] Hello, Florence! [*Jenny comes into view from the right hallway.*]

FLORENCE. [*Coming straight forward from the center door*] Am I the last? [*The front doorbell rings again, and Jenny turns and goes back into the right hallway again.*]

MRS. PAMPINELLI. No, but you're very close to it. How are you, dear?

FLORENCE. Rushed like mad. [*Flipping her lynx muff*] Hello, everybody. Hello, Nelly. [*She swings round to her left.*]

MRS. FELL. Hello, Flossie.

FLORENCE. How do you do, Mr. Spindler? [*Hossefrosse gets up and whispers something to Mrs. Pampinelli, in which she agrees.*]

SPINDLER. How do you do? [*Ritter bows very graciously to Florence, and Mrs. Ritter comes forward to her husband's right, eating a piece of cake.*]

FLORENCE. [*Extending the muff at arms-length at Ritter*] No, I don't speak to *you* at all. [*She removes her stole.*]

RITTER. What's the matter?

FLORENCE. Paula, did you know your husband is becoming very snooty? [*Hossefrosse resumes his seat on the piano stool.*]

MRS. RITTER. [*Sliding her hand through Ritter's right arm*] Why didn't you speak to Florence at the station today, Fred?

RITTER. I didn't see you today.

FLORENCE. Well, my dear, you *must* be getting old; for Irene Colter and I did everything but stand on our heads to attract your attention. [*On the last word of this sentence she flips one of the tails of the stole at him, and he ducks, as though afraid of getting hurt.*] Where shall I put these, Paula? [*Mrs. Pampinelli rises quietly from her chair at the right, and, lost in thought, proceeds slowly and majestically across in the front of Mrs. Fell to the middle of the room, tapping her lead pencil on the notebook.*]

MRS. RITTER. I'll take them. [*She takes the muff and stole from Florence and goes up and out into the right hallway with them.*]

FLORENCE. [*Espying Teddy up back of the piano, shading his eyes with his hand, as though trying to see her from a great distance*] Hello, Teddy dear! [*Goes towards him*] What are you doing away back here in the corner? [*She makes a sudden move as though to tickle him in the ribs, but he laughs and jumps away. Mrs. Pampinelli has by this time reached the center of the room, where she stands turning from side to side in a profound indecision as to the relationship of certain positions. She indicates her line of thought by diverse pointings and flippings of the lead pencil. Ritter watches her with narrow amusement; and, presently, Mrs. Fell, who is still occupied with the manuscript at the little table, looks up, distracted by the gyrations of the lead pencil.*]

MRS. FELL. What's the matter, Betty?

MRS. PAMPINELLI. I was just wondering about a little piece of business here.

SPINDLER. [*Stepping to the back of the armchair at the left and leaning over it towards Mrs. Pampinelli*] Can I help you, Mrs. P.?

MRS. PAMPINELLI. [*Without turning to him*] No, thank you; it's purely technical. [*He resumes his position at the left corner of the mantelpiece and glances at Ritter, who is obliged to use his handkerchief to hide his amusement. Mrs. Ritter comes in through the door at the right, above the piano.*]

MRS. FELL. Betty, did I tell you I saw Clara Sheppard today? [*But Mrs. Pampinelli is still deep in technical profundities, and simply silences her with a gesture of her right hand.*]

MRS. RITTER. [*Coming forward at the right of the piano*] Where did you see her, Nelly?

MRS. FELL. Darlington's, at the mourning counter.

MRS. PAMPINELLI. [*Coming suddenly out of her abstraction, and turning to Mrs. Fell*] Is she going in black?

MRS. FELL. My dear, she's *in* it already.

TWILLER. [*Coming in the right hallway*] Good evening!

MRS. PAMPINELLI. She's very foolish, under the circumstances.

MRS. FELL. That's just what I told her today.

TWILLER. [*Coming through the center door and forward at the left of the piano*] Good evening, Mrs. Ritter.

MRS. RITTER. Good evening, Mr. Twiller.

TWILLER. [*To Hossefrosse, casually*] Huxley.

HOSSEFROSSE. [*Shifting from the piano stool to the armchair, which Mrs. Pampinelli has just vacated, and proceeding to study his part, which he has taken from his pocket*] Hello, Ralph.

MRS. FELL. Hello Ralph.

TWILLER. Nelly!

MRS. PAMPINELLI. [*Still in the middle of the room*] You're the ten o'clock scholar again tonight, Mr. Twiller. [*Jenny crosses from the right hallway to the left, and goes out.*]

TWILLER. I'm awfully sorry, Mrs. P., really; but the fates seem to be against me. [*Teddy gives a little whistle at him. He turns and sees him, standing with Florence, up back of the piano.*] Hello, Teddy! [*He goes towards him, and Teddy shoots at him with his thumb and forefinger, by way of reply. Florence smiles and extends her left arm and hand towards him.*]

[*Mrs. Pampinelli and Twiller, together*]

MRS. PAMPINELLI. [*Moving over from the middle of the room to the left of Mrs. Fell, who is still at the table below the piano*] What was that you were saying, Nelly, about Clara Sheppard?

TWILLER. Flossie, dear, I didn't see you two up here! [*He takes Florence's hand and kisses it. Then he crosses to the left and shakes hands with Ritter; then over to Spindler, and then starts back towards Florence, at the piano. As he passes Ritter, Ritter taps him on the right shoulder; he turns, and Ritter asks him something. He replies, and they stand chatting for a moment; then Ritter indicates the partition-seat behind them and they sit down, to talk it over.*]

MRS. FELL. Why, I simply told her—I said, "Don't be spectacular, dear; it'll only make it more difficult for you when you want to marry again. And," I said, "you probably *will* marry again—" [*Spindler sits on the chair below the door at the left.*]

MRS. PAMPINELLI. Of course, she will.

MRS. FELL. For you're a comparatively young woman. "So," I said, "just get through the next few months as undramatically as possible. [*Jenny enters in the left hallway and takes empty glasses off.*] I know he was your *first* husband, and all that; but, after all," I said, "he was *only* your husband: it isn't as though you'd lost someone who was very *close* to you"—[*She turns her head and speaks directly to Mrs. Pampinelli.*] like one of your own people, [*Turning to Mrs. Ritter, who is standing at her right*] or something like that, I mean. "And," I said, "another thing, darling— *always remember*—he'd have very soon put another in *your* place if it had been you." [*She finishes the remark to Mrs. Pampinelli.*]

MRS. PAMPINELLI. [*Knowingly, and with conviction*] I should say he would.

MRS. FELL. [*Reaching for her handbag*] And I felt like saying, "And I could give you the names and addresses right now of *several* that he would have put in your place *long ago*, only for the law."

MRS. PAMPINELLI. [*With a shade of confidence*] She must have known it.

MRS. FELL. [*Reflecting the tone*] Of *course*, she knew it. [*Florence leaves Teddy, up at the piano, and crosses to Ritter and Twiller, to show them a piece of music. They rise, and she indicates a certain point on the sheet; then she continues down to Spindler, who rises at her approach, and shows it to him.*]

MRS. RITTER. How is she, Nelly?

MRS. FELL. My dear, she looks a perfect wreck. [*Florence sits on the arm of the armchair at the left and Spindler resumes the little chair below the left door, and drawing it a bit closer to the armchair. He appears to be telling Florence something very interesting.*]

MRS. RITTER. Poor soul.

MRS. FELL. She says no one will *ever* know how she feels—about losing that part. And she says she simply cannot *wait* until tomorrow night, [*She turns to Mrs. Pampinelli.*] to see Paula's interpre- tation of it. [*Mrs. Ritter gives an inane little laugh, and Mrs. Fell turns quickly to her.*] She's heard so much about it. [*Jenny comes in from the left hallway again with fresh glasses. She sets them down on the hallway table and proceeds to arrange them.*]

MRS. PAMPINELLI. Is she coming to the performance tomorrow night?

MRS. FELL. She says she'll see that performance, if she has to dis- guise herself.

MRS. RITTER. Doesn't that sound just like her? [*Nelly nods in agree- ment.*]

MRS. PAMPINELLI. Yes—she's so full of dramatic instinct.

MRS. FELL. [*With a touch of bitterness*] He never appreciated it though.

MRS. PAMPINELLI. My dear, has *any* artist *ever* been adequately appreciated?

MRS. RITTER. I understand he was very heavily insured.

MRS. FELL. Oh, yes!

MRS. PAMPINELLI. She *seemed* very optimistic when I spoke to her on the telephone.

MRS. FELL. I believe your husband's company had him insured for quite a lot, didn't they, Paula?

MRS. RITTER. [*Lowering her tone*] I believe they did, Nelly—but I couldn't say for just how much.

MRS. FELL. [*Quietly detaching herself*] I must find that out. [*She passes back of Mrs. Pampinelli and across towards Ritter. Mrs. Ritter and Mrs. Pampinelli continue in conversation*] Frederick, I want to ask you something. [*He steps forward, excusing himself to Twiller.*] Pardon me, Ralph.

TWILLER. That's all right, Nelly. [*He crosses again to Teddy.*]

MRS. FELL. Frederick, what did you think when you heard Jimmy Sheppard was dead?

RITTER. Why, I thought he was dead, of course. [*Mrs. Ritter leaves Mrs. Pampinelli, passing back of her, and goes up to assist Jenny with her arrangements. Mrs. Pampinelli busies herself with making nota- tions on the margin of the manuscript, at the little table.*]

MRS. FELL. [*Flipping the tip of her fan in his face*] Oh, did you, Smarty! [*Ritter raises his right hand, as though to ward off the blow*] Well, listen, Frederick. [*He attends, and she becomes confidential.*] He left quite a bit of insurance, didn't he?

RITTER. Yes—about three hundred thousand, I believe.

MRS. FELL. [*Becoming generally stoney*] Is there a will, do you know?

RITTER. I don't know, I suppose there is.

MRS. FELL. Well, I hope she was sharp enough to see that there is. Because if there isn't, you know, she's only entitled to a third in this state. That's all the widow's entitled to. And, you know, Frederick, Clara Sheppard could never in this world get along on a bare hundred thousand dollars; you know that as well as I do.

RITTER. Well, she has quite a bit of money of her own, hasn't she?

MRS. FELL. Oh, tons of it, yes; but there's no sense in using her own if she can use his. [*Ritter glances at her, but she has turned away slightly to cough, behind her fan. Jenny goes out at the left hallway.*] Was sudden, wasn't it?

RITTER. Yes, it was.

MRS. FELL. We were terribly inconvenienced. Because I'd simply *deluged* my friends with tickets. [*Mrs. Ritter is up at the punch bowl, sampling the punch and nibbling at the cakes.*]

RITTER. I can't understand why you didn't postpone the show.

MRS. FELL. That's what *I* wanted to do; but Mrs. P. here was superstitious.

MRS. PAMPINELLI. [*Catching her name, and straightening up from the manuscript, imperiously*] What are you saying about Mrs. P., Nelly Fell?

MRS. FELL. Why, Frederick was wondering why we didn't postpone the performance when Jimmy Sheppard died—and *I* told him you were superstitious about a postponement.

MRS. PAMPINELLI. No, Nelly, I was not superstitious, so please don't say that I was; I shouldn't care to have such an impression get abroad.

MRS. FELL. [*Touching her hair*] Well, you were something, Betty.

MRS. PAMPINELLI. Yes, Nelly, I admit that I was something—but it was not superstitious. I was—[*She looks out and away off, and feels for the word.*] intuitive. [*She turns her head and looks directly at Ritter, who drops his eyes to the tip of the cigar. Nelly Fell, following Mrs. Pampinelli's eyes, looks at Ritter also. Then everyone's eyes shift to Mrs. Pampinelli. Florence turns languidly and looks; and Mrs. Ritter, with a glass of punch in one hand, and a small cake in the other, moves forward, in the middle of the room, and stands looking and listening— and chewing. Hossefrosse steps over to the table behind which Mrs. Pampinelli is standing, and takes the manuscript—returning with it to the armchair, and becoming absorbed in a comparison of a certain page of it with his individual part.*] I have struggled so long to inaugurate a Little Theatre Movement in this community, that I had intuitively anticipated the occurrence of some obstacle to thwart me; so that, when the telephone bell rang, on the night of Mr. Sheppard's death, I said to myself, before I even took down the receiver, [*She plants her lead pencil on the table and assumes something of the aspect of a crusader.*] "*This* is my event. Something has happened—that is going to put my sincerity in this movement to the test. And I must remember, as Mr. Lincoln said at Gettysburg, 'It is better that we should perish, than that those ideals for which we struggle should perish.'" [*She turns her gaze in the direction of Ritter, but Mrs. Ritter is first in the line of vision, with her eyes full of the coast of Greenland, and her mouth full of cake. As she becomes suddenly conscious that Mrs. Pampinelli has stopped talking and is looking directly at her, she meets the looks and breaks into an utterly irrelevant little laugh.*]

RITTER. It's a singular thing, but I've noticed that invariably there's a *fatality* connected with these amateur performances.

MRS. PAMPINELLI. Unfortunately, that is true, Mr. Ritter, I agree with you. But then, we are not dismayed; we have the lessons of history to fortify us; for whenever the torch of essential culture has been raised, [*She raises the lead pencil as though it were a torch.*] there has unfailingly been the concomitant exactment of a human life. [*She stands holding the torch aloft until the little cuckoo-clock over the door at the left cuckoos the half-hour. Ritter looks at it,*] *and Nelly Fell gives it a glance. Florence, too, turns and looks up. Then Mrs. Pampinelli turns her eyes slowly upon it and withers it with a look.*] Well, children, it's eight-thirty—[*She gathers up her train and tosses it across her left arm, then comes around to the right in front of the table where she has been standing. Mrs. Ritter returns to the table in the hallway and sets down her empty glass. Ritter goes up after her and she fills him out a drink. Florence rises from the arm of the chair, and, passing in front of the table at the left, goes up and across back of the piano and out the door, at the right. As she passes above the piano she says something to Teddy, who has come down at the right of the piano, from his late position up near the door, and is crossing below it. Twiller turns and goes out through the center door and stands leaning over the partition in the right hallway. Hossefrosse rises, settles his clothes and clears his throat. Mr. Spindler, also, has risen, and is replacing his chair back against the wall, below the door.*] Time we went "unto the breach" once more.

MRS. FELL. [*Stepping forward a little to the center of the room, and stretching her hands towards Mr. Hossefrosse*] You have my props, Huxley.

HOSSEFROSSE. [*Crossing below the table, to give her the manuscript*] I beg your pardon, Nelly; I was just looking at something here.

MRS. FELL. Thanks. [*She pulls him towards her and whispers something.*]

MRS. PAMPINELLI. [*Standing at the left of the little table*] Have you my other pencil, Mr. Spindler?

SPINDLER. [*Hurrying across towards her*] I believe you left it over here on this little table. [*He passes below Teddy, who is just crossing to the left, and continues on between the piano and the table to the little table below the casement window. Nelly Fell breaks into a shrill giggle, pushes Hossefrosse towards the center door, and crosses to the left, passing below the table. She is in a violent state of laughter. Hossefrosse goes on up to the center door, and, excusing himself to Ritter, who is standing there drinking, passes out into the right hallway. Teddy comes around back of the armchair at the left and sits in the armchair. Mrs. Pampinelli has moved to the right of the table below the piano, where she stands reviewing her notes.*]

MRS. FELL. [*To Teddy, confidentially, as she takes up her position on the chair below the door at the left*] I'll tell you later. [*She sits down.*]

MRS. PAMPINELLI. [*Tapping her lead pencil on the table and addressing them generally*] Now, folks—[*Ritter sets his glass on the table and steps into the right hallway, where he converses with Twiller for a second, then stands listening; while Mrs. Ritter hurries in and settles herself on the partition-seat at the left and listens attentively.*] you understand, of course, that the setting will be just as it was at the Civic Club on the fourteenth; only, of course, as you know, the stage at Hutchy Kutchy is considerably larger. That, however, need not concern us particularly, as the entrances and exits will be relatively the same. [*She finishes this speech to Mr. Spindler, who is standing at her right, waiting for her to take the lead-pencil.*] Oh, thank you, Mr. Spindler. [*She gives him the one she has—simply an exchange of pencils, and he salutes and returns to a position below the casement window. Florence comes in at the right door again, wearing her furs, and comes down at the right of the piano. Mrs. Pampinelli moves a little towards the center door.*] Are you going to watch the rehearsal, Mr. Ritter?

MRS. FELL. Of course, he is!

MRS. RITTER. [*Coming through the center door*] If I wouldn't be in the way.

MRS. PAMPINELLI. Not at all—very glad to have you.

MRS. FELL. He can sit over here with the promptress. [*He crosses towards Nelly, picking up the little chair above the table at the left, as he passes. Hossefrosse emerges from the right hallway carrying a light, soft hat, a cane and gloves, and stands in the center door. Florence steps across below the piano and asks Mrs. Pampinelli something.*] If you can behave yourself. [*Florence returns to the corner of the piano nearest the window and drapes herself on it. She's a very gorgeous-looking thing, in a sleeveless gown of canary-colored metallic silk, made quite daringly severe, to exploit the long, lithe lines of her greyhound figure. There's a chain-effect girdle with the dress, of vivid jade, worn loose, and an ornament of the same jade on the left shoulder, from which the goods falls in a plain drape down in front of*

*the arm to the bottom of the skirt. She has a perfect shock of hair,—
rather striking—a kind of suspicious auburn; and she has it bobbed.
Her slippers and stockings are white.*]

MRS. PAMPINELLI. You needn't sit there yet, Teddy, I'm going to run
through the last scene first—

TEDDY. [*Rising*] Oh, all right.

MRS. PAMPINELLI. For Mr. Hossefrosse's lines. [*Teddy passes in front of
the table at the left and goes up to the center door and out into the
right hallway, where he chats with Twiller and watches the proceedings over the partition. Spindler comes over and asks Mrs. Pampinelli
something. Ritter places his chair beside Nelly's, above it, and sits
down, assuming the attitude of a lover.*]

MRS. FELL. [*Pushing Ritter's arm away*] Stop it, Frederick Ritter!
Paula! [*Spindler returns to his post.*]

MRS. RITTER. [*Inanely*] Behave yourself, Fred.

MRS. PAMPINELLI. Now, folks—[*She moves slowly down and across
towards the table at the left.*] Mr. Spindler will attend to the various
cues tonight, and at the performance tomorrow night as well.
[*Speaking directly to Nelly*] So we won't have to bother about that.
[*Turning round to her left and addressing the others*] He will do all
the rapping. [*She raps a little.*] And he has a little telephone bell of
his own, [*She moves across again towards the back of the table at the
right.*] which he has very kindly tendered the use of. Have you
that bell with you tonight, Mr. Spindler? [*He holds out a bell and
battery arrangement on a piece of wood, having taken it from his pocket
immediately she referred to it, and it rings twice.*] Splendid. [*She
passes above the table and comes forward at the right of it, very
thoughtfully.*] That's splendid. [*Spindler replaces the battery.*] Now,
children—[*She crosses in front of the table.*] I think, first, I should
like to take that scene at the finish, between Doctor Arlington
and his wife; [*She is standing at the left of the table, speaking directly
to Hossefrosse, who is standing in the center door, with his hat on, at a
rather absurd angle, and holding his cane in one hand and his gloves in
the other, in a very stilted fashion. Hossefrosse is a terribly well-fed-
looking person in dinner clothes, perhaps, thirty-eight years of age—*

flamingly florid of complexion, and with an effusiveness of manner that is probably only saved from absolute effervescence by the ponderous counterpoise of his dignity.] there are a few little things in there I want to correct. [*Crossing over back of the table at the left towards Mrs. Fell*] Page eighteen or nineteen, I think it is, Nelly. It's the scene at the finish between Mr. Hossefrosse and Miss McCrickett. [*Nelly looks for the place, through her lorgnon.*] Oh! [*Mrs. Pampinelli turns back to the others again.*] and one thing more I want to mention, boys and girls, before I forget it. [*She takes a funny little coughing spell.*] Pardon me. [*She coughs again.*] Oh, dear me! [*She closes her eyes tight and shivers her head.*]

MRS. FELL. Page eighteen did you say it was, Betty?

MRS. PAMPINELLI. Eighteen or nineteen, yes. It's somewhere right in there.

MRS. FELL. Oh, yes, here it is, I have it.

MRS. PAMPINELLI. [*Turning back to the people, and speaking with careful emphasis*] When you are going on and off the stage, be very careful of those little wooden strips that they have across the bottoms of the doors, and don't *trip.* [*Mrs. Ritter laughs self-consciously and Hossefrosse leans over and says something to her. Florence laughs, and turns and says something to Spindler, and Teddy and Twiller laugh and look toward Mrs. Ritter.*]

MRS. FELL. [*Looking out around Mrs. Pampinelli to see Mrs. Ritter*] Paula! [*Then she sits back, laughing, and says something to Ritter.*]

MRS. PAMPINELLI. I really think that was what made some of you so nervous at the Civic Club the last time. So, watch it, all of you, for they will probably have just the same thing down at Hutchy Kutchy—there is perhaps nothing quite so disconcerting as to trip—as one comes on a stage. Going off—is not so bad; but—coming on, I have found that it requires a *tremendous* artist to rise above it. [*She starts down towards the table at the right, below the piano.*] So, watch it, all of you. Now, is everybody in his place? [*She stops below the table and picks up her notebook.*]

MRS. FELL. [*Handing Ritter the manuscript and getting up suddenly*] Oh, just one moment, Betty! [*She teeters across to the table at the right.*]

I want to get my other glasses—they're right here in my bag. [*She picks up the bag and starts back to her place.*] I beg pardon, everybody, but I can't tell one letter from another without these glasses. [*This last sentence culminates in a flighty giggle, for no reason at all, and then she sits down, and heaves a deep sigh of amusement.*]

MRS. PAMPINELLI. [*Who has been looking at her steadily*] Now, is everybody ready? [*Mrs. Fell simply lifts her eyes and looks at her; then proceeds to get her glasses out of the bag.*] Use your voices, children, and try to do it tonight just as you are going to do it tomorrow night at Hutchy Kutchy. [*She moves a step or two nearer the middle of the room.*] Doctor Arlington is still in his office.

HOSSEFROSSE. Yes.

MRS. PAMPINELLI. Mr. Rush—

TWILLER. [*Coming in through the center door*] Yes.

MRS. PAMPINELLI. Is just about to make his exit. [*He crosses above the piano and stands waiting at the right door. He's a bald-headed youth, between thirty and thirty-five, in dinner clothes, excessively well groomed but utterly nondescript.*] And Mrs. Arlington is putting on the dead-latch. [*Florence straightens up.*] All ready, now? [*She holds up her hands for a second, then claps them once.*] All right. [*Twiller goes out through the right door and Mrs. Pampinelli moves over towards the right, watching Florence.*]

FLORENCE. [*Pretending to put on a dead-latch*] Dead-latch.

SPINDLER. [*Standing in rigid military fashion*] Click-click. [*Florence turns and starts across towards the middle of the room, passing between the piano and the table below it.*]

FLORENCE. [*Glancing toward the center door*] You can come out now, Clyde, they've gone. [*She continues to the table at the left and stands resting one hand upon it.*]

HOSSEFROSSE. [*Bustling forward from the center door, removing his hat as he comes*] Anybody here, David? [*Spindler whistles shrilly, takes a step forward and tries to attract Hossefrosse's attention, by holding up his right arm and flicking his fingers at him. Teddy laughs and*] turns to tell Twiller, who is just rejoining him from the right hallway, what has happened. Florence turns and looks at Hossefrosse, then at Mrs. Pampinelli, who is standing at the right of the table below the piano. Mrs. Ritter gets up and simply staggers laughing through the center door and out to Teddy and Twiller.]

FLORENCE. [Speaking to Mrs. Pampinelli] That isn't right, is it?

MRS. PAMPINELLI. [Turning to Spindler at her right and holding up her hand] Please don't whistle, Mr. Spindler! I can't stand whistling.

FLORENCE. I thought we were going to take the last scene first.

[Mrs. Pampinelli and Mrs. Fell, together]

MRS. PAMPINELLI. [Moving around in front of the table and going near to Hossefrosse] We are taking the last scene first, Mr. Hossefrosse, that is the first scene.

MRS. FELL. [Holding up her hand] Wait a moment, wait one moment, just one moment, somebody's off the track! [Twiller and Teddy laugh again and Hossefrosse turns and looks at them. Twiller shakes his head, flips his hand at him and walks away into the right hallway, as though delporing his stupidity. Ritter begins to laugh.]

MRS. PAMPINELLI. I thought I had made that sufficiently clear.

[Mrs. Pampinelli, Mrs. Fell, Spindler and Twiller, together]

MRS. PAMPINELLI. We are taking the scene at the finish, Mr. Hossefrosse, between you and Miss McCrickett.

MRS. FELL. [Rising] That's the first scene, Huxley, and we are taking the last scene, between you and Florence, on page nineteen, right here, [She indicates the place in the manuscript.]

SPINDLER. [Addressing Teddy] I hope he doesn't pull anything like that tomorrow night. [He returns to his place below the window.]

TWILLER. [Coming back into view from the hallway] Don't weaken, Huxley, you know what they say about a bad rehearsal.

MRS. PAMPINELLI. [Topping them all] Please, children, please!

MRS. FELL. Down at the bottom of the page. [Mrs. Ritter comes through the center door again and sits down on the left partition-seat]

MRS. PAMPINELLI. [Speaking directly to Mrs. Fell] Please—[Mrs. Fell sits down again, slowly, Mrs. Pampinelli looking at her stonily.] let us have one director, if you please. [She withdraws her eyes slowly,

and Nelly darts a bitter look at her.] Now, don't let us have everybody talking at once; it only confuses people, and wastes a lot
of time. [*Hossefrosse stands bewildered in the middle of the room.
Mrs. Pampinelli addresses him directly, speaking with measured
emphasis.*] We are taking the *last* scene *first*, Mr. Hossefrosse: it is
the scene at the finish, between you and Miss McCrickett, just
before Paula comes on—

HOSSEFROSSE. Oh, I beg your pardon!

MRS. PAMPINELLI. And *after* Mr. Rush has left the stage.

HOSSEFROSSE. I thought we were beginning right from the beginning.

MRS. PAMPINELLI. No, I'd like to run through the *last* scene *first*, if
you don't mind; there are a few little things in it I'd like to correct.

HOSSEFROSSE. [*Turning and starting for the center door*] This was the
wrong entrance for that line, anyway.

MRS. PAMPINELLI. And you won't need your hat and cane in this
scene.

HOSSEFROSSE. That's so, too.

TWILLER. [*Who is standing out just at the right of the center door*] I'll take
them, Hux.

HOSSEFROSSE. [*Handing him the hat, gloves and cane*] Thanks. [*Turning
to Mrs. Ritter*] I'll get straightened out after while. [*Paula laughs.*]

MRS. PAMPINELLI. Now, Florence dear, will you go back?

FLORENCE. [*Crossing back again to the window*] Certainly.

MRS. PAMPINELLI. [*Crossing back to the right, in front of the table*] And
take it right from Mr. Rush's exit.

FLORENCE. [*Looking round at Hossefrosse*] Ready?

HOSSEFROSSE. [*In the center door*] Yes, I'm ready.

MRS. PAMPINELLI. [*To Florence*] Go on.

FLORENCE. [*Repeating her former business of putting on a dead-latch*]
Dead-latch.

SPINDLER. [*Having again assumed his rigid military attitude*] Click-
click. [*Florence turns and crosses again between the piano and the
table.*]

FLORENCE. [*With a glance at the center door*] You can come out now, Clyde, they've gone. [*She continues to her former position at the right of the little table at the left. Hossefrosse steps resolutely through the center door, gives her a wicked look, glances toward the door at the right, then strides forward and plants himself directly opposite her, his head thrown back, his eyes ablaze, and his arms akimbo.*]

HOSSEFROSSE. Did you come here to make a scene!

FLORENCE. [*Languidly, and without turning*] Have I made one?

HOSSEFROSSE. [*Getting loud*] What are you doing here?

FLORENCE. [*Raising her hand to enjoin silence*] Sh-sh—[*He turns abruptly and looks toward the door at the right; then back to her again.*]

HOSSEFROSSE. I want an explanation of this!

FLORENCE. [*Turning to him, and rather casually*] So do I.

MRS. PAMPINELLI. [*Standing at the right of the table below the piano*] Oh, more imperious, Florence dear! [*Florence and Hossefrosse look at her.*] More of this. [*She lifts her shoulders, eyebrows and chin, to illustrate her idea of the general hauteur of the line.*] Much more.

FLORENCE. [*Vaguely*] Don't you think she would cry there? [*Mrs. Pampinelli looks at her steadily for a pause and thinks: then she rests her lead pencil on the table and tilts her head a bit to one side.*]

MRS. PAMPINELLI. Do you want to cry there, dear?

FLORENCE. No, but I can if you want me to.

MRS. PAMPINELLI. No—personally, I think she's speaking more in anger than in sorrow. You see, dear, you are impersonating a wronged wife. Now, you yourself, Florence darling, are an unmarried girl—it is difficult for you to realize how excessively annoyed with her husband a married woman can become. I think I would take it with more *lift*. More of this, you know. [*She repeats the former illustration.*]

FLORENCE. [*Endeavoring to imitate the manner of delivery, and speaking in a deep, tragic tone*] So do I.

MRS. PAMPINELLI. Perfect.

HOSSEFROSSE. [*Turning to Mrs. Pampinelli*] Go on?

MRS. PAMPINELLI. Yes, go on.

HOSSEFROSSE. [*Clearing his throat and trying to summon his attack*] What is your reason for sneaking into my office at this hour?

FLORENCE. Is it necessary that your wife have a reason for coming into your office?

HOSSEFROSSE. You wanted to embarrass Mrs. Rush, that was it, wasn't it?

MRS. PAMPINELLI. [*Waving her hand toward them with an upward movement*] Tempo, children!

FLORENCE. I wanted to meet my rival.

HOSSEFROSSE. You could have met Mrs. Rush under more candid circumstances.

MRS. PAMPINELLI. [*Moving around towards them, in front of the table*] Tempo, children!

FLORENCE. The present ones suited my purposes better.

HOSSEFROSSE. [*Turning away impatiently*] Naturally!—you wanted a scene! [*He starts over to the right, but Mrs. Pampinelli is standing right in his way. So he stops short, but maintains the physical tautness of his character. Florence, too, has turned away, to the left, and is moving across in front of the table towards the armchair.*]

MRS. PAMPINELLI. [*Oblivious of Hossefrosse, and still making her upward gesture over his shoulder*] Tempo, Florence! [*Suddenly becoming conscious that she is obstructing Hossefrosse's cross, and stepping below him*] I beg your pardon.

HOSSEFROSSE. [*Bowing stiffly*] Not at all. [*He continues over to the right and stops, right in front of Spindler, and they stand looking into each other's eyes; while Mrs. Pampinelli comes up to the left of the table to the piano.*]

FLORENCE. [*Sitting down in the armchair*] I think if I were a scenic woman I've had ample opportunity during the last fifteen minutes to indulge myself.

HOSSEFROSSE. [*Still looking into Spindler's eyes*] You did I think—

MRS. PAMPINELLI. [*Beckoning to Spindler*] Mr. Spindler.

HOSSEFROSSE. I had the pleasure of hearing you.

FLORENCE. Was it a pleasure, Clyde?

[*Mrs. Pampinelli and Hossefrosse, together*]

MRS. PAMPINELLI. [*Still beckoning to Spindler*] Mr. Spindler!

HOSSEFROSSE. [*Whirling around and glaring at Florence*] It appears to amuse you! [*Spindler steps below Hossefrosse and passes up in front of him to Mrs. Pampinelli, who whispers something to him.*]

FLORENCE. [*Unfastening her neckpiece*] I have an inopportune sense of humor.

HOSSEFROSSE. You should be able to appreciate the situation, you created it!

FLORENCE. [*Looking over at him*] I didn't create her husband.

HOSSEFROSSE. [*Making a little gesture of annoyance*] I'm afraid I'm stuck! [*He tries hard to think, and Mrs. Pampinelli makes a gesture toward Mrs. Fell to give him the line, but Nelly is occupied in telling Ritter a story.*] But, don't tell me! [*He feels for the line again, and Mrs. Pampinelli tries to attract Nelly's attention.*] I guess I'm gone. [*Suddenly Nelly bursts into a fit of laughing, having made the point of the story.*]

MRS. PAMPINELLI. What is the line, Nelly? [*Ritter nudges her.*]

MRS. FELL. [*Stopping suddenly in her laughter and hitting him with her fan*] Stop that!

RITTER. Get on your job, you're holding up the show. [*Nelly looks excitedly toward Mrs. Pampinelli.*]

MRS. PAMPINELLI. What is the line, Nelly, please?

MRS. FELL. What! Oh, I beg your pardon, is somebody stuck?

MRS. PAMPINELLI. Mr. Hossefrosse.

HOSSEFROSSE. Got another mind-blank.

MRS. FELL. Oh, well, now, just wait one minute, please, till I see where I'm at. [*She searches frantically through the manuscript.*] Oh, yes, here it is! [*Ritter indicates a place on the page. She pushes his arm out of the way.*] I didn't create her husband. [*Teddy and Twiller laugh.*]

[*Mrs. Pampinelli, Florence and Hossefrosse, together*]

MRS. PAMPINELLI. No, dear, we've passed that.

FLORENCE. I've already said that, Nelly.

HOSSEFROSSE. It's the next line.

MRS. FELL. [*Vaguely, and looking through her lorgnon and spectacles at the manuscript*] Oh, have we passed that!

MRS. PAMPINELLI. The next line after the one you just read.

MRS. FELL. Oh, I see now where we are! The next line after that is, "You've all been listening to a lot of damned, cheap gossip."

[*Mrs. Pampinelli and Hossefrosse, together*]

MRS. PAMPINELLI. That's it.

HOSSEFROSSE. [*To Mrs. Pampinelli*] That certainly is my Jonah line.

MRS. PAMPINELLI. You've all been list—[*Spindler goes around to the right and sits on the piano stool, looking near-sightedly at the music.*]

HOSSEFROSSE. [*Turning to Florence, and assuming his character again*] You've all been listening to a lot of damned, cheap gossip! [*He starts to cross towards the left, passing between the piano and the table, but Mrs. Pampinelli is right in his way again, so he is obliged to stop short and wait.*]

FLORENCE. Which should show you that people are talking. [*Mrs. Pampinelli turns to see why Hossefrosse is not picking up his line.*]

MRS. PAMPINELLI. [*Stepping out of his way*] I beg your pardon. [*She circles down at the left of the table again.*]

HOSSEFROSSE. [*Continuing over towards the mantelpiece*] My fault. One or two old women, perhaps.

FLORENCE. Will it confine itself to those?

HOSSEFROSSE. [*Turning at the mantelpiece and coming back to the middle of the room*] Well, I can't control that.

FLORENCE. Have you tried?

HOSSEFROSSE. [*Whirling upon her, and literally shouting*] No!

MRS. PAMPINELLI. [*Standing at the right of the table below the piano*] Excellent.

HOSSEFROSSE. [*Turning and bowing briefly to her*] Thank you very much. [*Resuming the scene with Florence*] And I don't intend to. People will always talk; it may as well be at my expense as anybody else's.

MRS. PAMPINELLI. [*Leaning towards him across the table, and speaking with poisonous sweetness*] Anybody's *else*, dear.

HOSSEFROSSE. Beg pardon?

MRS. PAMPINELLI. Would you say anybody's else; it sounds better.

HOSSEFROSSE. [*Turning back again to Florence*] It may as well be at my expense as anybody else's. [*Mr. Spindler's elbow slips off the piano onto the keyboard, striking a perfectly villainous chord, and causing everybody to turn and look in that direction.*]

MRS. PAMPINELLI. Mr. Spindler, please.

SPINDLER. [*Adjusting his goggles, which have been slightly dislodged by the incident*] I'm sorry. [*Mrs. Pampinelli turns back to Hossefrosse.*] Never mind, Mr. Hossefrosse, it will come.

FLORENCE. Your position can't afford it.

HOSSEFROSSE. [*Taking a step towards the right*] I've given them nothing to talk about.

FLORENCE. No? [*He stops abruptly and turns and looks at her.*]

HOSSEFROSSE. What? [*He takes a couple of steps towards her.*]

FLORENCE. [*Rising*] Please, Clyde!—[*She crosses in front of the table at the left and goes towards him. Mrs. Ritter gets up from the partition-seat and comes down to the table at the right, below the piano.*] You're not talking to your office boy—[*Mrs. Ritter picks up the little chair from the left of the table and starts back again towards the center door.*] Let us get to the point.

HOSSEFROSSE. Very well.

[*Mrs. Ritter and Hossefrosse, together*]

MRS. RITTER. Excuse me, Florence. [*Florence bows and smiles.*] And you, too, Mr. Hossefrosse.

HOSSEFROSSE. What brought you here tonight? [*He turns to see the cause of the movement behind him.*] Don't mention it. [*Mrs. Ritter places the chair in front of the partition where she has been sitting, then crosses to the piano and gets her sewing basket, returning with it to the chair and sitting down to sew.*]

FLORENCE. Not to quarrel with you, for one thing.

HOSSEFROSSE. You wanted to embarrass Mrs. Rush, that was it, wasn't it?

FLORENCE. Not at all—you misunderstood me; I said, "I wanted to *meet* Mrs. Rush." [*Teddy comes in through the center door from the right hallway and sits down on the partition-seat at the right. Teddy is a frail little wisp of a youth around twenty, in dinner clothes. He has big eyes and good teeth, and laughs on the slightest provocation. His forehead is defectively high, and his thin hair is plastered back and brilliantined. His type is always to be found draped upon the banisters or across the pianos in the houses of the rich—a kind of social annoyance, created by the wealthy connections and the usual lack of available men.*]

HOSSEFROSSE. What did you want to meet her for? [*Twiller steps through the center door from the right hallway and whispers something to Mrs. Ritter. She answers him, and he steps out into the hallway and fills himself out a glass of claret from the bowl, then goes up and sits on the landing of the stairway and watches the rehearsal.*]

FLORENCE. Why, I thought that we three might—reason together, [*He holds her eye for a second, then turns away, and reaches in his various pockets for his cigarettes.*] concerning our respective futures.

HOSSEFROSSE. [*In a lowered tone, to Mrs. Pampinelli*] Forgot my cigarettes.

MRS. PAMPINELLI. Never mind, I only want lines. Go on, Florence. [*Hossefrosse takes an imaginary cigarette from an imaginary case, replaces the case and taps the cigarette on the back of his hand, puts it in his mouth, strikes an imaginary match on his shoe, and lights the cigarette.*]

FLORENCE. I've deferred the discussion for a long time, but it may as well be today as tomorrow.

HOSSEFROSSE. Your plan didn't work out very well, did it?

FLORENCE. Oh, yes, very well, indeed; although hardly as I had anticipated; thanks to *her* husband and *your* lies. [*He blows out the imaginary match and tosses it onto the floor at the right; then snaps his head around and glares at Florence. Mrs. Pampinelli glances down onto the floor, as though to assure herself that Mr. Hossefrosse hasn't really thrown a lighted match onto the carpet.*] You've evidently told this boy here that Mrs. Rush is your wife.

HOSSEFROSSE. I've told him nothing of the kind! [*He starts to cross again to the right, but Mrs. Pampinelli is again right in his pathway, standing in front of the table below the piano.*]

MRS. PAMPINELLI. [*Stepping below him, and going a step or two nearer Florence*] I beg your pardon.

HOSSEFROSSE. I beg *your* pardon. [*He continues over to the table below the window at the right and stands there, pretending to smoke.*]

FLORENCE. Then, you've allowed him to think so.

HOSSEFROSSE. [*Looking straight ahead*] That's business.

FLORENCE. Perhaps it is. It has at least allowed you to be present at the passing of Mrs. Rush. [*She turns and goes towards the back. Mrs. Ritter calls her to her and they start discussing the hang of Florence's skirt.*]

HOSSEFROSSE. [*Whirling around*] You are deliberately misinterpreting this situation! [*He starts to move across towards her, passing between the piano and table.*] Yes you are! It's perfectly ridiculous that a physician cannot take a woman patient without being subjected to the whisperings of a lot of vulgar scandal-mongers! [*Nelly Fell goes into violent laughter at something Ritter has just finished telling her. Florence and Mrs. Ritter continue their discussion of the dress, and Mrs. Pampinelli tries by dint of gesturing to attract Florence's attention.*]

MRS. PAMPINELLI. Florence dear, please.

FLORENCE. [*Turning suddenly, and continuing her lines*] Oh, I beg your pardon! [*She moves slowly towards the mantelpiece.*] This is not a romantic age, Clyde.

HOSSEFROSSE. Mrs. Rush is a patient of mine!

FLORENCE. [*Moving down at the left towards Ritter and Mrs. Fell*] She may have been originally. [*Mrs. Fell bursts out afresh over something else that Ritter whispers.*]

MRS. PAMPINELLI. [*Flicking her finger at Nelly*] Sh-sh, Nelly.

MRS. FELL. [*To Florence, who is standing looking at her*] I beg your pardon.

HOSSEFROSSE. [*Standing in the middle of the room*] She is *now*!

FLORENCE. [*Resting one hand on the armchair*] I'm not disputing it. [*He turns away, and stands at the left of the table below the piano.*] But she must have a very persistent malady—

MRS. FELL. Just one minute, Flossie—one minute—

FLORENCE. That hasn't responded to a treatment of more than six years—

MRS. FELL. Flossie, Flossie, Flossie! [*Florence stops and looks at her.*] Just a minute. [*She looks sharply at her manuscript.*]

MRS. PAMPINELLI. What is the matter, Nelly?

MRS. FELL. Oh, I beg your pardon, I thought she'd omitted a line. [*To Florence*] I beg your pardon.

MRS. PAMPINELLI. Go on, Florence. [*Ritter says something to Nelly and she hits him with the manuscript.*]

FLORENCE. Not to speak of the innumerable changes of air that she's enjoyed—[*Mrs. Pampinelli, standing over at the right below the piano, takes quite a little coughing spell, and Mrs. Ritter promptly gets up and goes to the punch bowl to fill her out a glass of punch.*] at your expense; and under your personal escort. [*Hossefrosse looks over at her. She raises her hand understandingly and starts slowly across in front of the table towards him.*] I have the day and date of the majority of them. So, you see, your chivalry is a bit trying, under the circumstances. [*He looks straight ahead and tries to look sullen and defeated.*]

MRS. RITTER. [*Up in the center door, holding aloft a glass of punch*] Betty!

FLORENCE. But, I haven't come here to reproach you, or to plead for your return. Not at all. I think you *love* this woman.

MRS. RITTER. [*Coming a little further forward*] Betty! [*Mrs. Pampinelli has another coughing spell.*]

FLORENCE. And in that case, I want to offer you your freedom—

MRS. PAMPINELLI. Careful, now, children. [*Mrs. Ritter comes forward to the table at the left and tries to attract Mrs. Pampinelli's attention to the glass of punch.*]

FLORENCE. If you want it.

MRS. PAMPINELLI. [*Holding up her forefinger*] One, two, three.

HOSSEFROSSE. [*Snapping his head around and shouting at Florence*] Well, I don't want it!

MRS. PAMPINELLI. Good!

HOSSEFROSSE. And I see absolutely no occasion for any such talk. [*Mrs. Fell drops her bag and reaches for it.*]

FLORENCE. You are probably more broad-minded than I. [*Nelly Fell utters a piercing little shriek, having almost fallen off the chair in* reaching to pick up her bag. Everyone turns and looks, and Teddy laughs, as usual.]

MRS. PAMPINELLI. What's the matter, Nelly?

MRS. FELL. [Straightening up, with Ritter's assistance, and laughing] I nearly fell off the chair. [Mrs. Ritter laughs and returns to the center door and stands.]

MRS. PAMPINELLI. Go on, Florence.

FLORENCE. And, really, I don't think your freedom would be a very good thing for you. You have a form of respectability that requires a certain anchorage in conventions. But unless you can reconcile yourself in the future to a more literal observance of those conventions, I shall be obliged to insist that you take your freedom.

MRS. PAMPINELLI. Look at her, Mr. Hossefrosse.

HOSSEFROSSE. Beg pardon?

MRS. PAMPINELLI. [With a touch of impatience] Look at her! [She begins to cough again.]

HOSSEFROSSE. Oh, yes, yes! [He turns and glares at Florence, who is standing just a couple of feet away from him.]

MRS. RITTER. [Holding the glass of punch aloft again] Betty!

FLORENCE. I have a couple of growing boys—[Mrs. Pampinelli passes right up between Florence and Hossefrosse to Mrs. Ritter, and takes the glass of claret.] who are beginning to ask me questions which I find too difficult to answer: and I will neither lie to them—nor allow them to pity me.

HOSSEFROSSE. What do you want me to do?

MRS. PAMPINELLI. [Handing the claret glass back to Paula, who goes to the bowl and refills it, and the notebook and pencil to Teddy] Just a moment. [She turns and comes forward in the middle of the room. Florence turns and moves over to the table at the left, and Hossefrosse remains standing at the table at the right.] Just one moment. Listen, Florence, dear. [She uses her handkerchief, then stuffs it in the bosom of her dress.] I want you, if you can, to make just a little bit more of that last line. Within the limits of the characterization, of course; but if you can feel it, I'd like you to give me just the barest suggestion of a tear. Not too much; but just enough to show that—under all her courage—and her threatening, she is still a woman—and a Mother. You see what I mean, dear?

FLORENCE. More emotion.

MRS. PAMPINELLI. In that last line. You are doing splendidly, darling, [*Turning to Hossefrosse*] both of you; [*He acknowledges his excellence with a short bow.*] but I have always *felt* that that last line— was really the *big* moment—of the play. It seems to me— [*She toys with her necklace, narrows her eyes and looks away off.*] that it is there—that she makes her big plea, for her boys, for her home—for every woman's home. And even thought that plea *is* made in the form of a threat—somehow or other—I seem to hear her saying, sub-vocally, of course, "In God's *name, don't* make it necessary for me to do this thing!" [*She concludes this speech rather dramatically, her arms outstretched. Mr. Spindler, at this point, engaged in a too curious examination of the keyboard accidentally touches D flat above high C. Everybody turns and looks at him, but his consciousness of guilt does not permit of his meeting their eyes, so he remains bent over the keyboard in precisely the attitude he was in when he struck the note.*]

MRS. FELL. Oh, go away from that piano, Mr. Spindler! [*Mrs. Ritter comes forward at the left with a dish of cakes and a glass of claret.*]

MRS. PAMPINELLI. [*Withdrawing her eyes witheringly from Spindler and turning back to Florence*] Do you see what I mean, dear?

FLORENCE. I think I do. Do you want me to go back?

MRS. PAMPINELLI. No, that's quite all right. We'll take it right from Mr. Hossefrosse's line, [*She turns toward Hossefrosse. And Mrs. Ritter takes advantage of the circumstance to offer Florence a cake; which, of course, is declined with thanks. Then she turns to Mrs. Pampinelli and waits till the lady has finished directing Hossefrosse.*] "What do you want me to do?" [*Mrs. Pampinelli turns back, to be confronted with the cakes and claret; and she takes both. Then she and Paula move back towards the center door.*]

HOSSEFROSSE. [*Clearing his throat*] What do you want me to do? [*Paula gives a shriek of laughter, at something Mrs. Pampinelli whispers to her.*

*Then Paula goes out through the center door and offers Twiller, who is
still sitting halfway up the stairs, some cake, which he accepts, and then
Teddy, who declines, and finally, after taking another one herself, sets the
plate down on the hallway table and resumes her chair up at the left;
while Mrs. Pampinelli, cake and claret in hand, wanders forward at the
right, passing over between the piano and the table below it.*]

FLORENCE. I've already told you.

HOSSEFROSSE. Then, I suppose I'm simply to decline all women
patients in the future, [*She makes a little sound of amusement.*] or
else submit them for general approval. [*He now presses the imaginary fire out of the cigarette on the imaginary tray on the table.*]

FLORENCE. Stick to your guns, Clyde.

HOSSEFROSSE. That's the only thing I see to do. [*Mrs. Pampinelli
stands over at the right watching the scene, and eating and drinking.*]

FLORENCE. Your tenacity is commendable, but it's a lost cause.
[*Looking at him steadily*] I appreciate your embarrassment—

HOSSEFROSSE. [*Turning to her, thrusting his hands into his coat pockets,
tilting his chin, and looking at her with an absurdly perky expression*]
I'm not embarrassed.

FLORENCE. Desolation, then.

HOSSEFROSSE. [*Snapping his fingers at her*] Ha! [*He swings rather jaun-
tily across and up towards the mantelpiece.*]

MRS. PAMPINELLI. More nonchalance in the cross, Mr. Hossefrosse.

HOSSEFROSSE. [*Turning to her suddenly*] Me?

MRS. PAMPINELLI. More savoir faire, as we say in French. [*She illustrates the idea with a kind of floating gesture of the hand.*]

HOSSEFROSSE. I see. [*He continues over to the left and down towards Ritter
and Mrs. Fell, endeavoring to execute Mrs. Pampinelli's idea by raising
his shoulders, stiffening his arms, throwing his head back and swinging
his legs, as he walks. Nelly Fell is whispering something to Ritter behind
her fan, so that, when Hossefrosse reaches them, he is obliged to touch
Ritter on the shoulder and suggest with a nod and a smile that the exigencies of the play require that he shall sit where Ritter is sitting. So,
Ritter jumps up and tiptoes across in front of the table and up to the piano,
where he stands leaning—and watching—particularly Mrs. Pampinelli.*]

FLORENCE. [*Moving to the table below the piano*] But, I shall be magnanimous; having loved and lost myself. So that, really, it may not be nearly so difficult as you imagine.

HOSSEFROSSE. [*Sitting on the chair vacated by Ritter*] Well, I can't say that I relish the prospect, with any such misunderstanding as this between us.

FLORENCE. [*Crossing to the table at the left*] It's the portion of half the world, Clyde. [*Twiller gets up from the stairs and comes down into the right hallway, where he stands watching.*]

HOSSEFROSSE. [*Trying to look sullen, by resting one elbow on his knee and hunching his shoulders*] It certainly isn't a very inviting one. [*Nelly Fell starts to whisper something in his ear*]

FLORENCE. But it has its compensations. [*Mrs. Pampinelli, having finished her cake and claret, sets the empty glass down on the table below the piano and uses her handkerchief.*] You'll have your memories, and I shall have the wisdom of disillusionment—[*The telephone bell rings, up in the left hallway. Mrs. Ritter jumps up, places her sewing basket on the chair, and, touching her hair, comes forward quickly at the right to the table below the piano.*] as well as the consciousness of lots of company.

MRS. RITTER. [*Speaking directly to Mrs. Pampinelli*] Is that my cue? [*Florence stops and turns and looks at her.*]

MRS. PAMPINELLI. Which cue, dear?

MRS. RITTER. [*Taking a step towards Florence, and with a little questioning, bewildered gesture*] The telephone is my cue, isn't it?

MRS. PAMPINELLI. [*With a touch of impatience*] No, darling, you're not on in this scene at all. Go on, Florence. [*Mrs. Ritter puts her hand to her cheek and looks from one to the other in puzzled embarrassment.*]

FLORENCE. [*Turning and resuming her lines to Hossefrosse, who, by this time, is deep in conversation with Mrs. Fell*] For there are a million women exactly like me. [*Mrs. Ritter bursts out laughing. So does Teddy. Twiller reaches over the partition and flips Teddy on the head with his handkerchief. Jenny appears in the left hallway to answer the telephone.*]

[*Mrs. Ritter and Florence, together*]

MRS. RITTER. [*Turning to Mrs. Pampinelli*] Oh, I beg your pardon! [*She leans across the table explaining to Mrs. Pampinelli, who tries politely to silence her by suggestion that the scene is in progress.*] I thought that was my cue.

FLORENCE. Secondary women. [*She moves around above the table and stands just above Hossefrosse.*] So don't look so tragic; you haven't lost anything but a lot of time;

JENNY. [*At the telephone*] Hello?

[*Mrs. Ritter, Florence and Mrs. Fell, together*]

MRS. RITTER. I was thinking of something else, you know, and when I heard the telephone, I thought it was for me.

FLORENCE. And that's always lost when it's spent on things that are insusceptible of conclusion.

MRS. FELL. [*Bursting into a perfect shriek of laughter at something Hossefrosse had just finished telling her, and pushing him away from her*] Huxley Hossefrosse, you are perfectly dreadful! [*He laughs, too, and attempts to tell her something else, but she turns away and waves him aside.*] No, No, No.

MRS. PAMPINELLI. No, dear, that is your own telephone.

JENNY. [*At the telephone still*] Just a minute. [*Mrs. Ritter turns towards the back of the room.*]

MRS. RITTER. Oh, so it is! [*Directly to Ritter*] I knew I had one telephone cue. [*She goes laughing through the center door and on out into the right hallway.*]

JENNY. [*Trying to attract Ritter's attention*] Mr. Ritter! [*But Ritter is absorbed in watching Hossefrosse. Florence stands waiting for Hossefrosse and Nelly to stop laughing, but as it doesn't look as though they will ever stop, she gives Hossefrosse a little dig in the shoulder with her finger. He straightens up abruptly.*]

FLORENCE. [*Prompting him*] I've lost her.

JENNY. Mr. Ritter!

HOSSEFROSSE. I've lost her.

FLORENCE. That was inevitable in your case, Clyde; you have a conventional soul. [*Jenny asks Teddy in pantomime to attract Ritter's attention.*]

HOSSEFROSSE. [*In a tone intended to express abysmal despair*] I've lost you. [*Ritter bursts out laughing. Teddy reaches out and indicates that he is wanted on the telephone. Jenny holds the telephone up, and he steps quickly out into the hallway to take it from her.*]

FLORENCE. That was incidental, eh?

HOSSEFROSSE. But, it seems to me there should be some other way.

FLORENCE. [*Moving to the right, above the table*] There is, my dear boy—for lots of people—

RITTER. [*At the telephone*] Hello? [*Jenny goes out.*]

FLORENCE. But not for you.

RITTER. Yes.

FLORENCE. You're too respectable—physically, I mean. [*She laughs a little, and stands above the table looking at him.*]

RITTER. Well, wait a minute, I'll talk to you upstairs. [*He sets the telephone down and starts towards the right to go upstairs. As he passes the center door he speaks to Teddy, who is still sitting just inside the center door on the right partition-seat.*] Hang that up when I get on, will you, Teddy? [*Teddy jumps up and goes out to the telephone, and holds it, waiting till Ritter gets on the extension upstairs.*]

FLORENCE. And Mrs. Rush has what it appears to me to be a rather—primitive husband—[*Hossefrosse gives her a narrow look.*] and you have a very modern wife. So be wise, Clyde; you know what usually happens to him who "loves the danger." [*There is a loud knock at the right door. Hossefrosse jumps to his feet and stands looking fearfully toward it. Florence assumes all the dignity at her command, drawing herself up, placing her right hand upon her throat, her left hand on her hip, and waiting—the proud but outraged wife. Mrs. Pampinelli holds up both hands and looks in the direction of the door, to impress everybody with the dramatic value of the situation. Teddy hangs up the receiver and stands watching her. Nelly Fell straightens up briskly and sits watching the door, in expectant attention. Then Mrs. Pampinelli makes a gesture to Florence to go on with her lines.*] Go into your office, I'll talk to this woman. [*Hossefrosse drops his head and shoulders and slinks across in front of the table, a beaten man. He continues up to the center door and out, into the right hallway. The*] *knock is repeated at the right door. Mrs. Pampinelli motions to Teddy that that is his cue to open the door. He comes through the center door and crosses above the piano to the right door, Mrs. Pampinelli at the same time moving over to the armchair at the right and enshrining herself. Teddy opens the door; and Mrs. Ritter swishes self-consciously. Nelly Fell and Mr. Twiller give a little ripple of applause, but Mrs. Pampinelli holds one finger up toward Nelly and shushes her. Mrs. Ritter is wearing a rather bizarre-looking hat, set at something of a challenging angle, and as she comes forward at the right of the piano, she bursts into a self-conscious giggle. But Mrs. Pampinelli reproves her with a look. So she controls herself and crosses below the piano, Teddy, simultaneously, crossing above the piano. She stops at the corner of the piano and rests her left hand upon it. Then she places her right hand upon her hip, and, tilting her head back, looks at Teddy, who has stopped directly above her. Ritter appears on the stairway, and moves down a step or two, watching his wife, narrowly.]*

MRS. RITTER. [*Flipping her left hand at Teddy, in an attempt to give a fly impression*] Hello, kid.

TEDDY. Hello, Mrs. Arlington. [*Mrs. Ritter swishes down towards the left, shaking her head from side to side and holding her arms akimbo. She turns around to her left, gives Florence a look, supposed to be a very contemptuous look, and stands in the middle of the room again, facing Teddy.*]

MRS. RITTER. [*Speaking directly to Teddy*] Is my sweetie in? [*Ritter moves slowly down to the landing of the stairs, watching his wife as though she were some baffling phenomenon.*]

TEDDY. No, ma'm, he ain't.

MRS. RITTER. [*Drawing her shoulder up, and speaking in a high unnatural key*] What!

TEDDY. He went about six o'clock.

MRS. RITTER. Why, I had an appointment with *him*!

TEDDY. He might be back, maybe.

MRS. RITTER. But, I can't wait unless I'm *certain* that he's coming back.

TEDDY. He was expecting you.

MRS. RITTER. [*Still shaking her head and trying to generally to appear bold*] Yes, I know he was. [*Turning to the table at the left, back of which Florence is standing*] I suppose I'd better leave a note for him. [*She indicates the table with a waving gesture of her left hand.*]

TEDDY. You'll find that green one is the best pen.

MRS. RITTER. [*Stepping to the table*] Thanks. [*She looks at Florence, who gives her a withering look over her right shoulder and turns away to the mantelpiece at the left. Then Mrs. Ritter gives her a scornful laugh.*] Ha! Ha! Ha!

RITTER. [*Sweeping his hand across his brow, groaning, and falling down the stairs, into the right hallway*] Oh my God!

MRS. PAMPINELLI. [*Seeing him fall, and jumping up*] Oh, my dear! [*Everybody turns.*]

TWILLER. [*Trying to catch him*] Hold it! [*Spindler rushes past Mrs. Pampinelli and out the center door into the right hallway. Teddy jumps into a kneeling position on the right partition-seat and looks over the partition. Florence and Mrs. Fell rush up to the center door and try to see what's going on, Nelly dodging from one side of Florence to the other and peering through her lorgnon.*] Are you hurt, old man?

HOSSEFROSSE. [*Handing his cane and gloves to Spindler*] Hold those, please. [*Spindler takes them, and Hossefrosse prepares to assist Twiller to lift Ritter from the floor.*]

TWILLER. Get some water, somebody! [*Spindler rushes out the left hallway. Mrs. Pampinelli sweeps up from the table at the right to the center door.*]

MRS. RITTER. [*Bewildered, in the middle of the room, as Mrs. Pampinelli passes her*] What is it, Betty?

MRS. PAMPINELLI. Now don't get excited, Paula. [*Mrs. Ritter steps frantically across to the piano and turns, leaning against it, looking wide-eyed at Nelly Fell.*]

HOSSEFROSSE. Lift up his head.

MRS. PAMPINELLI. [*Looking eagerly out into the right hallway*] Is he hurt, boys?

TWILLER. I want to get him under the arms. [*They lift Ritter onto a bench in the hallway. Nelly Fell turns away from the center door with an exclamation of distress.*]

HOSSEFROSSE. We'd better lay him right here.

MRS. RITTER. Is it Fred, Nelly?

MRS. FELL. I don't know, dear

[*Mrs. Pampinelli and Mrs. Fell, together*]

MRS. PAMPINELLI. [*Addressing Hossefrosse and Twiller*] You can lay him right here, boys, I think it'll be as good as any.

MRS. FELL. What is it, Florence, did Mr. Ritter fall downstairs?

FLORENCE. I think so.

MRS. FELL. [*Covering her eyes and swaying*] Oh, dear child, don't! [*Florence puts her arm around her and guides her towards the armchair at the left.*]

MRS. PAMPINELLI. Give me one of those pillows, Teddy. [*He hands her a pillow from the partition-seat where he's kneeling.*]

MRS. FELL. [*Sinking into the armchair at the left*] Betty, I think I'm going to faint!

MRS. PAMPINELLI. [*Turning to her*] Sit down, dear, I'll get you some water. [*Calling and beckoning out into the hallway*] Jenny dear! Come here, please!

HOSSEFROSSE. [*Rushing across from the right to the left hallway*] I think I'd better call Dr. Wentworth. [*He snatches up the telephone and works the hook violently.*]

MRS. PAMPINELLI. Yes, I would. [*She turns around to her left and stands looking questioningly at Mrs. Ritter.*] Go on with your lines, Paula.

MRS. RITTER. Well, is he *dead*, Betty?

MRS. PAMPINELLI. [*With a definite little gesture of her right hand*] Never mind! [*The curtain commences to descend, and she sweeps forward.*] We will go right on from where Mr. Ritter fell downstairs.

THE CURTAIN IS DOWN

AS IT RISES AGAIN FOR THE PICTURE

HOSSEFROSSE. [*At the telephone*] Landsdowne 8, please—right away! [*Spindler rushes in from the left hallway carrying a glass of water, and followed immediately by Jenny. Twiller is ministering to Ritter. Mrs. Pampinelli is standing in the middle of the room, facing the cen-*

ter door, and holding up both her hands, as a signal to the various artists that the rehearsal is about to be resumed; so they quickly step to the various positions in which they respectively were when Ritter fell.]

MRS. RITTER. [*Addressing Teddy*] Yes, I know he was. I s'pose I'd better leave a note for him.

END OF THE ACT

⇨ ACT II ⇦

NOTE:—*The setting for this act consists simply of three wings set in the middle of the stage about four feet from the footlights, and parallel to the footlights, the wing in the middle, a plain one, and the one on either side of it, a door-wing. These doors open toward the footlights, and the one on the right is hinged to the right, and the one on the left, to the left. From these door-wings, regular plain wings oblique off to the back wall; and the whole thing is lashed and stage-screwed after the fashion of regulation stage setting. As the doors in the back flat open, there can be had a glimpse of footlights, and just beyond them, a neutral drop, in grayish black, to represent an auditorium. Between the back flat and the stage footlights (as distinguished from the regular footlights), the miniature stage is set to represent the interior of a doctor's waiting room. Through the door at the right can be seen a desk and revolving chair, and a couple of plain chairs against the wall; and through the left door, a table, littered with magazines, a cabinet, a revolving bookcase and two more chairs. There is a bright rug on the floor. Between the black flat and the regular footlights, over toward the left, there is a stage-screw sticking right up out of the floor; and between the two doors there is a plain chair with its back against the flat. Over the door on the right, there is a row of six electric bulbs with a cord and button depending from it; and further right, half-way back, there is a wood-wing, set as though it were the exterior backing for a window in the miniature set. Over at the left, away back, fastened about head-high against the back wall, there is a small switchboard arrangement. Just below this there is an old chair, without a back, with a newspaper lying upon it.*

A waltz is being played somewhere off at the right. Florence and Mrs. Ritter are standing in the middle of the stage, facing the flats, talking.

Florence is wearing a fawn-colored, one-piece coat-dress, buttoned high at the throat, military fashion, and a toque made of wine-colored velvet leaves. She wears fawn-colored slippers and stockings, and carries a fitch muff. Mrs. Ritter is wearing a very rich-looking coat-suit in blue serge, trimmed at the collar and cuffs with white monkey fur. Her hat is dark blue felt, quite large, with a bird of paradise set at a decidedly rakish tilt. Her slippers and stockings are black, and she carries an umbrella. Over at the extreme left, and forward, Mrs. Fell is hearing Mr. Twiller read his lines from the manuscript. Mrs. Fell is gowned in a brilliant creation of silver cloth trimmed with sea-green satin. There are numerous strings of crystal beads hanging in the front from the waist to the bottom of the skirt, and she has a spreading poinsetta in scarlet velvet fastened at her waist. There is a long, fish-tail train to the gown, lined with the green satin, and she has a heavy rope of pearls and sea-green beads around her neck, from which her lorgnon depends. There are diamonds in her hair, diamonds galore upon her arms and hands, and she's wearing her diamond dog collar. Her slippers and stockings are of pale green. Mr. Twiller has on a double-breasted blue serge suit, a black derby, black shoes and fawn-colored spats, and a perfectly villainous-looking black moustache, absurdly large, and obviously artificial. He stands leaning upon a cane, reciting his lines to Mrs. Fell. Mr. Spindler, in a dinner suit, is trying desperately to unfasten the stage-screw from the floor at the left, while Mr. Hossefrosse, wearing a light business suit, a light, soft hat, tan shoes and spats, and carrying a cane and gloves, is pacing back and forth between the left door and the extreme left, reciting his lines to himself. He is atrociously made up, with the carmine smeared heavily on his cheek bones. The stage manager, in a tan jumper and army shirt, dirty white running pumps, a battered old cap adorned with many tobacco tags, and carrying a hammer, wanders on from the right and crosses the stage, passing below Florence and Mrs. Ritter, who turn and look at him curiously, and continues on up at the left to the switch board, where he picks up the newspaper from the broken chair, and, after lighting his pipe, sits down to read. He is apparently disgusted with the world and utterly oblivious of his surroundings. The waltz music stops, and Mr. Hossefrosse comes to a halt in his pacing, right outside the left door. It is instantly flung open, knocking him toward the left, and disarranging his hat, and Mrs. Pampinelli sweeps out—in a princess gown of ruby-colored velvet, with a long train, and heavily trimmed about the upper part of the bodice with ornaments of ruby-colored beads. Her shoulders and arms are bare, she has a small string of rubies at her throat—a bracelet and several rings of rubies; as well as a high Spanish comb studded with rubies. Her slippers are of black velvet. Mrs. Ritter gives a little cry as Mr. Hossefrosse is struck by the door.

MRS. PAMPINELLI. [*Holding the door ajar*] Oh, did I hit you, Mr. Hossefrosse! I'm so sorry.

HOSSEFROSSE. [*Settling his hat*] That's all right.

MRS. PAMPINELLI. [*To the ladies*] The setting looks splendid, girls! [*Crossing quickly below Hossefrosse towards the left*] Will you come here for a moment, Mr. Spindler?

MRS. RITTER. [*Turning away to the right*] I don't want to see it till I go on.

FLORENCE. [*As Hossefrosse comes towards her*] You'd better keep away from that door, Mr. Hossefrosse. [*She and Mrs. Ritter laugh.*]

[*Hossefrosse and Mrs. Pampinelli, together*]

HOSSEFROSSE. Yes, I think I had.

MRS. PAMPINELLI. [*Up at the left, addressing the stage manager*] Are you ready, Mr. Stage Manager? [*He continues to read.*]

[*Hossefrosse and Mrs. Pampinelli, together*]

HOSSEFROSSE. [*Brushing his clothes*] I don't think a whisk broom'd be out of place on this stage either.

MRS. PAMPINELLI. [*Turning to Spindler, who is still occupied with the stage-screw*] Mr. Spindler, will you come here, please? [*Turning back to the stage manager*] Mr. Stage Manager! [*Spindler goes towards her, and Hossefrosse goes through the left door.*]

STAGE MANAGER. [*Looking up from his paper, very peevishly*] Yes?

MRS. PAMPINELLI. Are you all ready?

[*Stage Manager and Twiller, together*]

STAGE MANAGER. Yes, sure, I'm all ready. [*He resumes his newspaper.*]

TWILLER. [*Turning sharply to Spindler, who has stopped on his way to Mrs. Pampinelli to call Mrs. Fell's attention to the stage-screw, and to warn her to be careful of it*] Oh, go away! Can't you see we're busy.

MRS. PAMPINELLI. Mr. Spindler!

SPINDLER. [*Stepping briskly to her side*] Yes, ma'm?

MRS. PAMPINELLI. Come here, please, [*Turning to the stage manager*] Mr. Stage Manager—[*He looks up.*] this young man will give you the cue for the curtain, in case I am not here.

STAGE MANAGER. All right. [*He resumes his newspaper.*]

MRS. PAMPINELLI. [*Turning and coming forward again, holding her skirt up off the floor*] You stand right here, Mr. Spindler, and I'll give you the signal when I'm ready.

SPINDLER. All right.

MRS. PAMPINELLI. [*Hurrying towards the left door*] Now, is everybody all right?

FLORENCE. Yes.

MRS. RITTER. I think so.

MRS. PAMPINELLI. How are *you*, Paula?

MRS. RITTER. [*Giggling*] All right.

MRS. PAMPINELLI. Where's Mr. Hossefrosse? [*She glances frantically about.*]

[*Florence and Mrs. Ritter, together*]

FLORENCE. He's just stepped on to the stage.

MRS. RITTER. He was here a minute ago.

MRS. PAMPINELLI. Mr. Hossefrosse, where are you! [*She opens the left door.*]

MRS. RITTER. [*Calling*] Mr. Hossefrosse! [*He opens the right door and comes out.*]

HOSSEFROSSE. Yes?

[*Teddy and Mrs. Pampinelli, together*]

TEDDY. [*Sitting at the desk over at the right, in the miniature set beyond the flats, to Mrs. Pampinelli, as she comes through the left door*] There he is.

MRS. PAMPINELLI. [*To Teddy, as she steps into the miniature set, through the left door*] Where's Mr. Hossefrosse?

[*Florence and Mrs. Ritter, together*]

FLORENCE. [*To Hossefrosse*] Mrs. Pampinelli's looking for you.

MRS. RITTER. [*Calling*] Here he is, Mrs. Pampinelli! [*Hossefrosse steps quickly to the left door and starts in, just as Mrs. Pampinelli comes out through the right door. Florence steps over to the left door and catches Hossefrosse by the arm, and pulls him back.*]

MRS. PAMPINELLI. [*Coming through the right door*] Where *is* he?

MRS. RITTER. [*Pointing to Hossefrosse*] There he is! [*She laughs.*]

FLORENCE. [*Drawing Hossefrosse back*] Mrs. Pampinelli wants you!

HOSSEFROSSE. [*To Mrs. Pampinelli*] I beg your pardon.

MRS. PAMPINELLI. Oh, Mr. Hossefrosse!

HOSSEFROSSE. [*Crossing to the right towards her*] Yes?

MRS. PAMPINELLI. Are you all right?

HOSSEFROSSE. I think so, yes.

MRS. PAMPINELLI. How is your make-up?

HOSSEFROSSE. All right, I think.

MRS. PAMPINELLI. [*Indicating the right door*] Would you stand here for a moment under this light until I see it?

HOSSEFROSSE. Certainly. [*He goes to the right door and stands with his back against it. The light from the row of electric bulbs over the door shines down on his face. Mrs. Pampinelli stands off to his right, surveying his make-up critically.*]

MRS. PAMPINELLI. Very good.

HOSSEFROSSE. Not too much red?

MRS. PAMPINELLI. No, I shouldn't say so.

HOSSEFROSSE. [*Indicating his right cheek*] Up here, I mean.

MRS. PAMPINELLI. No, I think the contour of your face requires it. It heightens the expression. [*She starts across towards the left.*] It's very good. [*Hossefrosse comes over and chats with the ladies about his make-up.*] Mr. Twiller! [*Twiller turns from Mrs. Fell.*]

TWILLER. Yes? [*Turning back to Mrs. Fell*] Excuse me, Nelly.

MRS. FELL. Certainly.

MRS. PAMPINELLI. How is your moustache?

TWILLER. [*Touching it gingerly*] All right, I think.

MRS. PAMPINELLI. Is it quite secure?

TWILLER. I think so. [*Mrs. Ritter, Florence and Hossefrosse turn and look.*]

MRS. PAMPINELLI. [*Stepping back a step from him and looking at the mustache, with her head titled a bit to the left side*] You've made it a little smaller, haven't you?

TWILLER. [*Touching the left side of his mustache*] I cut it down a bit on this side.

MRS. PAMPINELLI. I thought you had.

TWILLER. I was a little conscious of it.

MRS. PAMPINELLI. Well—I don't know but that it's better for the characterization.

TWILLER. And how are my eyes? [*He turns and looks out and away off, widening his eyes as though he were having his picture taken.*]

MRS. PAMPINELLI. [*After looking keenly at his eyes for a second*] Very effective. [*She turns quickly away towards the right, and Twiller turns to his left to Mrs. Fell.*] Now, is everybody ready? [*They all smile and nod.*] Your gloves and cane, Mr. Hossefrosse?

HOSSEFROSSE. [*Crossing above Florence and Mrs. Ritter towards Mrs. Pampinelli, extending his cane and gloves*] Yes?

MRS. PAMPINELLI. [*Turning towards Mrs. Fell*] Places, Nelly! Get ready, Mr. Spindler!

SPINDLER. I'm all ready. [*Mrs. Fell closes the manuscript, excuses herself to Twiller, and crosses, above him, towards the right. He goes back at the left and says something to Spindler, then comes forward again.*]

MRS. PAMPINELLI. [*Calling through the left door*] Are you all right, Teddy?

TEDDY. [*Beyond the flats, over at the right*] All right. [*As Mrs. Fell passes above Florence and Mrs. Ritter, on her way over to the right, she whispers something to them which causes a general laugh—then she continues on over to the door at the right and takes up her official position, as promptress.*]

MRS. PAMPINELLI. [*Turning and addressing them generally*] Now, is everybody all right? [*They all nod.*] You both all right, girls? [*Mrs. Ritter nods.*]

FLORENCE. All right.

MRS. PAMPINELLI. [*Turning around to the left to Mr. Spindler, and with an authoritative gesture*] All right, then—take up the curtain!

SPINDLER. [*Waving his hand to the stage manager*] All right, Stage Manager!

STAGE MANAGER. [*Getting up, very reluctantly*] Are you ready?

[*Mrs. Pampinelli and Spindler, together*]

MRS. PAMPINELLI. Yes, all ready.

SPINDLER. Let her go!

MRS. PAMPINELLI. [*With a kind of ceremonious flourish of the hand*] Take up the curtain! [*The stage manager tosses his newspaper onto the chair and steps out of sight, to the left. There is an anxious pause. Then Mrs. Pampinelli starts violently and grabs the knob of the left door.*] Oh, wait one moment! [*Spindler rushes back at the left, whistling.*]

[*Florence, Mrs. Ritter, Twiller and Hossefrosse, together, as Mrs. Pampinelli pulls open the left door*]

FLORENCE. Wait a minute!

MRS. RITTER. Oh, wait!

TWILLER. Hold it!

HOSSEFROSSE. [*Grabbing the door and holding it open*] Not yet!

MRS. RITTER. [*Calling to the stage manager*] Just a minute!

MRS. PAMPINELLI. [*Going in through the left door*] One moment, please! [*She vanishes to the right, and there is a slight pause, during which the curtain, which has been raised four feet, can be seen through the door to descend again. They all exchange looks of distress and amused annoyance. Then Mrs. Pampinelli hurries out through the door again.*] All right!

SPINDLER. [*Who has come forward at the left*] Is it all right? [*Hossefrosse releases the door and it closes.*]

MRS. PAMPINELLI. Yes, it's all right. [*Spindler goes towards the back at the left and she follows him half-way.*]

SPINDLER. All right, Mr. Stage Manager.

STAGE MANAGER. [*Off at the left*] Are you ready?

[*Mrs. Pampinelli and Spindler, together*]

MRS. PAMPINELLI. Yes, all ready, Mr. Stage Manager!

SPINDLER. Let her go!

MRS. PAMPINELLI. [*Turning and coming forward at the left*] Take it up!
[*She stands just to the left of the left door, peering through the flats.
Spindler is farther back at the left, peering also; and Mrs. Fell is over
at the right, peering. There is a pause. Mr. Hossefrosse takes up his
position outside the left door, preparatory to making his entrance. He
settles his clothes generally, and clears his throat.*] The curtain is
going up, Mr. Hossefrosse, go on.

HOSSEFROSSE. Is it up?

MRS. PAMPINELLI. Yes, yes, go on! [*He opens the door, rather magnificently, and swings in. There is a ripple of applause, and the door closes
after him; and they all try to find a crevice behind the flats that will
afford a glimpse of the stage beyond. The stage manager appears from
the left carrying a regulation door-slam, which he brings forward and
drops, with a bang, just to the left of the left door. They all turn and
look at him, in resentful astonishment, but he simply gives them a look
of infinite disdain and returns to his chair at the back to read.*]

HOSSEFROSSE. [*Beyond the flats*] Anybody here, David?

TEDDY. [*Beyond the flats, over toward the right*] No, sir.

HOSSEFROSSE. [*Beyond the flats, moving towards the right*] No telephones?

TEDDY. No, sir.

HOSSEFROSSE. [*Coming through the right door, without his hat*] Nothing
at all, eh? [*Mrs. Ritter is standing right in front of the door.*]

MRS. PAMPINELLI. Get away from the door, Paula! [*Paula jumps to the
left. Mrs. Fell takes advantage of the crevice caused by the door being
open, to try to see the audience.*]

TEDDY. [*Who can see through the open door standing at the desk*] No, sir.

HOSSEFROSSE. [*Leaning over and laying his cane and gloves on the chair
between the doors*] All right, sir. [*The door begins to swing behind
him.*]

MRS. PAMPINELLI. Keep that door open, Mr. Hossefrosse! [*Spindler comes forward at the left to see what's the matter. Hossefrosse thrusts his foot back and kicks the door open.*]

HOSSEFROSSE. And I think that will do very nicely for this day. [*The door begins slowly to swing again.*]

MRS. PAMPINELLI. There it goes again, Mr. Hossefrosse!

HOSSEFROSSE. It won't *stay* open! [*Mrs. Fell looks around the door.*]

MRS. PAMPINELLI. Take hold of that door, Nelly! [*Nelly puts one foot around it, and stands looking at her manuscript. Spindler goes back at the left and looks through the wings again, at the stage.*]

HOSSEFROSSE. [*In a frantic whisper*] Telephone!

MRS. FELL. Telephone, somebody!

HOSSEFROSSE. Good Lord!

FLORENCE. Mr. Spindler, telephone! [*Spindler rushes forward to the left.*]

MRS. PAMPINELLI. Where is he?

SPINDLER. What?

FLORENCE. The telephone bell!

MRS. PAMPINELLI. Where's your bell?

SPINDLER. [*Pulling the battery arrangement out of his pocket*] Has the cue been given?

TEDDY. [*Picking up the telephone on the desk beyond the flats*] Hello?

MRS. PAMPINELLI. Ring it! Of course it's been given! [*He rings the bell, and Hossefrosse steps through the right door and watches Teddy anxiously.*]

SPINDLER. I didn't hear it!

MRS. PAMPINELLI. [*Annihilating him with a look, and starting over towards the right door*] Well, why aren't you over here when your cue's given and then you would hear it! [*Spindler trails over after her.*]

HOSSEFROSSE. [*Over his shoulder, to Mrs. Pampinelli*] Shush!

MRS. PAMPINELLI. [*Turning sharply back towards the left, and directly to Spindler, who is right behind her*] Shush! [*She passes below him and continues towards the left.*] Keep away from that door, they'll see you! [*In attempting to keep out of the way of the door, Spindler turns sharply and trips over the screw of a stage-brace, falling his length across the open door. Mrs. Ritter gives a little scream, and Mrs. Pampinelli whirls round and glares at him. He scrambles to his feet, and Mrs. Ritter giggles and pulls him to the left, away from the door.*]

HOSSEFROSSE. [*Standing in the open door, addressing Teddy*] Mrs. A.? [*Teddy nods, and Hossefrosse pretends to pick up an imaginary telephone from a desk just to the left of the right door.*] Yes? All right. [*He pretends to hang up and set the telephone down on the desk again.*] You can clear out of here now, David, any time you like—Mrs. Arlington is on her way up.

TEDDY. [*Rising, and settling the various papers on the desk*] All right.

MRS. RITTER. [*Helping Mr. Spindler to brush off his clothes*] Did you hurt yourself, Mr. Spindler? [*Mrs. Pampinelli tries to attract Spindler's attention to the door-slam*]

SPINDLER. No. [*He hurries over to the door-slam at the left and picks it up.*]

HOSSEFROSSE. I'll let you off early Monday. [*Florence stands anxiously outside the left door.*]

TEDDY. Oh, that's all right.

HOSSEFROSSE. And don't forget to leave that list with the Robinson people on your way down Monday.

TEDDY. No, sir, I won't; I have it right here in me pocket. [*Florence puts her lips against the left door and coughs hard. Then she shuffles her feet; so does Spindler. Hossefrosse steps through the right door and looks over toward the left door.*]

HOSSEFROSSE. [*Addressing Teddy, in a subdued tone*] Is that someone coming?

TEDDY. [*Looking toward the left door*] I think so. [*There is a slight pause, then Mrs. Pampinelli makes a decisive movement to Spindler and he brings the door-slam down with a thunderous bang. Mrs. Pampinelli starts violently.*]

MRS. PAMPINELLI. That's too loud Mr. Spindler!

SPINDLER. There's too much wood on it! [*He starts across to the right.*]

HOSSEFROSSE. [*Stepping down to Teddy's desk and picking up his hat*] That can't be Mrs. Arlington already. I won't see anyone else. [*He starts back towards the door.*] Tell them I've gone; and don't let anybody wait. [*He takes hold of the door as he steps through.*]

Say you're just locking up the office. [*He comes through the door and tries to close it, but Nelly's foot is still around it, and she is lost in the manuscript. He pulls at the door, but she is oblivious.*]

MRS. RITTER. Nelly! [*Spindler gives a little whistle to attract her attention.*]

MRS. PAMPINELLI. Let go of the door, Nelly!

MRS. FELL. [*Jumping out of the way, to the right*] Oh, I beg your pardon! [*Hossefrosse scowls at her and closes the door. Spindler jumps to the door and turns a key, which he has in his hand, in the lock, then touches the button at the end of the cord, extinguishing the row of lights over the door. Mrs. Ritter is right in his way as he rushes back, and they dodge each other twice before Mr. Spindler can get past. When he reaches the left door, he raps violently, Mrs. Pampinelli directing his activities with little nervous gestures. There is a pause: then the left door is opened by Teddy. Mrs. Ritter is right in front of it.*]

MRS. PAMPINELLI. [*Standing to the left of the door*] Get out of the way, Paula! [*Mrs. Ritter jumps out of the way, to the right, then looks back at Mrs. Pampinelli and giggles, but Mrs. Pampinelli puts her finger on her lips.*]

FLORENCE. [*Passing through the left door*] Good evening, son.

TEDDY. [*Reaching out and closing the door*] Good evening. [*There is prolonged applause from beyond the flats, and everybody, having seen Florence safely through the door, rushes to his favorite crevice between the wings, or rip in the scenery, to see how she is being received by the audience.*]

FLORENCE. [*Beyond the flats*] Isn't the Doctor in?

TEDDY. No, ma'm, he aint; he went about six o'clock.

FLORENCE. That's unfortunate, I wanted to see him. [*Hossefrosse turns away form the right door, where he's been peeking, and mops his brow: then he turns and puts his hat down on the chair.*]

SPINDLER. [*Stepping towards him from the left door*] How do you feel?

HOSSEFROSSE. All right; but that door and that telephone got me kind of rattled.

MRS. PAMPINELLI. [*Looking over from the extreme left of the back flat, where she has been peeking*] Shush, boys! [*Hossefrosse turns away and tiptoes towards the right, and the others resume their peeking.*]

MRS. FELL. [*Turning to Hossefrosse, as he passes below her*] What's the matter, Huxley, did something go wrong? [*Mrs. Pampinelli looks over again to see who's talking.*]

HOSSEFROSSE. [*Indicating the right door*] That door kind of got me rattled for a minute.

MRS. FELL. I don't think that the audience noticed it.

MRS. PAMPINELLI. Shush! [*Nelly consults her manuscript, listening at the same time to the dialogue beyond the flats, and Mr. Hossefrosse continues to the extreme right and forward, trying to make the squeak of his new shoes as inaudible as possible. Mrs. Pampinelli puts her ear to the flat and listens keenly.*]

TEDDY. [*Faintly, beyond the flats*] Why, he always asts me to wait whenever he's expectin' his wife downtown. [*Spindler suddenly turns from the wing where he has been peeking, and, breaking into quite a jaunty little whistle, starts across towards the left; but Mrs. Pampinelli turns abruptly and glares him into silence. He clasps his hand over his mouth and apologizes with an obsequious little gesture.*]

FLORENCE. [*Beyond the flats*] I see. And he was expecting her this evening?

TEDDY. Yes, ma'm.

FLORENCE. Do you know her? [*Spindler trips and almost falls over the stage-screw in the floor at the left. Twiller, who has been standing down at the extreme left, makes an impatient move and goes up towards the back.*]

MRS. PAMPINELLI. Oh, Mr. Spindler, for pity's sake do keep still for one moment!

SPINDLER. [*Squatting down and attempting to remove the screw*] We'd better get this thing out of here, before somebody gets hurt.

MRS. PAMPINELLI. Now, don't take that out of there, Mr. Spindler! You might loosen the scenery.

SPINDLER. This isn't connected with the scenery.

MRS. PAMPINELLI. You don't know whether it is or not! Leave it where it is.

SPINDLER. [*Getting up and moving over towards the right*] Somebody's going to get their neck broken, the first thing you know.

MRS. PAMPINELLI. Very well, then, that will be their misfortune!

We've simply got to be careful, that's all. Get ready, Paula. [*Mrs. Ritter giggles and takes up her position outside the left door.*]

MRS. FELL. [*As Spindler comes towards her*] What's the matter, Mr. Spindler?

SPINDLER. [*In quite a temper, and indicating the stage-screw over at the left*] Why, that thing there is sticking right up in the middle of the floor, and the first thing you know—

MRS. PAMPINELLI. Shush!—[*He turns and scowls at her, and she glares at him. He passes below Mrs. Fell and over to Hossefrosse, at the extreme right and forward, where he whispers his grievance.*]

MRS. FELL. You all right, Paula? [*Paula nods yes.*]

MRS. PAMPINELLI. Don't be nervous, now, Paula. [*Twiller comes forward at the left.*]

MRS. RITTER. I'm not the least bit, dear, really.

MRS. PAMPINELLI. Well, that's splendid, dear. I'll open the door for you. [*She takes hold of the knob of the left door.*]

MRS. RITTER. All right, thank you. [*They stand listening, keenly.*]

FLORENCE. [*Beyond the flats*] Do you mind if I wait a few minutes, in case he comes?

TEDDY. [*Beyond the flats*] Why, I was just going home.

FLORENCE. Oh, you were? [*Twiller lifts his hat and gives it a little wave at Mrs. Ritter, and she waves her hand back at him.*]

TEDDY. Yes, ma'm; and I have to lock up the office before I go.

MRS. PAMPINELLI. [*Suddenly*] There it is now, dear. [*She opens the door, and Mrs. Ritter steps back a bit, in order to make a more effective entrance.*] Good luck, darling.

MRS. RITTER. [*Turning to her.*] Thank you, dear. [*She steps through the door, tripping awkwardly over the door-strip. Mrs. Pampinelli makes a gesture of extreme annoyance. There is an outburst of applause; then Mrs. Pampinelli closes the door, and they all step to the flats and peek through, Mrs. Pampinelli's at the left door, Mrs. Fell at the right, Mr. Spindler between them, and Hossefrosse and Twiller about half-way back at the right and left, respectively. There is a pause; and then Mrs. Ritter can heard beyond the flats.*] Hello, kid!

TEDDY. Hello, Mrs. Arlington.

MRS. RITTER. Is my sweetie in?

TEDDY. No, ma'm, he ain't.

MRS. RITTER. [*With an unnatural inflection*] What!

MRS. FELL. [*Calling over in a whisper to Mrs. Pampinelli*] Betty! [*Mrs. Pampinelli doesn't hear her, so she tiptoes over towards her.*] Betty!

MRS. PAMPINELLI. What?

MRS. FELL. Did Paula trip?

MRS. PAMPINELLI. [*Coming away from the flat, and moving down to Mrs. Fell*] Yes. [*Mrs. Fell gives her an annoyed shake of her head.*] But I don't see how anyone can get onto *that* stage *without* tripping.

MRS. FELL. I don't either.

MRS. PAMPINELLI. It seems an utter impossibility to me for anyone, especially a woman, to get through those doors without catching her heel or her skirt or something. [*Spindler crosses to the left, back of the ladies, and speaks to Twiller.*]

MRS. FELL. [*Returning to the right door*] It's dreadful.

MRS. PAMPINELLI. [*Turning to her left and going back again to the left door*] I don't see the necessity of it.

MRS. FELL. [*Opening her manuscript*] I don't either.

MRS. PAMPINELLI. [*Listening keenly*] I'm afraid they're not hearing Paula at all.

MRS. FELL. What?

MRS. PAMPINELLI. I say, I'm afraid Paula isn't loud enough.

MRS. FELL. Well, why don't you speak to her, Betty, she's sitting right here. [*She indicates the point right inside the right door, and Mrs. Pampinelli, picking up her skirt, hurries over. Mrs. Fell out of the way, to the right.*]

MRS. PAMPINELLI. [*Putting her lips to the joining of the door-wing and the side wing*] Speak a little louder, Paula! I'm afraid they're not hearing you!

MRS. FELL. Can she hear you?

MRS. PAMPINELLI. A little louder dear! [*The right door is thrust open by Teddy.*]

TEDDY. [*In a frantic whisper*] There's no pen and ink on the desk! [*Spindler rushes over from the left.*]

SPINDLER. What? [*Mrs. Pampinelli, Mrs. Fell and Mr. Hossefrosse rush round to him from the right.*]

TEDDY. No pen and ink!

MRS. PAMPINELLI. What is it, Teddy?

[*Teddy and Spindler, together*]

TEDDY. No pen and ink on the desk!

SPINDLER. No pen and ink!

MRS. PAMPINELLI. My God!

MRS. FELL. Tell her to use a lead pencil.

[*Teddy and Mrs. Pampinelli, together*]

TEDDY. [*To Mrs. Fell*] There's none on there!

MRS. PAMPINELLI. Give him a lead pencil, Mr. Spindler!

SPINDLER. [*Whirling and springing towards the left*] Haven't got one! [*Teddy, Mrs. Pampinelli and Mrs. Fell rush after him.*]

[*Spindler and Mrs. Pampinelli, together*]

SPINDLER. Twiller!

MRS. PAMPINELLI. Oh, dear, dear!

TWILLER. [*Rushing towards them from the left*] What's the matter?

[*Spindler and Teddy, together*]

SPINDLER. Got a lead pencil?

TEDDY. Give him a lead pencil, Ralph!

TWILLER. [*Dropping his cane*] No! [*They fling him out of the way, to the left, and rush on back to the stage manager.*] What are you trying to do, knock me off my feet!

MRS. PAMPINELLI. Haven't you got one, Mr. Twiller?

[*Spindler and Mrs. Fell, together*]

SPINDLER. [*To the stage manager*] Got a lead pencil, old man?

MRS. FELL. [*At Mrs. Pampinelli's heels*] There's one in my bag somewhere!

[*Mrs. Pampinelli, Spindler and Teddy, together*]

MRS. PAMPINELLI. [*Turning to Mrs. Fell*] See what they're doing out there, Nelly!

SPINDLER. [*To the stage manager*] Or a fountain pen!

TEDDY. [*To the stage manager*] They need it on the stage!

[*Mrs. Fell and Stage Manager, together*]

MRS. FELL. [*Turning and rushing back towards the right door*] Certainly, darling!

STAGE MANAGER. [*Feeling his shirt pockets*] Well, now, wait a minute, wait a minute!

MRS. FELL. [*Turning with a despairing gesture, after having opened the right door and looked in*] My dear, they're not doing a thing, they're just sitting there!

MRS. PAMPINELLI. [*Turning to the left*] Hurry, boys! [*Turning to the right*] Tell them to say something, Nelly! Anything at all! Something about the weather! [*Nelly runs to the extreme right end of the flat. Teddy and Spindler come rushing forward at the left.*] Did you get it, Teddy?

[*Teddy and Spindler, together*]

TEDDY. Yes!

SPINDLER. Yes, he's got it!

MRS. PAMPINELLI. [*Indicating the left door*] Go on here, Teddy! [*He grabs the knob of the door, but it won't open.*]

MRS. FELL. [*Calling through the flats*] Say something, Paula!

MRS. PAMPINELLI. You should never leave the stage during a scene, Teddy!

[*Teddy and Mrs. Fell, together*]

TEDDY. [*Wrestling with the door*] Damn these doors!

MRS. FELL. [*Calling through the flats*] Something about the weather!

MRS. PAMPINELLI. Take hold of this, Mr. Spindler! [*He grabs the knob of the door and Teddy runs across to the right door.*]

TEDDY. I'll go on here!

MRS. FELL. [*As Teddy goes through the right door*] If you can't use one door, use the other! [*The door closes after him; and Mrs. Pampinelli turns and looks upon Spindler, who is trying to get the left door open.*]

MRS. PAMPINELLI. You know, this is *all your fault*, Mr. Spindler. [*He doesn't look up.*] You said you'd attend to all those properties!

MRS. FELL. What's the matter with the door, Betty?

MRS. PAMPINELLI. [*To Spindler*] Never mind it now. [*She moves towards the center of the stage.*]

SPINDLER. We'd better get it open before somebody has to use it again.

MRS. PAMPINELLI. Go away from it, I tell you! [*He walks away towards the left, sulking.*] It will probably open all right from the other side. [*She comes forward slowly, touching her hair and relaxing generally, then, suddenly, stands stock-still, and listens, wide-eyed. She looks quickly at Mrs. Fell, who is carefully settling her necklace, at the right door.*] What's wrong out there, Nelly? [*Nelly turns and looks through the flats then turns quickly to Mrs. Pampinelli.*]

MRS. FELL. I think he's up!

MRS. PAMPINELLI. [*Frozen to the spot*] Who? [*Nelly looks again, and then back to Mrs. Pampinelli.*]

MRS. FELL. All of them!

MRS. PAMPINELLI. [*Picking up her skirt and rushing towards the right door*] Let me see! [*Nelly jumps out of the way, to the right, and Twiller and Spindler rush to the left door and peek through. Mrs. Pampinelli peeks through, and then speaks through the flats*] What's the matter, Teddy? Go over and get your hat and coat! [*Turning frantically to Mrs. Fell*] He's up in his lines! What is it?

MRS. FELL. [*In a panic*] Up in his lines!

[*Mrs. Pampinelli and Mrs. Fell, together*]

MRS. PAMPINELLI. [*Speaking through the flats*] Go over and get your hat and coat, Teddy! Don't stand there like a jack!

MRS. FELL. [*Handing the manuscript to Hossefrosse, who is standing at her right*] Oh, find that for me, will you, Huxley! [*He takes the manuscript from her and turns it over furiously, while Nelly opens her lorgnon.*] About page eleven, I think it is! [*She assists him in finding the place.*]

MRS. PAMPINELLI. What was the last line, Nelly? This is dreadful!

MRS. FELL. Now, wait a minute, darling! Don't get me nervous, or I'll *never* be able to find it! [*Twiller and Spindler are in a panic of suspense over at the left door.*]

HOSSEFROSSE. Here's page eleven.

MRS. FELL. Is that eleven? Well, now, here it is, right here.—Why, a— I'll get you an envelope!

MRS. PAMPINELLI. What's the next?

MRS. FELL. The next is—a—why a—I've got to go now—

[*Mrs. Fell and Mrs. Pampinelli, together*]

MRS. FELL. It takes me nearly an hour to get home!

MRS. PAMPINELLI. [*Calling through the flats*] I've got to go now!

[*Teddy and Mrs. Pampinelli, together*]

TEDDY. [*Beyond the flats*] I've got to go now!

MRS. PAMPINELLI. [*Calling through the flats*] It takes me nearly an hour to get home.

TEDDY. It takes me an hour to get home!

MRS. FELL. Are they all right?

MRS. PAMPINELLI. [*Coming away from the flats*] Yes, they're all right now. But you'd better stand right here. I'm afraid of Paula. [*She moves towards the left.*]

SPINDLER. [*Coming towards her*] You know, I could have *sworn* I put a pen and ink on that desk!

MRS. PAMPINELLI. [*Imperiously*] Please, Mr. Spindler, don't explain anything! I am interested in results. [*She turns and moves back again towards the right, and Spindler goes over to the left. Just as he passes beyond the left door, the entire lock and knob fall to the floor. He turns nervously, only to find Mrs. Pampinelli, who has turned quite as nervously, looking at him dangerously.*]

SPINDLER. I didn't *touch* it!

MRS. PAMPINELLI. Will you go away before you ruin the entire performance! [*He snaps around and goes over to the left and up towards the back.*]

TEDDY. [*Opening the left door and swaying through*] Good night. [*He is dressed in a brown sack-suit and wears tan shoes.*]

FLORENCE. [*Beyond the flats*] Good night, son.

MRS. RITTER. [*Beyond the flats*] Good night, kid.

MRS. PAMPINELLI. [*Going towards him*] You should never walk off the stage, Teddy, in the middle of a scene! [*He closes the door behind him, and, pressing his hand to his brow, starts towards the left.*] Do something, no matter what it is! [*He falls backward in a full-length faint. She catches him.*] Oh, dear child! Mr. Spindler! Come here, Mr. Twiller, Teddy's fainted! [*Twiller, who has been standing over at the left, and forward, rushes towards her; and Mrs. Fell, followed by Hossefrosse, comes rushing from the right.*]

MRS. FELL. [*In a panic*] What's the matter, Betty!

MRS. PAMPINELLI. Take Teddy over to the door, Mr. Twiller, he's fainted!

TWILLER. [*Dropping his cane, in his excitement*] I *can't* take him now, I've got a cue coming right here in a minute! [*Spindler comes rushing down from the left.*]

MRS. PAMPINELLI. Here, Mr. Spindler, take Teddy over to the door, where he'll get some air! He's sick. Look at the color of him. [*She hands him to Spindler, who half carries him up at the left; and she and Twiller follow behind them.*] Hold on to him, now, Mr. Spindler.

MRS. FELL. [*Turning back towards the right door, and addressing Hossefrosse, who has returned to his former position down at the right*] I always said he wasn't strong enough for that part! [*She just gets past the right door when it is frantically opened and Mrs. Ritter thrusts her head out.*]

MRS. RITTER. [*Breathlessly*] Mr. Twiller! [*The door closes again.*]

MRS. FELL. [*Running towards the left*] Mr. Twiller! They're waiting for you!

MRS. PAMPINELLI. [*Rushing forward at the left*] What is it?

MRS. FELL. [*In a perfect frenzy*] They're waiting for Mr. Twiller!

MRS. PAMPINELLI. Mr. Twiller! [*He snatches up his cane from the floor, but the hook of it catches in the stage-brace, and he has considerable yanking to do to get it loose. Mrs. Fell raps on the left door.*] Go on, Mr. Twiller, for Heaven's Sake! The stage is waiting! [*She pulls the door open for him. He straightens his hat and then raps on the wing beside the door.*] Oh, go on! Never mind rapping! That's been done! [*He steps through the door and she slams it after him, catching his left arm and hand. The cane is in his left hand, and it falls at Mrs. Pampinelli's feet. She pulls the door open again to release his arm; then gives the door a definite slam. A burst of applause greets Twiller's entrance. Mrs. Pampinelli is in perfect wrath. She sweeps across towards the right, and back again all the way across to the left; then turns and starts back towards the right. As she passes the left door she sees Twiller's cane, and, realizing in a flash that he will have need of it in this scene, she picks it up, opens the door slightly, and flings it onto the stage. Then she continues on towards the right,*]

*turns and crosses back again to the left, holding up her skirt and
bristling with temper.*]

MRS. FELL. [*Back at the right door, speaking to Hossefrosse, down at the
right*] How are my eyes? Instead of paying attention to his part!

MRS. PAMPINELLI. [*Coming across to the right*] People rehearsing their
cues a thousand times, and then don't know them when they
hear them! It's positively disgusting! [*She turns and goes back
again to the left, turns, and starts back towards the right. Hossefrosse
tiptoes towards her.*]

HOSSEFROSSE. What happened to Teddy, did he get sick out there?

MRS. PAMPINELLI. No, just a little reaction. [*Hossefrosse nods comprehendingly.*] He gives too much to the scene. He doesn't understand emotional conversation yet. [*Hossefrosse shakes his head
knowingly and returns to the right, and Mrs. Pampinelli steps to the
left door and listens.*]

FLORENCE. [*Just audibly, beyond the flats*] She's waiting for my very
unpunctual husband. In fact, we are both waiting for him, to be
precise. But I've just been telling her I'm afraid we may as well
give it up, for he's never kept an appointment in his life. I'm
sorry he isn't here, if you wanted to see him.

TWILLER. [*Beyond the flats*] I don't know whether I wanted to see him
or not; it depends.

FLORENCE. I don't understand you.

TWILLER. I don't fully understand myself! [*There is a very general
laugh from beyond the flats. Mrs. Pampinelli looks anxiously at Nelly,
and Nelly looks up at her from the manuscript.*]

MRS. PAMPINELLI. What was *that?*

MRS. FELL. [*Not having caught what she said*] What?

MRS. PAMPINELLI. What was that the audience was laughing at?
[*Mrs. Fell peeks through at the door where she is standing, then turns
desperately to Mrs. Pampinelli.*]

MRS. FELL. Half of Mr. Twiller's mustache fell off! [*She looks through the
peek again. Mrs. Pampinelli put her hand against her brow and leans
upon the stage-brace, the picture of tragedy. Mrs. Fell turns to her again.*]
I don't think the audience noticed it, he stuck it right on again.

MRS. PAMPINELLI. That doesn't matter, there is absolutely no excuse for it! He's been here since four o'clock this afternoon! [*She crosses towards the left and back again.*]

FLORENCE. [*Beyond the flats*] What sort of a rumor was it, Mr. Rush, if I may ask?

TWILLER. [*Beyond the flats*] The usual kind. [*There's another laugh from beyond the flats, and Mrs. Pampinelli stands petrified, just below the left door. Mrs. Fell turns quickly and peeks, then turns quickly to Mrs. Pampinelli.*]

MRS. FELL. [*Dispairingly*] It fell off again! [*Mrs. Pampinelli raises her fists and shakes them.*]

MRS. PAMPINELLI. Well, why on earth hasn't he the brains to leave it off!

MRS. FELL. He has his hat on, too! [*Mrs. Pampinelli steps to the left door and speaks through it.*]

MRS. PAMPINELLI. Leave your mustache *off*, Mr. Twiller! Leave it *off!*—And take off your *hat*, you're inside. [*Hossefrosse tiptoes over from the right.*]

HOSSEFROSSE. What's the matter, did his mustache fall off?

MRS. PAMPINELLI. Yes, twice; he keeps sticking it back on. [*He shakes his head regretfully and tiptoes back to the right.*]

MRS. RITTER. [*Beyond the flats*] It's perfectly ridiculous!

FLORENCE. [*Beyond the flats*] Too bad my husband isn't here.

TWILLER. [*Beyond the flats*] Yes, it is; I had counted upon seeing him.

FLORENCE. I'm sure he'd be able to explain.

TWILLER. Well, I hope he would!—the thing is damned annoying! [*Mrs. Ritter gives an unearthly laugh, which is supposed to express derision. Mrs. Fell looks up from her manuscript, and Mrs. Pampinelli smiles and nods approvingly at her.*] Even it *you don't* appreciate it!

MRS. FELL. Wonderful. [*She turns and smiles and nods at Hossefrosse; then they all listen again. The stage manager, who has arisen from his chair at the sound of Mrs. Ritter's disdainful laughter, comes forward at the left, with his pipe in one hand and his newspaper in the other. He has a puzzled, inquiring expression, and looks from one to the*

other quizzically; but Mrs. Pampinelli has her back to him, Mrs. Fell
is looking at her manuscript, and Mr. Hossefrosse's face is, as usual,
utterly expressionless, so he steps to the juncture of the back flats with
the side wings and peeks through, curiously. Then he returns to his
chair up at the left, shaking his head from side to side.]

MRS. RITTER. [*Beyond the flats*] I don't know what it is, yet!

TWILLER. [*Beyond the flats*] You know very well what it is!

MRS. RITTER. You haven't told us.

TWILLER. You're here, aren't you!

MRS. RITTER. Yes.

TWILLER. Well, that's it, exactly! [*Mrs. Pampinelli smiles approvingly,*
and moves towards the right.]

MRS. PAMPINELLI. [*Calling Hossefrosse, who is engaged in studying his*
lines from a paper, over at the right] Mr. Hossefrosse.

MRS. FELL. [*Turning to him*] Huxley! [*He looks up, and tiptoes towards*
Mrs. Pampinelli.]

MRS. PAMPINELLI. How is this hall to speak in?

HOSSEFROSSE. Why, I shouldn't say it was good.

MRS. PAMPINELLI. I thought not.

HOSSEFROSSE. It's too big for the speaking voice.

MRS. PAMPINELLI. [*With a gesture*] You have to *project* the tone, do you
not?

HOSSEFROSSE. Oh, yes, absolutely.

MRS. PAMPINELLI. [*Taking a step towards the back flat, and listening*] I'm
afraid they're not hearing Paula at all.

HOSSEFROSSE. [*Putting his finger to his throat*] I'm using my upper register almost entirely.

MRS. PAMPINELLI. [*Glancing at him*] You're very fortunate to know
how to do it.

HOSSEFROSSE. Did it sound all right from back here?

MRS. PAMPINELLI. Oh, splendid, yes, Mr. Hossefrosse!—your voice is
beautiful. [*He raises his hand deprecatingly.*] Really—I was just
saying to Mrs. Fell, I'm so sorry there isn't another act, that you
might sing a solo between them. [*He beams and deprecates again,*
profusely, and turns to the right. Spindler comes down at the left and

towards Mrs. Pampinelli.] Really! Splendid. [*She sees Spindler.*] Where's Teddy?

SPINDLER. He's gone over to the drug store.

MRS. PAMPINELLI. With his make-up on?

SPINDLER. He said that he wanted to get some aromatic spirits of ammonia.

MRS. PAMPINELLI. You have a cue right here soon, haven't you?

SPINDLER. [*Taking the telephone arrangement from his pocket, and crossing towards the right door*] Where are they?

MRS. FELL. [*Suddenly looking up from her manuscript*] Telephone, Mr. Spindler!

MRS. PAMPINELLI. There it is now, ring it!

SPINDLER. [*Shaking it desperately*] It won't ring! [*Mrs. Fell turns to Hossefrosse in desperation.*]

[*Mrs. Pampinelli, Mrs. Fell and Hossefrosse, together*]

MRS. PAMPINELLI. Shake it harder, it rang before!

MRS. FELL. What's the matter with the fool thing!

HOSSEFROSSE. Hit it against something, Mr. Spindler!

SPINDLER. There's something the matter with the battery!

FLORENCE. [*Audibly, from beyond the flats*] Hello!

MRS. PAMPINELLI. [*Relaxing*] Let it go—it's too late now. [*Spindler continues to tinker with it.*] You've missed every other cue, [*She moves towards the left.*] you may as well be consistent for the rest of the evening.

SPINDLER. [*Following her*] Well, good night! I can't help it if the electricity won't work, can I?

MRS. PAMPINELLI. [*Turning upon him furiously*] You should have attended to it beforehand and then it *would* work! [*Mrs. Fell waves her hand at them, to be quiet.*]

SPINDLER. Well, My God! I can't be in a half-a-dozen places at the same time!

MRS. FELL. Shush! [*Hossefrosse tiptoes up to her and deplores the noise that Mrs. Pampinelli and Spindler are making.*]

MRS. PAMPINELLI. No one is asking you to be in half-a-dozen places at the same time! You've simply been asked to attend to your cues; and you've missed every one you've had!

MRS. FELL and HOSSEFROSSE, together. Shush!

SPINDLER. You told me to take care of Teddy, didn't you?

MRS. PAMPINELLI. I told you to take him to the door! I *didn't* say to take him all the way to the drug store!

SPINDLER. Did you want me to let the man wander off somewhere by himself, and maybe die!

MRS. FELL. [*Waving her manuscript at them*] Shus—sh!

[*Mrs. Pampinelli and Spindler, together*]

SPINDLER. Just for the sake of not missing a cue!

MRS. PAMPINELLI. [*With bitter amusement*] There is very little danger of his dying! And even if he did die, your duty is here! [*She points to the floor with an imperative gesture. The right door is quietly pushed open, and Twiller, with one-half of his mustache gone, pokes his head out.*]

TWILLER. Shush! [*He glances from one side to the other, withdraws his head, and quietly closes the door. Spindler crosses below Mrs. Pampinelli, to the left, then turns and looks at her angrily.*]

MRS. FELL. [*Turning to Hossefrosse*] What did I tell you! Making more noise out here than they are out there!

MRS. PAMPINELLI. [*Still holding her gesture, but following Spindler with her eyes.*] Performances are never interrupted simply because one of the artists happens to die! If you were a professional you'd know that; but you're not! [*She turns away from him, towards the right, and simultaneously, the left door is opened, almost striking her. She raises her arm to protect herself. Mrs. Ritter is standing in the doorway.*]

MRS. RITTER. [*Speaking to Twiller, who is still beyond the flats*] Look and see. [*The telephone arrangement in Spindler's hands suddenly rings wildly.*]

MRS. PAMPINELLI. [*Turning to him frantically*] Oh, stop that thing! [*Mrs. Ritter glances furtively over her left shoulder at Mrs. Pampinelli. Mrs. Fell comes rushing over, motioning to Spindler to stop the bell.*]

SPINDLER. [*Struggling with the bell*] I can't stop it! [*Mrs. Ritter hastily steps back through the door and pulls it to after her.*]

MRS. PAMPINELLI. Well, then, take it outside, where they can't hear it! [*Spindler scrambles towards the back and out of sight at the left. Mrs. Pampinelli starts back towards the right.*]

MRS. FELL. What's the matter with that Spindler man, anyway!

MRS. PAMPINELLI. I don't know what's the matter with him! I've given up thinking about him.

MRS. FELL. He acts to me like a person that wouldn't be in his right mind! [*She goes back towards the right door.*]

MRS. PAMPINELLI. [*Standing in the middle of the stage*] He's simply not a professional, that's all. [*The left door opens again and Mrs. Ritter is standing in it. Mrs. Pampinelli turns suddenly and looks at her. Mrs. Ritter repeats her unearthly laugh, which again arouses the curiosity of the stage manager, to the extent that he rises and comes forward again at the left to get a look at her. Then he returns to his chair, taking the door-slam with him, and standing it against the wing.*]

MRS. RITTER. [*Addressing Twiller, beyond the flats*] What about the gentlemen?

FLORENCE. [*Beyond the flats*] Jealous husbands, chiefly, aren't they? [*Twiller comes out through the left door, past Mrs. Ritter.*] Didn't you want to leave a message for the Doctor, Mr. Rush? [*Twiller turns right round and goes back to the door.*]

TWILLER. Who, me?

FLORENCE. If you wish.

MRS. RITTER. [*Having some difficulty seeing Florence over Twiller's right shoulder*] He might leave an apology.

MRS. PAMPINELLI. [*Very much annoyed, and stepping close to the flat, just to the right of the door*] Get out of the doorway, Mr. Twiller!

FLORENCE. [*Beyond the flats*] Perhaps we haven't convinced him of his mistake.

[*Mrs. Pampinelli and Mrs. Ritter, together*]

MRS. PAMPINELLI. [*Trying desperately to attract Twiller's attention, and becoming more emphatic*] Get out of the doorway, Mr. Twiller, you're covering Paula up!

MRS. RITTER. [*Trying to talk to Florence over Twiller's shoulder*] Well, he'll apologize to *me*, whether we've convinced him or not.

[*Mrs. Fell and Hossefrosse come over to see if they can be of any assistance.*]

[*Mrs. Pampinelli and Twiller, together*]

MRS. PAMPINELLI. [*Becoming desperate*] Paula! [*Paula gives her a nervous glance.*] Will one of you go farther in! Mr. Twiller!

TWILLER. [*Addressing Florence*] Have you convinced yourselves? [*He gives Mrs. Pampinelli an irritated look over his left shoulder.*]

FLORENCE. That there has been a mistake?

MRS. PAMPINELLI. Go farther in, one of you! [*Twiller gives her another look, then speaks to Florence.*]

TWILLER. Yes! [*Mrs. Pampinelli can contain herself no longer, so, picking up her skirt, and holding her hand against the left side of her, she darts across the open door, to the left, and speaks to them around the edge of the door. Mrs. Fell, taking advantage of the circumstance of Mrs. Pampinelli's crossing, tiptoes up to Twiller and strikes him on the left arm, quite viciously, with the rolled manuscript. As a polite remonstrance, he shakes his left hand and foot at her. But, she is not dismayed, and repeats the attack, even more viciously. Then he turns and glares at her, and she turns away towards the right, desperately.*]

FLORENCE. A great mistake.

MRS. RITTER. Disappointed? Because, you know, we can invent a scandal, if you insist.

MRS. FELL. Oh, what a man! What a man!

[*Florence and Mrs. Pampinelli, together*]

FLORENCE. I'm afraid *my* presence here would be a bit incongruous, even for that.

MRS. PAMPINELLI. Go farther in, Mr. Twiller, don't both of you stand wedged in the doorway that way, it looks dreadful!

TWILLER. [*Raising his arm and resting his hand against the jamb of the door, completely cutting off Mrs. Ritter's view of Florence*] That's the rub. [*Mrs. Ritter stands on her tiptoes to try and see over his arm, but being unsuccessful in this effort, stoops a bit, and tries to look under his arm.*]

MRS. PAMPINELLI. Take your arms down, Mr. Twiller! [*Mrs. Ritter reaches up and quietly but firmly draws Twiller's arm down. Mrs.*

Pampinelli turns away to the left, disgusted.] My God! I never gave any such direction as that!

FLORENCE. Be at ease, Mr. Rush; if you were not mistaken I should have known it—and so should you; I'm not a tragic woman. Did you want to leave any message for the Doctor, Mrs. Rush?

MRS. RITTER. [*At Twiller's right*] Yes—[*Twiller turns his head sharply and looks right into her eyes. She steps around back of him and speaks to Florence over his left shoulder.*] I wish you'd say that my husband called—[*Twiller turns and looks into her eyes again, and she steps around back of him again, to his right.*] for my bill. [*She reaches out and starts to draw the door to. Twiller, very ill at ease, and awkwardly looking from side to side, not knowing just how to get out gracefully, makes a full turn round to his right.*]

TWILLER. [*Raising his hat to Florence*] Good evening, Mrs. Arlington. [*Mrs. Ritter closed the door, causing him to drop his cane; but he's too excited to notice it.*]

HOSSEFROSSE. [*Standing at the right door, extending his hand*] Great, old man!

TWILLER. [*Dropping his gloves, as he shakes hands*] Thanks. [*He continues to the right.*]

MRS. FELL. [*As he passes below her*] Splendid, Ralph! What happened to your mustache? [*She laughs.*]

TWILLER. Can you beat that, Nelly! I couldn't *coax* that thing off before I went on!

HOSSEFROSSE. [*Holding the knob of the right door*] Shush!

MRS. FELL. I don't think the audience noticed it.

HOSSEFROSSE. [*Turning to them*] Shush! [*Twiller goes down to the right, and Mrs. Fell returns to her manuscript. The left door is flung open. They all watch eagerly.*]

MRS. RITTER. [*Inside the left door*] If you will, please?

FLORENCE. Certainly.

MRS. RITTER. Thanks.

FLORENCE. Don't mention it.

MRS. RITTER. [*Trying to appear very bold*] Good bye.

FLORENCE. Good bye. [*Mrs. Ritter gives another famous laugh, sways through the door, tripping over the door-strip, closes the door, looks at*

Mrs. Pampinelli, who is standing at the left, and bursts out laughing.
There is prolonged applause from beyond the flats.]

MRS. PAMPINELLI. Splendid, Paula!

HOSSEFROSSE. [Listening intently for his cue, from beyond the flats]
Shush-shush! [Mrs. Ritter looks at him, still laughing foolishly.]

MRS. FELL. [Waving at Paula] Lovely, dear!

MRS. RITTER. [Turning to Mrs. Pampinelli] I forgot my umbrella.

MRS. PAMPINELLI. Where is it?

MRS. RITTER. I left it on the stage.

MRS. PAMPINELLI. That doesn't matter. [Hossefrosse tries to silence them
by dint of impatient gesturing with his right hand.]

MRS. RITTER. Oh, Betty, I think I saw Clara Sheppard out there!

MRS. PAMPINELLI. Not really?

HOSSEFROSSE. Shush!

FLORENCE. [From beyond the flats] You can come out now, Clyde,
they've gone. [Hossefrosse yanks the right door open, causing the
wood-wing at the right to topple and fall forward.]

TWILLER. [Leaping to catch it, before it hits Mrs. Fell] Hold it! [Mrs. Fell
hunches her arm and shoulder and screams.]

MRS. PAMPINELLI. [Rushing over from the left] What is it?

TWILLER. [Struggling to set the wing up in place again] This thing
nearly fell! Just got it in time! [Mrs. Fell moves out of the way, over
the left, and Mrs. Pampinelli tries to assist Twiller.]

MRS. PAMPINELLI. Is it all right now?

TWILLER. [Brushing his hands and clothes, and coming forward at the
right] Yes, it's all right now. Just got it in time.

MRS. FELL. [Rushing up to Mrs. Ritter, who is coming towards her from
the left, and shaking her by the arms] Oh, you were marvelous,
darling! [Mrs. Ritter giggles foolishly.] I could just hug you!

MRS. RITTER. I forgot my umbrella.

MRS. FELL. Wonderful performance! [She steps to the right door and
opens her manuscript. Mrs. Ritter moves a little to the right and
stands looking at the wood-wing.]

MRS. PAMPINELLI. [Turning from a more precise adjustment of the wood-
wing] Oh, Mr. Twiller!

TWILLER. Yes?

MRS. PAMPINELLI. How did you and Paula get wedged in that door that way, over there a moment ago?

TWILLER. [*On Mrs. Pampinelli's right*] Oh, I'm awfully sorry about that! I got a little twisted on—[*Mrs. Ritter comes to Mrs. Pampinelli's left.*]

MRS. PAMPINELLI. [*Turning to Mrs. Ritter*] I was just asking Mr. Twiller about that business in the door.

[*Mrs. Pampinelli, Mrs. Ritter and Twiller, together*]

MRS. PAMPINELLI. Of course, it really didn't matter very much.

MRS. RITTER. Oh, my dear, wasn't that just too dreadful! But I didn't know what to do! I knew there was something wrong, but I didn't know what it was!

TWILLER. It was *my* fault. I got a little twisted there in my business cues. I got up to the door a couple of speeches too soon.

MRS. PAMPINELLI. I don't think the audience noticed it.

MRS. FELL. [*Frantically searching the manuscript*] Shush!

MRS. RITTER. Don't you think they did, Betty?

MRS. FELL. Shush! [*They all turn and look at her. Mrs. Pampinelli steps towards her.*]

MRS. PAMPINELLI. Is somebody up? [*Nelly simply silences her with a gesture, and opens the door slightly.*]

MRS. FELL. [*Prompting through the door*] You've all been listening to a lot of damned, cheap gossip!

HOSSEFROSSE. [*From beyond the flats*] You've all been listening to a lot of damned, cheap gossip!

FLORENCE. [*Beyond the flats*] Which should show you that people are talking.

MRS. PAMPINELLI. Somebody up? [*Nelly just shakes her head and relaxes.*] Mr. Hossefrosse?

MRS. FELL. The "damned, cheap gossip" line.

MRS. PAMPINELLI. [*Listening keenly*] Is he all right again?

MRS. FELL. Yes, he's all right now—but it's funny how that line has sent him up at every performance.

MRS. PAMPINELLI. [*Turning to rejoin Mrs. Ritter and Twiller*] It's purely mental.

HOSSEFROSSE. [*From beyond the flats, violently*] No! [*The stage manager, over at the left, jumps to his feet, causing the hammer to fall from his pocket. The door-slam also falls, with a bang. The stage manager has been dozing, and the thunder of Mr. Hossefrosse's outburst has considerably startled him. He comes forward at the left and looks over at Mrs. Fell, to inquire the cause of the disturbance.*]

MRS. FELL. [*Motioning to him with her manuscript*] Shush! [*He looks about and then goes back and picks up the hammer and door-slam. As he resumes his seat he takes another glance around.*]

MRS. RITTER. [*As Mrs. Pampinelli comes forward again at the right, between her and Twiller*] You know, I felt like a perfect fool standing there in that door, but I couldn't catch what *you* were saying. [*Twiller laughs.*]

MRS. PAMPINELLI. Well, dear, I *really* don't think the audience noticed it.

TWILLER. I hope they didn't.

MRS. RITTER. It must have looked awful.

MRS. PAMPINELLI. No, dear, it didn't, really; you both covered it up very nicely.

TWILLER. I *tried* to cover it up when my mustache fell off, too; but I had so many *lines* right in there. I held it on as long as I could, but I was afraid the audience would begin to notice it.

MRS. PAMPINELLI. I was so glad you had the presence of mind not to attempt to stick it on again when it fell off a *second* time.

TWILLER. I was afraid to take the time. I had a cue right there; so when it fell off the second time, I just—let it lie there. [*He makes a casual gesture with his right hand.*]

MRS. PAMPINELLI. That was quite right.

TWILLER. [*Laughing a little*] It's out there yet.

MRS. RITTER. [*Giggling*] So is my umbrella. [*They all laugh.*] Oh, listen, Betty dear! I think I'll just run upstairs for a minute and use that telephone—see how Fred is. [*She starts toward the left.*]

MRS. PAMPINELLI. [*Following her*] Yes, do, Paula.

MRS. RITTER. I'm kind of worried about him.

MRS. PAMPINELLI. See if he's regained consciousness yet.

MRS. RITTER. [*Regardless of the fact that a play is in progress*] Excuse me!

MRS. FELL. [*Looking up from her manuscript*] Shush!

MRS. PAMPINELLI. Certainly, dear. [*Twiller raises his hat towards her, and she waves back at him. Then he goes up at the right and peeks through the side wings*] Oh, Paula!

MRS. RITTER. [*Turning*] Yes, dear?

MRS. PAMPINELLI. Be sure and get down in time for the curtains.

MRS. RITTER. Oh, yes.

MRS. PAMPINELLI. I imagine there'll be a lot of flowers come over.

MRS. RITTER. [*Staring up at the left*] I'll be right down as soon as I telephone.

MRS. PAMPINELLI. Yes, do, dear. [*Mrs. Ritter goes out at the left, and Mrs. Pampinelli turns, touching her hair, and starts back towards the right. Something falls behind the flats. She stops dead, and listens. Mrs. Fell turns quickly and peeks through the right door. Twiller comes forward at the right and looks inquiringly.*]

FLORENCE. [*Just audible beyond the flats*] Then, you've allowed him to think so.

MRS. PAMPINELLI. What's that?

FLORENCE. [*Beyond the flats*] Perhaps it is.

MRS. FELL. [*Turning to Mrs. Pampinelli, and quite casually*] He knocked the ashtray over. [*Mrs. Pampinelli relaxes, and proceeds to arrange the beaded ornaments on her dress, while Mrs. Fell moves a bit farther over to the right and stands listening, manuscript and lorgnon in hand. Twiller crosses to the left, below Mrs. Fell, and gathers up his gloves and cane.*]

HOSSEFROSSE. [*Beyond the flats*] You are deliberately misinterpreting this situation! Yes you are! It's perfectly ridiculous that a physician cannot take a woman patient without being subjected to the whispering of a lot of vulgar scandal-mongers.

FLORENCE. This is not a romantic age, Clyde.

TWILLER. [*Coming to Mrs. Pampinelli's right*] Was that inflection of mine any better tonight on that line, "I'm puzzled."?

MRS. PAMPINELLI. Oh, very much better, I was listening for it.

TWILLER. [*Thoughtfully*] I never seemed to get the sense of that line until tonight. It just seemed to—come to me, out there on the stage.

MRS. PAMPINELLI. Oh, that is a very significant line, Mr. Twiller, coming where it does. [*Spindler comes wandering on from the left, comes forward, looks about, and goes up to the side wing and looks through.*]

TWILLER. I felt a great deal easier in that new business of turning—down at the bookcase that you gave me last night.

MRS. PAMPINELLI. [*With a touch of smugness*] Much better.

TWILLER. Did you notice it?

MRS. PAMPINELLI. Well, of course, I couldn't see it, I was here; but I could sense it; and I could tell from the *tone* of the scene that it was better. [*Spindler moves over to the extreme left, about half-way back, and, taking the refractory telephone bell arrangement from his pocket, starts to tinker with it.*]

TWILLER. I just turned my head *this* way, [*He turns his head sharply to the right, keeping his body and shoulders perfectly rigid.*]

MRS. PAMPINELLI. Excellent.

TWILLER. [*Turning back to her*] Without moving my body.

MRS. PAMPINELLI. Very good.

TWILLER. Instead of making the full swing around, [*He makes a complete swing around on his right foot.*] the way I had been doing. [*Mrs. Fell raises her lorgnon and looks over, curiously.*]

MRS. PAMPINELLI. A very good change.

TWILLER. [*Very seriously*] I *felt* that it got them.

MRS. PAMPINELLI. Well, you see, it gave them the full benefit of your expression. [*They nod agreement.*]

TWILLER. There's a great deal of light and shade in that part, right in there.

MRS. PAMPINELLI. [*Deprecatingly*] Ho! my dear—it is *all* light and shade—even to the gestures. [*She makes a Delsartian movement with her arms and hands. Mrs. Fell comes forward a little further and observes the gesture keenly, through her lorgnon.*]

TWILLER. [*Rather troubled, and shaking his head a bit*] I've got to put in a lit of work on *my* gestures—they're bad, I know.

MRS. PAMPINELLI. Well, I shouldn't exactly say that your gestures were bad; but I think, perhaps——

TWILLER. [*Leaning heavily on his cane*] I—ah—I think I try too hard to be natural.

MRS. PAMPINELLI. [*Smiling, biting her lip, and rolling her eyes*] That's exactly what I was going to say. Your gestures are, in a way, *too* natural. [*She gives a little mirthless laugh, and, out of courtesy, he joins her.*] Of course, that is a very virtuous fault; but it isn't pretty, is it? [*She laughs again.*]

TWILLER. No, it isn't. [*The stage manager gets up, stretches himself, and comes forward at the left.*]

MRS. PAMPINELLI. And, after all, the function of art is to be pretty, is it not? [*She repeats the floating gesture.*]

TWILLER. [*Trying to imitate her*] I don't seem to be able—to *do* that, the way you do. [*Mrs. Fell feels the call, and, putting the manuscript under her arm, tries rather unsuccessfully to copy the movement.*]

MRS. PAMPINELLI. Oh, it is purely a matter of experience, Mr. Twiller. But when you've been in the work as long as I have—you'll realize that the bird's-wing gesture is the *only* gesture. [*She illustrates again, for the edification of her disciples; and they attempt rather faithfully to imitate her. The stage manager stands looking at them.*]

FLORENCE. [*Beyond the flats*] But it has its compensations—you'll have your memories, [*There is a confusion of voices beyond the flats, and cries of "Sit Down!"*]

MRS. PAMPINELLI. [*Startled*] What's that? [*Mrs. Fell rushes to the right door and peeks through, Twiller goes over to the right and up, and the stage manager rushes back to his post and disappears at the left.*] What is it, Nelly?

MRS. FELL. [*Turning suddenly to Mrs. Pampinelli*] They're carrying a man out of the audience! [*She looks back again through the peek, and Mrs. Pampinelli steps to the left door and peeks. Mrs. Sheppard sweeps on up at the left, and comes forward. She is a slim brunette, in her thirties, very attractive, and wearing the very last whisper in widow's weeds. She looks around, rather dramatically, then sees the ladies. Mrs. Fell looks away from the peek-hole and sees her.*] Betty, there's Clara!

MRS. PAMPINELLI. [*Looking at Nelly*] What?

MRS. FELL. [*Not wishing to be heard*] Clara Sheppard. [*Mrs. Pampinelli turns quickly.*]

MRS. PAMPINELLI. Oh, Clara! [*She goes towards her, and Clara advances a little.*] I'm so glad to see you! [*Clara breaks down and weeps.*] Now, don't do that, dear. You know Jimmy wouldn't for anything in the world want you to feel that way. So be brave, honey. It was splendid of you to come here at all. And you look wonderful.

MRS. SHEPPARD. I must look perfectly dreadful.

MRS. PAMPINELLI. You don't look anything of the kind, darling, you look perfectly beautiful.

MRS. SHEPPARD. All I've done is cry.

MRS. PAMPINELLI. I know just how you feel.

MRS. SHEPPARD. But I didn't want you to think I'd entirely forsaken the cause.

MRS. PAMPINELLI. Oh, my dear, we understood perfectly.

MRS. SHEPPARD. But I just felt I *had* to come here tonight.

MRS. PAMPINELLI. Have you been out in front, Clara?

MRS. SHEPPARD. Yes, I just *had* to see it. I don't think anybody saw me; I came in late, and stood way in the back.

MRS. PAMPINELLI. They'd hardly see you.

MRS. SHEPPARD. I don't think so; I kept my veil lowered. Of course, I should *love* to have been right down there in front, where I could get all those *wonderful* little subtleties. But, you know how it is—I was afraid people might not understand my being here at all. It's only been three weeks, you know.

MRS. PAMPINELLI. They wouldn't, either.

MRS. SHEPPARD. That's what I thought.

MRS. PAMPINELLI. I don't suppose there's one person in *ten thousand* that has dramatic instinct enough to appreciate the way you feel. [*She turns to the left door and listens.*]

MRS. SHEPPARD. [*Beginning to cry again*] The flowers in the lobby are perfectly beautiful.

MRS. PAMPINELLI. [*Still listening*] Yes, but I'm not having them passed over the footlights tonight.

MRS. SHEPPARD. [*Drying her eyes*] No?

MRS. PAMPINELLI. Except one bouquet for each of the ladies. It took up too much time the last time.

MRS. SHEPPARD. [*Glancing about*] Where's Paula?

MRS. PAMPINELLI. She's upstairs, telephoning. She's rather annoyed about Fred, you know.

MRS. SHEPPARD. What about him? [*Mrs. Pampinelli turns from the door suddenly and looks at her.*]

FLORENCE. [*Beyond the flats*] There is, my dear boy—for lots of people—

MRS. PAMPINELLI. Why, my dear, didn't you hear?—about him falling downstairs last night?

MRS. SHEPPARD. Oh, not really!

MRS. PAMPINELLI. [*Coming towards her*] He fell almost the entire flight.

MRS. SHEPPARD. Oh, dear me!

MRS. PAMPINELLI. Poor Paula's terribly upset.

MRS. SHEPPARD. What was he doing, coming down the stairs?

MRS. PAMPINELLI. No, he was watching our rehearsal. You know, we held the final rehearsal at Paula's house last night—we couldn't get this place.

MRS. SHEPPARD. [*Solicitously*] Well, did he break any *bones*, Betty?

MRS. PAMPINELLI. No—Doctor Wentworth said—he was unconscious before he hit the floor. He said the fall was the result of a collapse; and that he would have fallen no matter where he had been. [*She turns back again to the left door.*]

MRS. SHEPPARD. [*Retrospectively*] I *thought* he looked pale when I saw him out there tonight. [*Mrs. Pampinelli turns suddenly and looks at her.*]

FLORENCE. [*Beyond the flats*] And you have a very modern wife.

MRS. PAMPINELLI. When you saw him out here, you mean? [*She indicates the audience beyond the flats.*]

MRS. SHEPPARD. Yes; he was standing out there at the back, right near *me*.

MRS. PAMPINELLI. [*Coming towards her again*] You *must* be mistaken, Clara.

MRS. SHEPPARD. No, Betty, I'm quite *sure* I saw him.

MRS. PAMPINELLI. Well, the only thing *I* know is that Paula said he hadn't regained consciousness when she left the house this evening at seven-thirty. [*Mrs. Ritter comes on up at the back, from the left, and comes forward.*] Here's Paula now!

MRS. SHEPPARD. [*Turning round to her left*] Poor dear, she must be terribly upset.

MRS. RITTER. [*Extending her arms*] Clara, dear! [*Mrs. Sheppard bursts into tears again.*] This is so nice of you! [*They embrace each other, and Mrs. Ritter starts to cry.*]

MRS. PAMPINELLI. Isn't she the sweet thing! [*The door at the right opens.*]

MRS. FELL. [*To the ladies*] Shush! [*They all turn and look toward the right door.*]

MRS. PAMPINELLI. [*With a gesture to Mrs. Ritter and Mrs. Sheppard*] Shush! [*Hossefrosse comes out the right door.*]

FLORENCE. [*Beyond the flats*] It's gotten very chilly.

HOSSEFROSSE. [*Picking up his hat, cane and gloves from the chair*] Yes, I know it has; I just came in a few minutes ago.

FLORENCE. You had tickets for the theatre, didn't you?

HOSSEFROSSE. [*Stepping back through the right door again*] Yes.

FLORENCE. Why not take me?—for a change. [*The door closes.*] You used to—years ago.

MRS. PAMPINELLI. [*Turning to Mrs. Ritter and Mrs. Sheppard*] Paula, Clara says she thinks she saw Mr. Ritter out there tonight.

MRS. RITTER. [*Standing at the left*] My dear, Jenny just told me over the telephone that he regained consciousness a half-hour after I left the house, and went out. Said she thought from the way he talked he was coming here.

MRS. SHEPPARD. [*In the center*] Yes, I was *sure* I saw him standing out there—[*Turning to Mrs. Ritter*] I was just telling Betty.

MRS. RITTER. I wonder if he's out there yet.

MRS. SHEPPARD. I don't know, dear.

MRS. PAMPINELLI. How much of the play did you see, Clara?

MRS. SHEPPARD. Why, I stayed just as long as I could, Betty. But when Paula came on, and I heard those lines again, I just couldn't stand it. [*She breaks down, and buries her face in her handkerchief.*]

MRS. PAMPINELLI. [*Laying her hand on her arm*] I know, Clara—you're such an artist.

MRS. SHEPPARD. [*Pressing her hands against her bosom*] Everything just seemed to come back on me.

MRS. PAMPINELLI. I know how it is, dear.

MRS. SHEPPARD. [*Speaking directly to Mrs. Pampinelli*] I got thinking how Jimmy would feel, if he could know, that *he* was the cause of standing in the way of my first *real* opportunity. [*She cries again.*]

MRS. PAMPINELLI. [*Raising her eyes to Heaven*] Perhaps he *does* know, dear.

MRS. SHEPPARD. [*Turning to her again*] I mean, you know, he was always so anxious about my getting *into* the work. And, somehow or other, I always *felt*—that I could have done so much with that part. [*Mrs. Ritter gives a vague little laugh, and Mrs. Sheppard turns to her quickly.*] Oh, of course, you were perfectly *adorable* in it, darling, I don't mean that—[*The left door opens, and Florence is standing in it, about to come out.*]

MRS. FELL. [*To Mrs. Pampinelli, Mrs. Ritter and Mrs. Sheppard*] Shush!

MRS. PAMPINELLI. [*Turning and going closer to the left door*] Excuse me, Clara.

MRS. SHEPPARD. Certainly, dear. [*Twiller comes forward at the right.*]

FLORENCE. [*Stepping through the door*] By the way, there was a Mr. Robinson telephoned this morning, after you'd left the house—[*Mrs. Sheppard waves her handkerchief at Florence, and Florence replies by quietly flicking her fingers at her. Then, still keeping in her character, she moves slowly towards the right, leaving the door open behind her.*] He said something about a list being correct.

HOSSEFROSSE. [*Appearing in the doorway, carrying his hat, cane and gloves*] Yes, I know. [*He reaches towards the left, beyond the flats, as though he were pushing an electric light button, then thrusts his head through the door and says in a fierce whisper.*] Lights.

FLORENCE. Lights out!

[*Mrs. Fell and Mrs. Pampinelli, together*]

MRS. FELL. Put out the lights, somebody!

MRS. PAMPINELLI. Lights, Mr. Stage Manager! [*The stage manager appears from the left, at the back.*]

SPINDLER. [*Springing from the left, where he has been engaged in trying to repair the telephone battery*] Lights out!

MRS. PAMPINELLI. Where are you! [*The stage manager reaches up and pulls one of the switches on the switchboard at the back, and the lights beyond the flats go out; then he disappears again at the left.*]

[*Spindler and Hossefrosse, together*]

SPINDLER. I was right here!

HOSSEFROSSE. [*Coming through the door*] Yes, I know—[*Closing the door behind him*] I talked to him. [*Puts his hat on*]

MRS. PAMPINELLI. Well, why aren't you right *here*, where you should be! Stand by for the curtain, now—see if you can do that much right. Surely, it's the old story of the lark—if you want a thing done, do it yourself! Curtain!

SPINDLER. [*Shouting*] Curtain! [*The curtain, beyond the flats, begins to roll down, and there is thunderous applause.*]

MRS. FELL. [*To Florence*] Marvelous, darling! [*Florence waves at her, turns, and rushes back towards the left.*] Just lovely, Huxley!

HOSSEFROSSE. Thanks. [*He turns to the left.*]

MRS. PAMPINELLI. Lights up! Splendid, children!

FLORENCE. I'm awfully glad to see you, Clara!

[*Mrs. Sheppard, Mrs. Pampinelli, Hossefrosse and Spindler, together*]

MRS. SHEPPARD. [*Shaking hands with Florence*] You were wonderful, Flossie!

MRS. PAMPINELLI. Take up the curtain, Mr. Stage Manager!

HOSSEFROSSE. Thank you very much.

SPINDLER. Lights up! [*The stage manager appears from the left and pulls the switch again, and the lights beyond the flats go on.*]

SPINDLER. Take it up! [*The stage manager darts off again to the left. The waltz music on the piano, beyond the flat, begins again.*]

HOSSEFROSSE. [*Lifting his hat and beaming*] Hello, Clara!

MRS. SHEPPARD. Wonderful! [*He deprecates profusely. The curtain rises again.*]

MRS. PAMPINELLI. Go on, Mr. Hossefrosse! [*He opens the right door, removing his hat.*] Wait a moment, Mr. Hossefrosse! Come on, Florence! [*Hossefrosse stops uncertainly in the doorway and looks at Mrs. Pampinelli.*] It's all right! Go on! [*She opens the left door.*] Here, go on here, Florence! [*They go on, bowing, and there is prolonged applause.*] Come on, Paula! Go on here! [*The curtain descends again. Paula scurries to the left door, giggling.*] Where's Mr. Twiller?

TWILLER. [*Springing over from the right, where he has been talking and laughing with Mrs. Fell*] Here I am!

MRS. PAMPINELLI. [*Turning to the left*] Take it up again, Mr. Stage Manager! [*Turning back to Twiller, and opening the door*] Here, Mr. Twiller, take Paula on! [*The curtain can be seen through the left door rising again.*] Come on, Paula! [*Twiller drops his cane, in shifting it from his right hand to his left.*] Hurry up! [*He snatches the cane up, and, taking Paula by the arm, escorts her through the door. But she trips over the door strip, nevertheless. And there is sustained applause. Mrs. Fell, over at the right, begins to preen herself feverishly. Mrs. Pampinelli closes the door slowly, and stands listening, smiling. Teddy appears up at the left and comes forward, pressing his violet handkerchief to his brow, and looking very wan. Mrs. Pampinelli turns to him.*] Come on, Teddy, hurry up! They're just going on! How do you feel? [*The curtain descends.*]

TEDDY. Only fair.

MRS. PAMPINELLI. [*Taking him by the right arm and urging him towards the right*] Here, Nelly, go on for a bow with Teddy! [*Rushing back towards the left.*] Take it up again, Mr. Stage Manager!

[*Mrs. Pampinelli, Teddy and Spindler, together*]

MRS. PAMPINELLI. Mr. Spindler!

TEDDY. [*Opening the right door*] Come on, Nelly!

SPINDLER. [*Half-way back, at the left*] Take it up! [*Rushing forward at the left.*] Yes?

[*Mrs. Pampinelli and Mrs. Fell, together*]

MRS. PAMPINELLI. [*To Spindler*] Keep it going up and down till I tell you to stop! And keep it up the next time till the gentlemen get the flowers!

MRS. FELL. [*Shrinking away a little more to the right of the door, but still preening herself, almost hysterically, and breaking into a little nervous laugh*] Oh, no, really, dear! I wouldn't *think* of it! [*Teddy goes through the right door. The curtain can be seen rising again; then the door closes right after him; and Mrs. Fell continues talking, to herself.*] Why, what have I done that I should go on. I wouldn't mind if I'd taken some part in the play—but I certainly don't see—

MRS. PAMPINELLI. [*Rushing back to the right*] Go on, Nelly! What are you waiting for? [*The curtain descends again. Mrs. Fell rushes towards Mrs. Pampinelli.*]

MRS. FELL. [*Handing Mrs. Pampinelli the rolled manuscript*] Hold this!

MRS. PAMPINELLI. Hurry, dear! [*Mrs. Fell rushes to the right door, settles herself finally, and flings the door open. The curtain is just rising. And, placing one hand upon her bosom, dropping her eyes and smiling, Nelly sways through the door, acknowledging the plaudits. Mrs. Pampinelli, standing in the middle of the stage, applauds, also, hitting the manuscript against her hand. The door closes after Mrs. Fell. Mrs. Sheppard, over at the left, suddenly bursts into tears and buries her face in her handkerchief. Mrs. Pampinelli turns quickly and looks at her, then crosses towards her.*] Do you want to take a bow, Clara?

MRS. SHEPPARD. Oh, no, thank you! [*Mrs. Pampinelli turns back to the left door.*]

MRS. PAMPINELLI. Get those flowers, boys! Keep it up, Mr. Stage Manager! Come on, Clara! Go on for a bow! [*Reaches for Mrs. Sheppard's hand*]

MRS. SHEPPARD. [*Giving Mrs. Pampinelli her hand, and allowing herself to be drawn towards the right*] Do you think they'll understand, Betty?

MRS. PAMPINELLI. Of course, they would, my dear! They know it isn't your fault that you're not appearing! [*Mrs. Fell thrusts open the right door. She has a basket of roses in her hand.*]

MRS. FELL. They are calling for you, Betty! [*Someone in the audience can be heard calling Mrs. Pampinelli's name.*]

MRS. PAMPINELLI. Here, Nelly, take Clara on for a bow!

MRS. FELL. [*Impatiently*] They're *calling* for you, dear! [*Mrs. Sheppard hastily throws her veil back dramatically.*]

MRS. PAMPINELLI. I'll take one alone, afterwards! [*The applause swells again.*] Go on, Clara!

MRS. FELL. [*Extending her right hand*] Come on, dear!

MRS. SHEPPARD. [*Giving Mrs. Fell her left hand*] Oh, I don't feel that I should! [*Mrs. Fell keeps the door open, and Clara droops through, bowing. Then Mrs. Fell closes the door and Mrs. Pampinelli turns to the left.*]

MRS. PAMPINELLI. Keep it up, Mr. Spindler!

SPINDLER. Keep it up!

HOSSEFROSSE. [*Thrusting open the left door*] Mrs. Pampinelli! [*There is a vision through the door of the various artists bowing towards the back wall, all the ladies laden with flowers.*]

MRS. PAMPINELLI. All right, dear! I'm coming! [*Hossefrosse closes the door, and Mrs. Pampinelli deftly touches her hair and flings her train out to its full length behind her. Then she speaks in a loud voice, so that she may be heard by those on the other side of the flats.*] Everybody stand to one side! Stand to one side, everybody! [*She pulls open the left door and stands, smiling; then she steps through the door; and instantly, the curtain falls with a deafening crash. The door closes after her. Nelly Fell gives a piercing scream. Spindler comes rushing down from the left to the left door.*]

TEDDY. [*Shouting, beyond the flats*] Curtain!

HOSSEFROSSE. Take up the curtain!

TWILLER. Take it up! [*There is a babel of voices beyond the flats. Then the left door is thrust violently open, and Mrs. Pampinelli looks out.*]

MRS. PAMPINELLI. [*Harshly, to Spindler*] What's the matter with the curtain?

SPINDLER. [*In a panic of excitement*] Something's broke! [*The stage manager rushes on from the left and comes forward.*]

MRS. PAMPINELLI. [*Coming through the door and calling to the stage manager, whom she hasn't seen yet*] Take up the curtain, Mr. Stage Manager!

STAGE MANAGER. I can't take it up, the guy rope's broken! [*He goes up at the left.*]

MRS. PAMPINELLI. What? [*Mrs. Fell comes running through the right door, carrying her basket of flowers, and crosses towards the left.*]

[*Mrs. Fell and Spindler, together*]

MRS. FELL. What is it, Betty?

SPINDLER. [*To Mrs. Pampinelli*] He says the guy rope's broken!

MRS. PAMPINELLI. [*Brushing him aside, to the left, and rushing up at the left*] My God! Did anyone ever hear of such stupidity!

[*Mrs. Pampinelli, Mrs. Fell and Spindler, together*]

MRS. PAMPINELLI. I'll go on at the side here!

MRS. FELL. What's the matter, Mr. Spindler?

SPINDLER. [*Shouting after Mrs. Pampinelli*] He says he can't get it up! [*Mrs. Sheppard comes through the right doorway with an armload of American Beauty roses, and stands looking anxiously from side to side. Teddy follows her out and stands at her right, discussing the incident. Florence opens the left door and comes out. Her arms are full of tiger-lilies. She moves to the right and speaks to Mrs. Sheppard, nervously.*]

STAGE MANAGER. You can't get through there, lady! [*Twiller comes out the left door.*]

[*Mrs. Pampinelli and Stage Manager, together*]

MRS. PAMPINELLI. I must get through somewhere!

STAGE MANAGER. That tormentor's too narrow there!

[*Mrs. Pampinelli, Stage Manager and Mrs. Fell, together*]

MRS. PAMPINELLI. [*Turning frantically and rushing forward again at the left*] I'll try the other side! He says it's too narrow there!

STAGE MANAGER. I don't know how you're going to do it!

MRS. FELL. [*As Mrs. Pampinelli sweeps between her and Spindler*] What is it he says is broken, Betty? [*Mrs. Pampinelli rushes over towards the right. She literally sweeps Twiller, who is in her path, out of the way, and he falls backward over a stage-brace, onto the floor. Mrs. Fell picks up her dress and runs after Mrs. Pampinelli.*]

SPINDLER. [*Outrunning Mrs. Fell*] The guy rope!

MRS. FELL. Well, why doesn't he fix it! Betty! Betty dear! [*Mrs. Pampinelli rushes up at the extreme right and tries desperately to find a way of getting through; but everything is solidly masked. Hossefrosse comes out the left door, and the stage manager comes forward at the left and stands looking after Mrs. Pampinelli.*]

HOSSEFROSSE. What's the matter, can't Mrs. Pampinelli get her bow?

STAGE MANAGER. She can't get on any more from that side than she can from this! [*Hossefrosse steps out through the door and looks towards the right. The door closes after him.*] There's the same opening over there as there is here! [*The applause beyond the flats, which has kept up throughout the debacle, begins to die. Mrs. Pampinelli comes sweeping back from the right with fire in her eye— Nelly Fell and Spindler still at her heels. She plants herself in the middle of the stage and glares at the stage manager.*]

MRS. PAMPINELLI. [*In a voice shrill with anger*] My God! What's the matter with your curtain!

STAGE MANAGER. [*Losing his temper*] The guy rope's broken! I've told you that about a dozen times! [*He turns doggedly away to the left, as though he were going up to his chair; but he stops short and finishes his remarks to her over his left shoulder.*] What do you want me to do, write you a letter! [*The left door is pushed quietly open; and Mrs. Ritter, with her face just visible above a perfect screen of roses, looks blankly at the stage manager.*]

MRS. RITTER. [*Vaguely*] There's something the matter with the curtain. [*The real stage curtain commences to descend.*]

STAGE MANAGER. [*Leaning towards her, assuming her general manner and tone, and flipping his hand at her*] Y-E-E-S! [*He goes up towards his chair, and Mrs. Ritter stands in wide-eyed astonishment.*]

END OF THE ACT

⇒ ACT III ⇐

NOTE:—*The setting for Act III is the same as for Act I except that the small chair which Jenny brings on at the opening of the play is eliminated.*

Jenny is seated at the table below the piano, reading the Pictorial Review. The door closes out at the right. She stops reading and listens. Then resumes. Ritter wanders in from the right hallway, wearing a black overcoat and a derby. The derby is a bit over one eye and his cigar is at a comic angle. Jenny sees him and rises immediately, circling around to the left to the middle of the room.

JENNY. Oh, Mr. Ritter! [*He comes into the center door and stands there, looking at nothing.*] I didn't hear you come in, sir. Is the show over?

RITTER. [*Removing his gloves*] It's all over town by this time.

JENNY. [*Standing slightly left of the center of the room, facing him*] Mrs. Ritter just telephoned a minute ago.

RITTER. Is she alive?

JENNY. Alive, Mr. Ritter?

RITTER. [*Moving down to the table below the piano, and thrusting his gloves into his overcoat pocket*] Because if she is, she's got a charmed life. [*Commencing to unfasten his coat*] The Seamen's Institute! God help them on a night like this.

JENNY. She was anxious to know if you were still unconscious.

RITTER. [*Taking off his overcoat*] If she telephones again, tell her yes. [*He is in a tuxedo suit.*]

JENNY. [*Crossing to him and helping him with the coat*] Ain't you feelin' well again, Mr. Ritter?

RITTER. No, Jenny, I'm not. [*He hands her his derby.*]

JENNY. [*Taking the hat and coat to the partition-seat above the piano*] Well, I'm sure I'm sorry, sir.

RITTER. [*Removing his scarf*] And after that exhibition tonight—I don't think I ever shall feel exactly well again.

JENNY. [*Coming down at his left and passing back of him*] Was it a sad play?

RITTER. [*Handing her his scarf, and speaking with measured conviction*] The saddest thing I've ever seen in my life.

JENNY. I allus cry when a show is sad.

RITTER. Is that so?

JENNY. Yes, sir; and a funny thing about me is—the sadder it is the more I cry.

RITTER. You'd have had a big night if you'd been with me. [*She passes back of him with the scarf, to put it with the other things.*] You'd better leave those things here, Jenny, I may leave town again tonight.

JENNY. I'll leave them right here. [*She turns from an arrangement of the things and comes forward to the middle of the room.*] Did they clap much when Mrs. Ritter finished?

RITTER. [*Still standing above the table near the piano, clipping the tip of a cigar which he has taken from his pocket*] I didn't wait for the finish; they carried me out.

JENNY. I'm dyin' till she gets home, for I know exactly how she felt. [*He looks at her keenly—she is looking straight ahead.*]

RITTER. Have you been on the stage, too, Jenny?

JENNY. [*Turning to him*] No, sir, I haven't, Mr. Ritter, not lately. But when I was at home in England I used to go on every once in a while. For a bit of a change, you know.

RITTER. Yes, I know.

JENNY. We had a little club in the town I lived in, and we used to give a show twice a year. [*Ritter nods slowly and comprehendingly.*] I always took off the comical parts.

RITTER. How is it they didn't get you into this show tonight?

JENNY. Oh, I haven't been on for a long time now, Mr. Ritter. My husband put a stop to it. [*She looks away off.*]

RITTER. [*Turning to her*] What was the matter?

JENNY. [*Turning to him, suddenly*] He died.

RITTER. [*Replacing his penknife*] I see.

JENNY. And I never felt much like cuttin' up after that. [*The telephone bell rings. She turns quickly and starts for the center door.*]

RITTER. [*Moving over toward the mantelpiece*] See who that is, Jenny.

JENNY. [*Hurrying out into the left hallway*] Yes, sir.

RITTER. [*Getting a match from the table below the mantelpiece*] Anybody for me, I've gone into permanent retirement.

JENNY. [*At the telephone*] Yes? [*He listens narrowly.*] Mr. Ritta? [*He makes a rapid movement towards her.*] Oh, Mrs. Ritta?

RITTER. [*In a subdued tone*] Who do they want?

JENNY. [*Into the telephone*] No, ma'm, she hasn't got home yet. [*Lowering the telephone and speaking to Ritter*] Mrs. Ritter.

RITTER. [*Casually*] Who is it, the police? [*He lights his cigar.*]

JENNY. [*Into the telephone*] All right, Mrs. Livingston, I'll give her your message as soon as she comes in. You're more than welcome I'm sure. [*She hangs up and comes to the center door.*]

RITTER. [*Looking at her*] Mrs. Livingston?

JENNY. Yes, sir.

RITTER. What did she want?

JENNY. She sez she wanted to congratulate Mrs. Ritter on her perfect performance tonight.

RITTER. Did she see the show?

JENNY. She didn't say, sir.

RITTER. [*Conclusively, and crossing in front of her down to the window at the right*] She didn't see it. If any of those women come back here with Mrs. Ritter, Jenny—say that I'm not home yet, do you understand.

JENNY. [*Settling the overcoat on the partition-seat*] Yes, sir.

RITTER. [*Looking through the window*] And that you haven't seen anything of me.

JENNY. Yes, sir, Mr. Ritter, all right.

RITTER. If my wife's alone, let me know as soon as she comes in.

JENNY. Yes, sir, I will. [*The telephone bell rings, and she hurries out to answer it.*]

RITTER. [*Half turning from the window*] You haven't seen anything of *me*, remember.

JENNY. No, sir. [*Into the telephone*] Yes, sir? [*He listens, without turning.*] No, sir, she hasn't got home yet. [*She lowers the telephone and looks at him, wide-eyed. He feels that she's looking at him and turns suddenly.*]

RITTER. [*Taking a step towards her, below the piano*] What is it?

JENNY. [*Into the telephone*] No, sir, *he* hasn't got home yet neither.

RITTER. [*Apprehensively*] Do they want me? [*She nods yes*] Who is it? [*She nods that she doesn't know.*] Police Headquarters I'll bet a ten dollar note! [*He crosses down below the table at the left and around up to the mantelpiece.*] Tell them that I had absolutely nothing to do with her going on! That I didn't hear about it until last night! [*He crosses back again down toward the table below the piano.*] And that I've been unconscious ever since.

JENNY. [*Into the telephone*] The Times?

RITTER. [*Stopping above the table*] My God, the newspapers have got hold of it!

JENNY. [*Into the telephone*] Well, just a minute, please.

RITTER. [*Turning suddenly to her*] Tell them she did it on a bet!

JENNY. The Times newspaper wants to know if Mrs. Ritter has a full-length photograph of herself for the morning paper.

RITTER. [*Emphatically, and going out through the center door into the right hallway and up the stairs*] Tell them NO!

JENNY. [*Into the telephone*] Hello.

RITTER. But that she'll have some taken as soon as she gets out of jail. [*He goes through the arched doorway at the head of the stairs.*]

JENNY. [*Into the telephone*] Why, I couldn't say, sir, whether Mrs. Ritter has a photograph of herself or not, sir; but I'll give her your message as soon as she comes in.

MRS. PAMPINELLI. [*In the right hallway*] Hurry, Theodore.

JENNY. [*Still at the telephone*] You're more than welcome I'm sure. [*She hangs up and hurries in through the center door, glancing out the right hallway as she comes and, gathering up Mr. Ritter's overcoat, derby and scarf, hurries over above the table at the left and out.*]

MRS. PAMPINELLI. [*In the right hallway*] Be careful of those jonquils. Now, be careful, Theodore! Now go back and fetch the others.

[*Coming into view, and seeing Jenny coming in again at the left door*] Oh, you're up, Jenny, aren't you! [*She comes through the center door, carrying her fan and an armload or orchids and red chrysanthemums, and wearing an enormous flowing cape of ruffled black lace, touched all over with tiny circular sequins in gold. Her dress, of course, is the ruby-velvet one of the preceding act.*]

JENNY. Yes, ma'm, I'm up.

MRS. PAMPINELLI. [*Hastening to the table below the piano*] I'm so glad; I hope I haven't roused you. [*She puts her fan on the piano and sets all the flowers on the table.*] Will you go out and get those flowers from my chauffeur, Jenny?

JENNY. [*Going out through the center door into the right hallway*] Yes, ma'm.

MRS. PAMPINELLI. [*Arranging the flowers on the table*] He's set them right down there in the hallway. I came right on in when I found the door unlocked; I was afraid you'd be asleep.

JENNY. No, ma'm, I was waitin' up.

MRS. PAMPINELLI. [*Sweeping around to her left and up to the center door*] Well, that's perfectly angelic of you I'm sure. [*She stands on the left side of the center door and looks out into the right hallway.*] Can you manage, dear?

JENNY. [*Appearing from the right side*] I think so. [*She struggles through the center door carrying an enormous horseshoe, made of red and white carnations and ferns. It is at least four feet high, set upon an easel, and across the front of it is a strip of white satin ribbon ten inches wide with the word "SUCCESS" inscribed upon it in blue velvet letters. She is also carrying a huge basket of jonquils, and a star made of white pansies. This last touch is fastened upon a violet easel.*]

MRS. PAMPINELLI. Let me help you, child. [*She takes the basket of jonquils and the star of pansies from Jenny.*] Now, set that right down there. [*She indicates a point in front of the mantelpiece for the horseshoe, and Jenny crosses in front with it.*] I want Mrs. Ritter to see it *first*, when she comes in—it's so appropriate. [*She sets the basket of jonquils on the piano.*] I suppose we can put these down anywhere here until she comes, can't we? [*She sets the easel of pansies down on the floor at the right of the table below the piano.*]

JENNY. [*Having set the horseshoe down in front of the mantelpiece*] This way, Mrs. Pampinelli?

MRS. PAMPINELLI. No, dear, *facing* the door.

JENNY. Oh, I see. [*She turns it round facing the center door.*]

MRS. PAMPINELLI. That's it. I want it to catch her eye as she comes in. And now will you go back and fetch the others, Jenny?

JENNY. [*Hurrying out through the center door*] Yes, ma'm.

MRS. PAMPINELLI. [*Gathering up the chrysanthemums from the table*] And these chrysanthemums, [*She sweeps across towards the mantelpiece and turns to her left, strewing the chrysanthemums through the center door and down toward the table at the left.*] I'll just strew in her pathway. [*Jenny comes in from the right hallway carrying a huge anchor of vivid red roses, with a broad band of navy blue ribbon running diagonally across it, and the words "SEAMEN'S INSTITUTE" in white velvet letters. She stands right in the center door, holding it, waiting for instructions as to its disposition from Mrs. Pampinelli. But Mrs. Pampinelli is lost in admiration of it, standing just to the left of the center door.*] Now, set that right down here, Jenny. [*She indicates a point at the extreme left, below the door, and Jenny hastens to place it there, setting it down half-facing the center door; and Mrs. Pampinelli stands up at the center door admiring it.*] Hope! [*Jenny turns to her and gives a faint little laugh.*] Hope, for the success [*She indicates the horseshoe with a gesture.*] of our enterprise. [*They both laugh, and Mrs. Pampinelli steps quickly down to the table below the piano and picks up the orchids.*] And these orchids, I think I shall just put right here on this table. [*She crosses to the table below the casement-window and puts them down; then straightens up and sighs.*] Ho, dear me, I'm warm! [*She crosses back between the piano and the table below it, picking up her fan as she goes.*]

JENNY. [*Moving up and across back of the table at the left, towards the center of the room*] 'Tis a bit warm.

MRS. PAMPINELLI. [*Fanning herself, as she moves towards the middle of the room*] And then I hurried so—foolishly.

JENNY. Did everything go along all right?

MRS. PAMPINELLI. Magnificently, my dear child! And Mrs. Ritter was a positive sensation.

JENNY. Did she get all these flowers?

MRS. PAMPINELLI. [*Deprecatingly*] Ho! This isn't the half of them! We sent three automobiles full to the various hospitals. And Mrs. Fell's car was still taking them when I left. [*Jenny shakes her head from side to side in wonderment.*] These are just a few that we rescued for Mrs. Ritter. [*She moves towards the center door.*] Sort of a little surprise for her, you know, when she gets home. [*She stands looking out into the right hallway, expectantly.*]

JENNY. They're certainly 'andsome.

MRS. PAMPINELLI. She doesn't even know that I've brought them.

JENNY. Is she comin' right home, do you know, Mrs. Pampinelli?

MRS. PAMPINELLI. [*Turning to Jenny*] Why, I *expect* her, yes. I was afraid she'd get here ahead of me. She was waiting for Mr. Ritter. [*Coming forward a little*] We heard at the hall that he was there, and she thought probably he'd come back and pick her up. He hasn't *come* home, has he?

JENNY. No, ma'm, I haven't seen anything of him.

MRS. PAMPINELLI. [*Laughing a little, indulgently, securing a hairpin, and moving over towards the right*] Poor man! His wife's success has very likely gone to his head. [*She glances out the window.*]

JENNY. He went out of here about eight o'clock.

MRS. PAMPINELLI. [*Turning and coming back towards Jenny*] Yes, we were so surprised to hear that he was there at all. Because Mrs. Ritter had said that he hadn't regained consciousness up to the time she left the house.

JENNY. He hadn't, neither. I thought I 'ad two heads on me when I came in and saw him puttin' on 'is 'at and coat.

MRS. PAMPINELLI. Well, did he seem all right?

JENNY. Yes, he seemed right enough; but he was awful pale-lookin'. And a couple of times I spoke to 'im, he gave me kind of a funny answer. So I got a bit frightened, you know; and I asked 'im if he know where he was goin'. And he said, "Yes," that he was goin' to see "The Torch-Bearers." Kind a flightly, you know.

MRS. PAMPINELLI. Well, he would be, naturally.

JENNY. So then—when he got to the door, he turned around—and he sez to me—"Jenny!—if you never see me again—I want you to know I *died* in the cause of Art."—And he went out.

MRS. PAMPINELLI. He was probably rambling a bit.

JENNY. But, he walked straight enough.

MRS. PAMPINELLI. [*Turning suddenly to the center door*] I think I hear a machine, Jenny.

JENNY. [*Stepping across quickly below the table to the casement window*] I'll see.

MRS. PAMPINELLI. Do quickly, dear.

JENNY. Is Mrs. Fell comin' back tonight?

MRS. PAMPINELLI. [*Looking out eagerly into the right hallway*] Yes, she's bringing the rest of the flowers. I've sent my car back for her.

JENNY. [*Turning abruptly from the window and hurrying across below the piano towards the center door*] Here's Mrs. Ritta now!

MRS. PAMPINELLI. Is Mr. Ritter with her? [*Intercepting Jenny*] No, don't go out, Jenny! I want to hear what they say when they see the flowers. [*Turning her round by the shoulder and indicating the door down at the left*] You go into the other room there, and I'll hide here—[*She moves forward at the right and across below the piano.*] in this window.

JENNY. [*Hurrying towards the door at the left*] All right, ma'm.

MRS. PAMPINELLI. [*Stopping near the window and turning to Jenny*] And Jenny, dear!

JENNY. [*Turning at the left door*] Yes, ma'm?

MRS. PAMPINELLI. Don't come out—until you hear *me* say "SURPRISE!"

JENNY. All right, Mrs. Pampinelli, I won't. [*Mrs. Pampinelli steps into the alcove of the window, then turns again to Jenny.*]

MRS. PAMPINELLI. Now remember, Jenny—"SURPRISE!"

JENNY. Yes, I know. [*She closes the door, and Mrs. Pampinelli conceals herself behind the window drapery. There is a slight pause; then Mrs. Ritter hurries in from the right hallway, carrying a marvelous bouquet of American Beauty roses. She comes in through the center door and stands, looking, with a touch of astonishment, at the horseshoe. Then her eyes wander down to the anchor; and then over to the easel at the right.*]

She is gowned in a very pale shade of gray lace, with gray-silk slippers and stockings; and around her head she is wearing a wreath of laurel in gold, touched with brilliants. Her cloak is of black chiffon-velvet, with a cape collar of black fox. She slides this cloak from her shoulders onto the partition-seat at the right, and starts across towards the door at the left.]

MRS. RITTER. [*Opening her door*] Are you up, Jenny?—Jenny! [*She closes the door again and crosses above the table at the left and over to the one below the piano. Here she sets down a few of the roses, then decides there is not sufficient room for all of them, and starts across to the table at the left. Ritter appears at the head of the stairs and starts down slowly. She sees him, and stops dead.*] Fred! [*She moves up towards the left of the center door.*] You don't mean to tell me you've been home here—and there I've been waiting at the hall since before ten o'clock. [*He wanders in through the center door and leans against the piano, holding a lighted cigar in his hand.*] Why didn't you come back for me? Irene Colter had to bring me home. [*She starts to cry.*] Clara Sheppard *told* me she saw you there, so, naturally, I waited for you. And when you didn't come back, why, of course, right away—I thought something had happened to you. [*She cries into her handkerchief.*]

RITTER. [*Without moving, and in a toneless voice*] Something *has* happened to me. [*She looks at him apprehensively.*]

MRS. RITTER . What happened to you, Fred?

RITTER. [*Stonily, and moving down and across below the piano*] I've seen you act.

MRS. RITTER. What? [*He raises his left hand solemnly and continues to the corner of the piano nearest the window, where he leans. She moves down a bit after him.*] What's the matter, Fred—did you have another of those spells that you had last night?

RITTER. Yes; only a great deal worse.

MRS. RITTER. Oh, isn't that dreadful! What do you think it is, dear?

RITTER. [*Turning slightly, and glancing at the violet easel and over at the anchor*] I don't know what it is. It looks like a *wake* to me. Who's dead?

MRS. RITTER. Dead?

RITTER. What are all these flowers doing here?

MRS. RITTER. Why, I imagine some of the ladies have been here from the show—to fix up a little surprise for *me*.

RITTER. They should have lighted a few candles, and completed the effect.

MRS. RITTER. But, these are just presents, Fred, from friends of ours.

RITTER. [*Straightening up, and moving across below the table*] They are tokens of sympathy, that's what they are. [*He crosses up and over above the table at the left.*]

MRS. RITTER. [*Following him over*] But, there's nobody *dead*, dear!

RITTER. [*Raising his left hand and solemnly again*] Oh, yes there is! Oh yes!

MRS. RITTER. *Really*, dear! [*He turns, just back of the armchair, and pins her with a look.*]

RITTER. You're dead. [*She stands perfectly still, looking at him, wide-eyed.*] You died tonight—down there on that stage at Horticulture Hall. And so did everybody that was up there with you.

MRS. RITTER. [*With a troubled, uncomprehending expression*] Why, how could I be dead, dear—when I'm here—talking to you? [*He stands looking straight ahead, smoking. She bursts out crying, and turns to the partition-seat at the right of the center door.*] Oh, Fred! it's terrible to see you this way!

RITTER. [*Sweeping his hand across his brow and starting across below the table towards the right*] The human brain can only stand so much.

MRS. RITTER. [*Setting her roses down on the partition-seat*] You've just been working yourself to death! But nobody could tell you anything! [*She starts out into the left hallway for the telephone.*]

RITTER. [*Stopping over near the window and turning*] What are you going to do?

MRS. RITTER. [*Turning to him*] Why, I'm going to call Doctor Wentworth, of course.

RITTER. What for?

MRS. RITTER. Why, because you *need* him!

RITTER. [*Taking a step or two towards her, between the piano and the table below it*] I won't see any doctor, now!

MRS. RITTER. [*Coming back through the center door*] Now—listen, Fred—

RITTER. [*Raising his hand, and crossing to the left*] I won't see any doctor, I tell you —there's nothing he can do for me: [*He stops above the armchair at the left and rests his hand upon the back of it.*] it's all been done. There's nothing left for me but to get out of town.

MRS. RITTER. [*Following him over*] Well, just let him come over and *see* you, dear.

RITTER. What would I let him come over and *see* me for? There's nothing the matter with me.

MRS. RITTER. Why, you're as pale as a ghost!

RITTER. That's nothing—I've had a scare.

MRS. RITTER. [*Solicitously*] What scared you, dear? [*He turns and looks at her.*]

RITTER. I was afraid every minute somebody was going to shoot *you*.

MRS. RITTER. [*After a bewildered pause*] But, why should anybody shoot *me*, darling?

RITTER. For trying to act. [*He moves forward and across in front of the table, to the right—she watching him blankly.*] Making a laughing-stock of yourselves in front of the community.

MRS. RITTER. Didn't you like me, Fred?

RITTER. [*Casually, as he nears the window*] I did till I saw you act. [*He turns around to his right and leans on the piano. She moves over towards the table below the piano.*]

MRS. RITTER. [*Rather helplessly, as the situation dawns upon her*] Why, Mrs. Pampinelli said I was a great artist.

RITTER. [*With vast amusement*] Ha! [*Then he looks at his wife and speaks very exactly.*] Mrs. Pampinelli is perhaps the world's greatest NUT. [*Mrs. Pampinelli, standing back in the window alcove at the right, in a state of puzzled irresolution, reacts, physically, to this last observation, causing an abrupt movement of the drapery. But, neither Ritter nor his wife are looking in that direction at the moment.*]

MRS. RITTER. [*Laying the remaining roses on the table*] She says I ought to go on with the work.

RITTER. [*Dryly*] She meant the housework. [*He replaces his cigar in his mouth.*]

MRS. RITTER. [*Looking at him with a touch of resentment*] No, she didn't mean anything of the kind. She says I ought to go to New York. [*He takes the cigar from his mouth and looks at her keenly.*]

RITTER. And what would you do when you'd *get* there?

MRS. RITTER. Why, I'd go on the stage, of course.

RITTER. [*Very level*] How?

MRS. RITTER. Why, I'd go to the people that have charge of it.

RITTER. And, do you think they'd put you on the stage simply because you wanted to *go* on it?

MRS. RITTER. Well, Mrs. Pampinelli could give me a letter—

RITTER. Hum!

MRS. RITTER. So that I'd have it when I'd *get* there.

RITTER. That'd do you a lot of good. You'd find a *thousand* there ahead of you, with letters from Mrs. Pampinellis. Nobody in New York knows Mrs. Pampinelli; and if they did, it'd probably *kill* any chance that a person *might* have otherwise. [*Mrs. Pampinelli can contain herself no longer. She flips the window drapery aside with a deft movement and stands looking at Ritter, from a great height. Mrs. Ritter, who is facing the window, utters an abrupt shriek of astonishment. Then Ritter turns, rather casually to see the cause of his wife's agitation, and finds himself looking into the frozen eyes of Mrs. Pampinelli. He regards her rather impersonally, and then quietly reaches up and secures his collar and tie. She steps majestically from the window alcove and moves a bit nearer to him, still holding him with an icy stare.*]

MRS. PAMPINELLI. [*After a devastating pause*] You creature.

RITTER. [*Turning smoothly away, to his left, as though he had been suddenly struck by something, in the right eye*] Another *actress*. [*He moves along a few steps to the left, in front of the table, then turns and speaks to Mrs. Pampinelli over his left shoulder.*] What did you do, come in through the window?

MRS. PAMPINELLI. I've been *hiding* here.

RITTER. [*Resuming his walk over to the left*] I don't blame you—after that show; I've been doing the same thing myself. [*He sits in the armchair over at the left.*]

MRS. RITTER. [*Who has been standing in a panic in the middle of the room, staring wide-eyed at Mrs. Pampinelli*] Oh, Mrs. Pampinelli—you *didn't* hear what he's been saying?

MRS. PAMPINELLI. Every word. [*She very regally deposits her fan upon the piano, and Mrs. Ritter, turning to Ritter, makes a long, moaning sound.*]

MRS. RITTER. Now, Fred Ritter, you see what you've done! [*She bursts into tears, and comes down to the chair at the left of the table below the piano and sits down.*]

MRS. PAMPINELLI. [*Moving to a point above the table*] And I wouldn't have missed it. I'll know how to regard this gentleman in the future. I came home hurriedly with these few flowers as a little acknowledgment of the appreciation your work deserved; and all I hear is abuse; and a very crude, but very venomous attempt at satire. [*Mrs. Ritter weeps aloud.*] Control yourself, darling, I wouldn't please him.

RITTER. [*Quietly*] She's acting again.

MRS. PAMPINELLI. [*Withering him with a glance*] You barbarian! [*To Mrs. Ritter*] Pull yourself together, dear.

MRS. RITTER. Oh, I just *can't*, Mrs. Pampinelli.

MRS. PAMPINELLI. [*Addressing Ritter directly, and indicating Mrs. Ritter*] Look at the state of emotion you've got this poor girl into!

RITTER. She's an emotional actress. [*Mrs. Ritter bursts forth again.*]

MRS. PAMPINELLI. Savage! [*To Mrs. Ritter*] Let me get you something, darling.

MRS. RITTER. Call Jenny.

MRS. PAMPINELLI. Yes, dear. [*She crosses to a point just to the left of the middle of the room, then stops and calls toward the door at the left*] Jenny dear, SURPRISE! [*Ritter listens, with a puzzled expression.*] Come here, Jenny—SURPRISE! [*Ritter turns around in the chair, to his right, and looks at her curiously. She meets his eyes with steady bitterness. Then he shifts his gaze to his wife.*]

RITTER. Why didn't you take your make-up off?

MRS. RITTER. I forgot it—I was so worried about you.

RITTER. You look like a Dutch squaw. [*She bursts into tears again.*]

MRS. PAMPINELLI. [*Hastening over to her*] Let her alone! Don't mind him, Paula!

RITTER. She's all made up! and it's coming off.

MRS. PAMPINELLI. Well, what if it is?

RITTER. [*Settling back into the armchair*] I don't want to be reminded of that show. [*Jenny enters hurriedly from the door at the left.*]

MRS. PAMPINELLI. Mrs. Ritter is ill, Jenny. [*Jenny comes quickly across, above the table at the left.*]

MRS. RITTER. [*Half turning to her*] My smelling salts, Jenny.

MRS. PAMPINELLI. [*Standing back of Mrs. Ritter*] Her smelling salts, dear.

JENNY. [*Hurrying out through the center door*] Yes, ma'm.

MRS. RITTER. They're in my bureau basket.

MRS. PAMPINELLI. [*Turning and calling after Jenny*] In her bureau basket, Jenny.

JENNY. [*Running up the stairs*] Yes, ma'm, I know where they are.

MRS. PAMPINELLI. [*Gathering up the roses from the table*] Let me take these flowers out of your way, dear. You've been treated abominably. Although your husband's attitude is entirely consistent with that of the average husband's, after his wife has distinguished herself. [*Ritter makes a little sound of amusement, and she glares at him.*] And any observations of Mr. Ritter's to the contrary, you *did* distinguish yourself tonight, Paula. [*She turns to her right and puts the roses on the piano.*]

RITTER. [*Sitting away down in the arm-chair, smoking*] So did the Cherry Sisters. [*Mrs. Ritter weeps again.*]

MRS. PAMPINELLI. [*Turning back again from the piano to Mrs. Ritter*] We are not talking to you at all, sir. [*Mrs. Ritter has a slight coughing spell.*]

MRS. RITTER. Will you get me a drink of water, please?

MRS. PAMPINELLI. Certainly, darling, where is it?

MRS. RITTER. You'll find it just inside the breakfast room. [*Mrs. Pampinelli sails across the room towards the left door. Just as she is*

*passing back of Ritter's chair, he turns and looks at her, and the exces-
sive grandeur of her manner causes him to burst out laughing. But
she simply freezes him with a look and goes out through the left door.
He continues to laugh; and Mrs. Ritter, not having seen the cause of
his laughter, stops crying and turns and looks at him, very troubled.]*
Fred Ritter, you're acting to me tonight—just like a man that'd
be losing his mind! *[He looks over at her.]* I really thought that
was what was the matter with you when I first came in!

RITTER. *[Very confidently]* Listen—When I didn't lose my mind
watching that show tonight, I couldn't go nutty if I tried.

MRS. RITTER. Well, if anybody else comes here tonight, you just keep
that kind of talk to yourself. There were lots of people there that
thought it was wonderful. Look at all these flowers.

RITTER. These flowers were all paid for long before anybody saw
that show. *[There is a staccato tap at the front doorbell. Jenny is hurrying down the stairs with the smelling salts.]*

MRS. RITTER. *[Rising, and trying to fix herself up a bit]* Well, that's only
your opinion. *[She starts for the center door.]* This is very likely
Nelly Fell. *[Turning back to him as she nears the center door.]* Now,
don't you say anything to *her*, remember! She likes you.

MRS. FELL. *[In the right hallway]* No, I think I can manage, Theodore.
[Jenny hands Mrs. Ritter the smelling salts, at the center door.]

MRS. RITTER. Thanks, Jenny.

JENNY. You're welcome. *[She hurries out into the right hallway, and
Mrs. Ritter comes forward to the chair below the piano, sniffing the
salts. Ritter rises and saunters around and up to the left of the armchair.]*

MRS. FELL. You can close that door, if you will! Couldn't wait for
you, Jenny! *[She rushes in from the right hallway.]* I'm too much
excited! *[She plants herself in the center door, holding aloft in her
right hand a beautiful basket of tulips, and in her left, a huge bouquet
of violets.]* Well, here *I* am, with *my* frankincense and myrrh! *[She
gives an hysterical giggle and teeters forward towards Mrs. Ritter.]*
Oh, there you are, Frederick Ritter! We thought something had
happened to you! Pauline, dear child, I've come to worship at

your shrine. [*She places the basket of tulips down on the floor to the left of Mrs. Ritter, then straightens up, regards Mrs. Ritter, giggles frantically, and looks over at Ritter.*]

MRS. RITTER. [*Laughing wanly, and trying generally not to appear as though she'd been crying*] You've been very sweet.

MRS. FELL. Not half as sweet as you were on that stage tonight! [*Speaking confidentially, and with great conviction*] Dear child, you're made! Absolutely made! [*Turning to Ritter*] Isn't she, Frederick? [*But he's busy getting rid of some of the ashes in the fireplace, so she returns to Mrs. Ritter.*] It's one of those overnight things that one reads about! [*She picks up the basket of tulips from the floor and teeters around above the table.*] Dear me, look at this wilderness of flowers! [*She sets the basket on the table.*]

MRS. RITTER. [*Trying not to cry*] Yes, yes, are'nt they beautiful! [*She darts a look at Ritter.*]

MRS. FELL. [*Rapturously*] Not another word until I've kissed you! [*She kisses her on the left side of the head.*] Oh, you sweet child! [*She shakes Mrs. Ritter by the shoulders.*] what can I *say* to you! [*Then she teeters to the middle of the room, addressing Ritter directly.*] See here, young man! Why aren't you just *pelting* your wife with these flowers? [*He tries to hide his appreciation of the situation by turning away his head.*] Answer me! [*He bursts out laughing, and Nelly teeters back towards Mrs. Ritter.*] My dear, the man is so pleased he can't talk! [*Ritter laughs a little more.*] And if you were any other woman but his wife, Paula, he'd be sending you mash notes! [*Ritter begins to laugh again, and Nelly teeters towards him.*] Oh, you can laugh all you like, Frederick Ritter, but you can't fool Nelly Fell! [*She comes back towards Mrs. Ritter, addressing her.*] I've had three husbands—I know their tricks. [*She places her finger on Mrs. Ritter's shoulder.*] Pauline, dear child, you may be sure that that young man is proud of you tonight if he never was before. [*Mrs. Ritter tries to laugh.*] And when he gets you alone—[*Mrs. Ritter's attempt at laughter is instantly abandoned, and she gives a startled glance toward Ritter, who turns away to his left and goes up toward the mantelpiece.*] oh, when he gets you alone! [*Mrs. Fell turns slowly and looks toward Ritter, with a roguish expression and a measured shaking of her finger at him.*] He's going to tell you you were the loveliest thing that ever stepped on a stage. If he hasn't done so already. Have you, Frederick? [*She looks at him with a mischievous eye.*] Have you? [*He laughs, at the irony of the situation. She crosses towards him.*] Come on, 'fess up!—I know the position is difficult! [*He laughs hard, and she laughs with him; then turns back to Mrs. Ritter. Jenny comes in from the right hallway.*] You see, my dear, the man is so pleased he can't talk! [*She sees Jenny passing along the hallway and steps quickly up to the center door.*] Oh, Jenny dear! Will you take these violets out and put them in some water?

JENNY. [*Taking the violets*] Yes, ma'm. [*Mrs. Pampinelli enters at the left door, with a glass of water.*]

MRS. FELL. I'm afraid they'll be all withered. [*Jenny continues on into the left hallway. Mrs. Fell turns around into the room again.*] Where's Mrs. P.? [*Seeing Mrs. Pampinelli*] Oh, there you are! I was just wondering where you were.

MRS. PAMPINELLI. [*Crossing above the table at the left, towards Mrs. Ritter*] Did you get the smelling salts, Jenny?

JENNY. Yes, ma'm, I gave them to Mrs. Ritter. [*She goes out at the left hallway.*]

MRS. RITTER. Yes, Betty, I have them.

MRS. FELL. [*Coming a step or two forward*] Well, Betty, you see we managed to get them all here.

MRS. PAMPINELLI. [*Back of the table below the piano, and at Mrs. Ritter's left*] Here, try and drink this, Paula. [*Mrs. Ritter takes the water and tries to drink it; and Mrs. Pampinelli leans solicitously over her. There is a pause.*]

MRS. FELL. [*Coming anxiously down at Mrs. Ritter's left*] What's the matter?—[*She looks at Mrs. Pampinelli.*] Is Paula sick?

MRS. PAMPINELLI. [*Straightening up, and very imperiously*] The *critic*— has been giving his impressions of our play.

MRS. FELL. Who? [*She turns towards Ritter.*] This critic here, you mean? [*She indicates Ritter and then looks at Mrs. Pampinelli. Mrs.

Pampinelli inclines her head, with the suggestion of a derisive smile, and passes up to the center door. Mrs. Fell crosses quickly towards Ritter.] What have you been saying, Frederick Ritter?—Huh?

MRS. RITTER. [*Laying the glass of water down on the table*] Oh, what does it matter, Nelly, what he's been saying!

MRS. FELL. [*Turning sharply to Mrs. Ritter*] What?

MRS. RITTER. [*Trying not to cry*] I say—I say [*She bursts into tears.*] I say what does it matter what he's been saying!

MRS. FELL. It doesn't matter in the least, as far as I'm concerned— [*Mrs. Pampinelli turns at the center door and comes forward slowly in the middle of the room.*] there's only one thing he *could* say, if he told the truth.

MRS. PAMPINELLI. [*Laying her hand on Mrs. Fell's left arm*] Eleanor, dear child—husbands are not always particular about telling the truth—where the abilities of their wives are concerned. If *I* had listened to the promptings of my own soul, instead of to my husband, when I was a younger woman, I should in all probability be one of the leading figures in the American Theatre today. But I was fool enough, like a lot of other women, to believe that my husband had my welfare at heart—when the fact of the matter was, as I see it now, when it's too late—he was simply jealous of my artistic promise. [*The cuckoo-clock strikes the midnight hour. Ritter turns and looks up at it, then glances at Mrs. Pampinelli. She is looking up at the clock distrustfully. Mrs. Fell raises here eyes discreetly to it, then drops them to the floor*] Why, the night I played Hazel Kirke, I had my best friends in tears: yet, when I returned from the hall, and the entire town of Cohoes ringing with my name—my husband had the effrontery to tell me that I was so terrific he was obliged to leave the hall before the end of the first act. So—[*She turns to Mrs. Ritter.*] if this gentleman here has set himself up as your critic, Paula—remember *my* story—the actress without honor in her own house. [*She sweeps across below the piano to the window.*] Is my car out here, Nelly?

MRS. FELL. [*Moving aver a bit towards Mrs. Ritter.*] Yes, it's there. I told

Matthew he needn't bother coming back for me, that you'd take me home. [*Mrs. Ritter begins to cry softly, and Mrs. Fell steps to her left and puts her hand on her shoulder.*] Don't do that, Paula. [*She turns sharply and goes towards Ritter.*] What was the matter with that performance, Frederick Ritter?

RITTER. [*Over at the left, below the mantelpiece*] Why, they didn't even know their lines!

MRS. RITTER. [*Straightening up abruptly and looking at him, reproachfully*] Oh!

MRS. PAMPINELLI. [*Turning sharply from the window*] That is a falsehood! They ran over every line last night, right here in this room—and they knew—practically all of them.

RITTER. What good was that, if they couldn't remember them on the stage.

[*Mrs. Ritter and Mrs. Pampinelli, together*]

MRS. RITTER. [*To Ritter*] I *could* remember them on the stage! [*Turning to Mrs. Pampinelli*] I never missed *one* line!

MRS. PAMPINELLI. [*To Ritter*] They *could* remember them on the stage!

MRS. PAMPINELLI. [*To Mrs. Ritter*] Not a line.

RITTER. She and that other woman sat there blinking at the audience like a couple of sparrow-hawks.

MRS. PAMPINELLI. They did nothing of the kind.

MRS. FELL. Of course they didn't!

RITTER. [*Speaking directly to Mrs. Fell*] How do you know? *You* weren't out there.

MRS. FELL. I could see them through the scenery, couldn't I? And they didn't look anything *like* a couple of sparrow-hawks—as you say.

MRS. PAMPINELLI. [*Contemptuously*] Well, as I have never seen a couple of sparrow-hawks, I cannot appreciate the comparison.

RITTER. Well, you'd have seen a couple tonight, if you'd been with me.

MRS. RITTER. Oh, don't argue with him, Betty! He's only trying to be smart.

RITTER. Why didn't one of them *say* something?

MRS. PAMPINELLI. What could they have said?

RITTER. Why, any commonplace! It'd have been better than just sitting there blinking. [*Mrs. Ritter weeps.*]

MRS. PAMPINELLI. One can't be commonplace in high comedy.

RITTER. Was that what it was?

MRS. PAMPINELLI. [*Bitterly*] What did you *think* it was?

RITTER. [*Turning and going up to the center door*] *You* tell her, Nelly; I haven't got the heart.

MRS. FELL. [*Moving a little towards the right*] You bold thing. [*Nelly is wearing the gown she wore in the preceding act, and a heavy cloak of old rose-colored velvet. She lays her hand on Mrs. Ritter's left shoulder.*] Don't let him upset you this way, Paula. [*There is a little pause. Ritter turns at the center door and comes forward again at the left.*]

MRS. PAMPINELLI. [*Picking up her fan from the piano*] I suppose *you* would have eclipsed Edwin Booth, if *you* had been up there.

RITTER. Well, I'd have known better than to sit there blinking at the audience.

MRS. RITTER. [*Turning sharply to him*] I didn't *blink* at the audience.

MRS. FELL. Don't answer him, honey.

MRS. PAMPINELLI. What could they have done under the circumstances?

RITTER. Why, they could have covered it up!—if they'd had any brains.

MRS. PAMPINELLI. Covered it up with *what?*

RITTER. Why, with anything! Impromptu conversation! [*Mrs Fell looks at Mrs. Pampinelli and smiles pityingly.*]

MRS. PAMPINELLI. And have the audience *laugh* at them?

RITTER. They laughed anyhow, didn't they?

MRS. FELL. [*Taking a step or two towards him*] That was not their fault!

RITTER. [*To Nelly.*] Whose fault *was* it?

MRS. PAMPINELLI. [*Imperiously, and moving over to a point above the table at which Mrs. Ritter is sitting*] It was Mr. Spindler's fault.

RITTER. Mr. Spindler.

MRS. PAMPINELLI. He promised to attend to the various properties and he did *not* attend to them.—There was supposed to be a pen and ink on the desk for Mrs. Rush to leave a note for

Doctor Arlington—and when Paula sat down to write the note, there was no pen—and no ink. So she simply had to go on sitting there until Mr. Spearing went off and got them.

RITTER. I thought he'd left town.

MRS. FELL. Oh, he wasn't gone so very long, Frederick Ritter!

MRS. PAMPINELLI. [*Bitterly, to Mrs. Fell*] Not five minutes.

RITTER. I thought the show 'ud be over before he'd get back.

MRS. PAMPINELLI. The door wouldn't open when he attempted to go back, so he was obliged to go around to the other side. [*She illustrates the circumstance by waving her fan in a circular gesture about the table. Ritter bursts out laughing. Nelly glares at him, then looks to Mrs. Pampinelli, who, with a deadly, level look, turns and moves haughtily up towards the center door.*]

RITTER. What happened to the skinny guy's mustache, that it kept falling off every other line?

MRS. PAMPINELLI. [*Turning to him, up near the center door*] It only fell off twice, don't exaggerate. [*Ritter laughs again.*]

MRS. FELL. You bold thing!

RITTER. How many times was it *supposed* to fall off?

MRS. PAMPINELLI. Well, what if it fell off a dozen times—everybody knew it wasn't for real! [*He roars.*]

MRS. FELL. It's a lucky thing for *you*, Frederick Ritter, that you're not *my* husband!

RITTER. [*Quietly*] That goes both ways, Nelly.

MRS. FELL. [*Moving across towards him*] Well—when you do something that you'll get so many flowers that my limousine will have to make three trips to get them to the various hospitals— we may pay more attention to what you have to say. [*She turns away and moves back towards the center of the room, where Mrs. Pampinelli is just moving forward from the center door.*]

RITTER. I suppose most of the audience have gone with the flowers, haven't they? [*Nelly whirls round to retort, but Mrs. Pampinelli lays a restraining hand upon her right arm.*]

MRS. PAMPINELLI. [*With immortal authority*] Don't answer him, Eleanor—"Envy loves a lofty mark." The next time we have a part that calls for a very limited intelligence, we'll engage Mr. Ritter for it. [*She moves a little down to the right towards Mrs. Ritter.*]

MRS. FELL. [*Looking at Ritter*] Now!

RITTER. [*Casually*] Well, if you do, he'll know how to walk across the stage without tripping every other step.

MRS. FELL. Who tripped every other step?

RITTER. [*Indicating his wife*] The weeping willow there. [*Mrs. Ritter begins to weep afresh.*]

MRS. FELL. It's a wonder to me you're not afraid to lie so!

RITTER. She tripped when she first came through the door! I was looking right at her!

MRS. PAMPINELLI. [*Turning to him*] She didn't *fall*, did she?

RITTER. No, but it looked for a while there as though she were going to. [*Mrs. Ritter's weeping becomes audible again.*] I very nearly had heart failure.

MRS. PAMPINELLI. [*Laying her hand on Paula's shoulder*] Don't mind him, Paula.

RITTER. She tripped when she came *on* the stage, she tripped when she went *off*, and she tripped over the rug when she went over to the desk!

MRS. PAMPINELLI. [*With measured finality*] She didn't trip any oftener than anybody else. [*He laughs.*]

MRS. FELL. [*Directly to Ritter*] No, nor half so often as some of the others—[*Turning towards Mrs. Pampinelli*] now that you speak of it! [*She turns and goes up to the hallway.*]

MRS. PAMPINELLI. I will admit that Mr. Hossefrosse is a bit unsteady—but that is due to his weak ankles.

RITTER. What was the star's unsteadiness due to?

MRS. RITTER. The rugs!

RITTER. [*Looking at her keenly*] What?

[*Mrs. Ritter and Mrs. Pampinelli, together*]

MRS. RITTER. The rugs.

MRS. PAMPINELLI. [*Moving to the center of the room*] The rugs!

MRS. PAMPINELLI. Those funny rugs—that they have down there. We didn't use them at the rehearsals—and, naturally, when it came to the performance—Paula wasn't accustomed to them.

RITTER. She was accustomed to rugs at home, wasn't she?

MRS. PAMPINELLI. [*Tersely*] Well, she wasn't at home on the stage.

RITTER. [*With a gesture of complete acquiescence, and moving up towards the center door*] That's my argument in a nutshell. [*Mrs. Pampinelli stands frozen in the middle of the room, with an expression very much as though she were trying mentally to assassinate him. He comes back down again at the left; to his former position.*] Why, I couldn't hear *two-thirds* of what she said.

MRS. PAMPINELLI. Well, evidently there were many people there who *could* hear what she said, for they laughed at all her points. [*She turns and goes to the piano, where she picks up several roses. Mrs. Fell comes forward through the center door and down towards the piano.*]

RITTER. I wanted to laugh, too, but I was afraid somebody'd turn around and *see* me.

MRS. PAMPINELLI. [*Turning to Mrs. Ritter*] Are you ready, Nelly?

MRS. FELL. Yes, I'm ready.

MRS. RITTER. Are you going, Betty?

MRS. PAMPINELLI. Yes, I must, darling, it's getting late. [*She places her hand on Mrs. Ritter's shoulder.*] Good night, dear. [*She passes up towards the center door.*]

MRS. RITTER. Good night, Betty.

MRS. FELL. [*Laying her hand on Mrs. Ritter's shoulder*] Good night, Paula child.

MRS. RITTER. Good night, Nelly. [*Nelly follows Mrs. Pampinelli.*]

MRS. PAMPINELLI. [*Stopping in the center door and turning to Ritter*] Perhaps, at out *next* performance—Mr. Ritter will favor us with the benefit of some of his suggestions. [*She regards him with a touch of lofty amusement. He turns his head towards her and looks at her with a kind of mischievous squint.*]

RITTER. [*Quite pleasantly*] There aren't going to be any more performances, Mrs. Pampinelli, as far as anybody in *this* house is concerned.

MRS. PAMPINELLI. [*After a steady pause*] No? [*He inclines his head in quiet emphasis.*]

RITTER. Not until there's a change in the management. [*There is another taut pause.*]

MRS. PAMPINELLI. [*Coldly*] Really? [*He inclines his head again.*] Then, I'm afraid we shan't have you with us, Mr. Ritter.

RITTER. [*Smiling*] I know very well you won't have *me* with you. And as far as Mrs. Ritter's concerned—she's got a very good home here—and I love her; and any time she feels any dramatic instinct coming on, there's a very nice roomy attic upstairs, and she can go up there and lock the door, and nobody'll ever see or hear her. But if she ever gets mixed up again in anything like that atrocity I saw tonight—I'm through. [*He speaks the last words with a quiet definiteness, and turns towards the door at the left.*] And she'll get killed in the bargain. [*He hits the door open with the palm of his hand and goes out. There is a slight pause; then Nelly Fell crosses quickly towards the mantelpiece, addressing Ritter as she goes.*]

MRS. FELL. Why, Fred Ritter!—I've heard you say yourself that you were n *favor* of a Little Theatre in this city!

RITTER. [*Coming in again through the door at the left, carrying his overcoat, derby and scarf*] So I am! I say so again. [*He stops inside the door.*] But in the light of that cataclysm tonight, you'll pardon me if I add, that I do not see the connection.

MRS. PAMPINELLI. [*Stepping forward to the middle of the room and challenging him with a lift of her head and brows*] What did you *expect* to *see*, Mr. Ritter—a finished performance from a group of comparative amateurs?

RITTER. I expected to see something almost as bad as what I saw— that's the reason I *fainted* last night and was unconscious for twenty-four hours at the prospect of it. [*He turns to Mrs. Fell and speaks quite colloquially.*] And that's the first time in my life I've ever fainted. [*Nelly just gives him a look and turns her head away.*]

MRS. RITTER. Don't mind him, Betty—he's only trying to show off.

MRS. PAMPINELLI. [*With bitter amusement*] No, but I'm a bit *curious*—

to know just *how* Mr. Ritter would expect to *accomplish* the establishment of a Little Theatre here, unless through the medium of such performances as this one this evening. How else is our local talent to be discovered—or developed?

RITTER. Well, I'm equally curious, Mrs. Pampinelli, as to your exact *qualifications*—as a discoverer or developer of talent for the theatre.

MRS. PAMPINELLI. That is a very familiar attitude. People who *do* things—are constantly having their ability to do them called into question. [*She moves up a step further forward and towards Mrs. Ritter.*]

RITTER. I'm afraid that's something you've read somewhere. [*She glares at him.*]

MRS. PAMPINELLI. The theatre is a matter of instinct.

RITTER. The theatre is a matter of qualifications—the same as any other profession; and it will only be *through* those particular qualifications that your Little Theatre will ever be brought about. [*He crosses over in front of Mrs. Fell and up towards the center door.*]

MRS. PAMPINELLI. Well, perhaps you will come to the rescue—you seem so familiar with the various necessities of the Little Theatre. [*He stops, just to the left of the center door, and looks at Mrs. Pampinelli straight.*]

RITTER. [*Quietly*] I am also familiar, Mrs. Pampinelli, with a little remark that Mr. Napoleon made on one occasion, a long time ago—about the immorality of assuming a position for which one is unqualified. [*There is a pause—he settles his coat on his arm, then moves slowly out through the center door into the hallway; while Mrs. Pampinelli, with an expression of eternal exclusion, moves over between the piano and the table towards the window.*]

MRS. RITTER. [*Turning*] Fred Ritter, where are you going?

RITTER. [*Lighting his cigar in the hallway, just outside the center door*] I haven't the faintest idea. But I shouldn't be surprised if I'd go on the stage.

MRS. FELL. [*Standing back of the armchair at the left*] One star is enough in the family.

RITTER. [*Bowing very graciously to her*] Applause—[*She turns away and looks straight ahead. Then Ritter bows towards Mrs. Pampinelli.*] and great laughter—[*Mrs. Pampinelli isn't looking at him, but she knows that that is meant for her, so she simply moves another step or two towards the window. Mrs. Ritter turns to see what Ritter is doing. He takes a step and leans towards her, speaking rather confidently.*] followed by booing. [*She turns back again and starts to cry, while he continues out into the right hallway and up the stairs. As he mounts the stairs, he holds aloft his lighted cigar, after the fashion of a zealous bearer of the torch.*]

MRS. PAMPINELLI. [*Picking up the orchids from the table below the window*] Paula, you should have Jenny put these orchids in water, they keep ever so long in a cool place. [*She comes across towards the left, below the piano.*]

MRS. RITTER. Will you call her, Nelly?

MRS. FELL. [*Crossing to meet Mrs. Pampinelli*] Give them to me, Betty. I'll take them out to her. [*Mrs. Pampinelli gives her the orchids.*]

MRS. PAMPINELLI. Tell her to put them in a cool place. [*Nelly starts up for the center door. The telephone bell rings.*]

MRS. RITTER. Will you answer that, Nelly?

MRS. FELL. [*Setting the orchids down on the chair in the left hallway*] Certainly, darling.

MRS. PAMPINELLI. [*Standing back of Mrs. Ritter's chair*] If it's anything concerning the play, I shall be at home on Tuesday at two.

MRS. FELL. [*At the telephone*] Yes?—Yes?—Who?—Oh—well, wait just one moment, please.

MRS. PAMPINELLI. What is it?

MRS. FELL. [*Holding the transmitter against her bosom and leaning over the partition towards Mrs. Pampinelli*] It's the Star Moving Picture Company.

MRS. PAMPINELLI. What do they want?

MRS. FELL. They want the address of Mrs. Ritter's manager. [*Mrs. Pampinelli gives a quick look at Mrs. Ritter.*]

MRS. PAMPINELLI. [*To Mrs. Ritter*] I anticipated this. [*She goes quickly towards the center door, laying her fan and roses on the left partition-*

seat, as she passes out into the hallway.] Give it to me, Nelly. [*Nelly hands her the telephone, and, picking up the orchids from the chair, tiptoes back of Mrs. Pampinelli and in through the center door.*]

MRS. FELL. [*In an excited whisper to Mrs. Ritter.*] What did I tell you! [*She giggles nervously, shakes her finger at Mrs. Ritter, and then watches Mrs. Pampinelli eagerly.*]

MRS. PAMPINELLI. [*Into the telephone*] Hello-hello—This is Mrs. Ritter's manager speaking. Mrs. Pampinelli. Pampinelli. Mrs. J. *Duro* Pampinelli. Capital P—a—m, p—i—n, e—double l—i.— Correct. Yes—I see—I see.—Well, how do you mean, a thousand dollars, a thousand dollars a day, or a thous—I see. Well, just one moment, please. [*She lowers the telephone and leans towards Mrs. Ritter, speaking in a subdued tone.*] The Star Moving Picture Company wants to know if Mrs. Ritter will appear in a special production of tonight's play before the camera.

MRS. FELL. [*Narrowing her left eye*] What's the figure?

MRS. PAMPINELLI. One thousand dollars per week.

MRS. FELL. Fifteen hundred.

MRS. PAMPINELLI. [*Into the telephone*] Hello-hello!

MRS. RITTER. [*Rising*] Maybe I'd better talk to them.

MRS. FELL. [*Suggesting with a gesture that she be quiet and resume her chair*] Please, dear. [*Mrs. Ritter meekly sits down again.*]

MRS. PAMPINELLI. [*Into the telephone*] Why, I'm sorry—but Mrs. Ritter does not appear under fifteen hundred dollars per week.

MRS. FELL. [*Watching her shrewdly*] Net! [*Mrs. Pampinelli turns and looks at her sharply, and Nelly emphasizes what she said by inclining her head: then Mrs. Pampinelli speaks into the telephone again.*]

MRS. PAMPINELLI. Net.

MRS. FELL. [*To Mrs. Pampinelli*] It's a bargain at that. [*She nods towards Mrs. Ritter.*]

MRS. PAMPINELLI. [*Into the telephone*] Twelve-fifty?

MRS. FELL. No compromise.

MRS. PAMPINELLI. [*Into the telephone*] Well, just one moment. [*Covering the transmitter and speaking to Mrs. Fell*] Twelve-fifty is offered.

MRS. FELL. [*Definitely*] Fifteen hundred dollars. They'll lift it.

MRS. PAMPINELLI. [*Turning back to the telephone*] Why, I'm very sorry—but Mrs. Ritter positively does not appear under fifteen hundred dollars. [*Nelly inclines her head towards her.*] Net. Well, how do you mean satisfactory? Satisfactory at our figure? [*Mrs. Pampinelli glances at Mrs. Fell and Mrs. Fell glances at Mrs. Ritter.*]

MRS. FELL. [*To Mrs. Pampinelli*] Sign!

MRS. PAMPINELLI. [*Into the telephone*] Very well, then—signed at fifteen hundred dollars per week—

MRS. FELL. Net!

MRS. PAMPINELLI. [*Into the telephone*] Net! And Mrs. Ritter appears. [*She stands holding the telephone and listening.*]

MRS. FELL. [*Whirling round and teetering down to Paula*] Our STAR! I always said it! [*She shakes Mrs. Ritter by the shoulders.*] I always said it! [*She whirls round and teeters up towards the center door.*] Haven't I always said it, Betty? [*Mrs. Pampinelli is listening on the telephone, and tries, by dint of thrusting the telephone towards Nelly, to silence her. But Nelly is irrepressible.*] That it was only a question of time? [*She turns and flies down towards Mrs. Ritter again.*] We must telephone Mrs. Livingston at once, Paula!

MRS. PAMPINELLI. Be quiet, Nelly, be quiet!

MRS. FELL. [*Rushing up towards the center door again*] She'll be so interested! We must call up Mrs. Livingston right away, Betty!

MRS. PAMPINELLI. Please, Nelly! [*Nelly is silenced. Mrs. Pampinelli listens sharply, Nelly and Mrs. Ritter watching her; and there is a dead pause.*] Beg pardon? [*There is another slight pause; and then Mrs. Pampinelli utters an abrupt shriek and sets down the telephone.*]

MRS. FELL. What is it, Betty? [*Mrs. Pampinelli looks at her, then straight ahead.*]

MRS. PAMPINELLI. [*With venomous enunciation*] It's Ritter! [*Mrs. Ritter rises slowly.*]

MRS. FELL. Ritter? [*Mrs. Pampinelli doesn't stir.*]

MRS. RITTER. [*Addressing Mrs. Pampinelli*] Fred?

MRS. PAMPINELLI. I recognized his voice. [*She moves along the left hallway and comes in through the center door and forward, a little to the left of the center of the room.*]

MRS. FELL. [*Up just to the right of the center door*] Why, where is he?

MRS. RITTER. [*Beginning to cry*] He must be on the extension upstairs. [*Nelly listens keenly.*]

MRS. FELL. It is he; I hear him laughing. [*She crosses down to the door at the left.*]

MRS. PAMPINELLI. [*Taking a step towards Mrs. Ritter*] Sit down, Paula. [*Mrs. Ritter sits down, rests her elbows on the table and weeps bitterly. Nelly stops over at the door and turns.*]

MRS. FELL. [*Positively*] Paula—if he were *my* husband, I should lose no time in having him arrested. [*She goes out, at the left door.*]

MRS. PAMPINELLI. [*Standing back of Mrs. Ritter's chair*] Paula dear, I do hope that you are not going to allow Mr. Ritter's flippancies to discourage you. [*Paula clasps her hands in her lap and looks tearfully at the backs of them.*] The way of the essential artist is always hard; and so very frequently the most serious obstacles are those to be encountered at home.

MRS. RITTER. But, I feel so unsuccessful.

MRS. PAMPINELLI. I know, dear—I know exactly how you feel. But you must *go on.* Just remember that art is the highest expression of truth—and you cannot fail. For you have everything in your favor, Paula.

MRS. RITTER. [*Weakly*] Thank you.

MRS. PAMPINELLI. And the masses need you, dear; you are an altogether *new note* in the theatre.

MRS. RITTER. But—I don't know whether Fred'll *want* me to go on any more—[*Mrs. Pampinelli suddenly becomes very still and stoney, and looks down at Mrs. Ritter with merciless inquiry. Mrs. Ritter senses the change and turns hastily to explain.*] the way he spoke.

MRS. PAMPINELLI. And, do you mean that you will allow him to *stop* you, Paula?

MRS. RITTER. [*Breaking down under Mrs. Pampinelli's frozen amusement*] Well, of course, he's my *husband,* Betty. [*She cries. Mrs. Pampinelli regards here with a kind of pained toleration; and settles her cloak, preparatory to going.*]

MRS. PAMPINELLI. Very well, then, Paula—if you feel *that* way about it, I should advise you to keep him; and I shan't waste any more of my time encouraging you. [*She sweeps around to her left and up towards the center door.*] There are far too many who are only too *willing* to make the necessary sacrifices without being urged. [*She picks up her fan and roses from the partition-seat, lays them across her left arm, and turns regnantly to Mrs. Ritter.*] Only remember this, Paula—there will be actresses when husbands are a thing of the past. [*She sweeps out through the center door and out into the right hallway. There is a slight pause; then Nelly Fell comes in at the left door. She misses Mrs. Pampinelli.*]

MRS. FELL. Where is Mrs. P., Paula?

MRS. RITTER. She's just gone out to the car, Nelly.

MRS. FELL. [*Stooping to pick up one of the chrysanthemums from the floor*] Do you mind if I take one of these flowers, Paula? [*She stands in the middle of the room, holding it, and looking at Mrs. Ritter.*] I want it for my dramatic shrine.

MRS. RITTER. You can take all of them, if you like.

MRS. FELL. Why, what would *you* do, dear?

MRS. RITTER. I don't want them.

MRS. FELL. [*Crossing towards her*] Now, you mustn't feel like that, Paula Ritter.

MRS. RITTER. [*Having all she can do to keep from crying*] I just can't help it.

MRS. FELL. I see in your husband's attitude—nothing but a desperate attempt to save his home—for he *must* know what your performance tonight will inevitably lead to. [*Mrs. Ritter turns with a puzzled expression and looks at her.*]

MRS. RITTER. I don't understand what you mean, Nelly.

MRS. FELL. Why, you must go to New York, dear; you can do nothing dramatically here.

MRS. RITTER. But, I have a husband.

MRS. FELL. [*Very casually*] Every married woman has that cross, darling. But you mustn't let it stand in the way of your career; he would very soon eliminate *you*, if you stood in the way of *his*.

MRS. RITTER. But, I don't like the thought of breaking up his home, Nelly. [*Nelly gives a hard, knowing little laugh.*]

MRS. FELL. Don't be unnecessarily sacrificial, darling. I made that mistake with my first *two* husbands; but I was *wiser* with the third. And I said to him, immediately we returned from the church, I said, "Now, Leonard, you and I have just been made one; and *I* am that one." [*She touches herself on the breastbone with her forefinger, then touches Paula on the left shoulder.*] And it worked out beautifully. So be sensible, darling. [*She skips up towards the hallway.*] I must run along, Mrs. Pampinelli's waiting! [*She teeters out through the center door into the right hallway.*] Cheerio, Paula darling!

MRS. RITTER. Good night.

MRS. FELL. Cheerio! [*She giggles and vanishes into the right hallway. Mrs. Ritter sits still for a second, looking from side to side, at nothing, particularly, and presently gets up. The horseshoe of "SUCCESS" over in front of the mantelpiece catches her eye, and she wanders slowly towards it. But the irony of it all overcomes her and she commences to cry again. Ritter appears at the head of the stairs and starts down. She turns and looks at him, as he comes through the center door.*]

MRS. RITTER. Fred Ritter, those women will never come inside that door again, the way you talked to them. [*He moves to the piano and leans against it.*]

RITTER. Well, I don't suppose that'll make very much difference.

MRS. RITTER. [*Looking straight ahead*] Well, it *should* make a difference.

RITTER. They'd hardly come here to see *me*, anyway.

MRS. RITTER. Well, they'd come to see me.

RITTER. But *you* won't be here. [*She turns and looks at him blankly.*]

MRS. RITTER. Why—what—what do you mean, I won't be here?

RITTER. [*With a touch of delicacy*] Why, aren't you going on with *The Work?*

MRS. RITTER. Well, I don't want to go unless you *want* me to.

RITTER. But, I *do* want you to. I don't think a talent like yours should be hidden; [*He looks straight out, thoughtfully.*] it's too unique.

MRS. RITTER. I thought you said a while ago you didn't like me?

RITTER. [*Raising his left hand and crossing over and down in front of her towards the armchair at the left*] You mustn't hold me responsible for what I said a while ago—[*He stops back of the armchair and rests his hand upon the back of it.*] I was panic-stricken at the thought of having my home broken up. [*She moves down to the center of the room.*] But I've been thinking it over upstairs, and

I've concluded that it's more important that the world should see you act, than that I should have a home to come to.

MRS. RITTER. But, I don't like the thought of breaking up your home, Fred.

RITTER. [*Raising his right hand to her with a touch of solemnity*] You mustn't consider me in the matter at all, dear. Every great gift has its victim—and I am, in a way, rather happy—to find myself chosen the victim of yours.

MRS. RITTER. What would *you* do, if I was to go?

RITTER. [*With the faintest shade of classic pose*] I'd go with you; you'd need someone to look after the flowers—see that they got to the various hospitals all right.

MRS. RITTER. [*Looking away out*] I might not like it, after I'd get there.

RITTER. Maybe not. I suppose fame becomes monotonous like everything else. But, I wouldn't want you in the future, to look back and feel that I had stood in your way.

MRS. RITTER. [*Carefully*] No, Fred—I really don't *know* whether I want to be a great actress or not.

RITTER. But, you are a great actress, dear.

MRS. RITTER. Thank you.

RITTER. [*Indicating the anchor of roses down at the left*] Look at this anchor—of hope. [*He steps back and picks up the horseshoe.*] And this horseshoe of "SUCCESS." [*He brings it forward and sets it down just to Mrs. Ritter's left. Then he steps across in front of it, takes her hand and slips his right arm around her waist.*] And I think, Paula, it might be a very sensible move, to just let the public *remember* you as a great actress—as they saw you *tonight—at your best.*

MRS. RITTER. [*Looking wistfully straight ahead*] Do you think they *will* remember, Fred?

RITTER. [*Inclining his head, with a suggestion of the obsequious*] Yes, I *think* they will. [*Curtain.*]

MRS. RITTER. [*Turning and sinking into his arms*] You're awfully sweet, Fred.

THE END OF THE PLAY.

The Same Racket

Near relatives of two famous playwrights are acting this week in "The Torch-Bearers."

One is Jennifer Howard (the Maid) who is the daughter of the late Sidney Howard, author of "Ned McCobbs Daughter," "The Silver Cord," "The Late Christopher Bean," etc. She was seen here last week also in "Ah Wilderness."

The other is Grace Kelly (Miss Florence McCrickett), niece of George Kelly, author of "The Torch-Bearers." Miss Kelly, daughter of John B. Kelly of Philadelphia, is making her professional stage debut here. She has just completed a course at the American Academy of Dramatic Art in New York. Her brother recently figured in the news by winning the Diamond Sculls at the Henley Regatta in England. Her father was a champion oarsman and is well known as the former chairman of the Democratic party in Philadelphia. (We hope Republicans won't be mad at us for engaging his daughter).

Miss Howard also made her stage debut in a George Kelly play "The Fatal Weakness," starring Ina Claire.

BUCKS COUNTY PLAYHOUSE

NEW HOPE, PA.   PHONE NEW HOPE 3541

1949 SUMMER SEASON

COMMENCING July 25th

HAILA STODDARD   **MARY WICKES**

in

"THE TORCH-BEARERS"

with

JESSIE BUSLEY

Henry Jones   John Harvey

The Cast

(in order of their appearance)

Mr. Frederick Ritter	John Harvey
Jenny	Jennifer Howard
Mrs. Paula Ritter	Haila Stoddard
Mrs. J. Duro Pampinelli	Mary Wickes
Mr. Spindler	Henry Jones
Mrs. Nelly Fell	Jessie Busley
Mr. Huxley Hossefrosse	Carl White
Teddy Spearing	Fred Beir
Miss Florence McCrickett	Grace Kelly
Mr. Ralph Twiller	Jared Reed
Stage Manager	Robert Caldwell
Mrs. Clara Sheppard	Ruth White

Cast of the July, 1949 summer production of *The Torch-Bearers* at the Bucks County (PA) Playhouse. Niece Grace Kelly (Florence McCrickett) is making one of her first professional appearances. Jessie Busley (Nelly Fell) had played the title role in Kelly's *Daisy Mayme* (1926).

THE

SHOW-OFF

THE ∫HOW-OFF

The *Show-Off* (1924) is Kelly's most successful play (571 performances) and, along with his next drama, *Craig's Wife*, his most memorable. In a preface to the play's first published edition, Heywood Broun called it "the finest comedy which has yet been written by an American."[*] Over forty years later, *New York Times* critic Clive Barnes hailed it as the best American play in several seasons.[†]

It is no coincidence that both critics stressed the word *American*, for *The Show-Off* is a close inspection of the country's working and lower-middle classes. The domestic comedy is set in a row house located in East Falls, the North Philadelphia section in which Kelly was raised. Into the provincial home of the Fishers comes the play's title figure, Aubrey Piper, a denizen from West Philadelphia—then a slightly more prosperous section of the city, separated from East Falls by the Schuylkill River (the scene of Kelly's Olympic-champion brother John's sculling triumphs).

Aubrey is larger than life with his loud voice, braying laugh, flatulent rhetoric, obvious toupee, and festive carnation. His nat-

---

[*]Heywood Broun, preface to George Kelly, *The Show-Off* (New York: Samuel French, 1951), ix.

[†]Clive Barnes, review of *The Show-Off*, *New York Times*, December 6, 1967.

ural foil is his future mother-in-law, Mrs. Fisher, tight-lipped, laconic, and a born protector of home and hearth who is instinctively suspicious of any intruder into her narrow world. She is the very essence of the provincial Philadelphia housewife of the period; the clash between her practical, conservative nature and Aubrey's flamboyant and improvident personality constitutes much of the play's humor as well as its action.

The genesis of *The Show-Off* is Kelly's *Poor Aubrey* (1919), a vaudeville sketch that toured the country before and even during the run of *The Show-Off*. Its location is the Fisher home, but the time is that of the third act of *The Show-Off*—the period after Pa Fisher's death, when Aubrey, having married Mrs. Fisher's daughter Amy, has moved into the Fisher home, along with his wife. Neither son Joe nor daughter Clara Fisher Hyland appears in Poor Aubrey, although they are integral to the plot of *The Show-Off*. Instead, Marion Brill, an old friend of Amy, is onstage for at least half of the play. She is the straight-faced, gracious recipient of Aubrey's boastful lies as well as of Mrs. Fisher's intimate family gossip, the first function that Gill, the factory worker, performs in *The Show-Off*. There is a farce bit in which Aubrey loses his toupee, and a final heated argument between Aubrey and Mrs. Fisher at the play's conclusion. Both plays end on the same tranquil note, with Aubrey requesting the financial page of the daily paper.

The "battle of the sexes" motif, used so effectively by Kelly in *The Torch-Bearers*, emerges comically in *The Show-Off* as the perennial "husband versus mother-in-law" clash, ending with the temporary victory of the male. However, Kelly tempers his conflict by making his opponents more believable and more universal than those in *The Torch-Bearers*. There are more Mrs. Fishers than Mrs. Pampanellis in the world, and Aubrey's counterpart is present in families of every generation. In addition, Kelly makes us genuinely fond of his adversaries. Aubrey, despite his lies, his self-absorption, and his other obnoxious personal traits, is almost childlike in his Micawberish optimism, and in his genuine concern for his wife's welfare. Mrs. Fisher may be querulous, hard-bitten, prejudiced, and bossy, but she is also fiercely maternal, watching over her children like a den mother, even though they are adults. Her family is her whole life—as a working man's wife, she has known little but her own home—and she is even willing to tolerate Aubrey under her roof if it will somehow contribute to her daughter's happiness.

The play's sub-rosa theme is emphasized in Mrs. Fisher's bitter comment to Clara: "There's nothing can be done by anything, Clara—when once the main thing is done. And that's the marriage. That's where all the trouble starts—gettin' married." For more than any other of his plays, including *Craig's Wife*, *The Deep Mrs. Sykes*, and *The Fatal Weakness*, *The Show-Off* is about marriage. There are three marriages in the play: that of Aubrey and Amy, of Clara and Frank Hyland, and of Mr. and Mrs. Fisher. Of the three, only the first is a happy one. Despite Aubrey's egotism and Amy's stubborn self-justification, there is a genuine affection in their union—a tender, even romantic side to their relationship, something that is glaringly absent in the other two cases. The marriage of Clara and Frank was doomed from the beginning; in a touching scene with her mother, Clara confesses that her husband only really loved a woman whom he foolishly lost some years before. He has tried to make up for his mistakes in this early relationship by being financially overgenerous to Aubrey and Amy, who share an intimacy he is unable to provide in his own marriage.

The prosaic marriage of Mr. and Mrs. Fisher may be the most moving of the three because its inevitable bleakness was so common among the working class in Kelly's time. Romance has departed early from the lives of the Fishers because of the grinding daily struggle of financial survival. Pa Fisher is a weekly wage earner in a tedious factory job, and his wife has occupied herself in the equally monotonous rearing of her children and the upkeep of an ordinary, slightly drab house. Meaningful dialogue between the pair barely exists; it is relegated to pointless observations occasionally prompted by newspaper items. However, with little communication, there is also little hostility; the Fishers have settled into a life of dull tranquillity, with the husband the de jure boss of the home, and the wife the de facto one. And there is still some sort of bond between them, the depth of which emerges when Mr. Fisher suffers a fatal stroke. Theirs is a sad marriage in many ways, but it has been a better one than Clara and Frank's. And Aubrey's permanent presence helps relieve the monotony of the Fisher home and lends some vitality to the family, a quality that has been missing for many years.

While Mrs. Fisher has more lines than Aubrey, it is clearly he who dominates the play. He is talked about from the opening curtain, and his early speeches, sprinkled with slang, pointless quotations, and outright lies, punctuated by loud laughter and accompanied by broad gestures and backslapping, enable him to capture our immediate attention. He is all the playwright promises us and more, and we instinctively sympathize with Amy in her early resentment of her family's rudeness when they deliberately walk out of the room on him. Mrs. Fisher never uses his first name, seldom his last, preferring pejoratives like "boy," "nut," "fool," and "blatherskite." (She refers to the less colorful but more reliable Frank Hyland by his full name.) To Mr. Fisher, Aubrey is "Windy"; to Joe, he is "the Pennsylvania Railroad" or "the Old Scientific American." Except for Amy, only Clara, the play's voice of reason, senses Aubrey's basic decency and sympathizes with his pathetic efforts at self-importance. Although Mrs. Fisher ignores Clara when she tells her mother of Aubrey's better qualities, the audience listens and concurs.

Like Aubrey, Mrs. Fisher is an ambivalent figure—a mixture of caring and cynicism. Her distrust of marriage and her resentment of Aubrey and Amy's overt demonstrations of affection spring from a naturally dour nature, hardened by experience and age. Yet she evidently loves her children, and she is fiercely protective of them against outsiders like Aubrey and even Frank, who makes the mistake of agreeing with Mrs. Fisher's criticism of Amy's spendthrift traits. She worries over Joe's health, and his planned move to nearby Trenton; she is concerned over her husband's failure to arrive promptly from work; and she shows sympathy for Clara's failing marriage. She even turns over her insurance check to pay for Aubrey's traffic fine. Her home is her life and she forever frets about it, making sure that doors are locked and heaters work properly. Much of her advice, jaundiced and too freely given, is ignored by her family, but she means well in offering it.

Percy Hammond in 1924,* and Walter Kerr in 1967,† commented on the moving personal effect on Mrs. Fisher of the news of her husband's stroke and subsequent death. She becomes badly shaken and temporarily disoriented, and the audience weeps for her and with her. But she soon recovers, for, above all, she is a survivor—her final "God help me from now on" is only a temporary concession of the initial round of what promises to be a lifetime bout with the swaggering Aubrey.

Although Foster Hirsch sees *The Show-Off* as an anticipation of Arthur Miller's *Death of a Salesman*, with both Willy Loman and Aubrey believing in a false American dream,‡ both Kelly's play and his hero lack the social significance of Miller's tragedy. Aubrey's problem is a personal one, springing, as Clara notes, from a combination of insecurity and egotism. His early bad-mouthing of capitalism and his later willingness to quote encouragement to the young from a company president are all part of the marvelous contradictions in his personality. That he should be able to talk a metal company into a large advance for Joe's invention was regarded by Arthur Hobson Quinn,§ John Corbin,‖ and other critics as improbable, although Heywood Broun liked the happy conclusion, arguing that Kelly had up to

*Percy Hammon, review of *The Show-Off*, *New York Herald Tribune*, February 6, 1924.

†Walter Kerr, "Which Death is Dramatic?" *New York Times*, December 17, 1967.

‡Foster Hirsch, *George Kelly* (Boston: Twayne, 1975), 63.

§Arthur Hobson Quinn, *A History of the American Drama from the Civil War to the Present Day*, rev. ed. (New York: Appleton-Century-Crofts, 1936), 225.

‖John Corbin, review of *The Show-Off*, *New York Times*, February 6, 1924.

then pursued Aubrey with a bit too much "venom and malignancy."* Perhaps Kelly is merely suggesting here that Aubrey's combined aggressiveness and bluff were at home in a business world that depends heavily on both characteristics for its very existence and survival.

Kelly insisted that *The Show-Off* was a "transcript of life." He uses a selective but not merely photographic technique to create an illusion of reality in this presentation of Philadelphia rowhouse existence. Alexander Woollcott, himself a native of Kelly's city, asserted that the play contained "the very flow of Philadelphia all the way through."† Stark Young noted Kelly's mastery of "the idioms, axioms, and catchwords . . . of ordinary speech" as well as the "alive and infectious" beat of the dialogue.‡ Walter Prichard Eaton felt that the play's "absolute veracity" showed the influence of Continental naturalism on the American drama more than any other play of the time, and he praised Kelly's realistic direction in achieving his effects.§ (Actually, Kelly had read few of the Continental dramatists.) An unsigned column in the *World* went so far as to assert that Kelly could recreate American life and speech better than Eugene O'Neill.‖

The panel of judges selected by Columbia University to nominate the 1924 Pulitzer Prize play voted heavily in favor of *The Show-Off*. However, the university, which officially awards the prize, turned down the recommendation in favor of *Hell-Bent fer Heaven*, a backwoods drama written by one of its theater faculty, Hatcher Hughes. A major controversy arose, but Columbia officials stood firm. Their decision was a foolish one. *Hell-Bent fer Heaven* remains only as a footnote in American literary history, while *The Show-Off* occupies a permanent position in traditional American theater. It richly deserved the Pulitzer, which eventually would be awarded to Kelly in 1926 for *Craig's Wife*.

---

*Heywood Broun, review of *The Show-Off*, the *World*, February 6, 1924.

†Alexander Woollcott, "The Stage," review of *The Show-Off*, *New York Herald Tribune*, February 6, 1924.

‡Stark Young, "The Show-Off," *New York Times*, February 14, 1925.

§Walter Prichard Eaton, *The Drama in English* (New York: Scribner, 1930), 319.

‖Untitled, unsigned column in the *World*, February 7, 1924, possibly by Heywood Broun.

The Show-Off is probably Kelly's best play; certainly it is his most beloved. In Aubrey Piper and Mrs. Fisher, he created two figures with enough universality to be recognized by every generation of playgoers, yet individual enough to divert the audience with their distinct, colorful personalities. Though technically the play falls into the category of domestic comedy, its incisive observations on marriage raise it to a higher level than that of mere entertainment. It is one of the few American dramas of the first quarter of the century that merits and receives frequent production. It is a genuine American theatrical classic.

CAST

"The Show-Off," as first produced at the Playhouse Theatre, New York, on February 4th, 1924:

CLARA	JULIETTE CROSBY
MRS. FISHER	HELEN LOWELL
AMY	REGINA WALLACE
FRANK HYLAND	GUY D'ENNERY
MR. FISHER	C. W. GOODRICH
JOE	LEE TRACY
AUBREY PIPER	LOUIS JOHN BARTELS
MR. GILL	FRANCIS PIERLOT
MR. ROGERS	JOSEPH CLAYTON

"If he's a wise bird, he'll let me handle that money for him . . ."
Aubrey Piper (Louis John Bartels) offers family financial counsel
to Mrs. Fisher (Helen Lowell). Clara (Juliette Crosby) registers
silent disapproval. *The Show-Off*

THE SHOW-OFF

 ACT I

After a slight pause a door out at the left is heard to close, and then Clara comes in carrying a fancy box of candy. She glances about the room and crosses to the kitchen door at the right.

CLARA. Anybody out there ? [*She crosses back again towards the left, laying the box of candy on the center table as she passes. Upon reaching the parlor doors, at the left, she opens them and calls into the parlor.*] You in there, Mom? [*Mrs. Fisher can be heard coming down the stairs. Clara turns, with a glance toward the hall door, and moves over to the mirror above the mantelpiece. Mrs. Fisher appears in the hall door and glances in at Clara.]*

MRS. FISHER. Oh, it's *you*, Clara. [*She peers on into the hall.*]

CLARA. Where is everybody?

MRS. FISHER. I thought I heard that front door open.

CLARA. Where are they all?

MRS. FISHER. [*Moving towards the parlor door*] Your Pop's gone over to Gillespie's for some tobacco: I don't know where Joe is. [*She glances into the parlor, then turns and kisses Clara. Clara moves down to the chair at the left of the center table and Mrs. Fisher moves over to the kitchen door at the right.*] I don't know how you can stand that fur on you, Clara, a night like this.

CLARA. It's rather cool out.

MRS. FISHER. [*Calling out through the kitchen door*] You out there, Joe?

CLARA. [*Sitting down*] He's not out there.

MRS. FISHER. [*Turning around to the cellar door at her left*] He must be around here somewhere; he was here not two minutes ago, when I went upstairs. [*Opening the cellar door and calling down*] You down there, Joey?

JOE. [*From the cellar*] Yes.

MRS. FISHER. All right. [*Closes the cellar door*]

JOE. What do you want?

MRS. FISHER. [*Turning to the cellar door again*] What?

[*Joe and Clara, speaking together*]

JOE. What do you want?

CLARA. He sez, "What do you went?"

MRS. FISHER. [*Opening the cellar door again*] I don't want anything; I was just wonderin' where you were. [*She closes the cellar door and comes a step or two forward, fastening an old-fashioned brooch that she wears on the front of her dress.*] He spends half his time down in that cellar foolin' with that old radio thing. He sez he can make one himself, but I sez, " I'll believe it when I see it."

CLARA. There's some of that candy you like.

MRS. FISHER. [*Crossing to the center table*] Oh, did you bring me some more of that nice candy? [*Beginning to untie the ribbon around the candy*] I never got a taste of that last you brought.

CLARA. Why not?

MRS. FISHER. Why, Lady Jane took it away with her down to the office, and never brought it back. She sez the girls down there et it. I sez, "I guess you're the girl that et it." She sez she didn't, but I know she did.

CLARA. Well, I hope you'll keep that out of sight, and don't let her take that too.

MRS. FISHER. [*Opening the candy*] Oh, she won't get her hands on this, I can promise you that. Let her buy her own candy if she's so fond of it.

CLARA. [*Opening the "Delineator"*] She won't buy much of *anything*, if she can get hold of it any *other* way.

MRS. FISHER. Oh, isn't that lovely! Look Clara.—[*Tilting the the box of candy towards Clara*] Don't that look nice?

CLARA. Yes, they do their candy up nice.

MRS. FISHER. [*Gingerly picking up the cover of lace paper*] That looks just like Irish point lace, don't it? [*Clara nods yes.*] I think I'll put that away somewhere—in a book or something. My, look at all the colors—look Clara—did you ever see so many colors?

CLARA. It's pretty, isn't it?

MRS. FISHER. It's beautiful—seems a pity to spoil it. Do you want a bit of it, Clara?

CLARA. Not now, Mom.

MRS. FISHER. I think I'll take this pink one here. I like the pink ones. [*She picks up the box and the lid and moves around to the chair at the right of the table.*] Mind how they all have this little fancy paper around them. You'd wonder they'd bother, wouldn't you?— just for a bit of candy. [*She tastes the candy and chews, critically.*] That's nice candy, isn't it?

CLARA. Yes, *I* like bonbons.

MRS. FISHER. [*Sitting down*] I do too—I think I like them better than most anything. [*Putting the box of candy down on the table*] I'm sorry these are not all bonbons.

CLARA. [*Looking up from the "Delineator"*] They are all bonbons. [*Her mother looks at her.*] There's nothing else in there.

MRS. FISHER. Oh, are they!—I thought only the pink ones were the bonbons.

CLARA. No, they're all bonbons.

MRS. FISHER. Well, that's lovely. I can eat any one of them I like, then, can't I? [*She sits back in her chair and rocks and chews.*] How is it you're not home tonight, Clara?

CLARA. Frank had to go to a dinner of some kind at the Glenwood Club; so I thought I'd stay in town and get something. He said he might call for me here around eight o'clock. I was in anyway about my lamp.

MRS. FISHER. [*Rocking*] Men are always going to dinners somewhere. Seems to me they can't talk about anything unless they've got a dinner in front of them. It's no wonder so many of them are fat.

CLARA. [*Turning a page of the "Delineator"*] Where's Amy—upstairs?

MRS. FISHER. Yes, she's gettin' dressed. I was just hookin' her when you came in.

CLARA. Is she going out?

MRS. FISHER. I don't know whether she is or not—I didn't hear her say. [*Leaning a bit towards Clara, and lowering her voice*] But it's Wednesday night, you know.

CLARA. Is that fellow still coming here?

MRS. FISHER. Oh, right on the dot—such as he is. Sunday nights too now, as well as Wednesdays. It looks like a steady thing. And you never in your life heard anybody talk so much, Clara—I don't know how she stands him. Your Pop can hardly stay in the room where he is. I believe in my heart that's the reason he went over to Gillespie's tonight—so he wouldn't be listenin' to him.

CLARA. Doesn't she take him into the parlor?

MRS. FISHER. She does, yes; but she might just as well leave him out here; for he's not in there five minutes till he's out here again-talkin' about Socialism. That's all you hear—Socialism—and capital and labor. You'd think he knew somethin' about it. And the Pennsylvania Railroad. He's always talkin, about that, too. That's where he works, you know. I don't know what he does down there. He sez himself he's head of the freight department; but as I sez to our Joe, I sez, "I don't know how *he* can be head of *anything*, from the talk of him. Joe sez he thinks he's a nut. And your Pop told him right to his face here last Sunday night—that he didn't know the meanin' of the word Socialism. [*She checks herself and gets up.*] I'd better not be talkin' so loud— he's apt to walk in on us. [*She moves up towards the hall door and glances out.*] He's a great joker, you know—that's what he did last Sunday night. [*Coming forward again to a point above the center table*] I never got such a fright in my life. Your Pop and me was sittin' here talkin', just the way we are now, when all of a sudden, I glanced up, and there he was—standin' in the doorway there, doin' this [*She points her forefinger and thumb at Clara*

and wiggles her thumb. Clara laughs faintly.]—as though he was a
bandit, you know. Well—I thought the breath'd leave my body.
Then he sez "Haha!—that's the time I fooled you!" I don't
know how long he'd been standin' there. But, as luck'd have it,
we wasn't talkin' about him at the time: although we *had* been
talkin' about him not five minutes before. I don't know whether
he heard us or not, for I don't know how long he'd been
standin' there. I hope he did: it'd just be the price of him, for
bein' so smart. [*With a glance toward the hall door, and speaking
very confidentially*] But, you know, what'd kill you, Clara, you
can't say a word about him in front of her. [*Clara moves.*] Oh, not
a word. No matter what he sez, she thinks it's lovely. When Joe
told her here the other night he thought he was a nut, she just
laughed, and said that Joe was jealous of him—because he
could express himself and *he* couldn't. [*Clara smiles.*] You never
heard such talk. And, you know, Clara, I think he wears a wig.
[*Clara laughs.*] I do, honestly. And our Joe sez he thinks he does
too. But when I asked *her* about it here one mornin', I thought
she'd take the head right off me. You never seen anybody get
themselves into such a temper. She sez, "It's a lie," she sez, "he
don't wear a wig." She sez, "People always say somethin' like
that about a fellow that makes a good appearance." But, *I* think
he does, just the same; and the first chance I get I'm goin' to
take a good look. [*She moves around to her chair again, at the right
of the table.*] He often sits right here, you know, under this light,
while he's talkin'; [*Selecting another piece of candy*] and I'm goin'
to look close the very first chance I get. [*She sits down.*] *I* can tell
a wig as good as anybody. [*She rocks and looks straight out, chewing.*] She won't make a liar out of me.

AMY. [*From the head of the stairs*] Mom, did you see anything of that
blue bar-pin of mine?

MRS. FISHER. [*Calling back to her*] Which blue bar-pin?

AMY. Well now, how many blue bar-pins have I got?

MRS. FISHER. I don't know how many you've got, and I don't care!
[*Turning back again and speaking rather to herself*] So don't be

botherin' me about it. [*Calling up to Amy again*] If you can't find it, go look for it. [*She resumes her rocking and her chewing.*] She thinks all she's got to do is come to the head of them stairs and holler and everybody'll jump.—But she'll get sadly left.—I've got somethin' else to do besides waitin' on her. [*She takes another bite of candy, and turns casually to Clara.*] Did you get your lamp yet?

CLARA. No, that's what I was in town today about. The girl sez they haven't been able to match the silk till yesterday.

MRS. FISHER. I wish I could get somethin' done to that one of mine there in the parlor; the wire's right out through the silk in two places.

CLARA. Why doesn't Amy take it in some day [*Mrs. Fisher makes a sound of amusement.*]—when she's going to work?

MRS. FISHER. Why don't she? It's all Amy can do to take herself into work these days. I've almost got to push her out the door every morning.

CLARA. Couldn't she take it over at lunchtime?

MRS. FISHER. She sez she hasn't time at lunchtime.

CLARA. Oh, she has no time.

MRS. FISHER. Of course she has.

CLARA. It's only at Ninth and Chestnut, and she's at Eighth.

MRS. FISHER. That's what I told her. I sez, "I bet if it was somethin' for yourself you'd have plenty of time." [*Leaning towards Clara*] But, you know—what *I* think, Clara—I think she's meetin' this fellow at lunchtime. Because in the mornin's here she stands fixin' herself there in front of that glass till it's a wonder to me she don't drop on the floor. And whenever you see them gettin' very particular that way all of a sudden—there's somethin' in the wind. I sez to her the other mornin', when she was settlin' herself there till I got tired lookin' at her, I sez, "You must be goin' to see him today, ain't you?" And she sez, "He must be on your mind, isn't he?" "No," I sez, "but by the looks of things, I think he's on yours. And," I sez, "maybe after you get him you won't think he was worth all the bother you went to." Because, you know, Clara, she

don't know a *thing* about him; except that he works in the
Pennsylvania freight office—I believe he did tell her that much.
But she don't know whether he works there or not. He could tell
her anything; and she'd believe it [*Taking another bite of candy and
settling herself in her chair*]—before she'd believe me.

CLARA. That's where he works [*Her mother looks at her sharply.*]—at
the Pennsylvania freight office.

MRS. FISHER. How do you know?

CLARA. Frank knows him.

MRS. FISHER. Frank Hyland?

CLARA. Yes—he sez he eats his lunch at the same place, there at
Fifteenth and Arch.

MRS. FISHER. And, does he say he knows him?

CLARA. Yes. He sez he's seen him around there for a long time. I've
often heard him speak of him, but I didn't know it was the
same fellow. Frank always called him Carnation Charlie. He sez
he's always got a big carnation in his buttonhole.

MRS. FISHER. [*Tapping the table conclusively*] That's the one; he's
always got it on when he comes here, too.

CLARA. Frank sez he's never seen him without it.

MRS. FISHER. I haven't either. And I believe in my heart, Clara, that's
what's turned her head. [*Clara smiles.*] You often see things like
that, you know. The worst fool of a man can put a carnation in
his coat or his hat over one eye, and half a dozen sensible
women'll be dyin' about him.

CLARA. Well, Frank sez this fellow's absolutely *crazy.*

MRS. FISHER. That's what your father sez.

CLARA. He sez they kid the life out of him down around the restaurant there.

MRS. FISHER. Well, he don't know who Frank Hyland *is*, does he?

CLARA. No, Frank didn't tell him. He sez he just happened to get
talking to him the other day and he mentioned that he was calling on a girl up this way named Fisher. So then Frank found out
what his right name was, and when he came home he asked me
about him.

MRS. FISHER. Well, is he sure it's the same fellow?

CLARA. He told him his name was Piper.

MRS. FISHER. [*With finality*] Thats the name—Aubrey Piper. I don't know where he got the Aubrey from; *I* never heard of such a name before, did you?

CLARA. Yes, I've heard the name of Aubrey.

MRS. FISHER. [*Rocking*] Well, I never did. Sounds to me more like a place than a name. [*Amy can be heard coming down the stairs.*] Here she comes. [*She snatches up the box of candy and puts it under her apron.*]

CLARA. Don't say anything, now.

MRS. FISHER. It'd be no use. [*Trying to be casual*] What color are you havin' your lampshade made, Clara?

AMY. [*Hurrying in at the hall door*] Mom, you must have seen something of that bar-pin of mine; I can't find it anywhere. [*She tosses a beaded bag onto the center table and turns to the mantelpiece and looks for the bar-pin.*]

MRS. FISHER. [*Abstractedly*] I saw a pin of yours in one of the drawers in the buffet there a few days ago, I don't know whether it's there yet or not.

AMY. [*Hurrying across to the buffet at the right*] How's it you're not home tonight, Clara? [*She starts to rummage in the buffet drawers.*]

CLARA. [*Casually*] I had my dinner in town.

AMY. Is that parlor all right, Mom?

MRS. FISHER. Certainly it's all right.

AMY. Well, did you side it?

MRS. FISHER. [*Sharply*] Certainly I sided it.

AMY. All right, Mom, don't make a speech about it.

MRS. FISHER. [*Considerably ruffled*] No, but you'd think the way she sez it that I sat here all day with my two hands as long as each other. [*Amy finds the pin and slams the drawer shut, leaving various ends of tape and pieces of lace hanging out. Then she starts back towards the mirror over the mantelpiece.*] Did you find it?

AMY. [*Disrespectfully*] Yes.

MRS. FISHER. [*Rising, still holding the candy under her apron, and step-*

ping over to the buffet] It's a wonder you wouldn't leave these drawers the way you found them. She does that every time she goes near this buffet. [*She puts various odds and ends back into the drawers and closes them.*] She's in such a great rush lately.

AMY. [*Settling herself at the mirror*] Isn't that a new dress on you, Clara?

CLARA. Yes.

MRS. FISHER. [*Coming back to her chair*] I'd like to see the kind of house you'll keep.

AMY. Well, I hope it won't be anything like this one, I'll tell you that.

MRS. FISHER. [*Stopping halfway to her chair*] Oh, go easy, lady! You might be very glad to have half as good, if you live long enough. [*Continuing to her chair, and looking keenly at Clara's dress*] I thought I hadn't seen that dress on you before. [*She sits down.*]

CLARA. No, I only got it last week.

MRS. FISHER. Stand up there till I see it. [*Clara gets up and takes a couple of steps towards the teft, pulling down her skirt, then turns around to her left and faces her mother. Amy comes down to the center table, looking sharply at Clara's dress.*]

CLARA. I got it at a sale in Strawbridge's. [*Amy opens her beaded purse on the table and looks at herself critically in the little inside mirror; then adds a touch of powder.*]

MRS. FISHER. It's a nice length.

CLARA. I didn't have to have a thing touched on it.

MRS. FISHER. That's what I was tellin' you about the other day, Amy.—Do you see the way that dress hangs?

AMY. Yeh.

MRS. FISHER. [*Speaking directly to Clara*] There was a dress on Queen Mary in last Sunday's Ledger that I was sayin' to Amy I thought'd look good on me. And it had all buttons up and down the front, the way that has.

CLARA. [*Coming back to her chair*] A lot of the new dresses are made that way.

MRS. FISHER. How much was it?

CLARA. [*Sitting down*] Forty-two seventy-five. [*Amy starts to polish her nails.*]

MRS. FISHER. [*Turning away, with a lift of her eyes to heaven*] You must have plenty of money.

AMY. Mom, Where'd you put those roses I brought home?

MRS. FISHER. They're out there in the dining room. [*Amy starts towards the right.*] I put them in some water. [*Amy goes out; and Mrs. Fisher rocks for a second or two; then she turns and calls after Amy.*] I think it's time you lit the light in that parlor, Amy, if that fellow of yours is comin' here tonight. [*She rocks a little bit more, then turns casually to Clara.*] What time is it by your watch there, Clara? [*With a glance toward the mantelpiece at the back*] That old clock of ours is stopped again.

CLARA. [*Looking at her wrist watch*] Quarter past eight.

MRS. FISHER. [*Getting up suddenly*] I must tell her. [*The box of candy lands on the floor.*] My God, there goes the candy! Pick that up, Clara, I can't stoop; and put it out of sight. [*Going towards the door up at the right*] It's a wonder I didn't do that while she was in here. [*Calling after Amy*] Amy!

AMY. Yes?

MRS. FISHER. Clara sez it's a quarter past eight by her watch—you'd better get some kind of a light in that parlor if that fellow's comin'. [*She moves back towards her chair, then speaks in a very subdued tone to Clara.*] She brings flowers home with her from the city now, every night he's coming. She must have flowers for him in the parlor. [*She sits down.*] I told her, I sez, "I bet it'd be a long time before you'd bring any flowers home from the city to me."

CLARA. That's another new dress on *her* tonight, isn't it?

MRS. FISHER. [*Straightening the magazines on the table*] She's had it about a week.

CLARA. What's she getting so many new dresses for lately?

MRS. FISHER. Heaven knows, I don't.

CLARA. That's the fourth I've seen on her since Easter.

MRS. FISHER. Tryin' to make him think she's rich, I guess. I told her the other night she might not get so many after she gets him.

AMY. [*Entering from the right, carrying a vase of roses, and crossing directly to the parlor doors at the left*] You need another box of matches out there, Mom.

MRS. FISHER. Is that box of matches gone already?

AMY. Pretty near. [*She goes into the parlor.*]

MRS. FISHER. I swear I don't know where all the matches go to—seems to me all I do is buy matches. [*Amy strikes a match in the parlor.*] Be careful of them lace curtains there, now, Amy, if you're goin' to light that lamp. [*The lamp is lit in the parlor; and Amy closes the parlor doors.*]

CLARA. [*Rising and handing her mother the box of candy, which she has been holding since she picked it up from the floor*] I think I'll go, before he comes.

MRS. FISHER. [*Rising*] You'd better, unless you want to be here all night. [*Clara moves up to the looking glass over the mantelpiece, and Mrs. Fisher crosses to the buffet with the candy.*] For if he ever starts talkin', you'll never get out. [*She puts the candy into one of the drawers, then starts across towards the hall door, up at the left.*] You wouldn't mind, you know, if he'd stay in there in the parlor—but the minute ever he hears a voice out here, he's out like a jumpin' jack. [*Amy can be heard coughing out in the hallway, and, as Mrs. Fisher passes back of Clara, Clara half turns and suggests with a movement of her hand that Amy might overhear her.*] Oh, he's not here yet; you'd know it if he was. [*She peers keenly out into the hallway, then turns and tiptoes back to Clara, and speaks in a very low tone.*] She stands out there in the vestibule until she sees him get off the trolley, then she comes in and lets him ring, so he won't think she's been waitin' for him. [*She tiptoes back and peers out into the hallway again, and Clara moves over to the right, adjusting her neckpiece. Mrs. Fisher comes back to the center table.*] You never seen anybody so crazy about a fellow.

CLARA. Well, I think somebody ought to tell her about him, Mom.

MRS. FISHER. [*Folding the ribbon and the paper from the candy box*] What's the good of tellin' her—she'd only give you a look if you said anything about him.

CLARA. Well, I'd say it anyway, whether she gave me a look or not; for, remember what I'm telling you, Mom, it's *you* that'll have them on your hands if she takes him. [*Her mother looks at her sharply.*]

MRS. FISHER. *I'll* have them on my hands?

CLARA. [*Turning to her mother*] Well now, who else will, Mom? You couldn't leave her out on the street; and that's exactly where she'll land if she takes *him*; for you know how long Amy could get along on a hundred and fifty dollars a month.

MRS. FISHER. Takes more than that to keep herself, never name a house and a husband.

CLARA. Well, that's exactly what he gets, for he's only a clerk down there.

MRS. FISHER. He told her he was the head of the department.

CLARA. He's a clerk, Mom—like a hundred others down there: Frank knows what he does.

MRS. FISHER. [*Moving a step or two nearer to Clara*] Well, why don't you say something to her, Clara?

CLARA. Now, you know how much attention she'd pay to anything I'd say.

MRS. FISHER. [*With measured definiteness*] She won't pay any attention to what anybody sez.

CLARA. Especially if she knew it was Frank Hyland that said it.

MRS. FISHER. She thinks everybody's jealous of him; and jealous of *her* because she's gettin' him. So let her get him. If she makes her bed, let her lie in it.

CLARA. [*Looking straight out*] Well, that's the trouble, Mom; it isn't always the person that makes the bed that lies in it.—Very often somebody else has to lie in it.

MRS. FISHER. [*Turning back to the table*] Well, it'll be nobody around here, I can promise you that.

CLARA. [*Turning to the buffet mirror*] Maybe not.

MRS. FISHER. No maybe about it.

CLARA. But you know what you are, Mom, where Amy's concerned.

MRS. FISHER. [*Taking a step towards Clara*] Why, don't be silly, Clara. Do you think your father'd be listenin' to that rattlebrain here every night?

CLARA. [*Turning and speaking directly to her mother*] He has to listen to him now, doesn't he—or go out, as he did tonight. [*The front door closes. They both turn and glance in the direction of the hallway.*] Maybe this is Frank now. [*There is a slight pause, then Frank Hyland comes in, and comes forward to the center table.*]

MRS. FISHER. Hello, Frank.

HYLAND. Hello, Mother. Hello, Clara. [*He puts his hat down on the table.*]

CLARA. I was just going; I thought maybe you weren't coming.

HYLAND. [*Looking at his watch*] I couldn't get away from there until nearly eight o'clock.

MRS. FISHER. Frank—Clara sez you know this fellow that's comin' to see our Amy.

HYLAND. Who, Piper?

MRS. FISHER. Yes—the one that does so much talkin'.

HYLAND. Yes, I know him. [*He moves to the left and sits down an the arm of the Morris chair.*]

MRS. FISHER. I think he's crazy, Frank; [*Hyland makes a sound of amusement.*] I do, honestly; and Pop and Joe sez they think he is, too.

CLARA. Mom sez he told Amy he was head of the freight department, Frank.

MRS. FISHER. He did, honestly, Frank; and she believes him. But Clara sez *you* say he's only a clerk down there.

CLARA. That's all he is, Mom.

MRS. FISHER. He isn't head of the freight department, is he, Frank? [*FRANK sits looking away off, dreamily.*]

CLARA. Frank—

HYLAND. [*Turning*] I beg your pardon, what did you say, dear?

MRS. FISHER. He isn't head of the freight department down there, is he?

HYLAND. No, he's just one of the clerks.

MRS. FISHER. [*Turning to Clara*] Now, you see that—and she'd only laugh at you if you told her that. [*Turning back to Hyland*] How much do them freight clerks get a month, Frank? [*Hyland is gazing out of the window at the left.*]

CLARA. Frank, Mom is talking to you.

HYLAND. [*Turning*] Oh, I beg your pardon, what did you say, Mother?

MRS. FISHER. I say, how much do them freight clerks get a month?

HYLAND. Why—about a hundred and forty or fifty dollars—I don't know exactly; but not any more than that. [*His eyes wander to the window again.*]

MRS. FISHER. What are we goin' to do about it, Frank?—It looks like a steady thing. He comes Wednesday and Sunday nights now—and if she ever takes him, she'll be the poorest woman in this city. You know how our Amy spends money. [*Turning to Clara*] She's got seven pairs of shoes up in that hall closet.

HYLAND. [*Abstractedly*] Amy certainly does let her money fly. [*Mrs. Fisher gives him a stoney look.*]

MRS. FISHER. Well, if she does she earns it. She might as well have a good time now while she's young—God knows what's ahead of her. [*The front doorbell rings—a series of funny little taps.*] Here he is now, I know his ring. [*She steps up to the mantelpiece and glances out into the hallway.*]

CLARA. [*Turning towards the kitchen door*] We'll go out the side door. Come on, Frank. [*Hyland rises and picks up his hat from the table, as he crosses below it.*]

HYLAND. Goodnight, Mother. [*Mrs. Fisher is too occupied with her interests out in the hallway.*] Do you want to go to a picture, Clara?

CLARA. [*Going out at the right*] I don't care.

HYLAND. [*Following her*] It's only about twenty after eight. [*He glances at his watch.*]

CLARA. We can get the second show at Broad and Columbia Avenue.

MRS. FISHER. [*Following them out*] Frank, I wish you'd talk to Amy some time, and tell her what you told me; she won't believe *me*.

HYLAND. I don't suppose she'd believe me either, Mother.

AUBREY. [*Out at the front door*] Right on the job!

AMY. Hello!

AUBREY. The pride of old West Philly! [*He laughs a bit, boisterously.*]

AMY. I'll take your hat, Aubrey.

AUBREY. Anything to please the ladies. [*The front door closes.*] The boy rode off with many thanks, and many a backward bow. [*He laughs again, rather wildly. Mrs. Fisher tiptoes into the room from the right and stands listening, keenly.*] Do you know, I think I'll have to get hold of an airship somewhere, Amy, to come out here to see you.

AMY. It is quite a trip for you, isn't it?

AUBREY. Just one shining hour and a half, if you say it quick; by the little old Brill special. And how is the Mother? [*Mrs. Fisher's face hardens, and a door closes. Then she tiptoes over to the double doors at the left and listens. Aubrey's voice can be heard fairly distinctly from beyond the doors.*] Say, Amy—wasn't that hold-up in last night's paper somewhere out this way?

AMY. Yes, it was right over here on Erie Avenue. [*Mr. Fisher appears in the hall door and stands, looking with amusement at his wife. He takes an old pipe and tobacco pouch from the pocket of his knit jacket and starts to fill the pipe.*]

AUBREY. A doctor's house, wasn't it?

AMY. Yes, Doctor Donnelly's. They got nearly two thousand dollars.

AUBREY. I don't believe that, Amy.

AMY. Why not?

AUBREY. I don't think there's that much money in North Philadelphia. [*He roars with laughter. Mr. Fisher gives his wife a little dig in the ribs and makes a sound like a startled cat. She starts violently, smothering a little shriek.*]

MRS. FISHER. Oh, you frightened me! [*Mr. Fisher continues to the center table and sets his newspaper down.*]

MR. FISHER. You ought to be pretty nearly frightened to death by this time, oughtn't you? [*He replaces the tobacco pouch in his pocket.*]

MRS. FISHER. Well, it's no wonder I'd be.

MR. FISHER. You've been jumpin' that way ever since I knew you.

MRS. FISHER. Well what do you come pussy-footin' in that way for, when you know how nervous I am?

MR. FISHER. I didn't come pussy-footin' in at all.

MRS. FISHER. You did so, or I'd have heard you.

MR. FISHER. You *would* have heard me, if you weren't so busy listenin' to somethin' that's none of your business.

MRS. FISHER. Well, it'll be somethin' of my business if you go spillin' any of that dirty old tobacco on my nice new table cloth, I tell you that. [*She resumes her listening at the door, and Mr. Fisher brushes the tobacco from the table cloth.*]

MR. FISHER. I'm not spillin' any of it. [*There's a burst of laughter from Aubrey in the parlor, and Mr. Fisher looks toward the parlor door.*] Who's in there—Windy? [*Mrs. Fisher nods, yes, and the old man moves down at the right of the center table, picking up the newspaper and reaching into his vest pocket for his spectacles.*] What's he doin', laughin' at some more of them West Philadelphia jokes of his? [*He sits down to read, in the chair at the right of the table, and Mrs. Fisher comes tiptoeing towards the chair at the left of the table.*]

MRS. FISHER. [*In a lowered tone*] He was astin' Amy about that robbery over at Doctor Donnelly's yesterday mornin'; and when she told him the bandits got away with nearly two thousand dollars, he said it couldn't be true, because there wasn't that much money in North Philadelphia.

MR. FISHER. [*With mock laughter*] Ha! Ha! Ha!

MRS. FISHER. [*Returning to the parlor doors to listen*] Shush! [*There's a Ha! Ha! Ha! from the parlor from Aubrey, and the old man looks quickly and distrustfully in that direction. Aubrey continues to laugh.*]

MR. FISHER. [*Settling himself to read*] I'll bet there wouldn't have to be much money up this way to be more than *he's* got. [*There's a sound of hammering in the cellar. Mrs. Fisher hurries across to the cellar door.*]

AUBREY. [*In the parlor*] You know, I discovered tonight, Amy, that I can save a full fifteen minutes on this trip over here, by transferring up Twenty-ninth to the Lehigh Avenue car, instead of going on in and up Nineteenth.

MRS. FISHER. [*Opening the cellar door and calling down, in a subdued voice*] Joe! Stop that hammering down there. We can't hear our ears up here. [*The old man gives a hard chuckle. Mrs. Fisher tiptoes back towards the parlor doors, looking at her husband stonily.*] What ails you?

AMY. [*In the parlor*] It is hard to get out here, unless you use the Park trolley. I hear some people say that's a great deal quicker. [*Mrs. Fisher listens keenly again with her ear against the parlor door.*]

AUBREY. I don't know how they ever found this place.

AMY. I don't know how *you* ever found West Philadelphia.

AUBREY. Lot of people think they haven't found it *yet*. [*He bursts into violent laughter.*] Lost somewhere between the Schuylkill River and Darby. [*He laughs some more. The old man looks piercingly over his spectacles at his wife.*]

MR. FISHER. [*Amost shouting*] Come away from there, Josie! [*Mrs. Fisher is startled almost to death. She places her hand on her bosom and moves away from the door toward the center of the room.*] Don't be listenin' to that damned blatherskite

MRS. FISHER. [*Trying to be casual*] I wasn't listenin' to him—I was just seein' what he was sayin'. [*She moves up to the little stand between the hall door and the mantelpiece and picks up her knitting bag. Amy is very much amused at something Aubrey has just said in the parlor. Mrs. Fisher glances toward the parlor doors, then comes down to her husband's right, and, with another glance toward the door, speaks very confidentially.*] He was astin' Amy how she ever found this part of town to live in; and she was astin' him how *he* ever found West Philadelphia. He sez West Philadelphia ain't *been* found yet—that it's lost somewhere between the Schuylkill River and Darby. [*She moves over to the armchair at the right, in front of the window, and sits down.*]

MR. FISHER. I wish to God *he'd* get lost some night, somewhere between here and the Schuylkill River.

MRS. FISHER. [*Taking the needles and the pink wool out of the knitting bag*] What'd kill you, too, you know, he always dies laughin' whenever he gets off one of them bum jokes.

MR. FISHER. Somebody's got to laugh.

AUBREY. [*From the parlor*] Ha! Ha! That's the time I fooled you, Amy!

Leave it to me to put it right over the plate. [*Amy has quite a laughing fit in the parlor. Her mother looks narrowly toward the parlor doors until Amy has finished laughing.*]

MRS. FISHER. He's got Amy laughin' now, too. [*She commenses to knit; and there is a slight pause. Then she glances at the clock on the mantelpiece.*] That old clock has stopped again, Neil.

MR. FISHER. [*Without moving*] Needs fixin'.

MRS. FISHER. It's been fixed twice—don't do no good. [*There is a pause, and Mrs. Fisher sighs.*] I think it's terrible lonesome not to hear the clock—it's too still in a room.—It always sounds to me like soap bubbles meltin'.

MR. FISHER. H'm—here's a fellow here's been left a quarter of a million dollars, and he won't take it.

MRS. FISHER. [*Sharply*] What's the matter with him?

MR. FISHER. Nothin' at all's the matter with him—he just won't take it.

MRS. FISHER. [*Resuming her knitting*] He mustn't be in his right mind, poor boy. I wisht somebody'd leave *me* with a quarter of a million dollars.

MR. FISHER. You wouldn't know what to do with it if they did.

MRS. FISHER. Well, I know *one* thing I'd do with it; and that'd be to have somethin' done to that old heater of ours downstairs, and not be freezin' to death all *next* winter, the way I was last. [*Aubrey laughs in the parlor. Mrs. Fisher glances toward the parlor doors; then shifts her knitting.*] Every sweater I start I swear it'll be the last—and then I start right in on another. [*She gives a faint little laugh and looks at her husband; but he's reading; so she subsides and continues to knit. Suddenly she stops and rests her knitting in her lap, and thinks; then turns to Mr. Fisher.*] Well now, what becomes of money like that, Neil, that people won't take?

MR. FISHER. [*Squinting at her over his glasses*] What'd you say?

MRS. FISHER. I say, what becomes of money that people won't take that way?

MR. FISHER. [*Resuming his paper*] Why, nothing at all becomes of it— they just come and get it. [*She looks at him steadily.*]

MRS. FISHER. *What* does?

MR. FISHER. The people that won't take it. [*Mrs. Fisher is puzzled for a second.*]

MRS. FISHER. [*Resuming her knitting*] Well, I'll bet if they left it to *me* they wouldn't have to come and take it.

MR. FISHER. [*Looking at her again with a shade of irritation*] Who wouldn't have to come and take it?

MRS. FISHER. [*Losing her temper*] Why, the people that won't take it!

MR. FISHER. What are you talking about, Josie, do you know?

MRS. FISHER. Yes, I do know very well what I'm talkin' about!—but I don't think *you* do.

MR. FISHER. Let me read the paper, will you?

MRS. FISHER. [*Knitting rapidly*] Go ahead and read it!—I'm sure I don't want to talk to you. It was you that started talkin' to me— readin' about that young man that took the money. [*Joe comes up from the cellar, carrying some kind of a radio arrangement on a flat baseboard and a screw driver.*] Joe, I'm goin' to have that light took out of that cellar, if you don't stop spendin' all your time down there.

JOE. [*Holding his work under the table lamp to look at it closely*] You don't want me hammerin' up here, do you?

MRS. FISHER. I don't want you hammerin' anywhere. I want you to go out at night and get some air, and not be cooped up in that dusty old cellar. [*There's a violent burst of laughter from Aubrey in the parlor. Joe glances toward the parlor doors, then turns, with something of distress in his expression, to his mother.*]

JOE. Who's *in* there—the Pennsylvania Railroad?

MRS. FISHER. Yes, and he's got about as much sense as yourself.

JOE. [*Moving around to the chair at the left of the center table and sitting down*] You won't say that when you're sittin' here listening' to the Grand Opera. [*He starts to tighten the small screws in the baseboard.*]

MRS. FISHER. I won't be listenin' to it, don't fret—I got something else to do besides listenin' to a lot of dagoes singin'.

MR. FISHER. [*Looking over at Joe's radio arrangement*] What is it?

MRS. FISHER. He sez when he gets that radio thing finished, I can sit here and listen to the Grand Opera.

MR. FISHER. What's that, them singin' people?

MRS. FISHER. Yes—them that goes away up high, you know—that Clara has on her Victrola. [*The parlor door opens, and Amy comes out, walking on air.*]

AMY. Oh, it's all right if you let it run for a minute. [*She crosses to the right to the kitchen door, glancing at herself in the mantlepiece mirror as she pauses.*]

MRS. FISHER. What's the matter?

AMY. Aubrey wants a drink of water. [*She goes out at the right.*]

MRS. FISHER. [*With a significant sound*] Oh.

AUBREY. [*Coming out of the parlor*] Stay right where you are, folks, right where you are. [*He moves to the mirror over the mantlepiece.*] Just a little social attention—going right out again on the next train. [*He surveys himself critically in the mirror, touching his tie and toupé gingerly. Mrs. Fisher gives him a smouldering look, and Joe looks at his father. Aubrey turns from the mirror, and indicates his reflection with a wide gesture.*] There you are, Mother! Any woman's fancy, what do you say? Even to the little old carnation. [*He gives the table a double tap with his knuckles, then laughs, and moves up towards the kitchen door, and calls out to Amy.*] Come on, Amy step on the United Gas out there; customer in here waiting for the old aqua pura. [*Moving down to Mr. Fisher's right*] Man's got to have something to drink—how about it, Pop? [*He gives Mr. Fisher a slap on the right shoulder.*] You'll stay with me on that, won't you? [*He laughs and moves up to the mirror again. Old man Fisher is very much annoyed.*] Yes, sir. [*Coming forward again at the right*] I want to tell those of you who hve ventured out this evening, that this is a very pretty little picture of domestic felicity. [*He laughs a little and looks from one to the other, patronizingly; but nobody pays the slightest attention to him.*] Father reading—Mother knitting; [*Mrs. Fisher withers him with a quick look.*] But then, Mama is *always* knitting. [*She knits rapidly and Aubrey laughs, and moves up and across back of the table.*] And little old Tommy Edison over here, working eighteen hours a day to make the rich man richer and the poor man poorer. [*He gives Joe a tap on the back, then moves back again towards Mr. Fisher.*] What about it, Popcorn? [*Slaps him on the back.*] Shake it up! Right or raving?

MR. FISHER. [*Starting to his feet violently*] God damn it, let me alone! And keep your hands to yourself. [*He crosses below the center table and up to the hall door.*] I never saw such a damn pest in my life! [*He goes up the stairs bristling with rage, and muttering to himself. Aubrey is vastly amused. He leans on the back of Mrs. Fisher's chair and roars with laughter.*]

AUBREY. Sign on the dotted line! And little old Popsy-Wopsy getting sore and going to leave us flat. [*He laughs again considerably; then turns to Mrs. Fisher.*] Nevertheless, and notwithstanding, Mrs. Fisher, I'd like to mention that the kid from West Philadelphia is giving the growing boy the said and done. [*He indicates Joe with a waving gesture. Amy comes in from the right with a glass of water. He turns and acknowledges her with even a wider gesture.*] And there she is herself, and not a moving picture. [*Amy extends the glass of water, laughing, and with a touch of self-consciousness.*] Blushing as she gave it, looking down—at her feet so bare, and her tattered gown. [*Amy giggles, and her mother looks sharply at Amy's shoes. Aubrey takes the glass of water and turns to Mrs. Fisher.*] How's that, Mother Fisher? Can't beat that little old Willie Shakespeare, can you? No, sir—I'd like to tell the brothers that that little old Shakespeare party shook a wicked spear. [*He laughs at his own comedy, and Amy is immeasurably delighted.*] Well, here's laughter, ladies! and, [*Turning to Joe*] Mr. Marconi—my best regards to you. [*He drinks.*]

AMY. I'm afraid it's not very cold. [*He just raises his hand, signifying that it's perfectly satisfactory.*]

MRS. FISHER. Why didn't you let it run?

AMY. I did, but it doesn't seem to get any colder.

AUBREY. [*Handing the glass gack to Amy*] Very nice, indeed. And a sweeter draught, from a fairer hand was never quaffed.

AMY. [*Flipping her hand at him*] Oh, you! [*She goes out at the right again with the empty glass.*]

AUBREY. [*Laughing a bit*] Thank you very much. [*He turns and moves across above the table towards Joe, drawing a gaily bordered handkerchief from his breast pocket and touching it to his lips.*] Yes, sir, Mr. Joseph, I want to tell you you're wasting time; for when you're all through, they'll offer you twenty cents for it, and sell it for twenty million [*He punctuates this last remark with a series of patronizing taps on Joe's back.*]—take it or leave it—sign on the dotted line. [*He taps his knuckles on the table, and moves back again to Mrs. Fisher's left.*] Yes, sir—that's exactly what they did to little old yours truly here. Twenty Lincoln Anacondas, for a formula that would have solved the greatest problem before the Industrial Chemical world today. [*Amy comes in from the right, and, looking at Aubrey wonderingly, moves across towards the left. Aubrey moves forward and across in front of the table towards Joe.*] A formula to prevent the rusting of iron and steel. [*Joe gets up and moves up and around above the table twoards the kitchen door at the right.*] A solution of vanadium and manganese, to be added to the metal in its molten state; [*Joe stops and looks back at him.*] instead of applied externally as they have been doing.

JOE. What did you say, Aubrey?

AUBREY. I said, a simple combination of chemical elements to be added to the metal in its *molten* state, instead of applied externally as they have been doing.

[*Joe and Aubrey, speaking together*]

JOE. [*Speaking to his mother*] Mom, do you know anything about that little screwdriver with the black handle?

AUBREY. But—simply because it was discovered by a workingman—that they saw they couldn't buy—

MRS. FISHER. Do you mean the one you fixed the sewing machine with?

[*Joe and Aubrey, speaking together*]

JOE. Yes, that little short one with the black handle.

AUBREY. They gave it the swinging door. [*Amy moves over to the parlor doors.*]

[*Mrs. Fisher and Aubrey, speaking together*]

MRS. FISHER. I think I saw it on that shelf out there, over the sink. And now, don't go upsettin' everything out there.

AUBREY. They'd rather go on paying a million dollars a year [*Joe goes out, and Aubrey follows him to the kitchen door.*]—to paint their steel and iron structures throughout the country, than pay *me*.

MRS. FISHER. Do you see it, Joe?

AUBREY. [*Coming down to Mrs. Fisher's left*] And do you know *why*, Mrs. Fisher?

JOE. [*Answering his mother from the kitchen*] No!

AUBREY. Then, I'll tell you. Because I work for my living. That's the said and done on the whole business. [*Mrs. Fisher starts to put her things into the knitting bag, preparatory to getting up.*] Keep them poor and get them married; and then, [*He looks away off.*] as my darling old Mother used to say, "You've got them on their beams and hinges."

MRS. FISHER. [*Getting up*] I don't see that anybody's tryin' to make anybody get married if they don't want to. [*She passes up to the kitchen door, putting her knitting bag on the buffet as she goes*].

AUBREY. [*Following her up*] But they do want to, Mrs. Fisher—but the capitalist wants to stop them.

MRS. FISHER. [*Turning at the kitchen door and speaking directly to him*] Well, I guess it'd be just as well to stop *some* of 'em. [*She goes out.*]

AUBREY. [*Calling after her through the kitchen door*] Ah, don't go back on little old William Jennings Bryan, Mother Fisher. Life, liberty and the pursuit of happiness, you know. [*He turns and comes forward a the right again, laughing a little.*] Sign on the dotted line.

AMY. [*Trying to conceal her temper*] Come in here, Aubrey.

AUBREY. [*Starting towards her*] Yes, sir, Amy, I want to tell you it's the poor man that gets it every time. I put a question up to Secretary Mellon, in a letter six weeks ago—that absolutely stumped him, because I haven't had a line from him since. [*Amy is smiling into his eyes. He passes in front of her and goes into the parlor. The curtain commences to descend slowly. Amy looks darkly toward the kitchen door, and stamps her foot with temper; then follows Aubrey into the parlor.*] I simply asked him to what extent his proposed program of Income Tax Revision would affect the great American Railroad Employee. [*The curtain is down.*]

THREE HOURS PASS

THE CURTAIN RISES AGAIN

Mrs. Fisher is sitting at the right of the table asleep, her knitting lying in her lap; and Joe, sitting at the left of the table, is endeavoring to pass the tip of a wire through a small eyelet in the baseboard. Amy starts to play the piano in the parlor; and, after the usual introduction, Aubrey begins to sing, "Rocked in the Cradle of the Deep," in a heavy bass voice.

AUBREY. [*Singing*]

"Rocked in the cradle of the deep,
  I lay me down—in peace to sleep—
  Secure I rest upon the wave,
  For Thou alone—

[*Mrs. Fisher starts slightly and wakens. Joe glances at her. Aubrey continues.*]
  has the power to save."

MRS. FISHER. Where'd you put it? What? Did you say something? [*Aubrey continues to sing.*]

JOE. Not a thing, Mom.

MRS. FISHER. [*Brushing back her hair*] I must have been dozin'.

JOE. You've been dead.

MRS. FISHER. What?

JOE. Since half-past nine. [*Mrs. Fisher becomes conscious of Aubrey singing.*]

MRS. FISHER. What time is it now, Joe? [*The singing becomes louder, and Mrs. Fisher rises, with her eyes fastened on the parlor door.*] Is that him singin' in there?

JOE. [*Reaching into his bell pocket for an Ingersoll watch*] The old Scientific American himself. A quarter of twelve.

MRS. FISHER. My God! what's he startin' to sing at this hour for! [*She steps to the buffet at the right and puts her knitting bag into one of the ___s.*]

                should never be suppressed at any time, Mother.

MRS. FISHER. It's a wonder Amy wouldn't have sense enough to stop him. [*She slams the buffet drawer shut, and starts across towards the parlor doors.*] I never saw a man yet that didn't think he could sing. Put that thing away, now, Joe, you've been at it long enough. And see that that back is locked. I don't think Amy has any idea what time it is or she'd shut him up.

JOE. Let the young man express himself. [*He gets up and crosses below the table towards the right, and up to the kitchen door.*]

MRS. FISHER. Oh, I wouldn't care if he bawled his head off, as far as I'm concerned—I'd be glad if he did; but I don't want him to waken your Father. [*She steps up to the hall door and listens, at the foot of the stairs.*] And that's what he'll be doin' the first thing you know, and then the fat'll be in the fire for sure. [*Aubrey reaches a high note, and Joe and his mother stand looking at each other. Then Joe bursts out laughing.*] Ain't that terrible, Joe? Do you think I ought to tell Amy what time it is?

JOE. No, give the boy a chance. [*Aubrey finishes on a high note and holds it.*] Hurray! [*Aubrey can be heard applauding himself. Joe applauds, also.*]

MRS. FISHER. [*Frantically, and going towards Joe*] Shush, Joe!

JOE. [*Going out through the door at right*] Sign on the dotted line!

MRS. FISHER. Don't encourage him, for God's sake, Joe, he's bad enought as it is.

MR. FISHER. [*Shouting from the top of the stairs*] Josie!

MRS. FISHER. [*Rushing back towards the hall door on her tiptoes*] Yes?

MR. FISHER. What the devil's goin' on down there! Do you know what time it is?

MRS. FISHER. [*Trying to pacify him*] Why, Joe was just cuttin' up here a minute ago.

MR. FISHER. What's Amy playin' the piano for, at this time of night?

MRS. FISHER. [*Trying not to be heard in the parlor*] Why, her and Joe was just foolin'—

MR. FISHER. Damn funny kind of foolin', at this time of night! The neighbors'll be wonderin' what kind of a house we're keepin' here!

MRS. FISHER. Well, they've stopped it now, Neil.

MR. FISHER. Well, tell them to see that it's *kept* stopped! And get them lights out down there and go to bed! It's nearly twelve o'clock.

[*Mrs. Fisher turns and looks at the parolor doors. Then there's a burst of wild laughter from Aubrey. This decides Mrs. Fisher. She steps resolutely towards the doors with the ostensible purpose of opening them, but, before she can reach the knob, the door is yanked open from the inside, and Amy steps out, looking resentfully at her.*]

AMY. What's the matter?

MRS. FISHER. [*A trifle disconcerted*] Why—a—I was just comin' to tell you to be sure and put them lights out; I'm just goin' up—it's nearly twelve o'clock.

AUBREY. [*Thrusting his head and shoulders out through the door*] I am also just about to take my reluctant leave, Mrs. Fisher.

MRS. FISHER. [*Trying to be polite*] Well, I don't want to hurry you, but—

AUBREY. In fact, the recent outburst was in the nature of a farewell concert. [*He breaks into a wild laugh and draws back into the parlor; and Mrs. Fisher, with a series of frantic gestures, intended to convey to Amy the imminence of her father at the head of the stairs, steps back out of the range of the parlor door. Amy makes an impatient movement of her body, and stamps her foot, then flounces into the parlor and slams the door.*] The little old song at twilight, you know, Mother Fisher—to soothe the savage breast. [*He gives vent to another gale of laughter; and Mrs. Fisher stands petrified, expected to hear her husband again.*]

MRS. FISHER. [*As Aubrey's laugh subsides*] The damn fool! [*She crosses to the right to the kitchen door and calls out to Joe.*] Joe!

JOE. Yeh?

MRS. FISHER. You'd better bring Gypsy Queen in and put her in the laundry there; she was shiverin' when I opened the door this mornin'. I think it's too cold for her on that back porch yet a while. [*She moves a little back towards the center of the room.*]

JOE. [*Out at the right*] Come on in here, Gypsy! Come on. [*He whistles.*]

MRS. FISHER. [*Turning around to her left and looking back toward the kitchen door*] Ain't she there?

JOE. I don't see her.

MRS. FISHER. [*Calling in a high voice*] Where *are* you, Gypsy?

JOE. Here she is. Come on in here, Gypsy! Come on! That's the old gypsy kid. [*The door out at the right closes.*]

MRS. FISHER. [*Going a step nearer the kitchen door*] Go into that laundry there, Gypsy.

JOE. Come back here, Gypsy.

MRS. FISHER. Make her go in there, Joe.

JOE. [*Stomping his foot*] Gypsy!

MRS. FISHER. [*Stamping her foot at the kitchen door*] Go back there, Gypsy! You bad girl! And go into that laundry this minute—

JOE. There she goes.

MRS. FISHER. And don't let me hear a sound out of you when you get in there either, or I'll come right straight out and give you what I gave you last Sunday afternoon. [*A door closes.*] You better put the ketch on that door, Joe, or she'll be pushin' it open again; she wants to lay out here on this rug. [*Going nearer to the door again, and calling*] Now, you remember what I told you, Gypsy; and don't let me have to speak to you again. [*Turning and moving across the room to the left*] Your father has her spoiled. [*A door out in the hallway at the left opens, and Amy can be heard laughing. Mrs. Fisher stops dead in the middle of the room and listens.*]

AUBREY. [*Calling from the hallway*] Goodnight, Mrs. Fisher. [*Mrs. Fisher turns and darts back into the cellar alcove at the right.*]

AMY. I guess she's gone up, Aubrey.

AUBREY. [*Coming in at the hall door, poising on one toe, hat and cane in hand, and looking about the room*] Montreal, Mother. [*Mrs. Fisher flattens herself against the wall at the head of the cellar stairs, and listens with a stoney expression.*]

AMY. I don't think she's in there, Aubrey.

AUBREY. And silence was her answer. [*He laughs wildly, turns, and starts out into the hallway again.*] Right you are, Amy—[*Glancing up the stairs*] On the right side she is sleeping. [*He goes laughing out into the hallway.*]

JOE. [*Coming in from the kitchen, mimicking Aubrey's laugh*] Ha! Ha! Ha! [*He passes his mother without seeing her.*]

MRS. FISHER. [*Coming out of the alcove*] Shush! Don't let them hear you, Joe. [*Joe turns and looks at his mother, then continues across to the left to the hall door.*]

JOE. Is he goin'?

MRS. FISHER. [*Following Joe to the center of the room*] At last! [*Joe glances out into the hallway.*] Don't let him see you, now, Joe, or we'll have him here for another hour.

JOE. [*Starting up the stairs*] I'm goin' to bed.

MRS. FISHER. Joe!

JOE. [*Leaning back and looking*] What?

MRS. FISHER. Come here! [*Amy can be heard giggling in the hallway. Joe comes back to his mother.*]

JOE. What?

MRS. FISHER. [*Very confidentially*] What was that he was sayin' here tonight, about discoverin' something to keep rust out of iron and steel?

JOE. [*Very much amused*] Wasn't that a scream?

MRS. FISHER. That's what *you're* always talkin' about, ain't it?

JOE. Yes, I was talkin' to *him* about it one night here, while he was waiting for Amy to come down; and he's forgot where he heard it.

MRS. FISHER. Can you imagine!

JOE. I was wonderin' if you were gettin' that tonight.

MRS. FISHER. No, it never struck me till afterwards.

JOE. [*With a shade of seriousness*] Did you get what he said tonight, Mom?

MRS. FISHER. Now, you know I never pay any attention to what *he* sez.

JOE. [*Turning away laughing*] He's a bird. [*He goes to the hall door and looks out into the hall.*]

MRS. FISHER. Don't let him see you, now, Joe.

JOE. The vestibule door's shut. [*He goes up the stairs. His mother follows him to the hall door.*]

MRS. FISHER. You'd better close that window at the head of your bed, Joe, and not have it blowin' in on you all night. [*She glances out into the hallway, then steps to the parlor door, opens it quietly and glances in, and starts across towards the right. The front door closes out in the hallway, then the vestibule door. Mrs. Fisher glances over her right shoulder toward the hallway, then continues to the kitchen door. Just as she reaches the kitchen door and glances out, the parlor door is flung open and Amy comes in. She takes a couple of steps towards the middle of the room, then stands still, looking bitterly at her mother. Mrs. Fisher speaks without looking at her.*] Did you put that light out in there?

AMY. [*In a quiet rage*] That was a *nice* trick you people did tonight! [*Her mother turns and looks at her.*]

MRS. FISHER. What?

AMY. Everybody walking out of the room, while Aubrey was talking.

MRS. FISHER. What did you *want* us to do, sit here all night listenin' to him?

AMY. You wouldn't have *had* to sit here all night listening to him; he was only in here five minutes.

MRS. FISHER. [*Moving back towards the center table*] That's no thanks to him; he'd have been here till mornin' if somebody didn't do somethin'.

AMY. [*Swinging to the mirror over the mantlepiece*] I was never so mortified in my life.

MRS. FISHER. [*Standing above the center table*] Oh, don't waste your sympathy, Amy! He don't have to have anybody listen to him; he'd talk to the wall if there wasn't anybody else around.

AMY. [*Coming forward at her mother's right*] What did Pop get into such a temper about?

MRS. FISHER. [*Getting mad*] Because he hit him on the back!

AMY. That was a lot to get mad about.

MRS. FISHER. Well, he's always hittin' *somebody!*—on the back—or

the shoulder—or someplace else. And your father *said* the next
time he did it he'd walk out of the room!—He can't say two
words *together* without *hittin'* somebody someplace.

AMY. Well, I'll bet you won't get a chance to insult him *again*, Mom,
I'll tell you that. [*She flounces down to the armchair at the extreme
right.*]

MRS. FISHER. Then, let him stop his silly talk! and he won't get
insulted. Sign on the dotted line! every two minutes. And
talkin' about Shakespeare. [*She crosses to the parlor door.*] What
kind of goin' on is that for a sensible man. [*She slams the parlor
door shut, and moves up to the hall door to listen for Mr. Fisher.*] It's
no wonder our Joe sez he's a nut!

AMY. Oh, everybody's a nut with the people around here!

MRS. FISHER. [*Coming back towards the center table*] Oh, it ain't only
the people around here that sez it; everybody that knows him
sez it. [*Amy makes a sound of derisive amusement.*] You needn't
laugh, for it's true.

AMY. [*Turning sharply to her mother*] Who do *you* know that knows
him?

MRS. FISHER. I know Frank Hyland. [*Amy is puzzled for the fraction of
a second.*]

AMY. You mean Clara's *husband?*

MRS. FISHER. Yes, I mean Clara's *husband.*

AMY. Oh, don't make up a lie, Mom! Frank Hyland never saw
Aubrey Piper!

MRS. FISHER. Oh, didn't he!

AMY. No, he didn't.

MRS. FISHER. Well now, my lady, you're so smart, he knows him better than you do.

AMY. I don't believe it.

MRS. FISHER. Doesn't matter whether you believe it or not, he knows
him just the same; he's been lookin' at him for years, down at
that restaurant at Fifteenth and Arch, where he eats his lunch.
And he sez he's as crazy as a *bass*-singer.

AMY. [*Whirling on her mother*] I suppose that's what Clara was here
to tell you, was it?

MRS. FISHER. What does it matter *who* was here to tell it, Amy, if it's true?

AMY. [*Stepping up close to her mother*] Well now, listen, Mom, I want to tell you something right now! You tell our Clara for me the next time you see her, to mind her own damn business—[*She taps the back of the chair twice with her knuckles, emphasizing the words "damn" and "business."*] as far as Aubrey Piper is concerned.

MRS. FISHER. [*Before Amy has finished speaking*] Oh, don't fly into a temper, if anybody speaks to you! [*She turns and crosses hurriedly to the hall door to listen.*]

AMY. [*Stamping her foot*] Well then, don't speak to me about things that *put* me in a temper!

MRS. FISHER. You're not frightenin' anybody around here. [*She looks up the stairs and listens.*]

AMY. No, and nobody around here is frightening *me*, either.—Our Clara took who *she* wanted. And I guess you took who *you* wanted. [*Mrs. Fisher moves steadily forward at the left to a point in front of the lower left hand corner of the center table.*] And if I want Aubrey Piper I'll take him!

MRS. FISHER. [*Taking Amy's tone*] Well, take him then!—and the sooner the better; for it's a pity to spoil two houses with you. [*She leans forward a little on the table and speaks with a steady precision.*] Only remember this, Amy—if you do take him—be sure that you keep him—and that—he—keeps—you. [*Amy looks at her keenly.*] And don't be comin' around here cryin' for your *Pop* to keep you.

AMY. [*With a sound of amused derision, and flouncing down to the armchair at the right*] Don't make me laugh.

MRS. FISHER. You can laugh all you like; there's a lot of that kind of laughin' goin' on these days. But they change their tune as soon as the rent begins to come due; and it's the mothers and fathers that has to listen to the changed tune. But nothin'll do but they'll get married.

AMY. [*Pinning her mother with a quick look*] *You* got married, didn't you?

MRS. FISHER. Yes I did.

AMY. [*Turning away again*] Well—

MRS. FISHER. To a man that was able to keep me.

AMY. [*Back to her mother again*] And how do *you* know that Aubrey Piper wouldn't be able to keep *his* wife?

MRS. FISHER. Because I know what he earns—[*She strikes the table with her fist.*] and it is isn't enough.

AMY. [*Stamping her foot*] Oh, don't go making up things, Mom!— You don't know anything *about* what he earns.

MRS. FISHER. [*With measured emphasis*] He earns a hundred and fifty dollars a month and not a penny more, for Frank Hyland sez so.

AMY. What does Frank Hyland know about it.

MRS. FISHER. He knows what he does!—His business takes him in there all the time.

AMY. And what does he say he does?

MRS. FISHER. Why, he sez he's a clerk, of course—[*Amy makes a sound of amusement.*] like a hundred others down there.

AMY. That shows how much he knows about it.

MRS. FISHER. But I suppose he told you he *owns* the Pennsylvania Railroad.

AMY. Well, I'd take his word before I'd take Frank Hyland's. [*Her mother looks at her narrowly, and there is a pause.*]

MRS. FISHER. [*Significantly*] Why would you take *his* word before you would take Frank Hyland's?

AMY. Well, why shouldn't I?

MRS. FISHER. [*Losing her temper*] Because he's a fool!—of a blather-skite.

AMY. That's only your opinion, Mom.

MRS. FISHER. It's the opinion of everybody that ever listened to him. But you'd believe *him* before you'd believe the word of a steady sensible man.

AMY. I don't know anything about Frank Hyland.

MRS. FISHER. You know he's been your brother-in-law for five years; and what do you know about this other clown?

AMY. Well, what do you *want* to know about him?

MRS. FISHER. I don't want to know anything about him; I know all I
    want to know about him. but before I'd get the name of havin' a
    fellow comin' to see me steady, there's a few things I'd want to
    know about him, I'll tell you that. [*She turns away and takes a step
    towards the back of the room.*]

AMY. I've told you where he lives and where he works—what else
    do you want to know about him?

MRS. FISHER. There's no use talkin' to you, Amy.

AMY. No, and there's no use talkin' to you, either.

MRS. FISHER. [*Turning to her sharply*] This fellow's got you so crazy
    mad about him, that I believe you'd take him if you knew he
    had a wife and family somewhere, and not two cents in his
    pocket. [*She moves towards the mantelpiece at the back, removing
    her spectacles.*]

AMY. Well, I guess we'd get along some way even if I did.

MRS. FISHER. All right.

AMY. Everybody else does.

MRS. FISHER. [*Turning upon Amy in a rage, and wiping the glasses on her
    apron.*] That's the kind of talk that leaves them livin' in garrets!
    And back at their jobs ten days after the weddin'.

AMY. Oh, you talk as though everybody that was married was
    starving to death.

MRS. FISHER. [*Lifting the glasses towards Amy with a quiet, knowing ges-
    ture*] There are ways of starvin' to death, Amy, besides not get-
    tin' enough to eat. [*With a change to great shrewdness of tone and
    manner*] And the funny part of it is, Amy—like a lot of others,
    you're very shrewd about money while you're at home, as far
    as what you give your mother and father is concerned; but the
    minute some clown, with a flower in his coat and patent-leather
    shoes, winks at you, you seem to forget there's such a thing in
    the world as a ton of coal. [*Crossing suddenly above the table
    towards Amy in quite a surge of temper*] And then it's just as Clara
    sez, it's your *people* that has to come to the rescue.

AMY. [*Furiously*] I wish I'd been here while she was talking! I bet I'd
    a told her a thing or two!

MRS. FISHER. Oh, you needn't try to turn it onto Clara—she wasn't talkin' at all.

AMY. [*Stomping her foot*] She must have been talking!

MRS. FISHER. She simply asked me where you were!—and I told her you were gettin' dressed—that this fellow was comin' here tonight: so then she told me that Frank Hyland knew him, and where he worked, and what he got and all about him. [*She turns away and moves to the left. There is a slight pause.*]

AMY. [*Half crying*] I'd just take him for *spite* now. [*Mrs. Fisher comes to a stop, and turns slowly—and looks at her.*]

MRS. FISHER. Well, let me tell *you*, Amy—the day a girl that's used to spendin' money the way you do, takes a thirty-five-dollar-a-week man—the only one she's spitin' is herself. [*She moves slowly to the mantelpiece at the back and puts her glasses down definitely, then turns and starts to remove her apron.*] There'll be no more permanent waves after that—[*She rolls her apron up.*] you can make up your mind to that. [*She flings the rolled apron onto the sofa at the right of the mantelpiece, and commences to unfasten the old-fashioned brooch in the front of her house dress.*] Nor fifty-five dollar beaded dresses, either.

AMY. [*In a crying temper*] Well, I'd never bother anybody around here if I needed anything, I'll tell you that.

MRS. FISHER. Maybe you won't.

AMY. I won't—you needn't worry.

MRS. FISHER. [*With a bitter levelness*] Time'll tell that, Lady Jane; I've heard the likes of you before. [*She detaches the brooch and goes to the hall door, glances out into the hallway, then turns and looks back at Amy.*] Put out that light and go to bed, it's twelve o'clock. [*She goes up the stairs. Amy stands for a second, fuming, over at the right; then she swings suddenly to the middle of the room and stops, with her hands on her hips, irresolute. Then she comes forward and stands above the table, thinking. As she clasps her hands together she becomes conscious of the ring in her hand. She tiptoes to the hall door, stands listening for a second, then looks up. Then she hurries back to the center table, looks at the ring, slides it onto the third finger of her*]

left hand and holds it so that the diamond will catch the light from the
chandelier. But, the reflection is evidently unsatisfactory; so, with a
furtive glance toward the hall door, she shifts her position to a point
nearer the table lamp and holds her hand so that the ring will reflect
the light. The curtain commences to descend slowly; and she stands,
holding her hand at arms length, lost in the melting wonder of her
engagement ring.]

THE CURTAIN IS DOWN.

⇤ ACT II ⇥

Same as preceding Act, six months later, about five-thirty on a Monday afternoon. Mrs. Fisher is sitting in the armchair below the buffet, over at the right, listening in on the radio. Suddenly the front door closes with a bang, and she starts, and looks in the direction of the hall door. Aubrey bounces into the room, very much done up, with the traditional carnation, as usual, and comes forward, putting his hat down on the table.

AUBREY. Hello, Mother—Amy here? [*He steps to the mirror at the back and gives himself a critical touch here and there.*]

MRS. FISHER. [*Commencing to remove the listeners*] Our Amy!

AUBREY. Yes, have you seen anything of her?

MRS. FISHER. [*Rising*] No, I haven't seen anything of her. [*She places the listeners on the buffet, and signs off.*]

AUBREY. [*Turning from the glass*] Wonder where she is?

MRS. FISHER. Isn't she home?

AUBREY. No, I just came by there.

MRS. FISHER. [*Picking up her knitting bag from the buffet*] She hasn't been here today.

AUBREY. She was saying this morning she thought she'd go out looking for a house today; I suppose she hasn't got back yet. [*He gives the chair at the left of the center table a double tap with his cane as he crosses down to the window at the left.*] I wanted to take her out to the Automobile Show tonight; I got the loan of Harry Albright's car.

MRS. FISHER. [*Moving to the chair at the right of the center table.*] Did you say she was out lookin' for a house?

AUBREY. [*Moving back, towards her*] Yes, we've got to get out of that place we're in. The LePage printing people have bought the whole block: they're going to put up a new building there.

MRS. FISHER. [*Standing with her hand on the back of the chair*] How soon do you have to get out?

AUBREY. Soon as we can find a place, I suppose. I understand they want to begin tearing down there about the first of the year.

MRS. FISHER. I'm afraid you won't find it so easy to get a place as reasonable as that again in a hurry. [*She sits down.*]

AUBREY. I don't *want* a place as reasonable as that, if I can get something better. [*He plants himself at the left of the table and looks away off, with a dreamy narrowing of his eyes, and balances hirmself on his toes.*] I want a home—something with a bit of ground around it—where I can do a bit of tennis in the evening—[*He makes a couple of leisurely passes at an imaginary tennis ball.*] if I feel like it.

MRS. FISHER. [*Beginning to knit on a green sweater*] Well, if you do you'll pay for it.

AUBREY. That is exactly what I expect to do, Mother Fisher, not giving you a short answer—that is exactly what I expect to do. [*He gives the table a double tap with the cane.*] But, I want what I'm paying for, I'll tell you that. No more of the old first of-the-month business for this bambino. He's all washed up, and signed on the dotted line. [*He moves lip to the mirror at the back.*]

MRS. FISHER. They're not puttin' *up* any more houses, from what I can hear.

AUBREY. Be yourself, now, Mother Fisher, be yourself.

MRS. FISHER. Well, where *are* they?

AUBREY. You ought to go out along the Boulevard some Sunday— see what they're doing out there.

MRS. FISHER. Well, there's no danger of you goin' out along the Boulevard, except for a walk.

AUBREY. [*Moving to the hall door and glancing out into the hallway*] Lot of people out that way, Mother.

MRS. FISHER. Well, if there is they're payin' more than you're able to
pay.

AUBREY. Man's got to live somewhere, Mother. [*He swings forward to
the window down at the left, and stands whistling to the canary.*]

MRS. FISHER. Well, if he's wise, he'll live where he's able to pay for
it—unless he wants to be breakin' up half a dozen times a
year—like a lot of them are doin'. Makin' a big show. Buyin'
ten thousand dollar houses, and puttin' fifty dollars down on
them. [*He turns to her.*] Besides, you haven't got any furniture
for a house, even if you got one—unless you want to be sittin'
on the floor.

AUBREY. The matter of furniture nowadays, Little Mother, is a very
inconsequential item, from what I can gather.

MRS. FISHER. You ought to price it sometime when you're in the city,
and see how unconsequent it is.

AUBREY. [*Settling himself for a golf shot, using his cane for a club*] I've
investigated the matter very thoroughly, Mrs. Fisher, and I find
that there are at least fifteen first-class establishments right
here in this city that will furnish a man's house from garret to
garage, and give him the rest of his life to pay for it. [*He hits the
imaginary golf ball and pretends to follow it straight out with his
eyes.*]

MRS. FISHER. They'd need to give some of them the rest of their
lives, at the rate they're goin' now.

AUBREY. Give the growing boy a chance, Mrs. Fisher, give the grow-
ing boy a chance. You know what Mr. L. D. Brophy of the
American Can Company said in the September number of the
American Magazine, don't you?

MRS. FISHER. No, I don't.

AUBREY. Well, I'll tell you. [*Mrs. Fisher shifts her knitting, giving him a
wearied glance.*] He said, "I would say, to that innumerable host
of young men, standing on the threshold of life, uncertain, and,
mayhap, dismayed—as they contemplate the stress of modern
industrial competition, 'Rome was not built in a day'." Those
were his very words, I wouldn't kid you, and I think the old

boy's got it right, if you ask me. [*He moves up to he hall door again and glances out.*]

MRS. FISHER. What are you goin' out to the Automobile Show for?

AUBREY. [*Turning and coming forward again*] Repeat the question, Mrs. Fisher, if you please.

MRS. FISHER. I say, what are you goin' out to the Automobile Show for?

AUBREY. [*Coming to a point above the center table*] Ha! Married five months ago today, Mother; got to celebrate the happy event. Besides, one never knows what a day will bring, in the way of an opportunity to satisfy a long-felt want. And since she knocks but once—[*He taps his cane on the table, causing Mrs. Fisher to start slightly.*] at each man's door, the kid here doesn't want to miss his chance by any uncertainty as to just what choo choo he prefers. [*Mrs. Fisher turns with an annoyed expression, to find him pointing at her with his forefinger and thunb. He laughs at her annoyance.*] Well, got to run along now, Mother, and see if Amy's back at the house yet. [*He picks up his hat from the table and starts for the hall door.*]

MRS. FISHER. What'll I'll tell her if she comes here after you're gone?

AUBREY. [*Stopping at the door*] Why, tell her I've got the loan of Harry Albright's car, and I want her to see that new Jordan Six that I was telling her about, out at the Show. And that I'll be at Childs' at Fifteenth and Chestnut until eight o'clock. [*He looks at his Ingersoll.*]

MRS. FISHER. Fifteenth and Chestnut?

AUBREY. That's the said and done, Mother. [*He laughs boisterously.*] The old Café Infanté. [*He laughs again.*] Olive oil, Mother. [*He goes out the hall door, breaking into another laugh, and in a second the front door closes with a bang, causing Mrs. Fisher to start again, end look irritatedly toward the hall door. Then she resumes her knitting. The parlor door opens again and Amy drifts in, and starts across towards the chair at the left of the table.*]

AMY. Hello! [*Mrs. Fisher starts again.*]

MRS. FISHER. Oh, you frightened me, Amy—walkin' in that way like a ghost ! When did you come in?

AMY. [*Sitting down, with a wearied air*] A couple of minutes ago—
  I've been in the parlor.

MRS. FISHER. Why, your man just left here, didn't you see him?

AMY. No, I heard him when I came in—I went in the parlor.

MRS. FISHER. He's lookin' for you.—He sez he wants you to go to
  some kind of an Automobile Show with him.

AMY. I know; I don't want to go; I'm too tired.

MRS. FISHER. What's he doin' about his supper?

AMY. I told him this morning to get something in town; I knew I
  wouldn't be home till late. [*Mrs. Fisher resumes her knitting; and
  there is a slight pause.*]

MRS. FISHER. He sez you've got to get out of that place you're in.

AMY. Yes, they're going to tear those houses down. That's what I
  was doing today—looking around for someplace.

MRS. FISHER. Did you see anything?

AMY. I saw a couple of places that were fair, but they want too
  much money.

MRS. FISHER. I'm afraid that's what you'll find, Amy, wherever you
  go.

AMY. Thirty-eight dollars a month—for a little two-story house—
  that didn't even have a front porch.

MRS. FISHER. Well, you're surely not lookin' for a house, Amy, are
  you?

AMY. Yes, if I can find one.

MRS. FISHER. And have you any idea what they're askin' for houses
  these days?

AMY. Well, Aubrey sez he will not live in rooms any longer.

MRS. FISHER. What the devil does it matter *what* he sez! He don't
  know what he's sayin' half the time, anyway. It's *you* that has
  to stretch the money, and it'll only go so far; and the money
  that *he* gets won't cover any forty-dollar rents, you can make
  up your mind to that right now, before you go any further.
  And that's what you'll be asked to pay, Amy, remember I'm
  tellin' you.

AMY. He doesn't want to pay rent—he wants to buy.

MRS. FISHER. What on, thirty-two dollars a week?

AMY. He sez he can put it into a new building society that he heard about, over in Frankford.

MRS. FISHER. Wouldn't he have to pay the building society?

AMY. Well, he wouldn't have have to pay it all at once.

MRS. FISHER. There'd be more onces than he'd be able to meet. I thought *you* had a *little* sense, but you're nearly as bad as him

AMY. No, but you talk awfully silly, Mother; you'd think everybody that was married was living out in the street.

MRS. FISHER. That's where a good many of them would be livin', Amy, only that somebody belongin' to them is givin' them a hand. Money'll only go so far, and I've been keepin' house too long not to know just how far that far is. Nobody can tell *me*.

AMY. There was a girl down in our office that was married, just before I was married, and the fellow she married didn't even get as much money as Aubrey gets; he got about twenty-five a week—he was a guard in the Corn Exchange Bank; and *they* bought a house, out in Kensington, and they say it's beautiful.

MRS. FISHER. She's back at her job, though, isn't she?

AMY. [*With reluctant admission*] She never left her job.

MRS. FISHER. Well—that's how she's doin' it. You told me yourself there were five girls in your office that have married within the last two years. Do you think they're hanging over books nine hours a day because they *like* it? And you haven't got any furniture even if you got a house.

AMY. Oh, you can always get furniture.

MRS. FISHER. You can if you pay for it. And I don't know how you expect to do all these wonders later on, when you find it so hard to make ends meet now, with only the rent of two rooms to pay for. You're everlastin' borrowin' from me as it is.

AMY. I always pay you, don't I?

MRS. FISHER. You do when you get it. But, that's not the point, Amy; it's that what you get one week don't last you till the next

AMY. The reason I was short last week, Aubrey bought that new overcoat.

MRS. FISHER. And next week it'll be something else.

AMY. Well, a man can't be shabby, Mom, in a position like Aubrey's. He sez he's got nearly eighty clerks down there in his department; and he sez unless he sets some kind of an example of personal appearance, he sez there are some of them down there that'd come in in overalls.

MRS. FISHER. [*Laying her knitting on the table and looking keenly at Amy*] How is it, Amy, that a girl like you—that was smart enough to keep books, has so little sense when it comes to what some man tells you? [*Amy looks at her mother steadily.*]

AMY. Who do you mean, Aubrey?

MRS. FISHER. Yes.

AMY. What does he tell me that I have so little sense about?

MRS. FISHER. That he has eighty clerks under him.

AMY. So he has.

MRS. FISHER. And gets thirty-two dollars a week?

AMY. He gets thirty-two fifty. [*Mrs. Fisher resumes her knitting, shaking her head hopelessly.*] Well now, Mom, you know yourself what the Pennsylvania Railroad pays its men.

MRS. FISHER. I don't know what anybody pays anybody.

AMY. Well, the Pennsylvania Railroad is notorious. Aubrey sez that only that a couple of things haven't panned out just right with him, he'd have left them *long* ago. He sez they just try to break your spirit. He sez that's one of the main reasons why he pays so much attention to his clothes.—He sez he just wouldn't *please* them.

MRS. FISHER. How much did he pay for that overcoat?

AMY. Twenty-eight dollars. [*Mrs. Fisher raises her eyes to Heaven.*] Oh, he didn't have to pay it all at once; the man said on account of it being so near Christmas he could let it go till the first of February.

MRS. FISHER. I guess he'll be wantin' a suit, now, the first you know, to go with the overcoat.

AMY. No, his suit's all right—yet a while. But this suit of mine is beginning to go; I 've worn it till I'm tired looking at it.

MRS. FISHER. People can't *get* things so handy once they're married.

AMY. I thought I'd be able to put something away out of this week, toward a suit; but I don't know where the money went to—it just seemed to go. Honestly, I had exactly *twelve cents* in my purse when Aubrey gave me his pay.

MRS. FISHER. I don't know what'll become of you, Amy, if ever you have a houseful of children to keep. [*Amy sits looking at nothing, with a rather troubled expression about the eyes, and her mother continues to knit. Suddenly Amy bursts into tears. Mrs. Fisher looks at her: she gets up quietly, laying her knitting on the table, and crosses in front of the table to her—and lays her hand on her arm.*] Now, there's no use a startin' that kind a thing, now, Amy; for it won't do you a bit of good. [*She continues across.*]

AMY. I don't know what I'm going to do, Mom—I'm nearly crazy.

MRS. FISHER. [*Turning*] I'll tell you what you're goin' to do, Amy, if you're a wise woman.—You're goin' to realize that you're married; and that you've got some kind of a house to keep up; and just how much money you're goin' to get each week to keep it up *on;* and then suit your ideas accordin'. And if you don't, you'll have plenty of cryin' to do. And you'll have nobody to thank but yourself, for you had nothing but impudence for them that tried to tell you—how many beans made five. [*The front door is heard to close.*] I guess this is your father. Go into the parlor there, and don't let him see you cryin'. [*Amy rises and steps quickly across and through the parlor doors at the left into the parlor; and Mrs. Fisher crosses above the center table to the buffet and puts her knitting into one of the drawers. Clara appears in the hall door.*]

CLARA. What's the matter? [*Mrs. Fisher turns and looks at her.*]

MRS. FISHER. There's nothing at all the matter,

CLARA. What did Joe telephone me for?

MRS. FISHER. *Our Joe,* do you mean?

CLARA. Yes; Bertha said he telephoned the house about four o'clock and told her to tell me to come right over home as soon as I came in.

MRS. FISHER. Well, I'm sure *I* don't know what he'd want you for, Clara; he didn't leave any word with me for you this morning.

CLARA. [*Coming forward towards the center table*] I was over paying my Electric, and just got back; so I came right over; I thought maybe something was wrong here, and he was calling from next door.

MRS. FISHER. No, he hasn't been home here today. [*Clara puzzles for a second, then tosses her purse onto the table.*]

CLARA. I wonder what he wanted me for. [*She turns to the mirror at the back and touches her hat.*]

MRS. FISHER. Is that girl at your house sure it was our Joe?

CLARA. [*Coming back to the table*] She said it was; and I suppose she knows his voice—she's often answered the phone when he's called. [*She picks up a book from the table and glances casually at it.*]

MRS. FISHER. Well, maybe he wants to see you about something; I'd wait a while; he'll be here at six.

CLARA. [*Looking suddenly at her mother*] Maybe he's heard some news about that formula that those people are interested in.

MRS. FISHER. [*Coming over to the table*] Oh, I guess he'll be an old man before he ever hears anything from that. [*She folds and settles various things on the table, and Clara glances through the book. Then, as she moves over to settle the upper left hand corner of the table cover, she gives Clara a little push.*] Look out of my way, Clara, till I fix this cloth. [*Clara just moves without looking up from the book.*] That's a book Joe brought home last night: about that woman that was left up on the North Pole. He sez it's very nice. I've got to put those potatoes on, for your father's supper; he'll be here around six. [*She moves to the door at the right.*]

CLARA. [*Standing at the left of the table, still looking at the book*] Did you know that Amy's got to get out of those rooms she's in?

MRS. FISHER. [*From the kitchen*] Yes.

CLARA. They're going to tear those houses down.

MRS. FISHER. [*Coming back into the room*] So she was telling me.

CLARA. [*Moving to the chair at the left of the table*] What's she going to do? [*Tossing the book onto the table*] come in here to live? [*She sits down.*]

MRS. FISHER. Now that's a sensible question for you to ask, Clara—you know how much she's comin' in here to live.

CLARA. [*Commencing to remove her gloves*] I don't know where else she'll go—with rents the way they are now—unless she goes back to work.

MRS. FISHER. She'll have to look around.

CLARA. What good will it do her to look around—she certainly won't find anything as reasonable as where she is now: and when she's not able to pay that, how does she expect to pay any more? [*The parlor door is whipped open and Amy is standing between the curtains looking tight-lipped at Clara.*]

AMY. How do *you* know I'm not able to pay my rent where I am?

MRS. FISHER. [*Moving towards the hall door*] Now, don't start a fight, Amy, your Pop'll be in here any minute. [*She looks out into the hallway.*]

AMY. [*Speaking to her mother, and indicating Clara with a gesture*] No, but I'd like to know what business it is of hers whether I can pay my rent or not. I don't see that anybody's asking her to pay it for me.

CLARA. [*Very sure of her ground*] It's a bit late in the day to talk that way, Amy; your husband's been to Frank Hyland *twice* already to pay it for you. [*Amy looks at her aghast, and Mrs. Fisher comes forward between them.*] It's time you quit this posing in front of me; *I* know how you're fixed better than you do yourself. [*She turns sharply away and flings her gloves onto the table.*]

AMY. [*Almost crying*] Now, do you hear that, Mom!

MRS. FISHER. Stop your talk, Amy! Do you want your father to walk in and hear you?

AMY. [*Lowering her voice, but still speaking with angry rapidity*] She sez that Aubrey Piper's been to Frank Hyland twice, for the loan of *our* rent.

CLARA. So he has.

AMY. You're a liar, [*Mrs. Fisher gives her a slap on the back; and there is a vibrant pause. Then Amy moves down towards the window at the left and bursts out crying.*]

MRS. FISHER. [*With controlled excitement*] Will you stop when I speak to *you!* [*There is a pause.*] What kind of talk do you call that! [*She steps to the hall door again and glances out into the hallway.*]

AMY. [*Whirling again upon Clara*] Well, that's what she is! Aubrey Piper never asked Frank Hyland for a cent in his life.

CLARA. He's asked him a dozen times, and got it, too; till I put a stop to it.

MRS. FISHER. [*Coming forward again, and speaking with authority*] Now, that'll do, Clara—I don't want to hear another word—out of either one of you—I had enough of that when the two of you were at home.

AMY. Well, I'll make her prove what she sez about about Aubrey Piper, just the same!

CLARA. It's very easily proved. Just come over to the house some night and I'll show you a few of his letters.

AMY. What do you do, open them?

CLARA. I do now, yes—since I found out who they're from.

MRS. FISHER. Do you mean to tell me, Clara, that he's writin' to Frank Hyland for money?

AMY. No, he doesn't do anything of the kind, Mom, that's another of her lies!

MRS. FISHER. [*Before Amy has finished speaking*] I'm not talkin' to you, Amy.

AMY. She just makes those things up.

CLARA. I make them *up!*

AMY. [*Crying*] Yes!

CLARA. And I've got at least twelve letters right in my bureau drawer this minute that he's written within the last two months.

MRS. FISHER. What does he write letters for?

CLARA. For money, so he can pay seven dollars for a seat out at the football game—as he did Thanksgiving afternoon—Frank saw him there.

MRS. FISHER. Why don't he just ast Frank Hyland for the money when he sees him, instead of writin' to him?

CLARA. I suppose he thinks a written request is more appropriate, coming from one of the heads of the Pennsylvania Railroad.

MRS. FISHER. How much does he ast for, when he asts him?

CLARA. There was one a couple of weeks ago, for three hundred. [*Amy makes a sound of bitter amusement, and turns away.*]

MRS. FISHER. [*Aghast*] Three hundred dollars?

CLARA. That's what the letter said. [*Mrs. Fisher turns and looks at Amy.*]

MRS. FISHER. What would he have wanted three hundred dollars for, Amy?

AMY. Oh, ask her, Mom; she's good at making things up. [*She sweeps towards the parlor doors.*]

MRS. FISHER. [*Taking a step or two after her*] Oh, you wouldn't believe it, even if it was true, if it was against him.

AMY. Well, I wouldn't believe her, anyway. [*Amy slams the parlor door with a bang.*]

MRS. FISHER. [*Raising her voice*] You wouldn't believe your own mother—never name your sister. [*She turns to Clara.*] She flew at me like a wildcat, when I told her he wore a wig. I guess she knows it herself by this time.

CLARA. She's for *him*, Mom; and the sooner you get that into your head the better.

MRS. FISHER. [*Moving towards the right, above the table*] I know very well she is, you needn't tell me. And she'd turn on everyone belongin' to her for him. The idea of askin' anybody for three hundred dollars. [*She continues towards the kitchen door, fuming; then turns.*] I suppose he wanted to buy an automobile or something. That's where he is tonight, out at the Automobile Show—and not two cents in his pocket—like a lot of others that'll be out there I guess.—And I'll bet he'll be doin' more talk out there than them that'll buy a dozen cars.

CLARA. I think that's what he *did* want the money for.

MRS. FISHER. It wouldn't surprise me—the damned fool. [*She steps to the mantelpiece and glances out into the hallway.*] It'd be fitter for him to be thinkin' about getting a house to live in.

CLARA. He doesn't think he *needs* to think about that; he thinks he's coming in here.

MRS. FISHER. [*Turning sharply, on her way back to the kitchen door*] Comin' in here to *live*, do you mean?

CLARA. That's what he told Frank, the day before yesterday.

MRS. FISHER. Well, he's very much mistaken if he does, I can tell you that. I'd like to be listenin' to that fellow seven days in the week I'd rather go over and live with your Aunt Ellie in Newark.

CLARA. [*Rising, and picking up her gloves from the table*] Well, that's about what you'll have to do, Mom, if you ever let them in on you. [*She stands looking straight out, unfastening her neckpiece.*]

MRS. FISHER. I won't let them in on me, don't fret. Your father 'ud have something to say about that.

CLARA. [*Slipping off her neckpiece*] Pop may not always *be* here, Mom. [*She turns around to her left and moves to a point above the table, and puts her fur and gloves down.*]

MRS. FISHER. Well, I'll be here, if he isn't; and the furniture is mine. And there's very little danger of my walkin' off and leavin' it to any son-in-law. [*The front door closes.*] I guess this is your Pop now, and I haven't even got the kettle on. [*She hurries out at the right. Clara glances at the hall door, Joe appears in it, and stands for the fraction of a second, irresolute.*]

JOE. Where's Mom?

CLARA. Out in the kitchen—why?

JOE. [*Motioning to her, causing the paper to drop from his hand*] Come here—don't let her hear you. [*Clara steps towards him, with a shade of apprehension in her face and manner.*] Listen Clara—Pop had some kind of a stroke this afternoon at his work.

CLARA. *Pop* did?

JOE. They found him layin' in front of one of the boilers.

CLARA. Oh, my God!

JOE. I tried to get you on the phone about four o'clock.

CLARA. I know—I came right over as soon as I came in.

JOE. *You* better tell Mom. [*He starts for the stairs, and Clara turns towards the kitchen door.*]

CLARA. [*Turning sharply back again*] Joe!

JOE. [*Stopping abruptly on the first step of the stairs*] What?

CLARA. Where's Pop now?

JOE. They took him to the Samaritan Hospital. I just came from there—they telephoned me to the office.

CLARA. Well, is he very bad?

JOE. *I* think he's done.

CLARA. Oh, don't say that, Joe!

JOE. That's what the doctor at the hospital sez.—He hasn't regained consciousness since three o'clock. So you'd better tell Mom to get her things on and go right down there. I've got to change my clothes; I went right up there from work. [*He starts up the stairs; and Clara moves vaguely towards the kitchen door. She stops and stands looking toward the kitchen in a controlled panic of indecision. Then, abruptly she whirls round and steps quickly back to the hall door.*]

CLARA. [*In a subdued voice*] Joe!

JOE. What?

CLARA. That Samaritan Hospital's at Broad and Ontario, isn't it?

JOE. Yes. [*She turns slowly and looks out, irresolute. Then she stoops down abstractedly and picks up the newspaper that Joe dropped. The parlor door opens sharply and Amy stands looking at her apprehensively. Their eyes meet.*]

AMY. What is it? [*Mrs. Fisher appears in the door at the right drying an agate-ware plate.*]

MRS. FISHER. Wasn't that your Pop that came in, Clara? [*Clara makes a deft, silencing gesture with her left hand to Amy, and moves towards the center table.*]

CLARA. No, it wasn't, Mom, it was the boy with the paper.

MRS. FISHER. [*Coming further into the room to see the clock*] I wonder what's keepin' him; he's late tonight. [*Clara leans against the center table, keeping her face averted from her mother.*] He's nearly always here before this. [*She moves back again towards the kitchen.*]

AMY. [*Crossing quickly down to Clara's left*] What is it, Clara?

MRS. FISHER. [*Turning and looking at Clara*] What's the matter with her? [*Clara tries to control her feelings.*]

AMY. I don't know what's the matter with her, Mom! Something *Joe* just told her—he's just gone upstairs.

MRS. FISHER. [*Coming forward apprehensively at Clara's right*] What is it, Clara—somethin' about your father? Is that what you're cryin' for?

AMY. Why don't you tell her, Clara?

MRS. FISHER. Go to the foot of the stairs, Amy, and call Joe. [*Amy steps towards the foot of the stairs.*] Something's happened to your father, I know it.

CLARA. [*Moving a step or two towards her mother*] Now, it's nothing to get upset about, Mom; he just took a little spell of some kind at his work this afternoon, and they had to take him to the hospital. [*Amy comes forward eagerly, and crosses to a point below the table.*] Joe just came from there, and he sez we'd better get our things on right away and go down there. [*Mrs. Fisher sways a step forward, letting the agate-ware plate slide from her hands to the floor. Amy steps towards her mother, lifting the chair from the right of the table and guiding her mother into it.*] Here, sit down here, Mom.

MRS. FISHER. [*Slightly dazed*] What is it she's sayin' happened to your Father, Amy? [*Amy passes back of the chair to her mother's right, and Clara comes to her left.*]

CLARA. Now, it's nothing to get excited about, Mom; it might be just a little heart attack or something that he took. [*She takes the towel from her mother's hand and hands it to Amy.*] Put this over there. [*Amy turns to the buffet.*]

MRS. FISHER. There was never anything the matter with your father's heart, Clara.

CLARA. Well, it's pretty hot in there where he works, you know that. [*Mrs. Fisher shakes her head up and down, knowingly.*] And men at Pop's age are always taking little spells of some kind.

MRS. FISHER. [*With a long, heavy sigh*] Ah, I guess it's a stroke, Clara.

CLARA. It might not be, Mom, you can't tell.

MRS. FISHER. That's how his two brothers went, you know.

CLARA. Amy, you'd better go to the telephone next door and tell Frank Hyland I won't be home. [*Amy hurries across towards the hall door, and Clara follows her, continuing her instructions.*] If he isn't home yet, tell Bertha to tell him to come right down to the Samaritan Hospital as soon as he comes. And tell Johnny Harbison to go to the corner for a taxi. [*The front door closes after Amy and Clara steps back to her mother's side.*]

MRS. FISHER. Is that where your father is, Clara, the Samaritan Hospital?

CLARA. Yes; it's right down there near where he works, at Broad and Ontario.

MRS. FISHER. [*Starting to cry*] Your poor father—I wonder what happened to him. [*Clara reflects her mother's sentiment.*]

CLARA. [*Picking up the plate*] Now, there's no use looking on the dark side of it already, Mom.

MRS. FISHER. No, but me gettin' his supper out there, and him not comin' home to it at all. And maybe *never* comin' home to it again, Clara, for all we know.

CLARA. He'll be home again, Mom—Pop is a strong man. [*She puts the plate on the buffet.*]

MRS. FISHER. [*Suddenly*] I guess he's dead, now, and you're not tellin' me.

CLARA. [*Coming to her mother's left*] He isn't dead, Mom; I'd have told you if he was.

MRS. FISHER. What did Joe say?

CLARA. Just what I told you; that he'd had a spell of some kind.

MRS. FISHER. Well, why didn't he tell me? What's he doin' upstairs, anyway?

CLARA. He's changing his clothes; he's got to go right back down there again.

MRS. FISHER. He's cryin' I guess. You know, it'll kill our poor Joe, Clara, if anything happens to your father.

CLARA. He sez we'd better go right down there, too, Mom; so you'd better go upstairs and fix yourself up a bit. Give me your apron.

MRS. FISHER. [*Rising and commencing to remove her apron*] I don't know whether I'll be able to dress myself now or not; my hands are like lead.

CLARA. You don't need to get all dressed up, Mom—just put on your black silk waist; that skirt's good enough. [*She goes towards the door at the right with the apron and goes out.*]

MRS. FISHER. [*Taking the comb from the back of her head and commencing to comb her hair*] Well, I'm not goin' down there lookin' like a dago woman.

CLARA. [*Coming quickly in again*] Nobody'll see you in the dark. [*She picks up the plate and towel from the buffet and straightens the runner.*]

MRS. FISHER. [*Moving aimlessly about in front of the mantelpiece*] It won't be dark in the *hospital* unless somethin' happens to the lights. [*Clara goes out again.*] Put that gas out under them potatoes, Clara, I just lit it. And you'd better pick up this room a bit while I'm upstairs, you don't know who might be comin' here if they hear about your father. [*She stops and looks helplessly about the room.*] Oh, dear, oh, dear, oh, dear! I don't know what I'm doin'. [*Clara comes in again.*] Take all them papers off that table, Clara, and put them in the kitchen.

CLARA. [*Crossing to the table and folding and gatherering up the various papers*] You'd better bring your umbrella down with you, Mom, when you go up—it looked like rain when I came in.

MRS. FISHER. Oh, and I let our Amy take my rubbers the last day she was here, and she never brings anything back.

CLARA. [*Taking the papers out into the kitchen*] You won't need rubbers.

MRS. FISHER. Oh, I get all my feet wet, when I don't have rubbers. [*She is facing the hall door, fastening the old-fashioned brooch at her throat. Aubrey frames himself in the door, with a bandage around his head, and looking a bit battered.*] My God, what happened to you, now?

AUBREY. [*Coming forward at the left, removing his hat*] It's beginning to rain. [*He places his hat and cane on the table, and stands in front of the table removing his gloves.*]

MRS. FISHER. [*Following him with her eyes*] Never mind the rain, the rain didn't do that to you. [*She comes forward at his left. Clara comes in and stands over near the door at the right, looking at him.*] I guess you ran into somebody, didn't you?

AUBREY. [*With a shade of nonchalance*] Don't get excited, Mother—just a little misunderstanding on the part of the traffic officer.

MRS. FISHER. You don't mean to tell me that you ran into a traffic officer! [*Clara comes forward at the right.*]

AUBREY. Control, now, Little Mother, I assure there is no occasion for undue solicitation. [*He turns and sees Clara.*] Good evening, Mrs. Hyland.

AUBREY. Hello! What happened to your head?

MRS. FISHER. You look like a bandit.

AUBREY. The veriest trifle, Mrs. Hyland—just a little spray from the windshield.

MRS. FISHER. Where's the car you borrowed? Smashed, I guess, ain't it?

AUBREY. The car I borrowed, Mother Fisher, is now in the hands of the bandits of the law. The judicial gentlemen, who have entered into a conspiracy with the regulators of traffic—to collect fines from motorists—by ordering them to go one way—and then swearing that they told them to go another.

MRS. FISHER. Never mind your fancy talk, we've heard too much of that already! I want to know who you killed—or what you did run into; for I know you ran into somethin'. And where's the automobile that someone was fool enough to lend you?

AUBREY. The automobile, Little Mother, is perfectly safe-parked and pasturing—in the courtyard of the Twenty-second and Hunting Park Avenue Police Station.

MRS. FISHER. Did you get arrested, too?

AUBREY. I accompanied the officer as far an the station house, yes; and I told them a few things while I was there, too, about the condition of traffic in this city.

MRS. FISHER. I guess they told you a few things, too, didn't they?

AUBREY. Beg pardon?

MRS. FISHER. [*Starting abruptly for the hall door*] Never mind; you're welcome.

CLARA. You'd better change your shoes, Mom; you can't go down there with those.

MRS. FISHER. [*Pointing toward the cellar door*] See if my long black coat's in the cellarway there. [*Clara goes quickly to the cellar door, opens it, and looks for the coat.*] That fellow's got me so upset I don't know what I'm doin'. [*She goes out the hall door and to her left, up the stairs. Aubrey moves over to the chair at the right where Mrs. Fisher collapsed, and sits down—quite ruffled in his dignity. Clara closes the cellar door and, with a glance toward the hall door, comes quckly forward at Aubrey's left.*]

CLARA. What did they do, fine you, Aubrey?

AUBREY. They were all set to fine me; but when I got through with them they didn't have a leg to stand on. So they tried to cover themselves up as gracefully as possible, by trumping up a charge against me of driving an automobile without a license.

CLARA. What did they do, take the automobile *away* from you?

AUBREY. Nothing of the sort; they simply complied with the usual procedure in a case of this kind—which is to release the defendent on bond, pending the extent of the victim's injuries.

CLARA. Was there somebody injured?

AUBREY. The traffic cop that ran into me, yes.

CLARA. For God's sake, couldn't you find anybody but the traffic cop to run into!

AUBREY. I did not run into him, Mrs. Hyland—you don't understand the circumstances of the case.

CLARA. Well, I understand this much about them—that they can give you ten years for a thing like that. And it'd just serve you right if they did, too. Borrowin' people's automobiles, and knowing no more about running them than I do. [*She turns away to her right and moves across above the table towards the hall door.*]

AUBREY. No time like the present to learn, Mrs. Hyland.

CLARA. [*Turning to him sharply*] Well, you'll very likely have plenty of time, from now on—if that officer is seriously injured. [*She continues over and down to the window at the left, where she draws the drape aside and looks anxiously down the street for the taxi.*]

AUBREY. He was faking a broken arm around there when I left—but it's a wonder to me the poor straw ride wasn't signed on the dotted line; for he ran head on right into me.

CLARA. [*Crossing back towards him, in front of the Morris chair*] Was *he* in a car, too?

AUBREY. No, he was jaywalking—trying to beat me to the crossing, after giving me the right of way.

CLARA. Where did this thing happen?

AUBREY. Broad and Erie Avenue, I wouldn't kid you.

CLARA. Did they take the cop to the hospital?

AUBREY. Yes, we took him over there in the car.

CLARA. Did they let *you* run it?

AUBREY. Repeat the question, Mrs. Hyland.

CLARA. You heard me—I don't need to repeat it. And take that silly-lookin' bandage off your head, before Amy sees you; and don't frighten the life out of her. [*She steps up to the hall door and glances out.*] She's got enough to worry her now without looking at you. [*Aubrey rises, and, detaching the handkerchief from around his head, moves across to a point above the center table.*]

AUBREY. Is my wife here?

CLARA. She's next door, telephoning, yes; and she'll be back in a minute. [*Coming forward a step or two at the left*] Pop just had a stroke of some kind at his work this afternoon, Joe just told us.

AUBREY. What are you doing, kidding me?

CLARA. [*Starting to cry*] No, of course I'm not kidding you! What would I be kidding you about a thing like that for? [*She crosses down and across in front of the center table. The front door closes.*]

AUBREY. Where is he now?

CLARA. They took him to the Samaritan Hospital; we're just going down there. [*Amy appears in the hall door, and stands looking questioningly at Aubrey.*]

AMY. What's the matter, Aubrey? [*He turns and looks at her.*]

AUBREY. [*Extending his arm and hand in a magnificent gesture*] Well! [*Amy comes forward to her husband.*] The old kid herself!

AMY. What is it, Aubrey?

AUBREY. [*Taking her in his arms*] Nothing in the world but this, Baby. [*He kisses her affectionately.*]

CLARA. Did you get Frank on the phone, Amy? [*Mrs. Fisher can be heard hurrying down the stairs.*]

AMY. [*Crossing above Aubrey and speaking directly to Clara*] He wasn't home yet; I told the girl to tell him as soon as he came in.

MRS. FISHER. [*Coming through the hall door, and tossing her little knit-jacket onto the small stand at the left of the mantelpiece.*] Clara, is that automobile-cab here yet?

CLARA. It'll be here in a minute, Mom.

MRS. FISHER. What do you think of this fellow, Amy—runnin' wild through the city breakin' policemen's bones! We didn't have enough trouble without that—with your poor father layin' dead for all we know—down in the Jewish hospital. [*She starts to cry and steps down to the window at the left to look out for the taxi-cab.*] It's enough to make a body light-headed.

CLARA. Where's your coat, Mom?

MRS. FISHER. [*Turning to her*] Isn't it there in the cellarway?

CLARA. No, I just looked.

MRS. FISHER. [*Going up to the hall door*] It must be upstairs. Joe!

AMY. [*At Aubrey's right*] I thought you were out at the Automobile Show, Aubrey.

MRS. FISHER. [*At the foot of the stairs*] Listen, Joe—

AUBREY. I had a little mix up at Broad and Erie Avenue.

AMY. You didn't get hurt, did you?

[*Mrs. Fisher and Aubrey, speaking together*]

MRS. FISHER. Throw down my long black coat; you'll find it on a hook there in the hall closet. [*She starts for the buffet.*]

AUBREY. Nothing but a scratch or two, here on my forehead, from the glass in the windshield. Just a little shake-up.

MRS. FISHER. [*Stopping and turning sharply at the right of the center table*] He nearly killed a traffic officer!—That's how much of a little shake-up it was. [*She continues to the buffet, where Clara is standing.*] Get out of my way, Clara, till I get a clean handkerchief out of here. [*She pushes Clara out of her way and opens the left hand drawer of the buffet and rummages for a handkerchief. Clara passes across in front of the center table to the window at the left.*]

AMY. You *didn't*, Aubrey, did you?

AUBREY. Certainly not, Amy—your mother's raving. [*Mrs. Fisher finds the handkerchief, slams the drawer shut and turns.*]

MRS. FISHER. The man's in the hospital!—I don't know what more you want. [*The big black coat lands at the foot of the stairs with a thud, causing Mrs. Fisher to start nervously, then she hurries across at the back towards the hall door, tucking the folded handkerchief at her waist.*]

AMY. Is he, Aubrey?

AUBREY. Do you think I'd be here, Kid, if he was?

MRS. FISHER. [*On the way over*] You *wouldn't* be here, only that someone was fool enough to bail you out; instead of lettin' you stay in where you couldn't be killin' people. [*Clara has stepped up to the foot of the stairs and picked the coat up immediately it fell, and now stands holding it for her mother to put on; but Mrs. Fisher disregards her, going straight out to the foot of the stairs and calling shrilly up to Joe.*] Joe, why don't you tell a body when you're goin' to throw a thing down that way, and not be frightenin' the life out of people! [*She comes back into the room again and Clara assists her. Amy stands above the center table looking wide-eyed at Aubrey, who sways forward at the left, and, crossing below the center table to the chair at the right, where he has been previously seated, sits down.*]

CLARA. Aren't you going to put on another waist, Mom?

MRS. FISHER. No, this one is good enough—I'll keep the coat buttoned up. Put that collar inside.

AMY. [*In a lowered tone*] Are you out on bail, Aubrey?

AUBREY. They always bail a man in a case like this, Amy; they've got my car on their hands.

MRS. FISHER. [*Buttoning the coat, and moving to the mirror over the mantelpiece*] Get my hat, will you, Clara?

CLARA. [*Starting for the hall door*] Where is it, upstairs?

MRS. FISHER. No, it's in the parlor there, inside the top of the Victrola. [*Clara comes back and goes into the parlor.*]

AMY. Why didn't you bring the car back with you, Aubrey?—That fellow might want it tomorrow.

AUBREY. I'll have it for him all right; I've got to call around there for it Monday morning at ten o'clock. [*Mrs. Fisher turns sharply from her primping at the mirror.*]

MRS. FISHER. I guess you've got to go down there to a hearing Monday morning at ten o'clock—[*Amy turns and looks at her mother.*] and pay your fine! [*Speaking directly to Amy*] I guess that's the automobile he's got to call for. [*Clara hurries out of the parlor brushing the dust off an old black hat, with a bunch of cherries on it.*]

CLARA. I'd better go out and get a whisk broom and dust this, Mom.

MRS. FISHER. [*Turning to her nervously*] No, nevermind, it's good enough, give it to me.

CLARA. [*Crossing below her mother, to the right*] Your coat needs dusting. [*She takes a whisk broom from hook just inside the kitchen door.*]

AMY. How much did they fine you, Aubrey?

AUBREY. They didn't fine me at all.

MRS. FISHER. [*Settling her hat*] They'll do that Monday.

AUBREY. Time'll tell that, Mother Fisher. [*Clara hurries back and starts brushing her mother's coat.*]

MRS. FISHER. And you'll pay it, too, or go to jail; and it'ud just be the price of you.

AUBREY. They didn't seem very anxious to do any fining today, after I got through telling it to them.

MRS. FISHER. Am I all right, Clara?

AUBREY. I took a slam at the Pennsylvania Railroad, too, while I was at it.

MRS. FISHER. You're always takin' slams at somethin'; that's what's leavin' you under bail right now. Are you ready, Clara? [*She hurries to the foot of the stairs.*]

CLARA. [*Hurrying back to the kitchen with the whisk broom*] Yes, I'm ready.

AUBREY. Nevermind about that, Mother Fisher.

MRS. FISHER. [*Calling up the stairs*] Are you goin' down there with us, Joe?

JOE. [*From upstairs*] Comin' right down. [*Mrs. Fisher comes in to the mantelpiece and picks up her gloves. Clara hurries in from the kitchen again to the center table and picks up her neckpiece and gloves.*]

AUBREY. Only don't be surprised if you hear of a very quiet little shake-up very soon—in the Department of Public Safety.

MRS. FISHER. Are you warm enough with that coat, Clara?

CLARA. Yes, I'm all right. How about the umbrella?

MRS. FISHER. I think it's out there in the hall rack; look and see. [*Clara hurries out into the hallway, and Mrs. Fisher stands putting on her gloves. Amy crosses Aubrey's left.*]

AMY. [*Very quietly*] How much bail did they put you under, Aubrey?

AUBREY. One thousand berries, Amy. [*Mrs. Fisher looks over at them keenly.*]

AMY. A thousand dollars!

AUBREY. That's regulation—[*Amy turns and gives her mother a troubled look, and Mrs. Fisher moves forward at the left to a point where she can see Aubrey.*] A little chickenfeed for the stoolpigeons.

MRS. FISHER. Did *he* say they put him under a thousand dollars' bail?

AUBREY. That's what I said, Mrs. Fisher, one thousand trifles—I wouldn't kid you.

MRS. FISHER. You wouldn't kid anybody that'd listen to you for five minutes. And who did you get to *go* a thousand dollars bail for you?

AUBREY. Don't be alarmed, Little Mother—I saw that the affair was kept strictly within the family

MRS. FISHER. What do you mean?

AUBREY. Your other son-in-law—was kind enough to come forward. [*Clara hurries in from the hallway with the umbrella, and comes forward at the extreme left.*]

MRS. FISHER. Clara's husband!

AUBREY. That's the gentleman, Mrs. Fisher—Mr. Francis X. Hyland.

MRS. FISHER. [*Helplessly*] My God! [*She turns around to her right till she locates Clara.*] Do you hear that, Clara?

CLARA. What?

MRS. FISHER. He got Frank Hyland to go his bail for a thousand dollars.

CLARA. [*Looking bitterly at Aubrey*] What did you do, write him another letter?

AUBREY. That was not necessary, Mrs. Hyland, not giving you a short answer. Your husband was fortunate enough to see the whole affair from the trolley car. He was just returning from his business, and happened to be on the trolley car that ran into me.

MRS. FISHER. How many more things ran into you—besides traffic cops and trolley cars! I suppose a couple of the buildin's ran into you too, didn't they? [*Joe hurries in from the hall door buttoning his overcoat.*]

JOE. Are you ready, Mom?

CLARA. [*Going up to the hall door*] Yes, we're ready. [*Joe comes forward at the extreme left, looking questioningly from one to the other. Clara goes out into the hall.*]

AUBREY. You'll find out all about that Monday morning, Mrs. Fisher.

MRS. FISHER. [*Moving up towards the hall door*] Well, see that nothin' else runs into you between now and Monday.

JOE. What's the matter?

MRS. FISHER. We don't want Frank Hyland losin' any thousand-dollar bills on account of you.

JOE. What's happened, Mom?

MRS. FISHER. [*Turning to Joe, and pointing at Aubrey with a wide gesture*] Why, this crazy Jack here's been runnin' into everything in the city but ourselves; and he got himself arrested; and Frank Hyland had to bail him out for a thousand dollars. [*She starts to cry.*]

JOE. What were you doin', Aubrey, joy-ridin'?

MRS. FISHER. No!—he was trolley-ridin'—and traffie cop-ridin'—and every other kind of ridin'—in an automobile that he borrowed.

CLARA. [*Hurrying in from the hallway*] I think I see that taxi coming, Mom.

MRS. FISHER. [*Starting towards the hall door*] Come on here, Joe. [*Joe crosses up at the left of the center table to the mirror over the mantelpiece, looking disapprovingly at Aubrey. Aubrey rises and strolls over to a point in front of the center table.*] How do we get down there, Clara?

CLARA. Right down Erie Ave.

AUBREY. Too bad I left that car down there at the station house, I could have run you down there. [*They all turn and look at him; and Mrs. Fisher, with poison in her right eye, moves forward at the left of the center table, with a level, ominous slowness.*]

MRS. FISHER. *You* wouldn't run *me* down there—don't fret—not if you had a thousand cars. There's enough of us in the hospital as it is. [*Aubrey simply regards her from a great height.*] And don't you come down there neither—for you'd only start talkin', and that'd finish Pop quicker than a stroke. [*There's a startling hoot from the taxicab horn outside, which almost throws Mrs. Fisher from her balance.*]

CLARA. [*Going out*] Come on, Joe.

JOE. [*Following her out*] Ain't you comin' down to the hospital, Amy?

MRS. FISHER. [*Going out*] No, you'd better stay here, Amy—there'd better be some one of us here—or that fellow'll be runnin' into somethin' else. You ought to have somethin' heavier on you than that fur, Clara. [*Aubrey sits down at the left of the center table.*]

CLARA. [*In the hallway*] I'm all right, we'll be down there in a few minutes.

MRS. FISHER. Have you got your coat buttoned up good, Joe? [*The front door closes after them. Amy turns from the hall door, where she has been standing, seeing them out, and comes forward to the back of the chair at the left of the center table, where Aubrey is sitting.*]

AMY. Where's your toupé, Aubrey? [*Touching the sticking-plasters on his forehead*]

AUBREY. In my pocket here.

AMY. [*Stroking his hair*] Is your head hurting you?

AUBREY. [*Reaching for her hand and drawing it down over his left shoulder*] Not a bit, Honey—just a couple of little scratches. [*He kisses her hand. She raises her eyes and looks straight ahead, with a troubled expression.*]

AMY. Aubrey, what do you think they'll do to you down there Monday?

AUBREY. Now, don't you worry about that, Sweetheart; I'll be right there if they try to pull anything. [*She moves over thoughtfully towards the upper right hand corner of the center table. Then a new thought occurs to her, and she turns her head and looks at him narrowly.*]

AMY. You hadn't had anything to drink, had you, Aubrey?

AUBREY. [*Looking at her quickly*] Who, me?

AMY. I mean I thought somebody might have treated you or something.

AUBREY. [*Making a statement*] I had a glass of Champagne six months ago with a friend of mine in his suite at the Ritz-Carlton Hotel, and I haven't had a drink of anything since.

AMY. You better take off your overcoat, Aubrey; we'll have to stay here till they get back. [*He gets up end commences to remove the overcoat.*]

AUBREY. Yes, I guess we will.—I wonder how your Father is.

AMY. [*Taking the overcoat from him*] Pretty bad I guess—or they wouldn't have sent for Joe. [*She takes the coat up to the sofa at the right of the mantelpiece, and Aubrey takes a huge cigar from his vest pocket and feels for a match.*] I'll get you a match, Aubrey. [*She goes out into the kitchen, and Aubrey moves to a point above the center table, biting the tip of his cigar.*]

AUBREY. I thought I had some here, but I guess I haven't. Did they send for Joe?

AMY. Yes, they telephoned for him, to the place where he works.

AUBREY. Your mother said it was a stroke.

AMY. [*Entering with some matches*] I guess that's what it is, too; his two brothers died that way.

AUBREY. [*Taking the matches from her*] I'm sorry to hear that, Amy. But, you mustn't worry, now, Kid.

AMY. It isn't only that I'm worried about, Aubrey—I'm thinking about you—Monday. [*She takes hold of the lapels of his coat and almost cries.*]

AUBREY. [*Putting his arm around her*] Now, listen to me, Baby—you know I'd tell you, don't you, if there was anything to worry about.

AMY. But, they're getting awfully strict in this city; there's been so many automobile accidents lately.

AUBREY. They're only strict, Honey, when a man is driving under the influence of liquor. [*There's a slight pause, and Amy thinks hard.*]

AMY. What if that traffic cop is hurt bad, Aubrey?

AUBREY. It'd only be a fine for reckless driving, even if they could prove it *was* reckless driving; and I can prove it was the copper's fault. [*Detaching himself from her*] So they'll very likely be *apologizing* to me around there Monday morning, instead of fining me. [*He moves across and down to the window at the left—with ever so slight a touch of swagger.*]

AMY. Oh, I wouldn't care if they only fined you, Aubrey; because I could go back to work until it was paid.

AUBREY. [*Looking out the window*] You'll never go back to work, Kid, while I'm on the boat.

AMY. I wouldn't mind it, Aubrey.

AUBREY. Not while your *my* wife, Amy. [*He half turns to her, with considerable consequence.*] I'd rather leave the Pennsylvania Railroad *flat*; and go out and take one of the jobs that have been offered me where they pay a man what he's worth.

AMY. You don't think they might do anything else to you, do you, Aubrey?

AUBREY. [*Turning to her*] Oh, they might try to take away my license.

AMY. You haven't got a license, have you?

AUBREY. [*Turning back to the window*] No, I neglected to attend to it this year.

AMY. They can fine you for that, can't they?

AUBREY. Driving an automobile without a license, you mean?

AMY. Yes.

AUBREY. Sure—they can fine you for anything unless you know

how to beat them to it. [*He strikes the match on the arm of the Morris chair at his right. Amy rests her hands on the center table, and looks straight out, wretchedly.*]

AMY. [*Tonelessly*] What is it they send them to prison for, Aubrey? [*He is just holding the lighted match to the cigar, and, consequently, is unable to answer her immediately. The front doorbell rings. She glances apprehensively in the direction of the hall door, then meets his eyes.*] I wonder who that is.

AUBREY. [*Tossing the burnt match into the window at his left*] Do you want me to answer it?

AMY. I wish you would, Aubrey; it might be something about Pop. [*He crosses in front of the Morris chair and up at the left of the center table to the mirror over the mantelpiece, where he stands settling his tie and vest. Amy turns to the couch and gathers up his coat, then steps forward to the center table and picks up his hat and the bandage that he took off his head.*]

AUBREY. [*Touching the plasters on his forehead*] Does my head look all right?

AMY. [*Glancing at him, as she goes towards the hooks at the head of the cellar stairs*] Yes, it's all right, Aubrey.

AUBREY. Wait a minute—[*He steps to her side and takes the carnation from the buttonhole of his overcoat, then steps back to the mirror and fixes it in his sack coat.*]

AMY. Hurry up, Aubrey. [*The doorbell rings again.*]

AUBREY. [*Going out into the hallway*] All right—all right. [*Amy hangs the overcoat and hat up, then turns, opens the cellar door, and tosses the bandage down the cellar stairs. Then she crosses quickly to a point in front of the mantelpiece and listens intently.*]

GILL. [*At the front door*] Good evenin'.

AUBREY. Good evening, sir.

GILL. Is this where Mr. Fisher lives?

AUBREY. This is Mr. Fisher's is residence, yes, sir. What can I do for you?

GILL. Why, I got some things of his here that the boss ast me to leave.

AUBREY. Oh, just step inside for a minute. Getting a little colder I think. [*The front door closes.*]

GILL. Well, we can look for it any time, now.

AUBREY. Will you just step in this way, please? [*Aubrey enters from the hallway.*] There's a gentleman here, Amy, with some things belonging to your father. Just come right in. [*Aubrey comes forward a few steps at the left; and Gill enters.*]

GILL. Good evenin'.

AMY. Good evening.

AUBREY. This is my wife, Mrs. Piper.

GILL. [*Nodding*] How do you do. [*Amy nods.*]

AUBREY. Mrs. Piper is Mr. Fisher's daughter. The rest of the folks have gone down to the hospital.

GILL. I see. [*Turning to Amy*] Have you *heard* anything from the hospital yet?

AMY. Not yet, no.

AUBREY. We didn't know anything about it at all, till fifteen minutes ago.

GILL. It's too bad.

AUBREY. Those hospitals won't tell you anything.

AMY. Do you work with my father?

GILL. No, ma'm, I'm a twister on the second floor. But, one of the machinist's-helpers that works with your father knows I live out this way, so he ast me to stop by with these things on my way home. [*He crosses towards Amy, with a hat and overcoat, and a more or less discolored lunch box.*]

AMY. [*Taking the things*] Thanks ever so much.

GILL. There's just the overcoat and hat, and his lunch box.

AMY. Thanks.

GILL. McMahon sez if he comes across anything else he'll let me know.

AMY. [*Crossing to the sofa with the things*] No, I don't imagine there's anything else.

GILL. If there is, I'll bring it up.

AMY. Well, that's very nice of you; I'm ever so much obliged to you. [*She comes back towards Gill.*]

AUBREY. Who is this McMahon?

GILL. He's one of the machinist's-helpers down there.

AUBREY. I see.

AMY. Were you there when my father was taken sick?

GILL. No, ma'm, I wasn't. I don't think there was anybody there, to tell you the truth. McMahon sez he was talkin' to him at a quarter of three, and he sez when he came back from the annex at three o'clock, he found Mr. Fisher layin' in front of number five.

AUBREY. [*With a suggestion of professionalism*] Very likely a little touch of Angina Pectoria. [*Gill looks at him.*]

GILL. The doctor down there sez he thought it was a stroke.

AUBREY. Same thing.

AMY. Won't you sit down, Mr.—a—

GILL. No, thank you, ma'm, I can't stay; I've got to get along out home. [*There's a rapping out at the right. They all look in the direction of the kitchen.*]

AMY. Oh, I guess it's Mrs. Harbison—I'll go. [*She goes out at the right.*]

AUBREY. [*Crossing above Gill towards the right*] Don't stand out there talking, now, Amy, with nothing around you. [*Surveying himself in the buffet mirror at the right*] Do you live up this way, Governor?

GILL. No, sir, I live out Richmond way.

AUBREY. I see.

GILL. I take number thirty-two over Allegheny Avenue.

AUBREY. [*Turning and moving over towards the center table*] Too bad my car's laid up, I could run you out there.

GILL. Oh, that's all right; the trolley takes me right to the door.

AUBREY. I had to turn it in Thursday to have the valves ground.

AMY. [*Appearing in the kitchen door*] I'm wanted on the telephone, Aubrey; I'll be right in. Will you excuse me for a minute?

GILL. That's all right, ma'm; I'm goin' right along meself.

AUBREY. Very likely some word from the hospital.

GILL. I hope it ain't any bad news.

AUBREY. Well, you've got to be prepared for most anything, Governor, when a man gets up around the old three-score mark.

GILL. That's true, a lot of them push off about that age.

AUBREY. Especially when a man's worked hard all his life.

GILL. Yes, I guess Mr. Fisher's worked pretty hard.

AUBREY. Not an excuse in the world for it, either.—I've said to him a thousand times if I've said to him once, "Well, Pop, when are you going to take the big rest?" "Oh," he'd say, "I'll have lots of time to rest when I'm through." "All right," I'd say, "go ahead; only let me tell you, Pop, you're going to be through ahead of schedule if you don't take it soon."

GILL. Well, I guess it comes pretty hard on a man that's been active all his life to quit all of a sudden.

AUBREY. Well, he wouldn't have to quit exactly.—I mean, he's a handy man; he could putter around the house. There are lots of little things here and there that I'm not any too well satisfied with. [*He glances around the room.*]

GILL. Is Mr. Fisher's wife livin'?

AUBREY. Yes, she's here with us too.

GILL. Well, that makes it nice.

AUBREY. Well, it's a pretty big house here; so when I married last June, I said, "Come ahead, the more the merrier." [*He laughs a little.*]

GILL. 'Tis a pretty big house this.

AUBREY. Yes, they don't make them like this anymore, Governor. Put up by the McNeil people out here in Jenkintown.

GILL. Oh, yes.

AUBREY. They just put up the twenty of them—kind of sample houses—ten on that side and ten on this. Of course, these on this side have the southern exposure—so a man's got to do quite a bit of wire-pulling to get hold of one of these.

GILL. You've got to do some wire-pullin' to get hold of *any* kind of a house these days.

AUBREY. Well, I have a friend here in town that's very close to the city architect, and he was able to fix it for me.

GILL. [*Glancing toward the window, at the left*] It's a nice street.

AUBREY. Nice in summer.

GILL. I was surprised when I saw it, because when I ast a taxicab-driver down here where it was, he said he never heard of it.

AUBREY. [*Looking at him keenly*] Never heard of Cresson Street?

GILL. He said not.

AUBREY. [*With pitying amusement*] He must be an awful straw-ride.

GILL. I had to ast a police officer.

AUBREY. Well, I'll tell you, Governor—I don't suppose they have many *calls* for taxicabs out this way. You see, most everybody in through here has his own *car*.

GILL. I see

AUBREY. Some of them have a half dozen, for that matter. [*He laughs, a bit consequentially.*]

GILL. [*Starting for the parlor doors*] There certainly is plenty of them knockin' around.

AUBREY. All over the ice. [*Aubrey indicates the hall door.*] This way, Governor.

GILL. [*Turning towards the hall door*] Oh, excuse me.

AUBREY. [*Moving towards the hall door*] Those doors go into the parlor.

GILL. I see. [*He turns at the hall door*] A fellow was tellin' me over here in the cigar store that there was quite a smash-up about a half hour ago down here at Broad and Erie Avenue.

AUBREY. That so?

GILL. He sez there was some *nut* down there runnin' into everything in sight. He sez he even ran into the traffic cop; and broke his arm. Can you imagine what they'll *do* to that guy, knockin' the traffic cop down!

AUBREY. What was the matter with him, was he stewed?

GILL. *No*—the fellow in the cigar store sez he was just a nut. He sez they didn't know where he got hold of this car; he sez it didn't belong to him. I guess he picked it up somewhere. They took it away from him and pinched him. [*Starting to go out*] So I guess he won't be runnin' into anything else for a while.

AUBREY. [*Following him out*] Traffic's in pretty bad shape in this town right now.

GILL. Certainly is. Why, a man's not safe walkin' along the sidewalk, these days. I hope your wife'll hear some good news.

AUBREY. Well, while there's life there's hope, you know.

GILL. That's right. No use lookin' on the dark side of things. [*Amy enters from the right, with a wide-eyed, wan expression, and comes slowly down to the center table.*]

AUBREY. Where do you get your car, Governor?

GILL. Why, I can get one right at the corner here, and transfer.

AUBREY. Oh, that's right, so you can. Well, we're ever so much obliged to you.

GILL. Don't mention it.

AUBREY. Goodnight, sir.

GILL. Goodnight. [*The door closes.*]

AUBREY. [*Coming in from the hall door*] When did *you* come in, Amy? [*He stops to look at himself in the mantelpiece mirror.*]

AMY. [*Without turning*] I came in the side door; I thought that man'd be still here.

AUBREY. [*Coming down to her*] Well, Kid, what's the good word?

AMY. [*Breaking down*] Aubrey, Pop is dead. [*She buries her face in the lapel of his coat. He takes her in his arms, looks straight ahead, and there is a long pause—during which Amy cries hard.*]

AUBREY. Don't let it get you, Honey—you have nothing to regret; and nothing to fear. The Kid from West Philly'll never go back on you—you know that, don't you, Baby? [*She continues to cry.*] You know that, don't you, Amy? [*She doesn't answer him.*] Amy.

AMY. What?

AUBREY. You know I'm with you, don't you?

AMY. Yes. [*He kisses her hair affectionately.*]

AUBREY. Don't cry, Honey; the old man's better off than we are. He knows all about it now. [*He kisses her again; then detaches himself and moves over and down at the left of the center table.*]

AMY. What do you think we ought to do, Aubrey?

AUBREY. There's nothing at all that you can do that I can see, Sweetheart; except to sit tight till the folks get back. They'll be

down there themselves in a few minutes, and they'll know all
about it.

AMY. They said that Pop died at a quarter of six.

AUBREY. Was that the hospital on the telephone?

AMY. Yes.

AUBREY. [*Moving up to a point above the center table again*] Something
we ought to have in here, Amy; a telephone—not be letting the
whole neighborhood in on our business. [*Amy leans on the back
of the chair at the right and cries softly.*]

AUBREY. Now, pull yourself together, Sweetheart. [*He crosses to her
and puts his arm around her shoulders.*]

AMY. This is where Pop always used to sit in the evening.—It'll
seem funny not to see him here anymore. [*She breaks down
again.*]

AUBREY. [*After a slight pause*] The old gent had to go some time. [*He
passes back of her, comes forward at the right and stands, looking at
the tip of his cigar.*] Your mother'll have you and me to comfort
her now. [*He strolls across below the center table and stops, thinking
profoundly. Amy sinks down on the chair dejectedly.*]

AMY. I don't know how Mom'll keep this house going now, just on
Joe's pay.

AUBREY. Why don't you say something to your mother about letting
us come in here? She'll need a man in the house. And my salary
'ud cover the rent.

AMY. Mom doesn't have to pay rent, Aubrey—she owns this house.
Pop left it to her. He made his will out the week after we were
married. [*Aubrey looks at her keenly.*] Clara got him to do it.

AUBREY. Who's the executor, do you know?

AMY. Clara is. [*Aubrey nods comprehendingly.*]

AUBREY. [*Looking away off*] Too bad your father didn't make *me* the
executor of that will—I could have saved him a lot of money.
[*He replaces the cigar in his mouth.*]

AMY. I suppose he thought on account of Clara being the oldest.

AUBREY. I wonder why your father never *liked* me.

AMY. Pop never said he didn't like you, Aubrey.

AUBREY. I always tried to be clubby with him. I used to slap him on the back whenever I spoke to him.

AMY. Pop was always very quiet.

AUBREY. And the Kid from West Philly had too much to say. Well—forgive and forget.—It's all over now.—And the old man can be as quiet as he likes. [*Amy cries again, and there is a pause. Aubrey stands smoking.*]

AMY. [*Pulling herself together and getting up*] You haven't had anything to eat tonight yet, have you, Aubrey?

AUBREY. [*Coming out of his abstraction, and sauntering up at the left of the center table*] Don't worry about me, Sweetheart.

AMY. [*Going to the buffet drawer at the right for an apron*] I'll get you something.

AUBREY. It'll be all the same at the finish—whether I've had my dinner or not. [*He rests his fist on the table, throws his head back, and looks to the stars.*] "Sic transit gloria mundi." And we never get used to it. [*He moves across to the upper right hand corner of the center table.*] The paths of glory lead but to the grave. [*He stops again, leans on the table and looks out and away off.*] And yet we go on,—building up big fortunes—only to leave them to the generations yet unborn. Well [*He moves forward to the chair at the right.*]—so it goes. [*He sits down, throws one leg across his knee, and shakes his head up and down slowly.*] And so it will always go, I suppose. "Sic transit gloria mundi."

AMY. [*Standing at his right*] What does that mean, Aubrey? "Sic transit gloria mundi"?

AUBREY. [*Casually*] It's an old saying from the French—meaning, "we're here today, and gone tomorrow."

AMY. [*Looking out, wretchedly*] I'm worried about tomorrow, Aubrey. [*He looks at her*]

AUBREY. What are you worried about, Sweetheart?

AMY. I mean Monday.

AUBREY. [*Extending his hand towards her*] Now—"sufficient unto the day is the evil thereof"—you know that, don't you, Baby? [*She takes his hand and moves over to the back of his chair.*]

AMY. But, you didn't have a license, Aubrey. And if that traffic officer should be seriously injured—

AUBREY. Don't you worry about that, Sweetheart—we're here today; and if he's seriously injured—we'll know all about it on Monday. [*The curtain commences to descend slowly.*] "Sic transit gloria mundi."

THE CURTAIN IS DOWN

⇛ ACT III ⇚

Same as preceding Act—the following Monday, about four o'clock in the afternoon. Mrs. Fisher is seated at the right of the center table, in black, watching Mr. Rogers, the insurance agent opposite her, writing on various papers. Clara, also in mourning, is standing in back of her father's chair, watching Mr. Rogers.

ROGERS. [*Handing Mrs. Fisher an insurance receipt*] Now, will you just sign that, Mrs. Fisher. Right on that line there. [*He hands her his fountain pen.*]

MRS. FISHER. [*After a sincere attempt to write with the fountain pen*] It won't write.

CLARA. Press on it a bit, Mom.

MRS. FISHER. I *am* pressin' on it.

ROGERS. Just let me have it a second, Mrs. Fisher. [*She hands him the pen.*]

MRS. FISHER. I never saw one of them fountain pens yet that'd write.

ROGERS. [*Holding the pen out and shaking it, in an attempt to force the ink forward*] They cut up a little once in a while. [*Mrs. Fisher looks keenly to see if her carpet is being stained.*]

MRS. FISHER. I gave one to my son the Christmas before last, and it's been in that drawer there from that day to this.

ROGERS. [*Handing her the pen again*] There we are. I think you'll find that all right.

MRS. FISHER. Right here?

ROGERS. That's right. [*He commences to collect his papers.*]

MRS. FISHER. [*Writing*] It's writin' now all right.

ROGERS. It's usually pretty satisfactory. [*She hands him the receipt, and he hands her another.*] And that one also, Mrs. Fisher, if you please.

MRS. FISHER. In the same place?

ROGERS. Yes; right on the dotted line. It's just a duplicate. [*She looks at him sharply, then signs it and hands it back to him; and he puts it into his wallet. Mrs. Fisher looks distrustfully at the point of the fountain pen.*]

MRS. FISHER. Here's the pen.

ROGERS. Thank you. [*He signs a check and looks at it.*]

MRS. FISHER. [*Half-turning towards the cellar door*] See if that cellar door is closed, Clara, I feel a draught from somewhere. [*Clara goes and sees that the door is closed.*]

ROGERS. [*Handing a check*] There you are, Mrs. Fisher, one thousand dollars.

MRS. FISHER. Thank you. [*Clara comes forward again.*]

ROGERS. [*Collecting his things*] That's money we like to pay, Mrs. Fisher, and money we don't like to pay.

MRS. FISHER. No, things are never very pleasant when this kind of money is bein' paid.

ROGERS. [*Rising, and putting his wallet into his inside pocket*] Well, at least, it doesn't make things any less pleasant, Mrs. Fisher.

MRS. FISHER. [*Rising*] No, I'm sure I don't know what a lot of folks 'ud do without it.

ROGERS. Pretty hard to make a good many of them see it that way, Mrs. Fisher.

MRS. FISHER. [*Moving around to a point above the table*] Yes, I guess we don't think much about trouble when we're not havin' it.

ROGERS. Lot of people think they're never going to have trouble; [*Mrs. Fisher shakes her head knowingly.*] and never going to need a dollar.

MRS. FISHER. They're very foolish.

ROGERS. Very foolish indeed.

MRS. FISHER. Everybody'll have trouble if they live long enough.

ROGERS. Yes, indeed.

MRS. FISHER. Well now, what do I do with this check, Mr. Rogers?

ROGERS. Why, you can deposit it if you like, Mrs. Fisher, or have it cashed—just whatever you like.

CLARA. Frank'll get it cashed for you, Mom, downtown.

MRS. FISHER. I'm not used to thousand-dollar checks, you know, Mr. Rogers.

ROGERS. I'm not very used to them myself, Mrs. Fisher, except to pay them out to somebody else. [*He laughs a little.*]

MRS. FISHER. Well, will you take this, then, Clara, and give it to Frank Hyland?

CLARA. [*Advancing*] Yes; I'll give it to him tonight, Mom. [*Rogers moves to the window at the left and takes a paper from his pocket.*]

MRS. FISHER. Don't go layin' it down somewhere, now, and forgettin' where you left it—the way you're always doin' with your gloves.

CLARA. [*Crossing to the buffet where her purse is lying*] I'll put it in my purse here. [*Mrs. Fisher comes forward at the right of the Morris chair*].

ROGERS. [*Turning and coming back a little from the window*] Oh, by the way, Mrs. Fisher—would you give this to your son-in-law, Mr. Piper? [*He hands her the paper.*]

MRS. FISHER. What is it?

ROGERS. Why, it's a little explanation of some of the features of a very attractive *accident* policy that our company has brought out recently—and I was talking to Mr. Piper about it the day I called for Mr. Fisher's policy. He seemed to be very much interested. In fact, I find that people are usually a little more susceptible to the advantages of a good insurance policy, when they actually see it being paid to somebody else. Now, that particular policy there—is a kind of combination of accident and life insurance policy—as well as disability and dividend features. In fact, we contend that there is no investment on the market today [*Clara sits down in the armchair at the right window.*] that offers the security or return that that particular policy described there does. The thing is really almost benevolent.

MRS. FISHER. How much is it for?

ROGERS. Why, we *have* them as low as ten thousand dollars; but the policy that Mr. Piper was most interested in, was one of our fifty *thousand*-dollar policies. [*Clara laughs faintly, and her mother looks over at her.*]

MRS. FISHER. [*Turning back to Rogers*] It's no wonder she's laughin', Mr. Rogers; for if you knew Mr. Piper as well as she knows him, you'd laugh too. He has just about as much notion of takin' out a fifty thousand-dollar insurance policy as I have. And just about as much chance of payin' for it.

ROGERS. Why, he seemed very much interested, Mrs. Fisher.

MRS. FISHER. He was showin' off Mr. Rogers, what he's always doin'. Why, that fellow don't make enough salary in six months to pay one year's premium on a policy like this. So, if I was you, I'd just put this paper right back in my pocket, for you're only wastin' it to be givin' it to him.

ROGERS. [*Taking the paper*] Seems rather funny that he'd talk about it at all—I mean, if he had no idea of taking it.

MRS. FISHER. He never has any idea when *he* talks, Mr. Rogers— that's the reason he talks so much; it's no effort. That's the reason he's gettin' thirty-two dollars a week, down here in the Pennsylvania Freight Office. And it's a wonder to me they give him *that* much, after listenin' to him for five minutes.

ROGERS. It's particularly funny, because I spoke to Mr. Piper first about one of our ten thousand-dollar policies; but he didn't seem to be interested in anything but the *fifty* thousand-dollar life and *accident* policy.

MRS. FISHER. Well, I can understand him being interested in the accident part of it, after last Monday. I suppose you heard about him runnin' into everything here last Monday evening, didn't you? Down here at Broad and Erie Avenue.

ROGERS. Oh, was that Mr. Piper?

MRS. FISHER. That was him. He ran into a traffic cop, and broke his arm.

ROGERS. Yes, I saw that in the paper; but the name was spelled Pepper in my paper.

MRS. FISHER. Well, it was spelled Piper in our paper.

ROGERS. Well, what did they do about that, Mrs. Fisher?

MRS. FISHER. Why, he's down there today, at the Magistrate's, gettin' his hearin'. God knows what they'll do with him; for he didn't own the car he was drivin', and didn't have a license to drive it.

ROGERS. Well, that's very unfortunate.

MRS. FISHER. But, he'll very likely tire the magistrate out so with his talk, that the man'll discharge him just to get rid of him.

ROGERS. [*Laughing*] I'm afraid Mr. Piper won't want to see me today when he comes back.

MRS. FISHER. He may not *be* back, for six months.

ROGERS. [*Starting for the hall door*] Oh, well, let's hope it won't be anything like that. Good afternoon, Mrs. Hyland.

CLARA. [*Rising*] Good afternoon, Mr. Rogers. [*He goes out into hallway.*]

ROGERS. Good afternoon, Mrs. Fisher.

MRS. FISHER. Good afternoon, Mr. Rogers. [*Calling after him from the hall door*] Will you close that vestibule door tight after you, Mr. Rogers—

ROGERS. Yes, I will, Mrs. Fisher.

MRS. FISHER. This hallway gets awful cold when that vestibule door isn't shut tight. [*A door closes in the hallway, then another door. And then Mrs. Fisher turns, removing her glasses, and moves towards the mantelpiece.*] I'm glad you were here; I don't understand them insurance papers. [*She puts her glasses on the mantelpiece.*]

CLARA. [*Moving to the chair at the right of the center table*] What do you think you'll do with that money, Mom?

MRS. FISHER. Why, I think I'll just put it into a bank somewhere; everything is paid. And then I'll have something in my old days. [*She comes forward to the chair at the left of the center table.*]

CLARA. Do you want me to put the check right into the bank?

MRS. FISHER. No—I want to see the money first. [*She sits down.*] But, can you imagine that clown, Clara, takin' up that man's time talkin' about a fifty thousand-dollar policy; and him in debt to his eyes.

CLARA. [*Sitting down*] What does it matter, Mom; you can never change a man like Piper.

MRS. FISHER. No, but I hate to see him makin' such a fool of Amy; and of all of us—with his name in all the papers, and the whole city laughin' at him.

CLARA. He doesn't mind that, he likes it.

MRS. FISHER. But, Amy's married to him, Clara—that's the trouble.

CLARA. Amy doesn't mind it either, Mom, as long as its Aubrey.

MRS. FISHER. Well, she ought to mind it, if she's got any pride.

CLARA. [*Looking straight ahead, wistfully*] She's in love with him, Mom—she doesn't see him through the same eyes that other people do.

MRS. FISHER. You're always talkin' about love; you give me a pain.

CLARA. Well, don't you think she is?

MRS. FISHER. How do *I* know whether she is or not? I don't know anything about when people are in love; except that they act silly—most everybody that I ever knew that was. I'm sure *she* acted silly enough when she took *him*.

CLARA. She might have taken worse, Mom. [*Mrs. Fisher looks at her; and Clara meets the look.*] He does his best. He works every day, and he gives her his money; and nobody ever heard of him looking at another woman.

MRS. FISHER. But, he's such a rattlebrain, Clara.

CLARA. Oh, there are lots of things that are harder to put up with in a man than that, Mom. I know he's terribly silly, and has too much to say, and all that, but—I don't know, I feel kind of sorry for him sometimes. He'd so love to be important; and, of course, he never will be.

MRS. FISHER. Well, I swear I don't know how Amy stands the everlastin' talk of him. He's been here now only a week, and I'm tellin' you, Clara, I'm nearly light-headed. I'll be glad when they go.

CLARA. I'd rather have a man that talked too much than one of those silent ones. Honestly, Mom, I think sometimes if Frank Hyland doesn't *say* something I'll go out of my mind.

MRS. FISHER. What do you want him to say?

CLARA. Anything; just so I'd know he had a voice.

MRS. FISHER. He's too sensible a man, Clara, to be talkin' when he has nothin' to say.

CLARA. I don't think it's so sensible, Mom, never to have anything to say.

MRS. FISHER. Well, lot's of men are that way in the house.

CLARA. But there are usually children there—it isn't so bad.

MRS. FISHER. Well, if Amy ever has any children, and they have as much to say as their father, I don't know what'll become of her.

CLARA. She'll get along some way; people always do.

MRS. FISHER. Leanin' on somebody else—*that's* how they get along.

CLARA. There are always the Leaners and the Bearers, Mom. But, if she's in love with the man she's married to—and he's in love with her—and there are children—

MRS. FISHER. I never saw a married woman so full of love.

CLARA. I suppose that's because I never had any of it, Mom. [*Her Mother looks over at her.*]

MRS. FISHER. Don't your man love you? [*Clara looks straight out, shaking her head slowly.*]

CLARA. He loved someone else before he met me.

MRS. FISHER. How do you know?

CLARA. The way he talks sometimes.

MRS. FISHER. Why didn't he marry her?

CLARA. I think he lost her. I remember he said to me one time "Always be kind, Clara, to anybody that loves you; for," he said, "a person always loses what he doesn't appreciate. And," he said, "it's a *terrible* thing to lose love." He said, "You never realize what it was worth until you've lost it." I think that's the reason he gives Piper a hand once in a while—because he sees Amy's in love with him, and he wants to make it easy for her; because I have an idea he made it pretty hard for the woman that loved him. [*Mrs. Fisher leans back and rocks slowly.*]

MRS. FISHER. Well, a body can't have everything in this world, Clara. [*There is a pause: and Clara touches her handkerchief to her eyes. Then the front door closes softly, and Mrs. Fisher gets up.*] Maybe this is them now. [*She moves up to the hall door. Amy comes in, looking wearied. She is in mourning.*] What happened, Amy? [*Amy wanders down to the chair at left of table and sits down, and her mother follows her down at the left.*] Where's Aubrey Piper?

AMY. He's coming.

CLARA. Is Frank with him?

AMY. Yes.

MRS. FISHER. Where are they?

AMY. Aubrey stopped at the corner to get some cigars.

CLARA. What happened down there?

AMY. Oh, a lot of talk.

MRS. FISHER. [*Leaning towards her, solicitously*] Are you sick?

AMY. No.

MRS. FISHER. Well, you look sick.

AMY. I have a headache; we had to wait there so long.

CLARA. Why don't you take off your hat? [*Amy starts to remove her hat.*]

MRS. FISHER. Will I make you a cup of tea?

AMY. No, don't bother, Mom; I can get it myself.

MRS. FISHER. [*Going towards the right door*] It won't take a minute. [*Amy takes her handkerchief from her bag. Clara glances toward the right door.*]

CLARA. [*In a subdued tone*] What did they do to Aubrey?

AMY. [*Confidentially*] Fined him—a thousand dollars. Don't let Mom know. Recklessness, and driving without a license.

CLARA. Did Frank pay it?

AMY. Yes; I told him I'd be responsible for it.

CLARA. How can *you* ever pay him a thousand dollars, Amy?

AMY. I can go back to work for a while. I can always go back to the office. [*Clara moves.*] Well, it was either that or six months in jail. And Frank said we couldn't have that.

CLARA. Was there anybody there that we know?

AMY. I didn't see anybody.

CLARA. Was the traffic cop there?

AMY. Yes, there were fourteen witnesses. The traffic cop's arm was broken. The fellow that owned car was there, too.

CLARA. When do you think you'll go back to work?

AMY. [*After a troubled pause*] As soon as I get settled. There's no use in my going back now; I'd only have to be leaving again pretty soon. [*Clara looks at her.*]

CLARA. Does Mom know?

AMY. No, I haven't told her. [*There is a pause. Clara gets up; and, with a glance toward the kitchen door, moves around and crosses towards the left, above the center table. She stops back of Amy's chair and looks at her for a second compassionately; then she steps forward and lays her hand on her shoulder.*]

CLARA. Don't worry about it, Amy. [*She moves towards the window at the left.*] I wish to God it was me. [*There is a murmur of voices at the front door; then Aubrey's laugh rings through the house. Amy rises quickly, picks up her hat from the table, and signifies to Clara with a gesture, that she will go into the parlor. Clara moves across in front of the center table.*]

AUBREY. [*Entering, all dressed up, and with a little flourish of his cane to Clara*] Hello Clara!

CLARA. Hello.

AUBREY. [*Hanging up his hat and cane on the hooks at the head of the cellar stairs*] Where's Amy?

CLARA. She's just gone in the parlor there. [*Frank Hyland appears in the hall door and comes forward to the chair at the left of the table.*]

HYLAND. Hello! [*Aubrey crosses to the parlor, removing his gloves.*]

AUBREY. You in there, Amy?

AMY. Yes. [*He goes into the parlor; and Clara moves across above the center table to Hyland's left.*]

CLARA. How is it you didn't go back to the office, Frank? [*Aubrey hurries out of the parlor again and across to the hooks, removing his overcoat. Mrs. Fisher appears in the kitchen door, and stands, looking at him.*]

HYLAND. It was so late when we got through down there I didn't think it was worth while.

AUBREY. Hello, Mother.

MRS. FISHER. I see you're back again. [*He hangs up his overcoat.*]

AUBREY. Right on the job, Mother—doing business at the old stand. [*He takes the carnation from the overcoat and fastens it in the sack coat. Mrs. Fisher comes forward at the right.*]

HYLAND. Hello, Mother!

MRS. FISHER. Hello, Frank.

HYLAND. You're lookin' good, Mother.

MRS. FISHER. Well, I'm not feelin' good, Frank, I can tell you that.

HYLAND. What's the trouble?

MRS. FISHER. Why, I'm troubled to think of all the bother you've been put to in this business.

HYLAND. Don't worry about that, Mother—we've got to have a little bother once in a while.

MRS. FISHER. What did they do down there today, Frank?

HYLAND. Why—they—

AUBREY. [*Coming forward, adjusting the carnation*] I'll tell you what they *tried* to do.

MRS. FISHER. Oh, shut up, you! Nobody wants to hear what you've got to say about it at all. [*Clara crosses above the Morris chair and looks out the window at the left.*]

AUBREY. Well, I *told* them down there what I had to say about it, whether they wanted to hear it or not. [*He goes up to the mirror at the back.*]

MRS. FISHER. I guess they let you go just to get rid of you. [*He turns to his left and looks at her; then starts for the parlor doors.*]

CLARA. Why don't you take your coat off, Frank? [*Aubrey goes into the parlor, looking back over his shoulder at his Mother-in-law, who has not taken her eyes off him.*]

HYLAND. [*Looking at his watch*] I've got to meet that fellow at North Philadelphia Station at four o'clock.

MRS. FISHER. [*Coming a step or two nearer to the table*] What did they say to that fellow down there today, Frank?

HYLAND. Why, nothing very much, Mother—just a little reprimand, for driving without a license.

MRS. FISHER. Didn't they fine him at all, for breakin' that man's arm?

HYLAND. A little bit, not very much.—You see, that was more or less in the nature of an accident.

MRS. FISHER. How much was it?

HYLAND. Now, Mrs. Fisher, as Aubrey says, "It's all washed up, and signed on the dotted line." [*He laughs.*]

MRS. FISHER. How much was it, Clara, do *you* know?

CLARA. He hasn't told me, Mom.

MRS. FISHER. Well, I'll bet you paid it, Frank, whatever it was; for I know he didn't have it. [*She sits at the right of the table.*]

HYLAND. [*Rising*] Well, you know, it's getting near Christmas, Mother—got to give some kind of a little present here and there.

MRS. FISHER. Well, I don't think it's right that you should have to be goin' around payin' for that fellow's mistakes.

HYLAND. [*Standing up a bit toward the hall door, putting on his gloves*] That's about all any of us is doin' in this world, Mother—payin' for somebody's mistakes—and somebody payin' for ours, I suppose.

MRS. FISHER. Well, it don't seem right to me,

HYLAND. Well, I'll tell you, Mother—when you've made a couple of mistakes that *can't* be paid for, why, then you try to forget about them by payin' for the kind that can. [*He makes a little pallid sound of amusement. And there is a pause. Mrs. Fisher rocks back and forth.*]

CLARA. Will you be home for dinner tonight, Frank?

HYLAND. [*Coming suddenly out of an abstraction*] What'd you say?

CLARA. I say, will you be home for dinner tonight?

HYLAND. [*Picking up his hat from the table*] I don't think so; I'll very likely have to go to dinner with *him*. [*He goes towards the hall door.*] Goodbye, Mother.

MRS. FISHER. Goodbye, Frank.

HYLAND. [*Going out into the hallway*] Goodbye, dear. [*Clara wanders up to the hall door and looks out after him.*]

CLARA. Goodbye. [*The vestibule door is heard to close. And there is a significant pause; during which Clara stands looking wistfully out into the hallway.*]

MRS. FISHER. [*Rising, and moving to a point above the table*] Listen, Clara. [*Clara comes towards her.*]

CLARA. What?

MRS. FISHER. Didn't he tell you how much they fined Aubrey?

CLARA. No, he didn't, Mom, really.

MRS. FISHER. Didn't *she* tell you, while I was out puttin' the tea on?

CLARA. [*Moving forward to the chair at the left of the table*] Well now, what does it matter, Mom? You won't have to pay it. [*She sits down.*]

MRS. FISHER. Well, I'll find out; it'll very likely be in the evening paper.

CLARA. Well, I wouldn't say anything to Amy about it, even if it is; she has enough to bother her now.

MRS. FISHER. Well, she brought it on herself if she has—nobody could tell her anything.

CLARA. Well, there's nothing can be done by fighting with her, Mom.

MRS. FISHER. [*With conviction*] There's nothing can be done by *anything*, Clara—when once the *main* thing is done. And that's the marriage. That's where all the trouble starts—gettin' married.

CLARA. If there were no marriages, Mom, there'd be no world.

MRS. FISHER. [*Moving around to the chair at the right of the table again*] Oh, everybody sez that!—if there were no marriages there'd be no world.

CLARA. Well, would there?

MRS. FISHER. Well, what if there wouldn't, [*She sits down.*] Do you think it'd be any worse than it is now? I think there'll be no world pretty soon, anyway, the way things are goin'. A lot of whiffets gettin' married, and not two cents to their names, and then throwin' themselves on their people to keep them. They're so full of love before they're married. You're about the only one I've *heard* talkin' about love *after* they were married. It's a wonder to me you have a roof over you; for they never have, with that kind of talk. Like the two in the parlor there—that has to *kiss* each other, every time they meet on the floor. [*She bristles for a second or two; and there there is a silence.*]

CLARA. [*Quietly*] Amy's going to have a child, Mom. [*Her mother looks at her.*]

MRS. FISHER. How do you know?

CLARA. She told me so.

MRS. FISHER. [*Softening a bit*] Why didn't she tell me?

CLARA. I suppose she thought it'd start a fight.

MRS. FISHER. [*Indignant again*] I don't know why it'd start a fight; *I* never fight with anybody; except him, and I wouldn't fight with *him* only for his impudence.

CLARA. Has Amy said anything to you about coming in here to live?

MRS. FISHER. She said something to me the night your father was laid out, but I wasn't payin' much attention to her.

CLARA. I think you ought to let her come in here, Mom. [*Her mother looks at her.*] She'd be company for you, now that Pop is gone. And you don't know what day Joe might take a notion to get married.

MRS. FISHER. What's changed *your* ideas so much about lettin' her come in here? You were very much against it when she was married.

CLARA. I'd be against it now, if things around here were the way they were then. You didn't even own this house, Mom, when Amy was married: it was Pop's; and I knew if anything ever happened to him, and there was no will—you might not find it so easy to order anybody out of it.

MRS. FISHER. It isn't that I'd mind lettin' Amy come in here, Clara— but I wouldn't like to please him; for I know the first thing I'd know, he'd very likely be tellin' somebody that he'd let *me* come in. [*Clara smiles faintly.*] Oh, I wouldn't put it past him; he's told bigger lies than that. And if I ever found out that he said that—he'd go out of here inside of five minutes, bag and baggage. [*The front doorbell rings.*] See who that is, Clara. [*They rise; and Clara goes out into the hallway, and Mrs. Fisher crosses below the table to the parlor doors.*] Are you in there, Amy? [*She opens the door.*]

AMY. Yes; what is it, Mom?

MRS. FISHER. This kettle's boilin' out here, if you want a cup of tea.

AMY. All right, Mom, I'll be right out.

MRS. FISHER. [*Crossing to the kitchen door*] I'm goin' to make it right away, so you'd better come out if you want it hot. [*She goes out at the right.*]

AMY. [*Coming out of the parlor*] Do you want a cup of tea Aubrey? [*She crosses to the mirror over the mantelpiece and touches her hair.*]

AUBREY. [*Coming out of the parlor*] No, thanks, Honey, I don't care for any just now. [*He strolls to the hall door, glances out, then moves to Amy's side and puts his hands on her shoulders and kisses her affectionately. Then he pats her on the shoulder. She moves towards the kitchen door.*]

AUBREY. [*Patting her hand*] Everything'll be all right, Kid. You know me. [*She goes out into the kitchen, and he settles himself at the mirror over the buffet at the right.*]

CLARA. [*In the hallway*] Yes, I think it is myself. [*Appearing in the hall door.*] Just come right in, I'll call my mother. Is she out in the kitchen, Aubrey?

AUBREY. [*Turning*] Yes, she's getting some tea. [*Gill appears in the hall door.*]

GILL. Well, you needn't bother, ma'm, if she's busy. I just wanted to leave this watch.

AUBREY. How do you do.

GILL. How do you do. [*Clara stops and looks back at the watch.*]

AUBREY. And how is the young man?

GILL. I can't complain.

CLARA. Is that my father's watch?

GILL. Yes, ma'm. Are you Mr. Fisher's daughter?

CLARA. Yes. Close that door, Aubrey, will you?—I don't want Mom to see it. [*To Gill*] I'd rather my mother wouldn't see it. [*She takes the watch, and Aubrey closes the kitchen door.*]

GILL. That's right.

CLARA. I believe she gave him this watch when they were married. [*Aubrey comes forward again, at the right.*]

GILL. Yes, it'd make her feel bad.

CLARA. Thanks ever so much.

GILL. McMahon didn't notice it when he was gettin' the rest of Mr. Fisher's things together.

CLARA. I see.

GILL. He said it was hangin' under the time chart, back of number five.

AUBREY. This is the gentleman that brought Pop's lunchbox home.

CLARA. Oh, is that so?

GILL. I stopped by the day Mr. Fisher died.

CLARA. Did you work with my father?

GILL. No, ma'm; I'm a twister; but I live out this way.

AUBREY. How is it you're not working today, Governor?

GILL. Mondays and Tuesdays is my earlies as a rule.

AUBREY. I see.

GILL. But the hunkies don't always get the stuff up to us. You got to keep right after them. Well, I guess I'll be gettin' along. [*He starts for the parlor doors, then remembers that that is not the way out, and turns to his left towards the hall door.*]

CLARA. I'm ever so much obliged to you, for bringing this watch up.

GILL. [*Turning to her, at the hall door*] Oh, that's all right. I'm only sorry for the reason I have to do it.

CLARA. Yes, it was very sad.

GILL. Mr. Fisher was a hard-workin' man.

CLARA. I suppose he worked *too* hard, for his age.

GILL. Yes, I guess he did.

CLARA. You couldn't stop him, though.

GILL. No, that's what your brother-in-law here was sayin' the day I was here. He was tellin' me about all the times *he* tried to get him to quit, and take a rest. [*Aubrey turns to the buffet mirror.*] But, I guess when a man's worked as hard all life as Mr. Fisher did, it ain't so easy for him to quit.

CLARA. No, I guess not.

GILL. [*Stepping a little forward again*] I didn't know that was you, Mr. Piper, that was in that automobile smash-up that I was tellin' you about the day I was here.

AUBREY. [*Turning*] That so?

GILL. I didn't know it till I saw your picture in the paper the next day.

AUBREY. What paper did you see it in?

GILL. I saw it in the Record.

AUBREY. Wasn't a very good picture of me, was it?

GILL. I knew it was you, though, the minute I saw it.

AUBREY. A friend of mine loaned me his car while mine was laid up, and something went wrong with the steering gear.

GILL. How did you make out about that traffic cop?

AUBREY. Oh, I squared that up all right.

CLARA. Where do you live up here, Mr. a—

GILL. I live out Richmond way. I'd like to get a house over this way more, on account of bein' a little nearer my work, but I don't see much chance.

CLARA. No, I don't know of any vacant houses around here right now.

GILL. No, your brother-in-law was tellin' me about the time *he* had gettin' hold of *this* one. [*Aubrey turns to the buffet mirror again and smooths his toupé with considerable precision.*] Well, I'll be gettin' along. [*He starts out into the hallway.*]

CLARA. [*With a bitter look over her shoulder at Aubrey, and following Gill out into the hallway*] Well, thanks, ever so much, Mr. a—[*She puts the watch back of the statuette on the little stand at the left of the mantelpiece.*]

GILL. Don't mention it.

CLARA. I'm sure Mother'll be glad to have this watch. [*Aubrey turns and looks after them. Then, with a glance toward the kitchen door, he moves carefully to the mantelpiece and tries to see what is going on at the front door.*]

GILL. Yes; she might as well have it as one of them hunkies down there.

CLARA. Can you open it?

GILL. Yes, I got it. Goodbye.

CLARA. Goodbye; and thank you.

GILL. You're welcome. [*The front door closes; and Aubrey glides hastily for the parlor doors, in an attempt to avoid Clara—but just as he reaches the parlor doors, she appears the the hall door, and with a quick glance toward the kitchen door, comes forward to the back of the Morris chair.*]

CLARA. Come here, Aubrey, I want to talk to you. [*He turns towards her; with an attempt at nonchalance.*] What do you mean by telling people that this is your house?

AUBREY. I didn't tell anybody it was my house.

CLARA. You *must* have told this man, or he wouldn't have said so.

AUBREY. What do you think I am, a liar?

CLARA. Yes, I do; one of the best I know.

AUBREY. Well, ask Amy what I said to him, she was here when I was talking to him.

CLARA. [*Before he has finished speaking*] I don't have to ask anybody anything!—you were lying to him here today, right in front of me.

AUBREY. [*With a shade of challenge in his manner*] What'd I say?

CLARA. That you'd fixed the automobile thing up.

AUBREY. It's fixed up, isn't it?

CLARA. *You* didn't fix it up. [*There is a slight pause, during which Aubrey, his dignity considerably outraged, moves forward and crosses in front of her to the front of the center table, where he stops. Clara moves down at the right of the Morris chair to a point near him.*] You'd have gone to jail for six months only for Frank Hyland. And telling this man that you tried to pursuade Pop to stop working.

AUBREY. [*Over his left shoulder*] So I did.

CLARA. When?

AUBREY. I didn't say it to him. But I told Amy he ought to stop. And I think he'd be right here today if he'd taken my advice.

CLARA. He wouldn't be right here today if he'd stopped expecting *you* to keep him. [*He moves further over to the right, and she follows him.*] And now, listen to me, Aubrey; I want to talk seriously to you. You've made a lot of trouble for us since you've been in this family; and I want you to stop it. There's no reason my husband, because he happens to have a few dollars, should be going around paying *your* bills.

AUBREY. [*Half-turning to her*] What do you want me to do?

CLARA. I want you to stop telling *lies;* for that's about all everything you do amounts to. Trying to make people believe your something that you're not—when if you'd just stop your talking and your showing-off, you *might* be the thing that you are trying to make them believe you are. [*She glances toward the kitchen door, and then speaks to him again, in a slightly lower tone.*] Your wife's going to have a child one of these days, Aubrey, and you want to pull yourself together and try to be sensible, like the man of a family *should* be. You're smart enough—there's no reason why a fellow like you should be living in two rooms over a barber shop. I should think you'd have more respect for your wife. [*She turns and moves a few steps up towards the kitchen door.*]

AUBREY. A man doesn't stand much chance of getting ahead, Clara, when the boss has got a grudge against him.

CLARA. [*Turning sharply to her right, and moving to the upper right hand corner of the center table*] Well, stop your silly talk, and get rid of that carnation, and the boss might get rid of his grudge. [*She glances toward the kitchen door again, leans across the table towards him, and lowers her voice.*] But, what I wanted to tell you was this, Aubrey—I've asked Mom to let you and Amy come in here; and she sez she wouldn't mind it only that she knows that the first thing she'd *hear* is that you'd told someone that you'd taken *her* in. And, you see, that's exactly what you've done already—to this man that brought the watch. If I told Mom that there'd be war.

AUBREY. Are you going to tell her?

CLARA. [*With authoritative levelness*] I'm going to put that up to you. And the very first time I hear that you've told anybody that this is *your* house—I'll see to it that you'll get a house that *will* be your own. [*Aubrey smiles, a bit smugly, and looks at her out of the sides of his eyes.*]

AUBREY. I guess your mother 'ud have something to say about that, Clara.

CLARA. [*With a measured evenness*] Well, the only thing that needs to worry you, is what *I'll* have to say about it. [*Aubrey's smugness begins to fade—into a questioning narrowness.*] This is my house— Pop left it to me; so that Mom 'ud always have a roof over her. For he knew how long she'd have it if Amy ever got round her.

And if Amy ever got hold of it, he knew what she'd do if it ever came to a choice between you and Mom.

AUBREY. What are you doing, kidding me? [*Clara holds his eyes steadily for a fraction of a second.*]

CLARA. I'm giving you a tip—see that you keep it to yourself. [*Aubrey withdraws his eyes slowly and looks straight out, weighing this new bit of intelligence carefully in his mind.*] Be wise, now, Aubrey—you've got a chance to sit *in* here and live like a human being; and if you throw it away, you'll have nobody to blame but yourself. [*There is a sound at the front-door of a newspaper being thrown into the vestibule, and a man's voice says, "Paper!" Then the front door is heard to close.*] Open that door there, Mom'll be wondering what it's doing shut. [*She crosses up to the hall door and goes out for the newspaper. Aubrey stands for a second thinking; and then Amy opens the kitchen door and comes in. She glances about the room.*]

AMY. Where's Clara, Aubrey?

AUBREY. I think she's out on the front porch. [*Amy glances toward the hall door, then turns to her husband.*] How are you feeling?

AMY. All right, I just had some tea. Listen, Aubrey—[*She takes hold of the lapels of his coat.*] Mom said we could come in here to live.

AUBREY. Yes, I got Clara to fix it up.

AMY. She said we could have *my* room.

AUBREY. Is it a front room?

AMY. No, it's that one at the head of the stairs.

AUBREY. Will we put that bureau of ours in there?

AMY. I think the one that's in there is better looking. Let's go up and see. [*She starts up towards the hall door.*]

AUBREY. [*Following her*] You look nice in black, Amy.

AMY. [*Glancing in the mantelpiece mirror as she passes it*] This is the dress that Clara gave me. [*Clara appears in the hall door with the evening paper in her hand.*]

CLARA. It's in the paper here about that trial today. [*Amy takes the paper.*] Keep it out of sight and don't let Mom see it.

AMY. [*Going out the hall door and to her left up the stairs*] I'll take it upstairs. [*Clara moves down towards the center table, and Aubrey crosses above her towards the hall door. As he passes her he excludes her with a look.*]

AUBREY. [*Calling after Amy as he starts up the stairs*] Has it got my picture in it? [*Clara looks after him, rather hopelessly. Mrs. Fisher comes in from the kitchen and moves down to the buffet at the right for her knitting bag.*]

MRS. FISHER. You goin' to stay here for supper tonight, Clara?

CLARA. Yes, I might as well, Mom; Frank won't be home. I think I'll run in next door and tell Bertha I won't be home. [*She starts toward the kitchen door.*]

MRS. FISHER. [*Crossing up to the mantlepiece for her spectacles*] Yes, you'd better; she'll be expectin' you. Put somethin' around you.

CLARA. [*Stopping at the hooks at the head of the cellar stairs*] Is there something here?

MRS. FISHER. Put that old raincoat of Joe's around you; it's good enough. [*She moves forward to the chair at the right of the center table.*] And go to the side door, Clara; and don't be bringin' Mrs. Harbison to the front. [*She sits down and puts on her spectacles; and Clara shakes the old raincoat out and puts it around her shoulders.*] I told Amy she could have that side room upstairs.

CLARA. She might as well be using it, Mom.

MRS. FISHER. But I know I'm not goin' to hit it with *him*.

CLARA. Well, it's better to be fighting than lonesome, Mom. [*She goes out at the right, and Mrs. Fisher takes a purple sweater that she's working on, out of the knitting bag. A door out at the right closes after Clara. Mrs. Fisher commences to knit, when suddenly there is a shout of laughter from Aubrey upstairs. Mrs. Fisher freezes instantly into a stoney stillness, and listens narrowly. There is another gale of laughter from Aubrey, and this decides Mrs. Fisher. She puts her knitting back into the bag, very definitely, puts the bag on the table, gets up and marches resolutely across in front of the table and up to the hall door. Just as she reaches the hall door, with the ostensible purpose of reminding Aubrey that this is not his house, there is another roar from him. Amy can be heard laughing this time, also. Mrs. Fisher subsides, and*] *thinks. She appears to suddenly realize the futility of all remonstrances against the irresponsibility of Aubrey; and, after a thoughtful pause, to accept the situation. And as she moves back across the room, in front of the mantlepiece, to resume her chair at the right of the table, she seems a little older. Just as she reaches a point above the center table, the front-door closes, with a bang. She starts nervously, and steps back to the mantepiece to peer out into the hallway.*]

MRS. FISHER. Is that you, Joe?

JOE. [*From the hallway*] Yes.

MRS. FISHER. [*Continuing to her chair at the right of the table*] It's a wonder you wouldn't take the door off the hinges, and be done with it. [*Joe hurries in from the hallway.*]

JOE. How did they make out down there today, Mom? [*He tosses the evening paper onto the center table and continues on over and up to the hooks at the head of the cellar stairs, to hang up his hat and overcoat.*]

MRS. FISHER. [*Sitting down*] Who do you mean, Aubrey Piper?

JOE. Yes. Are they back yet?

MRS. FISHER. They're upstairs.

JOE. What'd they do to him?

MRS. FISHER. They fined him.

JOE. How much?

MRS. FISHER. [*Taking her knitting out of the bag*] I don't know; they wouldn't tell me. Frank paid it. But, I'll find out; it'll very likely be in the evening paper. [*Joe comes forward to the center table.*]

JOE. [*Picking up the paper from the table*] It isn't in this paper, I looked.

MRS. FISHER. I'll find out.

JOE. But, there's something else in tonight's paper, Mom.

MRS. FISHER. [*Knitting*] What?

JOE. [*Indicating a certain point on the paper*] Just cast your eyes on this, right here.

MRS. FISHER. [*Looking casually*] What is it?

JOE. [*Reading*] "Philadelphia Youth Makes Important Chemical Discovery. Mr. Joseph Fisher of North Philadelphia Perfects Rust-Prevention Solution." [*He gives his mother a squeeze and a kiss.*]

MRS. FISHER. [*Startled, and giving him a little slap*] Stop it, Joe! [*He laughs exultantly, strikes the palms of his hands together, and strides across above the table towards the left.*] Did they buy the thing from you, Joe?

JOE. [*Turning to her, at the left of the center table*] One hundred thousand dollars, Mother! They signed for it this afternoon in the lawyer's office. [*He becomes aware that the shoelace of his right shoe is untied, and puts his foot up on the chair to tie it.*]

MRS. FISHER. [*Leaning towards him*] The Meyers and Stevens people?

JOE. Yeh. They sent for me to come over there this afternoon about two o'clock, so I knocked off and got hold of Farley right away, and we went over there. And they had the contracts all drawn up and everything.

MRS. FISHER. What did you say about a hundred thousand dollars, Joe?

JOE. That's what they paid for it this afternoon, on account—[*He starts across above the center table and up to the hooks again at the right, removing his coat.*] then they're to market it for me from their laboratories, and give *me* half the net.

MRS. FISHER. [*Talking over her right shoulder*] What's the net?

JOE. [*Hanging his coat up*] Whatever's left after all expenses are paid. [*Mrs. Fisher tries to encompass the situation.*]

MRS. FISHER. I guess they'll see that there ain't much left, won't they?

JOE. [*Coming forward again to the center table*] Why, there'll be a fortune out of this thing, Mom. Have you any idea what a rust-preventive means as an industrial chemical problem? Why, they'll make a million dollars out of this, within the next five years. [*He moves over to the left, removing his tie.*]

MRS. FISHER. Well, how much of that are you goin' to get, Joe?

JOE. I'll get the same as they get, that's the contract.

MRS. FISHER. A million dollars?

JOE. Easy, I got a hundred thousand today. [*Mrs. Fisher shifts her eyes and tries to concentrate.*]

MRS. FISHER. How many noughts is a hundred thousand?

JOE. [*Coming back to her left, taking a pencil from his vest pocket*] It's a one, [*He leans over the table and writes it on the margin of the news-paper.*] and two noughts, and three more noughts. [*Mrs. Fisher looks at it closely. Joe replaces the pencil in his pocket and moves across again towards the left.*] They paid that today on account. I knew it was coming, though; their head chemist out at Bristol told me six weeks ago it was all set. I've got to go over there to their offices right away; they made an appointment for the newspaper and magazine people over there at five o'clock. [*He starts for the hall door.*] I've got to talk to them.

MRS. FISHER. Did they give you any of the money, Joe?

JOE. [*Stopping at the hall door*] A hundred thousand dollars, sure.

MRS. FISHER. Not in money, though?

JOE. [*Laughing, and coming back towards the center table*] Not in dollar bills, no; they gave me a check for it.

MRS. FISHER. Where is it?

JOE. Farley has it in his safe, down in the office.

MRS. FISHER. How much do you have to give *him*, half of it?

JOE. No, he's not a partner, he's just my lawyer. I give him five per cent of all monies received. [*He moves forward at the left of the center table.*]

MRS. FISHER. How much will that be?

JOE. Well, that was five thousand dollars right off the bat, today. Pretty soft for that bird. When I first talked to him he wanted to stick me for ten per cent; but I nailed that quick; I knew what this was goin' to be worth.

MRS. FISHER. What are you goin' to do now, Joe, stop workin?

JOE. No, of course not, I'm not goin' to stop working; I've got that oil paint thing on the carpet, now.

MRS. FISHER. Well, won't you have to go to Washington or some-place?

JOE. [*Rolling his tie up on his finger, and stuffing it into his vest pocket*] No, that's all been attended to. But I'll tell you, Mom—I might go to Trenton.

MRS. FISHER. New Jersey?

JOE. Yes.

MRS. FISHER. Not to live, surely?

JOE. I might—till I put this oil paint thing through.

MRS. FISHER. Well, I think you'd be very foolish, Joe, to go to Trenton at *your* age.

JOE. [*Removing his cuff links and dropping them into his vest pocket*] Well, the Meyers and Stevens people made me a proposition this afternoon that looks pretty good. They've got one of the most perfectly equipped experimenting laboratories in the world, just outside of Trenton; and it's open day and night; and that's what I want. I'd have had this rust-preventive through six months sooner, if I could have had the use of a laboratory somewhere at night. So they want me to go up there on a salary, with a first look at anything I strike; but I didn't want to say anything till I talked to *you*.

MRS. FISHER. What do you mean?

JOE. I mean, I wouldn't like the idea of goin' away, and leavin' you alone in the house.

MRS. FISHER. [*Resuming her knitting*] Oh, you go ahead, Joe—if it's for your good. Nevermind me—I'll get along some way.

JOE. I don't like the idea of leavin' you here alone.

MRS. FISHER. Nearly every mother is left alone, Joe, if she lives long enough. [*Joe looks straight out and thinks.*]

JOE. I was wonderin', Mom—why Amy couldn't come in here: she seems to be havin' a pretty tough time of it. [*There is slight pause, during which Mrs. Fisher knits.*]

MRS. FISHER. She's *in* here already; and her man with her.

JOE. I mean, to stay.

MRS. FISHER. They're goin' to stay—she can have that room at the head of the stairs. [*She stops knitting and thinks, looking steadily at the floor in front of her.*] They'll have to live somewhere; and I guess it'll have to be here. It's just as our Clara said here one night—I remember it as if it was yesterday. She said, "Remember what I'm telling you, Mom—it's *you* that'll have them on your hands if she takes him." And I suppose that's true. She made her bed—and I guess it's me that'll have to lie in it.

JOE. [*Starting up and across towards the hooks at the head of the cellar stairs, to get a paper out of his coat pocket*] They want me to go to Trenton right away.

MRS. FISHER. What would you do, Joe, come home over Sundays?

JOE. Sure, it's only thirty-eight miles from here.

MRS. FISHER. [*Astonished*] Is that all the further Trenton is from Philadelphia?

JOE. [*Starting across towards the left to the hall door, removing his vest*] That's all.

MRS. FISHER. It always seemed very far away to me. I guess it's the name.

JOE. I'm goin' up to get fixed up a bit before I go over to that office.

MRS. FISHER. [*Suddenly putting her knitting on the table, preparatory to getting up*] Well, listen, Joe!

JOE. [*Stopping, with his foot on the first step of the stairs*] What?

MRS. FISHER. [*Getting up and moving across in front of the center table*] Come here. [*Joe comes down to her left.*] Don't say anything about this to him, Joe, or he'll be wantin' to go up and talk to the newspaper men, too. [*Joe laughs faintly, then looks away off and thinks.*]

JOE. You know, Mom—I kinda feel that there's something comin' to that nut out of this thing.

MRS. FISHER. How do you mean?

JOE. *He* gave me an idea here one night.

MRS. FISHER. [*Seizing him suddenly by both arms*] Well, for God's sake, don't tell *him* that, Joe!—or, as sure as you live, he'll be tellin' everybody that he done the whole thing.

JOE. You remember the night he was sayin' here about bein' at work on a solution for the prevention of rust in iron and steel?

MRS. FISHER. Yes.

JOE. Well, you know, I'd been tellin' him somethin' about it a week or so before—

MRS. FISHER. Yes, you told me.

JOE. While he was waitin' here for Amy one night.

MRS. FISHER. Yes.

JOE. Well, he forgot that night he was tellin' *me* about it that it was me that had been tellin' *him* about it; and he got it mixed.

MRS. FISHER. That's the way he does with everything.

JOE. And it was the way he got it mixed, Mom, that gave me the idea. *He* said—that it was a combination of chemical elements to be added to the metal in it's *molten state*, instead of applied *externally*, as they *had* been doin'. And I *landed* on it—the way Howe did when he dreamed of puttin' the eye in the point of the needle instead of the other end. That was exactly what *I'd* been doin'—applying the solution *externally*—in a mixture of paint. But the next day, I tried adding parts of it to the molten state of the metal, and it did the trick. Of course, he didn't know what he was sayin' when he said it—

MRS. FISHER. He never does.

JOE. And he didn't know anything about the solution formula.—But it was the way he got what I'd been tellin' him *twisted*, Mom— that put the thing over.

MRS. FISHER. Well, that's no credit to him, Joe.

JOE. I know.

MRS. FISHER. He was only blowin' when he said it.

JOE. Sure.

MRS. FISHER. He don't know what a formula means. And I'd have told him where he heard it, too, if I'd been you.

JOE. [*Thoughtfully*] I'd like to give him a little present of some kind. [*His mother looks at him sharply.*]

MRS. FISHER. What would you give him a present for?

JOE. [*Breaking into a little laugh*] For makin' a mistake.

MRS. FISHER. That's all everybody's doin' around here—givin' that fellow presents for makin' mistakes. That's what Frank Hyland said here today, when I ast him why he paid his fine. He said, "Oh, you've got to give a little present here and there once in a while." There's no use tryin'to be sensible anymore.

JOE. I'd like to give him *somethin'*. [*She looks at him again keenly, and thinks for a second.*]

MRS. FISHER. I'll tell you what you can do, Joe, if you're so anxious to *give* him somethin'.—Find out what fine Frank Hyland paid for him this afternoon, and tell him you're goin' to give him that. But don't tell him what you're givin' it to him *for*, Joe, or we won't be able to live in the house with him. And don't give him money, Joe; for he'd only be goin' from one room to another here in an automobile. And don't give it to her neither, Joe; for she'll only hand it right over to him.—Give it to me. [*Joe looks at her.*] And I'll give it to them when I think they need it. [*A door closes out at the right; and Joe steps up towards the mantelpiece to look off.*] That's Clara; she's been next door telephonin'. [*She turns to her left and picks up her knitting from the table and sits down again. Clara comes in, slipping off the raincoat.*]

JOE. Hello!

CLARA. [*Hanging the raincoat up on the hook*] How's it you're home so early, Joe? [*Aubrey enters from the hall door, smoking a cigar.*]

JOE. The long threatening has come at last!

CLARA. [*Coming forward, looking at him seriously*] What?

JOE. The big news.

CLARA. The steel thing? [*Joe laughs.*] Did they buy it, Joe?

JOE. One hundred thousand dollars!—first payment—they gave me the check this afternoon.

CLARA. Joe, you're not telling me the truth!

AUBREY. [*Coming forward*] Something about the invention, Joe?

JOE. Hello, Aubrey!

CLARA. [*Coming down to her mother's right*] Did they, Mom?

[*Joe and Mrs. Fisher, speaking together*]

MRS. FISHER. So he sez.

JOE. They bought it this afternoon.

CLARA. Isn't that wonderful!

AUBREY. [*Extending his hand to Joe*] Congratulations!

JOE. [*Laughing*] Thanks.

AUBREY. So we put it over! [*Mrs. Fisher poisons him with a look.*]

JOE. To the tune of one hundred thousand clackers. [*He swings Aubrey towards the hall door.*]

AUBREY. [*Turning and following him*] No kidding?

JOE. [*Running up the stairs*] The check's in the safe, down in the lawyer's office.

AUBREY. [*Calling up the stairs after him*] Well, Kid, you know what I always told you!

[*Joe and Clara, speaking together*]

JOE. Leave it to you to call the turn, Aubrey.

CLARA. [*Running up to the hall door*] Joe! Come here and tell us something about it.

JOE. [*Calling back*] I've got to get dressed, Clara, I'll tell you about it later. [*Aubrey comes forward at the left, laughing; but suddenly he becomes conscious of Mrs. Fisher's left eye, and his laugh freezes into a detached gaze out the window at the left.*]

MRS. FISHER. [*Speaking to Clara*] He's got to go down to see them people that bought the thing from him.

CLARA. [*Coming forward to the center table*] Why, what will Joe *do* with all that money, Mom?

MRS. FISHER. [*Knitting*] Heaven knows, I don't.

CLARA. Have you any idea how much a hundred thousand dollars is?

MRS. FISHER. Joe sez it's a one and two noughts, and then three more noughts.

CLARA. Why, it's a fortune!

MRS. FISHER. Well, he brought it on himself; he'll have to tend to it; I'm sure I won't.

AUBREY. [*Coming towards the center table from the left*] If he's a *wise bird*, he'll let *me* handle that money for him. [*Mrs. Fisher pins him with a look, and her knitting slides to her lap.*] I could give him a couple of very fly tips on that.

MRS. FISHER. [*With dangerous steadiness*] He don't want *your* tips; nor your *taps* neither. We *know* about one tip *you* gave a man, and his arm has been in a sling ever since. [*Clara picks up the "Delineator" from the table and moves over to the right to the buffet, to look at the styles.*]

AUBREY. That s all right, Mrs. Fisher; but if he's a wise Bimbo—he'll take the drooping left, [*He lowers the lid of his left eye, very mysteriously.*] and I'll *double* that money for him, within the next two weeks; [*Mrs. Fisher resumes her knitting.*] and give him an extra pair of trousers.

MRS. FISHER. I guess he'd *need* an extra pair of trousers, if he was sittin' around waitin' for *you* to double his money for him.

AUBREY. Well, I'm telling you, Mother—he's an awful straw ride if he doesn't get in on some of that copper-clipping that those people are writing me about. [*She looks at him, hard.*]

MRS. FISHER. What is it, a copper mine this time?

AUBREY. 'Tain't a mine at all—it's a mint.

MRS. FISHER. What are they writin' to *you* about it for?

AUBREY. They're writing to everybody.

MRS. FISHER. They must be. [*She resumes her knitting.*]

AUBREY. Prospective Investors—they hear a man's got a few dollars laying around idle, and they get in touch with him.

MRS. FISHER. Well, nobody's heard that you have any dollars layin' around idle, have they?

AUBREY. [*With a touch of consequence*] Oh—I don't know—they may have. [*Mrs. Fisher stops knitting and leans towards him, stonily— her left elbow resting on the table.*]

MRS. FISHER. Listen, Boy—if you've got any dollars layin' around idle, it'd be fitter for you to pay Frank Hyland the money he paid to keep you out of jail, than to be lookin' around for an investment for it—in some old copper mine, out in God-Knows-Where—that you don't know no more about than them that's writin' to you about it. [*She knits again, indignantly.*]

AUBREY. I know a whole lot about this proposition, Mrs. Fisher; and so do a lot of other people. Why—they say they can see enough copper in those rocks, right now, to keep this thing going for the next ten years.

MRS. FISHER. [*Almost violently*] They *shoot* that in there.

AUBREY. Shoot copper into solid rocks, eh?

MRS. FISHER. [*Putting her knitting down on the table and picking up the newspaper that Joe has left there*] That's what I said. [*Aubrey turns away, with a gesture of helplessness, and moves across in front of the Morris chair to the window at the left.*] I read all about just how they do it, in a magazine not two weeks ago. [*Looking at the paper*] Then they shoot a lot of letters to the likes of you, and you *shoot off* about it.

AMY. [*Entering hurriedly from the hall door and coming forward to the center table*] Mom, is it true what Joe sez about the invention?

MRS. FISHER. [*Looking sharply at something in the paper*] Here it is in the paper. [*Aubrey moves across above the Morris chair towards the center table*]

AMY. Isn't that wonderful, Aubrey? [*Aubrey nods and smiles.*]

MRS. FISHER. [*To Clara*] I thought our Joe said it wasn't *in* here.

CLARA. [*Moving a step or two from the buffet*] What is it?

AMY. [*Leaning over her mother's left shoulder, looking at the paper*] What does it say, Mom?

MRS. FISHER. [*Reading*] Mad Motorist Fined One Thousand Dollars for Reckless Driving. [*Aubrey glides forward and crosses in front of the Morris chair to the window at the left again. Amy straightens up and gives a distressed look at Clara, who suggests, with a nod, that she go into the kitchen.*] Mr. Aubrey Piper, of 903 Lehigh Avenue, was arranged today before Magistrate Lister of the 22nd and Huntington Park Avenue Police Station, to answer to the charge of having disregarded traffic signals at Broad Street and Erie Avenue last Monday evening; resulting in rather serious injuries to Mr. Joseph Hart, a traffic officer. The defendant was fined one thousand dollars for recklessness, disregard of traffic signals, and operating an automobile without a license. [*She lowers the paper to her lap and looks at Aubrey.*]

AUBREY. [*Turning from the window and with a magnificent gesture*] That's the law for you. [*He folds his arms and leans on the back of the Morris chair, looking straight out.*]

MRS. FISHER. What do you think of that, Clara?

CLARA. [*Moving to the armchair below the buffet at the right*] Well, it's all over now, Mom—Frank paid it.

MRS. FISHER. What did he pay it *for?*

CLARA. [*Sitting down*] Well, it was either that or go to jail, Mom; and you wouldn't want that, on account of Amy. [*She opens the "Delineator".*]

MRS. FISHER. Well, Frank Hyland didn't have to pay it—[*She sits looking straight out, fuming.*] Amy's got a mother. [*Turning sharply to Clara*] And you take that thousand-dollar insurance check that I gave you and give it to him as soon as ever you see him. I don't want Frank Hyland goin' around payin' out thousand-dollar bills on account of this clown. [*She looks bitterly at Aubrey, who looks at her with an expression as though he were trying to come to some conclusion as to the most effectual means of putting her in her place.*] It's bad enough for me to have to do it.

CLARA. [*Calling to Amy*] Amy.

AMY. [*From the kitchen*] What?

CLARA. Come here a minute. [*Mrs Fisher puts the newspaper back onto the table and resumes her knitting. Aubrey strolls over and sits down at the left of the center table, reaching for the newspaper which Mrs. Fisher has just put down. Amy comes in from the kitchen.*]

AMY. What?

CLARA. Here's that skirt I was telling you about. [*Amy comes forward to Clara's left and they look at a certain skirt in the "Delineator." Aubrey deposits some ashes from his cigar on the little tray on the table, then sits back, takes a pair of tortoise-shell rimmed glasses, with a black tape attachment for over the ear, from his vest pocket, and settles them on his nose. His mother-in-law gives him a look.*]

AUBREY. Was that Insurance man here today? [*Amy opens the left hand drawer of the buffet and takes out a package of Life-Savers. She takes one herself, then offers Clara one; Clara takes it; and the two continue their discussion of the styles in the "Delineator."*]

MRS. FISHER. What do you want to know for?

AUBREY. [*Glancing over the evening paper*] Nothing—I was just wondering if he got around this way today.—Did he leave a paper here for me?

MRS. FISHER. [*Knitting*] He *wanted* to; but I told him not to waste his time [*Aubrey looks at her narrowly.*] talkin' to *you* about fifty thousand-dollar policies.

AUBREY. Well, what about it?

MRS. FISHER. [*Looking at him*] Nothin' at *all* about it; only the man was laughin' up his sleeve at you.

AUBREY. Is that so?

MRS. FISHER. What else *could* he do? He knows you haven't the faintest idea of takin' out any such policy.

AUBREY. How do you know he does?

MRS. FISHER. Because he knows you're only a clerk; and that you don't get enough salary in *six months*—to pay one year's premium on a policy like that.

AUBREY. What were you doing, handing out a line of gab about my business?

MRS. FISHER. [*Quietly knitting again*] You haven't got any business for anybody to hand out a line of gab about—that I ever heard of. [*Amy moves slowly across above the center table towards the left, picking up a newspaper.*]

AUBREY. Well, whether I have any line of business or not, it isn't necessary for you to be gabbing to perfect strangers about it.

MRS. FISHER. [*Getting mad*] Then, you stop gabbin' to people about fifty thousand-dollar policies!—On your thirty-two dollars a week. [*Turning to him furiously*] I told him *that*, too.

AMY. [*Touching Aubrey on the left shoulder, as she passes back of him*] Keep quiet, Aubrey.

MRS. FISHER. So he'd know how much attention to pay to you the *next* time you start. [*Amy moves forward to the Morris chair at the left and sits down.*]

AUBREY. What else did you tell him?

MRS. FISHER. I told him the truth!—whatever I told him.—And I guess that's more than can be said for a whole lot *you* told him. [*She knits again.*]

AUBREY. [*Resuming his paper*] A man 'ud certainly have a swell chance trying to make anything of himself around *this* hut. [*Mrs. Fisher stops knitting, and leans her elbow on the table.*]

MRS. FISHER. Listen, Boy—any time you don't like this *hut*, you go right straight back to Lehigh Avenue to your two rooms over the dago barber shop. And I'll be glad to see your heels.

CLARA. Stop talking, Mom.

MRS. FISHER. Nobody around here's tryin' to stop you from makin' somethin' of yourself.

AUBREY. No, and nobody's trying to help me any, either; only trying to make me look like a *pin-head*—every chance they get.

MRS. FISHER. Nobody'll have to try very hard to make *you* look like a pin-head; your own silly talk'll do that for you, any time at all.

AUBREY. I suppose it's silly talk to try to make a good impression.

MRS. FISHER. [*Turning to him and speaking definitely*] Yes; it's silly to try to make an impression of any kind; for the only one that'll be made'll be the right one—and that'll make itself.

AUBREY. Well, if you were out in the world as much as *I* am, you'd very soon see how much easier it is for a fellow to get along—if people think he's got something.

MRS. FISHER. Well, anybody that 'ud listen to *you* very long'ud know you *couldn't* have very much.

AUBREY. Is that so.

MRS. FISHER. [*Tersely*] You heard me. [*Clara rises and moves towards her mother.*]

AUBREY. [*Reaching over to dispose of some more cigar ashes*] People that are smart enough to be able to make it easier for you—

CLARA. Aubrey—that'll do. [*He is silenced; and resumes his paper. Clara shows her mother a particular pattern to the "Delineator."*] Mom, that'd look good for that new black crepe de chine of yours, No. 18, there in the middle.

MRS. FISHER. But, I wouldn't want that bunch of fullness like that right there, Clara. [*Joe enters hurriedly from the hall door, wearing a clean shirt and collar, and with his face washed and hair combed.*]

CLARA. Well, you're always saying you look too thin; and I think— Joe, tell me something about the invention.

JOE. [*Crossing quickly to the hooks at the right for his coat*] They telephoned for me this afternoon about two o'clock, and I got hold of Farley and we went right over there. And they had the contracts all drawn up and everything.

CLARA. [*Having moved up towards the hooks with him*] Well, did they really give you a hundred thousand dollars for it? [*Aubrey gets up and moves around and up to the upper left hand corner of the table.*]

JOE. [*Coming forward, putting on his coat*] Check's in the safe, down in Farley's office.

AUBREY. [*Flicking some ashes from his cigar*] Joe!—what do you think we ought to do with that money? [*Joe tries to hide his laughter, and steps down to his mother's right; and Clara comes forward and leans on the buffet.*]

JOE. You know, it was a funny thing, Mom—when I first talked to the Meyers and Stevens people, I was only to get *fifty* thousand dollars advance; and when I went up there today they had the contracts all made out for a *hundred* thousand.

AUBREY. And they're getting away with murder at that.

MRS. FISHER. [*Turning to him impatiently*] Oh, keep still, you!—You don't know anything about this at all.

AUBREY. I made *them* think I knew something about it.

MRS. FISHER. You made *who* think?

AUBREY. The Meyers and Stevens people.

JOE. What are you talkin' about, Aubrey, do you know?

AUBREY. Certainly, I know what I'm talking about. *I* went to see those people, last Saturday afternoon, after you told me they'd talked to you.

JOE. [*Crossing towards him, to a point above the center table*] And, what'd you do up there?

AUBREY. Why, I told them—that they'd have to double the advance, if they wanted to do business with us.

MRS. FISHER. And, what business was it of yours?

AUBREY. Well—I'm Joe's guardian, ain't I?

MRS. FISHER. Who told you you were?

AUBREY. Well—he's got to have somebody tend to his business, doesn't he?—He's only a lad.

MRS. FISHER. Well, he doesn't need *you* to tend to his business for him.—He tended to his business long before he ever saw *you*.

AUBREY. He never landed a hundred thousand dollars, though, till he saw me, did he?

JOE. Well, what did you say to them, Aubrey?

AUBREY. Why—I simply told them that your father was dead—and that I was acting in the capacity of *business* adviser to you: and that, if this discovery of yours was as important as you had led me to believe it was, they were simply taking advantage your youth by offering you fifty thousand dollars for it. And that I refused to allow you to negotiate further—unless they doubled the advance, market it at their expense, and one half the net— *sign* on the dotted line. [*He flicks more ashes from his cigar.*]

JOE. Well, did they know who you were?

AUBREY. I told them—that I was head of the house here; [*Mrs. Fisher grips the edge of the table, threateningly.*] *and* that I was also connected with the Pennsylvania Railroad.

MRS. FISHER. It's too bad they didn't know what you do down there; and call your bluff.

AUBREY. I beat them to it; I called theirs first. [*He strolls towards the left, with a bit of swagger.*]

JOE. Well, I certainly have to give you credit, Aubrey; that's the way the contract reads.

AUBREY. [*Strolling back again*] I told it to them; and I told it to your lawyer, too.

JOE. I'll have to give you a little present of some kind out of this, Aubrey.

AUBREY. [*Dismissing the suggestion with a touch of ceremony*] You'll not give *me* any present, Joe—give it to your mother. [*He strolls over to the left again*]. She'll need it more than I will. [*He comes forward at the left of the Morris chair.*] Amy—have you got the financial page there?

AMY. [*Handing him the newspaper*] Is this it, Aubrey?

AUBREY. [*Taking it*] Thank you. [*He crosses in front of her to the chair at the left of the center table and sits down. Amy gets up, looking at him wonderfully.*]

AMY. Aubrey, you're wonderful!

AUBREY. [*Settling himself to look over the bond market*] A little bit of bluff goes a long way sometimes, Amy.

AMY. Isn't he wonderful, Mom? [*Mrs. Fisher prepares to resume her knitting.*]

MRS. FISHER. [*After a long sigh*] God help me, from now on. [*The curtain descends slowly, with Amy standing lost in admiration of the wonder of Aubrey. When the curtain rises again Aubrey is reading, Mrs. Fisher is knitting, Clara is sitting reading the "Delineator," over on the arm of the armchair at the right, Joe is putting or his overcoat and hat at the mantelpiece mirror, and Amy is sitting in the Morris chair at the left just looking at Aubrey.*]

THE END OF THE PLAY

CRAIG'S WIFE

Craig's Wife (1925), Kelly's first serious full-length play, is a domestic tragedy featuring a protagonist, Harriet Craig, whose tragic flaw is a need to possess and to dominate both a home and a husband. Attendant to this urge is a smug sense of arrogant pride, which leads her to reveal her true nature to too many people, ultimately causing her destruction.

While *The Torch-Bearers* and *The Show-Off* uses the home as their basic setting, the domestic milieu in each play is largely secondary to the plot and characterization. In *Craig's Wife*, however, the setting, an upper-middle-class home, is more than a background—it is consciously used as a device to develop character. The cold, fanatically neat condition of Mrs. Craig's parlor in the one-set play exists as a permanent reminder of the basic frigidity of the mistress of the house. It also stands as a symbol of her self-imposed isolation, and at the play's conclusion, its icy atmosphere becomes that of a tomb for its sole occupant.

In the process of research for his book *Freud on Broadway*, W. David Sievers sent questionnaires to the major American playwrights, requesting information concerning their use of Freudian concepts in their work. Kelly denied any such influence; still, Sievers contended that, while avoiding Freudian terms, Kelly presented "a valid picture of the mechanism of reaction—formation, the explanation for which is suggested by childhood factors."* Sievers alluded to Harriet's first-act scene with her niece, Ethel, in which she advises the young girl against her planned marriage to Mr. Fredericks, a college professor of limited financial means. Harriet boldly asserts that she herself has married to get a home— a symbol of a security that has heretofore been denied her because of her victimization by male-dominated society. In an age when it was usual for the husband's name alone to be on the deed of a house, her father mortgaged their home to subsidize an affair with another woman, causing Harriet's mother to die of a broken heart. Her youthful years were spent in unhappiness with the father and stepmother, after which she was forced to live as a boarder with her married sister.

Harriet's fanatical desire to live in a home that only she really possesses explains her mania for neatness and her suspicion of any outsiders who would intrude on her domain, even the kindly, plain widow next door. She has determined to exercise an "independence of authority" over both spouse and house, while keeping Mr. Craig unaware of her real motives. In return, she has set out to be a perfect housekeeper and faithful wife, always one who, as she describes herself, "regards her husband and her home as more or less ultimate conditions."

Harriet's fiercely possessive nature alienates her from everyone around her. She resents Walter's Aunt Austen because she has claimed some of Harriet's husband's love, and she has virtually imprisoned the aunt in her room. She has also managed to drive Craig's poker-playing friends from the house, and to jeopardize his insurance career by acting as a subtle barrier between him and his business associates. And because of her inquisitive nature, she almost involves him as a suspect in the murder-suicide of a friend and his wife.

*W. David Sievers, *Freud on Broadway* (New York: Hermitage House, 1955), 161.

As the final curtain falls with a deliberate slowness, both the audience and Harriet are suddenly aware of the play's mordant irony: she is left alone, shut up in the home she so desired for herself. The only symbols of real life in the play, Walter, Aunt Austen, Ethel, and the servants, have left her, one by one, like mourners at a funeral service. Aunt Austen's warning, "People who live to themselves, Harriet, are generally left to themselves," has come to pass. She stands alone onstage, with a "wide and despairing" stare, aimlessly clutching a gift bunch of roses, unaware that their petals are dropping on the floor. She is experiencing a limited type of anagnorisis—an awareness of her fate, but no *evident* recognition of the personal flaw in her character that has destroyed her: a self-centeredness that has caused her to exclude the entire outside world. Though Kelly has explained her to his audience, he has not excused her; he has punished her.

Chrystal Herne, who played the original Mrs. Craig, described Harriet as ". . . cruel, as cruel as a Borgia or Medici,"[*] but blamed her husband, for being "weak." She suggested that had he demanded "more compromises" from his firm wife, there might not have been a tragedy.[†] Stark Young thought Walter "something of an ass,"[‡] Gilbert Gabriel called him a "natty ninny,"[§] and R. Dana Skinner felt that Craig's departure argued to a lack of "manhood," predicting that his next wife would probably be another version of his first.[||] An exasperated Robert Garland, reacting to a 1947 revival, suggested a more physical Mr. Craig (". . . there's nothing the matter with Harriet Craig that a good sock on the jaw won't cure").[#] For Harriet has had no respect for Walter, but, rather, an undisguised contempt, calling him to his face "a romantic fool."

The worst thing one can really say about Walter is that he is obtuse—he has been blinded by love, as Aunt Austen, the play's choral figure, tells him early in the play. It takes his wife's will-

---

[*]Chrystal Herne, "Playing the Shrew," *Theatre Magazine*, October 1926, 9.
[†]Ibid., 62.
[‡]Stark Young, "Craig's Wife," review of *Craig's Wife*, *The New Republic*, November 4, 1925, 281.
[§]Gilbert Gabriel, review of *Craig's Wife*, *New York Sun*, October 13, 1925.
[||]R. Dana Skinner, "The Play," review of *Craig's Wife*, *Commonweal*, November 4, 1925, 651.
[#]Robert Garland, review of *Craig's Wife*, *New York Journal-American*, February 13, 1947.

ingness to involve him in suspicion of murder to shock him into
an awareness of her true nature; from then on, nothing can deter
him from his final decision. His smashing of Harriet's vase (a gesture that has always provoked audience applause) and his litter-
ing of the fireplace with cigarette butts are only dramatic devices
used by Kelly to fool the audience into anticipation of Walter's
sudden transformation into the traditional he-man who, like
Petruchio, will probably put his wife in her place in the next act.

But Walter's strength is moral, not physical. He is not a
brute, and Kelly would not have seen mere physical force as a
solution to a complex marital problem, anyhow. He has too
much manhood in him to live with the status quo. The only possible solution for him is to leave a Harriet who he realizes will
never change, but to leave her as a gentleman would—completely, but with all her material needs provided for, including
her home.

One of the saddest lines in the play is Walter's response to
Harriet when she asks where he is going: "Where a lot like me
are going, Harriet—out of fashion, probably." He is aware that
Harriet's description of him as "romantic" is accurate, and that
in the "changing Social Order" (a term used by Kelly in his subti-
tle to the play), the gentle, somewhat idealistic male was being
phased out as a popular image of masculinity. And it is not without a touch of sadness that he leaves his wife, who "neither loved
nor honored" him.

Joseph Wood Krutch* and Foster Hirsch† are quite right in
describing *Craig's Wife* as a "well-made play," although the term
has unfortunately come to suggest a dramatist's preoccupation
with structure over all other dramatic elements. The drama certainly observes the unity of time (twenty-four hours), place (a
room in the Craig household), and action (the Harriet-Walter
conflict is the central plot; the Passmore murder case is only inci-

*Joseph Wood Krutch, "Drama," review of *Craig's Wife*, *The Nation*, March 1, 1947, 256.
†Foster Hirsch, *George Kelly* (Boston: Twayne, 1975), 71.

dental). The concept of a beginning, middle, and end is also beautifully illustrated in all three acts. A central critical question is, of course, whether such a deliberate structure hurts or helps the play. *Craig's Wife* clearly benefits from it. There is nothing extraneous to direct the audience's attention away from the protagonist, who is talked about even before we meet her. Kelly builds his conflict up to the vase-breaking scene at the close of the second act, and the audience's emotions, but not its curiosity as to Harriet's ultimate fate, are allowed to subside gradually until its last glimpse of the forlorn heroine. And the usual audience reaction when the lowering curtain reaches its eyes is a collective gasp of recognition of the play's ultimate irony.

Kelly's unforgettable but disturbing presentation of his unpleasant heroine led to the charge of misogynism, which haunted him all the rest of his career. Critics would, on one hand, praise his instinctive understanding of feminine psychology, yet accuse his mind of being "over-ridden by the selfishness of the feminine sex," as did academic critic Montrose Moses, as early as 1930.* John Gassner observed that Kelly built up a case against Harriet and her type as meticulously as a prosecuting attorney seeking a hanging sentence for a defendant.† Edward Maisel saw Harriet as an example of women who hold men back from their careers,‡ and Arthur Wills saw Kelly's depictions of "cunning, hard, and cynical women" as an indication of his basic distrust of the tender emotions.§ Kappo Phelan, the *Commonweal* critic, called Kelly "simply a woman-hater."‖

Kelly never answered these charges; indeed, he made a point of seldom replying to critics. However, one explanation for his gallery of selfish, egocentric, foolish women may simply be their dramatic effectiveness. Joseph Wood Krutch, quoting the old adage "Lilies that fester smell far worse than weeds," insists that Kelly uses women to dramatize his resentment of a "kind of meanness

*Montrose Moses, "George Kelly," *Theater Guild Magazine*, July 1930, 17.

†John Gassner, ed., *Twenty-Five Best Plays of the Modern American Theatre: Early Series* (New York: Crown Publishers, 1949), 162.

‡Edward Maisel, "The Theater of George Kelly," *Theater Arts*, February 1947, 41.

§Arthur Wills, "The Kelly Play," *Modern Drama*, December 1963, 254.

‖Kappo Phelan, "Craig's Wife," review of *Craig's Wife*, *Commonweal*, February 28, 1947, 492.

which strikes him always as a sort of vulgarity of the soul."*

Kelly's expert ear for dialogue does not fail him in *Craig's Wife*. The speech of his characters varies according to their social background. The servants speak ungrammatical, frequently humorous lower-class English, after the manner of Mr. and Mrs. Fisher in *The Show-Off*; the police employ a breezy station house slang. The rest of the characters in the play use a middle-class diction, polished but not artificial, causing an anonymous *Variety* critic to wonder at a vaudeville-trained playwright's ability to reproduce cultured speech.†

But what made the play is Kelly's portrait of his heroine, which caused generations of Americans to allude to any excessively neat housewife as a "Craig's Wife." Harriet is certainly a type, a character that Alexander Woollcott was sure that everyone would recognize "with something of a start"‡; yet, as John Mason Brown observed, she is still an individual, never descending into a mere stereotype.§ Robert Coleman likened her to *The Show-Off*'s Aubrey Piper in this respect.‖ She is a superbly well-rounded character who is peculiar to neither time nor place—a vivid presentation of a woman whose existence, theatrical and actual, would never fail to provoke recognition and controversy. She is Kelly's most memorable creation.

Craig's Wife received the Pulitzer Prize in 1926. While there were the inevitable whispers that the honor might have been a consolation gesture for *The Show-Off*'s failure to receive the justly deserved 1924 prize, his 1925 drama stands up admirably on its own merits. The play also became a critical point in Kelly's development as a playwright. In *The Torch-Bearers* and *The Show-Off*, he had proven his ability to write satire and domestic comedy. From 1925 on, he would concern himself with a more serious type of drama; he would use comedy sparingly and subtly. But he would also have a problem keeping the large audience that he had won in his first three successes.

---

*Joseph Wood Krutch, *The American Drama Since 1918* (New York: Random House, 1939), 65.

†Unsigned review of *Craig's Wife*, *Variety*, October 7, 1925.

‡Alexander Woollcott, review of *Craig's Wife*, *The World*, October 1925.

§John Mason Brown, "Ramifications of Realism," *The Saturday Review*, March 8, 1947, 33.

‖Robert Coleman, review of *Craig's Wife*, *Daily Mirror* October 14, 1925.

CAST

MISS AUSTEN	ANNE SUTHERLAND
MRS. HAROLD	JOSEPHINE WILLIAMS
MAZIE	MARY GILDEA
MRS. CRAIG	CHRYSTAL HERNE
ETHEL LANDRETH	ELEANOR MISH
WALTER CRAIG	CHARLES TROWBRIDGE
MRS. FRAZIER	JOSEPHINE HULL
BILLY BIRKMIRE	ARLING ALCINE
JOSEPH CATELLE	ARTHUR SHAW
HARRY	J. A. CURTIS
EUGENE FREDERICKS	NELAN JAAP

Play staged by the Author.

"... I thought Miss Austen'd be on the front porch, and I
wanted to bring her these roses." Mrs. Frazier (Josephine Hull)
pays a neighborly visit to Mrs. Craig (Chrystal Herne) in the
final moments of *Craig's Wife*.

CRAIG'S WIFE

✴ ACT I ✦

The entire action of the play transpires between five-thirty in the evening and nine o'clock the following morning, in the living room in the home of Mr. Walter Craig. This room, like all the other rooms in the house, reflects the very excellent taste and fanatical orderliness of its mistress. It is a kind of frozen grandeur, in dark, highly polished wood—strewn with gorgeous, gold-colored rugs and draped in rich brocaded satins. The piano scarf and the scarf on the oblong center table are canary-colored, and the draperies on the bay window at the left, and on the curving window on the stair landing at the back, are dark green. This curving window has a beautiful built-in seat at the right of the staircase, from which the balustrade curves upwards. On the right, at the back, there is a wide door hung with brown velvet portières; and the rest of the room at the right is taken up with an ornamental mantelpiece, fancy mirror and fireplace. In front of this fireplace there is a beautiful high-backed chair. There is another big chair at the left of the center table, a small fancy chair beside the piano, and a chair at either side of the room, forward. There are two fancy benches, one immediately above the center table, and one in front of the center table. There is sufficient room between the table and this forward bench to permit of the business of passing between them. Up at the left there is a glass vestibule, one door of which opens into the room and the other out on to the front porch. As

Mrs. Craig enters, she appears to have been dressed for this particular room. She wears an extremely fashionable fawn-colored ensemble suit, brown slippers and stockings, and a small, dark brown velvet toque. She carries a brown leather pocketbook and a brown silk umbrella.

Miss Austen hurries down the stairs and out through the portières at the right. Mrs. Harold comes in through the door up at the left, carrying the evening newspaper and some tabourette doilies, and moves down towards the center table.

MRS. HAROLD. [*Stopping halfway to the table and peering out after Miss Austen*] Is there something you wanted, Miss Austen?

MISS AUSTEN. No, thanks, dear, I'm just looking for that pattern that I sent for the other day: I wanted to show it to Mrs. Frazier.

MRS. HAROLD. Lift up the lid of that worktable there, Miss Austen; I think I saw a pattern of some kind in there this morning. [*Continuing to the table and putting down the newspaper and doilies*]

MISS AUSTEN. Yes, here it is, I have it. [*There is a sound from the right.*] I knew I left it right here somewhere. [*She hurries in through the portières and up the stairs.*]

MRS. HAROLD. [*Moving up to the door at the left*] I gave those roses she brought to Mazie to put in some water.

MISS AUSTEN. Oh, did you—thanks ever so much.

MRS. HAROLD. She's gettin' a vase for them.

MISS AUSTEN. They're lovely, aren't they?

MRS. HAROLD. Yes, they're handsome. [*She goes out on to the porch again, and Mazie comes in through the portières, carrying a vase of pink roses, which she puts on the upper corner of the small grand piano at the left.*]

MAZIE. [*Calling out through the French windows to Mrs. Harold*] Did the paper come yet, Mrs. Harold?

MRS. HAROLD. Yes, I just brought it in—it's there on the table. [*Mazie turns and comes back to the table, picks up the paper, and strolls for-*

ward, holding it up as though to allow the light from a window at the right to fall upon it.]

MAZIE. More rain again tomorrow.

MRS. HAROLD. [*Answering her from the front porch*] Does it say so?

MAZIE. Unsettled tonight and Friday—probably thunder showers. Slightly cooler, with moderate winds.

MRS. HAROLD. [*Coming in*] I don't know where all the rain is comin' from.

MAZIE. It isn't very nice weather for Mrs. Craig, is it?

MRS. HAROLD. [*Moving forward to the piano*] You can't tell; it might not be rainin' in Albany. Aren't these roses beautiful?

MAZIE. Yes, they're lovely. [*Mrs. Harold smells the roses.*]

MRS. HAROLD. [*Crossing to the foot of the stairs*] I heard her telling Miss Austen she's got over two hundred rose bushes in her garden.

MAZIE. [*Turning and looking at Mrs. Harold*] Is she still upstairs?

MRS. HAROLD. Yeh. I guess she's talkin' poor Miss Austen to death. [*Mazie laughs and resumes her paper, and Mrs. Harold gives an eye around the room.*] Bring that paper out with you when you're comin', Mazie; don't leave it layin' around in here.

MAZIE. All right.

MRS. HAROLD. [*Moving up to the door at the left and looking out*] It 'ud be just like the lady to walk in on us. [*Mazie turns sharply and looks at her.*]

MAZIE. Mrs. Craig, do you mean?

MRS. HAROLD. She might, you can't tell.

MAZIE. I thought you said she wouldn't be back before Saturday.

MRS. HAROLD. [*Coming back to the table and picking up the doilies*] That's what she told me when she was goin' away. But it's just as well to keep a day or two ahead of a woman like Mrs. Craig, Mazie, [*She flicks the dust from the table with the doilies.*] if she gets an idea up there that there's a pin out of place around here— she'll take the first train out of Albany. [*Mazie makes a sound of amusement and resumes her paper and Mrs. Harold starts for the door at the right.*] Oh, there's plenty like her—I've worked for three of them; you'd think their houses were God Almighty. [*She goes into the other room.*]

MAZIE. Didn't you tell me, Mrs. Harold, that you worked out on Willows Avenue one time?

MRS. HAROLD. [*Calling from the other room*] Yes, I worked out there for two years, at Doctor Nicholson's.

MAZIE. Did you know any people out that way by the name of Passmore?

MRS. HAROLD. [*Appearing between the portières*] By the name of what?

MAZIE. Passmore. Capital P-a-double s-m-o-r-e. Mr. J. Fergus Passmore and wife.

MRS. HAROLD. [*Coming forward at the right*] No, I don't remember anybody by that name; why?

MAZIE. Nothing.—It says here they were both found dead this morning in their home on Willows Avenue.

MRS. HAROLD. Oh, Lord have mercy on them! What happened to them?

MAZIE. [*Reading*] Why, it sez: "Fashionable Willows Avenue Residence Scene of Double Tragedy—Bodies of J. Fergus Passmore and Wife, Socially Prominent in This City, Found Dead in Library from Bullet Wounds—Empty Revolver Near Fireplace—Cause of Death Shrouded in Mystery—Police Working upon Identity of Gentleman Visitor Seen Leaving Premises in Automobile Shortly After Midnight." [*Mazie looks fearfully at Mrs. Harold, who shakes her head dolefully.*] "About eight o'clock this morning upon entering the library in the home of Mr. J. Fergus Passmore of 2214 Willows Avenue, Miss Selma Coates, a colored maid—"

MRS. HAROLD. Twenty-two fourteen must be out near the lake. [*The front doorbell rings incisively.*] See who that is, Mazie. [*Mrs. Harold disappears into the other room and Mazie crosses up to the door at the left, putting down the newspaper on the table as she passes.*]

MRS. CRAIG. [*Out on the porch*] We can leave these right here, Ethel—Mazie'll bring them in.

MAZIE. Oh, how do you do, Mrs. Craig.

MRS. CRAIG. Hello, Mazie.

MAZIE. [*Going out*] You're back a little ahead of time. [*Mrs. Harold comes in through the portières, peering out toward the front porch.*]

MRS. CRAIG. Yes, a little. Will you take these thing, Mazie?

MAZIE. Yes, ma'm. [*Mrs. Harold sees that it is Mrs. Craig, gives a quick glance around the room, snatches up the paper from the table, and, with another glance over her right shoulder toward the front door, vanishes into the other room.*]

MRS. CRAIG. And will you see that that catch is on that screen door, Mazie—

MAZIE. Yes, ma'm.

MRS. CRAIG. [*Appearing in the door*] It was half open when I came in. [*She comes into the room, sweeping it with a narrow eye, and crosses to the table to put down her handbag and umbrella. Ethel wanders in after her and stands at the upper corner of the piano. The screen door closes outside.*] Take you things off, dear, and sit down; you look tired. [*She moves across to the mirror over the mantelpiece at the right, and Ethel puts her handbag on the piano and commences to remove her coat and hat.*] I think there's nothing in the world so exhausting as train riding. [*Mazie comes in, carrying a lady's satchel and a suitcase. Mrs. Craig turns.*] You may as well take those things right upstairs, Mazie.

MAZIE. Yes, ma'm.

MRS. CRAIG. [*Crossing up and over to Ethel*] Put that suitcase in the corner room, Mazie—Miss Landreth'll occupy that room for the next few days.

MAZIE. [*Going up the stairs*] Yes, ma'm.

MRS. CRAIG. [*Taking Ethel's hat and coat*] I'll take them, dear.

ETHEL. Thanks.

MRS. CRAIG. I'll have Mazie take them right up to your room. [*She puts them down on the table carefully and Ethel crosses down towards the mirror, settling her hair.*]

ETHEL. I suppose I look terrible, don't I?

MRS. CRAIG. [*Crossing and taking Ethel's bag from the piano*] No, dear, you look quite all right. Would you like a drink of something?

ETHEL. I would like a drink of water, yes, if you don't mind. [*Mrs. Harold appears between the portières.*]

MRS. CRAIG. Hello, Mrs. Harold.

MRS. HAROLD. I see you're back again.

MRS. CRAIG. This is Mrs. Harold, Ethel.

ETHEL. How do you do. [*Mrs. Harold bows and Ethel moves back again to the roses on the piano.*]

MRS. CRAIG. Miss Landreth will be staying here with us for a week or two, Mrs. Harold, so I wish you'd see that everything is all right in that corner room.

MRS. HAROLD. All right, I will. [*Mazie comes down the stairs.*]

MRS. CRAIG. [*Moving down to the mirror, removing her coat*] And will you bring a glass of water, please, Mrs. Harold?

MRS. HAROLD. Yes, ma'm. Just one glass?

MRS. CRAIG. Yes, I don't want any. [*Mrs. Harold goes out again.*]

ETHEL. Aren't these roses beautiful? [*Mrs. Craig shifts her eyes from Mazie, who is gathering Ethel's things up from the table, and looks steadily at the roses.*] I don't think I've ever seen such lovely roses.

MRS. CRAIG. Yes, they're very nice. Take those things upstairs, Mazie.

MAZIE. [*Starting up the stairs*] Yes, ma'm.

MRS. CRAIG. And I wish you'd use that back way when you go up and down stairs, Mazie.

MAZIE. [*Coming down again*] I always keep forgettin' that. [*Ethel turns and looks at Mazie, and Mrs. Craig, laying her coat across Mazie's arm as she passes her, moves up to look at the stairs closely. Mazie goes out at the right.*]

MRS. CRAIG. This stairway'll soon look the way it did before, with everybody tramping up and down it every five minutes. [*She turns to Ethel with a kind of apologetic smile, and commences to remove her gloves.*] It doesn't seem ever to occur to anybody in the house, Ethel, to use the back stairway. It's the funniest thing you've ever seen in your life, really. We might just as well not have one. No matter how many times they have to go up or down stairs, they must go tramping up and down this front way. And you know what stairs look like after they've been tramped up and down a few times. [*Mrs. Harold comes in with a glass of water on a small silver tray.*] Thanks, Mrs. Harold.

ETHEL. [*Picking up a framed photograph from the piano*] Isn't this Mother's picture, Aunt Harriet? [*Mrs. Harold goes out.*]

MRS. CRAIG. [*Crossing to Ethel*] Yes, that's your mother.

ETHEL. I thought it looked something like her.

MRS. CRAIG. [*Taking the picture*] She had it taken at Lakewood one summer, and I always like it. I like that dress; it never seemed to get old-fashioned.

ETHEL. [*Starting to cry*] It doesn't look much like her now, does it? [*She moves forward to the chair beside the piano and sits down.*]

MRS. CRAIG. [*Putting the picture back on the piano*] Now, Ethel dear, you mustn't start that. Your mother's been through this very same kind of thing many times before.

ETHEL. But, I should *be* there, Aunt Harriet. Supposing something should happen.

MRS. CRAIG. But, nothing is going to happen, dear child. I haven't the slightest doubt but that your mother will come through this little spell just as she's come through all the others.

ETHEL. I don't think the others have been as serious as this, though.

MRS. CRAIG. Listen, Ethel dear, I've seen your mother at least a dozen times at what I was perfectly sure was the point of death, and she's always come around all right.

ETHEL. Well, why did Doctor Wood send for me, if he didn't think it was serious?

MRS. CRAIG. Because your mother asked him to, I suppose, dear; just as she asked him to send for me. But he certainly couldn't have thought it was so very serious when he suggested you come away with me.

ETHEL. It wasn't the doctor that suggested that, Aunt Harriet, it was the night nurse—I heard her tell him so. She said it upset Mother too much to see me, and if I were there she'd want to see me.

MRS. CRAIG. Well, that's very true, dear; but you know how she cried when you came in. And there's nothing in the world so upsetting to the heart as crying.

ETHEL. But, I should be there; it seems terrible to me now to have walked away and left Mother in that condition.

MRS. CRAIG. But, what could you do if you stayed, dear?

ETHEL. [*With a touch of desperation*] I'd at least know what was going on.

MRS. CRAIG. [*Handing her a glass of water, and putting her arm around her shoulder*] Now, don't upset yourself, Ethel. Here, take a sip of this water. I'm perfectly sure you're magnifying the seriousness of you mother's condition, dear. And I most certainly should never have come away myself only that I've seen this same thing over and over again. [*She turns and settles the photograph on the piano.*] Besides, there isn't a solitary thing we could do if we'd stayed; those nurses won't allow it. [*Taking the glass from Ethel*] And the doctor said I was upsetting you mother— simply because I told her a few things I thought she should be told. [*She crosses to the table and sets down the glass.*]

ETHEL. There was something I wanted to tell her, too, but he said he thought I'd better wait.

MRS. CRAIG. Well, I'd have told her anyway, if I'd been you.

ETHEL. I'm rather sorry now I didn't—I think it would have made her easier in her mind.

MRS. CRAIG. [*Taking her handkerchief from her bag*] Was it something important?

ETHEL. It was about Professor Fredericks, at school. Mother met him last year when she was up there at Commencement, and she liked him very much. And when we got home she said if he ever said anything to me, she'd be glad if I could like him well enough to marry him. She said she'd feel easier about me, in case anything ever happened to *her*. And I wanted to tell her.

MRS. CRAIG. You mean he *had* said something?

ETHEL. Yes, he asked me to marry him right after Easter. But I didn't write anything about it to Mother, I thought I'd wait until she'd be up there in June for my Commencement, and then I'd tell her.

MRS. CRAIG. I don't know why your mother should be so panicky about your future, Ethel; you're only nineteen.

ETHEL. She said she'd like to feel that I'd *have* somebody.

MRS. CRAIG. Why does a person need anybody, dear, if he has money enough to get along on? [*She turns and crosses to the mirror to remove her hat.*] And, as a matter of fact, you wouldn't be left absolutely desolate even if something *did* happen to your mother. You'd always have me—I'm you mother's sister. So that, really, I think you're a very foolish girl, Ethel, if you allow your mother's apprehensions to rush you into marriage. Unless, of course, it were an advantageous marriage.

ETHEL. She didn't want to rush me into it—she simply said she thought it would be better for me to be settled.

MRS. CRAIG. [*Bringing her hat back to the table, and taking a powder puff from her bag*] Well, naturally, I can understand that, of course. But, after all, simply being settled isn't everything, Ethel—a girl can be a great deal worse off being settled than when she was unsettled. And, personally, I can't conceive of being very much worse off than married to a college professor—stuck away in some dreadful place like Poughkeepsie or Northampton—with not a ten-cent piece to bless yourself with—unless you used your own money. I'm constantly reading agitations in the newspapers about the poor pay of college professors. And your marrying one of them will hardly improve the situation. [*She flips the bag back on to the table, and moves forward to a small ornamental bench in front of the center table, where she kneels.*] Did you accept this man when he asked you?

ETHEL. Practically, yes. We'd rather thought of being married sometime during the summer.

MRS. CRAIG. Then, you mean you're engaged to him?

ETHEL. Yes. I knew Mother liked him, for she said so. The only thing was, she wanted me to be sure that *I* liked him.

MRS. CRAIG. Well, that's all very nice, Ethel, but simply liking a man isn't going to go very far toward keeping things going, is it?

ETHEL. Well, I have money of my own, Aunt Harriet.

MRS. CRAIG. I know that, dear child, but surely he isn't marrying you because of that?

ETHEL. No, of course not; he doesn't know anything about that.

MRS. CRAIG. Well, I hope not—he surely wouldn't expect you to use your own money to keep *his* house going. If a man marries a girl he certainly must expect to support her, at least.

ETHEL. Well, he does expect to support me, naturally.

MRS. CRAIG. How, dear—on a professor's salary?

ETHEL. Why, lots of professors are married, Aunt Harriet.

MRS. CRAIG. But their wives are not living the way you've been accustomed to living, Ethel: not the wives of young professors, at least. And I suppose this man is young, isn't he?

ETHEL. He's twenty-seven.

MRS. CRAIG. Well, there you are. He's very lucky if he's getting two hundred dollars a month: unless he's some very extraordinary kind of professor; and he can scarcely be that at twenty-seven years of age.

ETHEL. He's professor of the Romance Languages.

MRS. CRAIG. Naturally. And I suppose he's told you he loves you in all of them.

ETHEL. Well, I certainly shouldn't care to think about marriage at all, Aunt Harriet, unless I were at least in love with the man. [*Mrs. Craig gives a little smile of pained amusement, and moves towards Ethel.*]

MRS. CRAIG. That is your age, Ethel darling: we all pass through that. It's the snare of romance,—that the later experience of life shows us to have been nothing more than the most impractical sentimentality. [*She arranges the piano scarf more precisely.*] Only the majority of women are caught with the spell of it, unfortunately; and then they are obliged to revert right back to the almost primitive feminine dependence and subjection that they've been trying to emancipate themselves from for centuries. [*She crosses to the big chair at the left of the center table and straightens it.*]

ETHEL. Well, *you* married, Aunt Harriet.

MRS. CRAIG. [*Leaning on the back of the chair*] But not with any romantic illusions, dear. I saw to it that my marriage should be a way toward emancipation for *me*. I had no private fortune like you, Ethel; and no special equipment—outside of a few more or less inapplicable college theories. So the only road to independence for *me*, that *I* could see, was through the man I married. I know that must sound extremely materialistic to *you*, after listening to the professor of romantic languages—but it isn't really; because it isn't financial independence that I speak of particularly. I know that would come—as the result of *another* kind of independence; and that is the independence of authority—*over* the man I married. And that doesn't necessarily imply any dishonesty of attitude toward that man, either. I have a full appreciation of Mr. Craig—he's a very good man; but he's a husband—a lord and master—*my* master. And I married to be independent.

ETHEL. Independent of your husband too, do you mean?

MRS. CRAIG. Independent of everybody. I lived with a stepmother, Ethel, for nearly twelve years, and with your mother after she was married for over five; I know what it is to be on someone else's floor. And I married to be on my own—in every sense of the word. I haven't entirely achieved the condition yet—but I know it can be done. [*She turns and glances up the stairs and out through the portières, to assure herself that no one is listening.*]

ETHEL. I don't understand what you mean, exactly, Aunt Harriet.

MRS. CRAIG. [*Turning to Ethel again*] I mean that I'm simply exacting my share of a bargain. Mr. Craig wanted a wife and a home; and he has them. And he can be perfectly sure of them, because the wife that he got happens to be one the kind that regards her husband and home as more or less ultimate conditions. And my share of the bargain was the security and protection that those conditions imply. And I have *them*. But, unlike Mr. Craig, I can't be absolutely sure of them; because I know that, to a very great extent, they are at the mercy of the *mood* of a *man*. [*She smiles knowingly.*] And I suppose I'm too practical-minded to accept that as a sufficient guarantee of their permanence. So I must secure their permanence for myself.

ETHEL. How?

MRS. CRAIG. By securing into my own hands the control of the man upon which they are founded.

ETHEL. How are you ever going to do a thing like that, Aunt Harriet?

MRS. CRAIG. Haven't you ever made Mr. Fredericks do something you wanted him to do?

ETHEL. Yes, but I always told him that I wanted him to do it.

MRS. CRAIG. [*Half-sitting on the arm of the big chair*] But there are certain things that men can't be told, Ethel; they don't understand them; particularly romantic men; and Mr. Craig is inveterately idealistic.

ETHEL. But, supposing he were to find out sometime?

MRS. CRAIG. Find out what?

ETHEL. What you've just been telling me—that you wanted to control him.

MRS. CRAIG. One never comprehends, dear, what it is not in one's nature to comprehend. And even if it were possible, what about it? It's such an absolutely unprovable thing; that is, I mean to say, it isn't a thing that one does or says, specifically; it's a matter of—interpretation. [*She is amused.*] And that's where women have such a tremendous advantage over men; so few men are capable of interpreting them. But, they can always interpret themselves, if they're so disposed. And if the interpretation is for the instruction of a romantic husband, a woman can always keep it safely within the exigencies of the moment. [*She laughs a little, and moves over to Ethel, resting her hand on Ethel's shoulder.*] I know you're mentally deploring my lack of nobility.

ETHEL. No, I'm not at all, Aunt Harriet.

MRS. CRAIG. Yes, you are, I see it in your face. [*She crosses to the front of the center table.*] You think I'm a very sordid woman.

ETHEL. No, I don't think anything of the kind.

MRS. CRAIG. [*Turning to Ethel*] Well, what *do* you think?

ETHEL. Well, frankly, Aunt Harriet, I don't think it's quite honest.

MRS. CRAIG. But it's very much safer, dear—for everybody. Because, as I say, if a woman is the right kind of a woman, it's better that the destiny of her home should be in *her* hands—than in any man's. [*Mrs. Harold appears between the portières.*] Did you want to see me about something, Mrs. Harold?

MRS. HAROLD. It'll do after a while, Mrs. Craig; I thought the young lady had gone upstairs.

MRS. CRAIG. No, not yet, she's going up immediately. [*Turning to Ethel*] That's what I want you to do, Ethel—go upstairs and lie down for an hour or so; you'll feel ever so much better. I'll call you in time for dinner. [*Ethel rises and moves towards the stairs.*]

ETHEL. I don't think I'll be able to eat any dinner, Aunt Harriet.

MRS. CRAIG. [*Guiding Ethel towards the stairs*] Well, now, you might feel very different after you've had a bit of a rest.

ETHEL. I'm so terribly worried, Aunt Harriet.

MRS. CRAIG. I know, dear child, it's very trying; but it's one of the things we've got to go through with, I suppose. Besides, worrying can't possibly help her, dear. [*Mrs. Craig continues with Ethel up to the landing, and Ethel goes on up the stairs.*]

ETHEL. Oh, how can I help worrying.

MRS. CRAIG. You can't help it, of course, dear; that's the reason I want you to lie down for a while. I'll be up in a few minutes—just as soon as I've seen to a few things down here. It's the room straight down the hall, to the right. Mazie's very likely in there now. And don't worry, dear. [*Ethel disappears at the head of the stairs, and Mrs. Craig looks closely at the landing, to see if she can discover any fresh scratches upon it. Mrs. Harold comes in at the right.*] What was it you wanted to see me about, Mrs. Harold? [*She comes down into the room again.*]

MRS. HAROLD. Why, I wanted to tell you, Mrs. Craig, that the cook left on Thursday. She went away and didn't come back.

MRS. CRAIG. Did she get her wages?

MRS. HAROLD. I paid her up till Tuesday.

MRS. CRAIG. Did she take her things with her?

MRS. HAROLD. Why, she only had a suitcase and a small grapho-phone; she took *them*. But I didn't think anything about it, because she took *them* every Thursday.

MRS. CRAIG. Have you been doing the cooking since, Mrs. Harold?

MRS. HAROLD. Yes, we've been managin' between us. Mazie's a pretty good cook. I called up the Camac Agency on Saturday to send somebody out, but Miss Hewlitt said she wanted to see you first. [*Mrs. Craig looks at her.*] She sez she's sent so many, she wants to find out what's the matter before she sends any more.

MRS. CRAIG. [*Crossing to the piano*] She ought to have a few of them cook for her; she'd *know* what was the matter. Where did these roses come from, Mrs. Harold?

MRS. HAROLD. Why, that woman across the street brought them over to Miss Austen.

MRS. CRAIG. Mrs. Frazier, you mean?

MRS. HAROLD. Yes, ma'm, she brought them over to the porch—Miss Austen was sitting out there sewing.

MRS. CRAIG. Well, you'd better take them out of here, Mrs. Harold: the petals'll be all over the room. [*Mrs. Harold moves across to the roses, and Mrs. Craig busies herself with the draperies in the bay window beyond the piano.*]

MRS. HAROLD. You didn't have to stay away as long as you thought, did you?

MRS. CRAIG. Well, I suppose I *could* have stayed away indefinitely, if I had allowed myself to become sentimental. But I'm afraid I haven't very much patience with sick people, Mrs. Harold. [*Mrs. Harold takes the vase of roses and starts back across towards the portières.*]

MRS. HAROLD. Well, I suppose it takes all kinds to make a world.

MRS. CRAIG. I suppose so.

MRS. HAROLD. [*Stopping, and turning*] Where do you want these roses put, Mrs. Craig?

MRS. CRAIG. I don't care where you put them, Mrs. Harold, as long as they're not in the rooms; I don't want to be picking up petals every two minutes.

MRS. HAROLD. Maybe Miss Austen 'ud like them in her room.

MRS. CRAIG. [*Moving down to examine the spot where the vase stood*] Maybe she would; you can ask her. Is she up there now?

MRS. HAROLD. Yes, ma'm; Mrs. Frazier is showing her something about a pattern that she has. [*Mrs. Craig looks at her.*]

MRS. CRAIG. Do you mean to tell me that Mrs. Frazier is upstairs, Mrs. Harold?

MRS. HAROLD. Yes, ma'm, she's up there.

MRS. CRAIG. And how did she happen to *get* up there?

MRS. HAROLD. Well, I don't know, I'm sure, Mrs. Craig, unless Miss Austen asked her.

MRS. CRAIG. All right. [*She crosses to the foot of the stairs and looks up, and Mrs. Harold goes out through the portières.*] Have there been any letters or messages for me, Mrs. Harold, since I've been away?

MRS. HAROLD. Why, there were two letters, yes; I left them in your room. [*Coming into the room again*] One came this morning, and one came Tuesday. And there was a gentleman called Mr. Craig last night about eight o'clock, but he'd gone out. So I gave him the telephone number that Mr. Craig gave me in case anybody called him.

MRS. CRAIG. Who was the gentleman? Did you get his name?

MRS. HAROLD. Yes, ma'm, he said his name was Birkmire.

MRS. CRAIG. Do you know if he got Mr. Craig all right?

MRS. HAROLD. Yes, ma'm, he did; because when I told Mr. Craig this morning about him calling, he said it was all right, that he'd talked to him last night. [*Mrs. Craig nods and moves down to the center table.*] And then he called again this afternoon about half-past four. [*Mrs. Craig turns and looks at her.*]

MRS. CRAIG. Mr. Birkmire did?

MRS. HAROLD. Yes, ma'm; he said he wanted Mr. Craig to get in touch with him as soon as he came in.

MRS. CRAIG. What number was it Mr. Craig gave you last night, Mrs. Harold, to have Mr. Birkmire call him at?

MRS. HAROLD. Why, it was Levering three, one hundred. I wrote it down on a piece of paper, so I wouldn't forget it.

MRS. CRAIG. All right, Mrs. Harold, I'll tell him when he comes. [*Mrs. Harold goes out.*] And will you get another vase for those roses, Mrs. Harold, before you take them up—

MRS. HAROLD. All right, I will.

MRS. CRAIG. That one belongs down here. [*She stands and thinks quietly for a second; then, with a glance up the stairs and out after Mrs. Harold, she moves to the telephone and picks it up.*] Give me Information, please. [*She waits, glancing toward the other room and up the stairs. Mazie comes down the stairs.*]

MAZIE. Miss Landreth sent me down for her bag.

MRS. CRAIG. It's there on the table [*Mazie picks up the bag from the table and starts for the stairs again. Mrs. Craig looks steadily at her and is about to speak when Mazie thinks of herself and turns back, crossing towards the portières.*] Take that glass out, too, Mazie.

MAZIE. [*Picking up the glass from the table as she goes*] Yes, ma'm.

MRS. CRAIG. [*Into the telephone*] Information? Why, could you give me the address of the telephone number, Levering three, one hundred? Oh, don't you?—All right, it isn't important—thank you very much. [*She stands thinking for a second. Then the screen door outside bangs, and she sets down the telephone and moves towards the door. Mr. Craig comes in briskly, wearing a Panama hat and carrying a newspaper.*]

CRAIG. Well, look who's here, bright and smiling! [*He advances, removing his hat, and she moves a step or two towards him.*]

MRS. CRAIG. You almost beat me home.

CRAIG. How did this happen? [*He kisses her affectionately.*] When did you get in, Harriet?

MRS. CRAIG. [*Taking his hat and the newspaper from him and putting them on the table*] A few minutes ago. I left Albany at noon.

CRAIG. [*Tossing his gloves on the piano*] And how is it you didn't wire or something?

MRS. CRAIG. [*Picking up her own gloves from the table and straightening out the fingers*] I never thought of it, to tell the truth; there was so much to be done around there—getting Ethel's things together, and one thing and another.

CRAIG. Was Ethel there?

MRS. CRAIG. Yes, Estelle insisted that she be sent for last Saturday. And for the life of me I don't know why she did such a thing;

for it upset her terribly. So the doctor said he thought the best thing to do would be to get Ethel out of her sight for a few days: so I brought her back with me. She's upstairs, lying down.

CRAIG. How is Estelle?

MRS. CRAIG. Why, I couldn't see that there was anything the matter with her—any more than usual. But you'd think from her letter she was dying. And then I have to walk out, and leave my house for a whole week, and go racing up to Albany.

CRAIG. Has she a trained nurse?

MRS. CRAIG. [*Picking up his hat from the table*] My dear, she's had two of them, for over six weeks. But you know what trained nurses are.

CRAIG. Well, I'm sorry to hear Estelle is so bad.

MRS. CRAIG. [*Handing him his hat*] Here, take this, Walter.

CRAIG. [*Drawing her back into his arms*] But I'm glad to have you back again.

MRS. CRAIG. [*Laughing lightly*] Stop it, Walter.

CRAIG. Seems you've been away a month instead of a week. [*He kisses the side of her head.*]

MRS. CRAIG. Don't break my bones, Walter!

CRAIG. That's what I think I'd like to do sometimes.

MRS. CRAIG. Now, stop it. [*He releases her and she straightens up, touching her hair.*] Stop. Here, take this hat and put it where it belongs. [*He takes the hat and crosses above her to the portières.*] And take this paper out of here too; this rooms a sight. [*He steps back and takes the paper, then goes out into the other room.*] You aunt's company will be scandalized.

CRAIG. [*From the other room*] Has Auntie Austen got some company?

MRS. CRAIG. [*Moving up to arrange the pillows on the fancy seat at the right of the stairway*] So Mrs. Harold says. She's upstairs with her.

CRAIG. [*Re-entering, and crossing directly over to the bay window at the left*] Who is it?

MRS. CRAIG. The lady of the roses, across the street there.

CRAIG. Mrs. Frazier?

MRS. CRAIG. Yes. She's getting very sociable.

CRAIG. She certainly has some beautiful roses over there, hasn't she?

MRS. CRAIG. She ought to have; she has nothing to do but look after them.

CRAIG. Those ramblers make a pretty effect, down at the side there, don't they?

MRS. CRAIG. Wait till you see them a week from now.

CRAIG. [*Turning to her*] Why?

MRS. CRAIG. Why, there'll be petals all over the place over there.

CRAIG. That ought to be prettier than the way it is now.

MRS. CRAIG. Well, you might not think it was so pretty if you had to sweep them up.

CRAIG. [*Taking some papers from his inside pocket, and moving to the chair beside the piano*] I wouldn't sweep them up. [*Mrs. Craig makes a sound of vast amusement.*] I can't think of anything much prettier than to have rose petals scattered all over the lawn. [*He sits down.*]

MRS. CRAIG. [*Straightening the big chair in front of the fireplace*] You'd have a nice looking place, I must say.

CRAIG. It's a wonder she wouldn't bring a few of those roses over here to Auntie Austen.

MRS. CRAIG. I guess she has sense enough to know that if we wanted roses we could plant some. [*She starts across towards him, above the center table, glancing toward the head of the stairs.*] Listen; she's apt to be down here any minute, Walter, and if I were you I wouldn't be sitting there when she comes; for if she sees you you'll never get away till she's told you her entire history. I've just escaped it twice. [*She gathers her things together on the table.*]

CRAIG. I've talked to her a couple of times on the way up from the garage.

MRS. CRAIG. You mean she's talked to you.

CRAIG. No, she was out there fixing the roses when I came by.

MRS. CRAIG. Of course she was. That's where she is most of the time. [*Becoming confidential, and moving towards him, below the table*]

And the funny part of it is, Walter, I don't think she realizes that people know exactly why she does it. Really, it's the most transparently obvious thing I've ever seen in my life.

CRAIG. Well, why do you think she does it?

MRS. CRAIG. Why do I think she does it?

CRAIG. Yes. [*Mrs. Craig laughs, with a shade of amused impatience.*]

MRS. CRAIG. Well now, Walter—why do certain women go about all the time with a child by the hand, or a dog on a leash. To facilitate the—approach. [*She returns to the table and puts her gloves in her pocketbook; and Craig sits looking at her, mystified.*] Only the lady upstairs uses roses. So, really, I wouldn't be sitting there when she comes down, if I were you, Walter; you know there *is* a danger in propinquity.

CRAIG. [*Resuming his letters*] I guess she could have gotten plenty of men if she'd wanted them.

MRS. CRAIG. But she may not have been able to get the kind she wanted. And *you* may be the kind. [*He looks at her and laughs.*] And this little visit this afternoon, laden with flowers, may be simply the initial attack in a very highly premeditated campaign.

CRAIG. Did you say she brought some flowers over this afternoon?

MRS. CRAIG. I said, "highly premeditated." I believe you told me you'd stopped a number of times to talk to her.

CRAIG. I've stopped twice, as a matter of fact.

MRS. CRAIG. And admired her roses?

CRAIG. There was nothing much else to talk about.

MRS. CRAIG. Of course there wasn't; that's the point. And if there hadn't been any roses, there wouldn't have been anything at all to talk about. And you wouldn't have stopped, and talked. [*She looks at him directly and smiles.*] But since you did, why—it isn't at all inconceivable that she should conclude that you probably liked roses. And that you might regard it as a very charming little gesture if she were to just bring a few over sometime—to your aunt—when your wife was out of the city.

CRAIG. [*Leaning back against the piano and looking at his letters*] What are you trying to do, kid me, Harriet?

MRS. CRAIG. Not at all. Don't lean back against that piano that way, Walter, you might scratch it.

CRAIG. My coat won't scratch it.

MRS. CRAIG. [*Crossing hurriedly*] Well, there might be something in you pocket that will. [*She pushes him away from the piano.*] Now, sit up. [*She gives him a little slap on the back.*] Sit over there. [*She indicates the big chair at the left of the center table, and he rises good-naturedly and crosses to it. Then she busies herself examining the spot on the piano where he leaned, and settling the piano scarf carefully.*]

CRAIG. Yes, sir, I think that's what you're trying to do, Harriet, just kid me.

MRS. CRAIG. Well now, do you think what I've been saying is at all improbable?

CRAIG. No, it isn't improbable; it's just funny.

MRS. CRAIG. [*Crossing back to the table and gathering all her things up*] The flowers were on the piano when I came in.

CRAIG. Well, if they were they were for Auntie Austen.

MRS. CRAIG. Maybe they were. I sent them up to her room, anyway. So Mrs. Frazier probably thinks I *thought* they were for Auntie Austen. [*She starts for the portières at the right, and he looks after her and laughs. She turns and looks at him.*] What are you laughing at?

CRAIG. You.

MRS. CRAIG. Really?

CRAIG. You're very amusing tonight.

MRS. CRAIG. [*Coming forward at the right of the table*] And I think you're just a little bit reckless, Walter—sitting there tempting the temptress.

CRAIG. You know, I think you're getting jealous of me, Harriet.

MRS. CRAIG. [*Amused*] Not at all, dear boy; I'm simply suspicious of rich, middle-aged divorcees, who specialize in wayside roses. [*She leans on her umbrella.*]

CRAIG. Mrs. Frazier isn't a divorcee.

MRS. CRAIG. Isn't she?

CRAIG. No, her husband was killed in an automobile accident in 1915. She told me so herself. She was in the car with him.

MRS. CRAIG. And how is it she wasn't killed?

CRAIG. [*Laughing a little*] Well now, does everybody have to be killed in automobile accidents?

MRS. CRAIG. No, there's always the Galveston Flood, for husbands. You're a very guileless young man, Walter; and I'm sorry your mind doesn't work just a little bit more rapidly.

CRAIG. It works pretty thoroughly, though, when it sees the point.

MRS. CRAIG. But, that's a very slight advantage, Walter, if the point is made before you see it.

CRAIG. Do you know, I'd like to be able to see just what's going on in your mind tonight.

MRS. CRAIG. Well, if you could, I daresay you'd find something very similar to what's going on in the minds of most of our neighbors these days.

CRAIG. Now, just what do you mean by that?

MRS. CRAIG. They have eyes, Walter; and they use them. And I wish you'd use yours. And I also wish you'd tell me whose telephone number Levering three, one hundred is.

CRAIG. Fergus Passmore, why?

MRS. CRAIG. Nothing, I was just wondering. Mrs. Harold told me you gave her that number last night in case anybody wanted you, and I was wondering where it was. [*She moves towards the door again.*]

CRAIG. Fergus Passmore's. I was playing cards out there last night. I ran into him yesterday in front of the First National, and he asked me to come out there last night and play a little poker.

MRS. CRAIG. What did Billy Birkmire want you for?

CRAIG. Why, a—

MRS. CRAIG. Mrs. Harold said he called you up.

CRAIG. Yes, Fergus told me to get hold of him, too, and bring him out there; so I did; but he called me up later to tell me that his father had just come in from St. Paul, and he wouldn't be able to make it. I wasn't here when he called, so I talked to him from there.

MRS. CRAIG. I hope you're not going to get into card playing again, Walter.

CRAIG. Why, I never gave up card playing.

MRS. CRAIG. Well, you haven't played in nearly a year.

CRAIG. Well, I suppose that's because *you* don't play. And most of the folks know that, so they don't ask *me*. I don't suppose Fergus would have asked me yesterday, only that I happened to mention that *you* were away.

MRS. CRAIG. Was his wife there?

CRAIG. She was for a while, but she didn't play; she was going out somewhere.

MRS. CRAIG. I suppose that's the reason Fergus asked you, wasn't it?

CRAIG. What do you mean?

MRS. CRAIG. Why, you know how insanely jealous of her he used to be.

CRAIG. Well, I'm sure he was never jealous of me.

MRS. CRAIG. He was jealous of everybody, from what I could see.

CRAIG. Oh, don't be silly, Harriet.

MRS. CRAIG. Well, you wouldn't know it, Walter, even if he were.

CRAIG. Well, I'm glad I wouldn't.

MRS. CRAIG. And you come to find out, I'll bet that's just the reason Billy Birkmire dodged it. I'll bet that's just what he called you up to tell you.

CRAIG. He didn't call me up to tell me anything of the kind, now, Harriet; he simply called me to tell me that his father had come in unexpectedly from—

MRS. CRAIG. I don't mean last night; I mean when he called you to-day.

CRAIG. He didn't call me today.

MRS. CRAIG. He did, this afternoon, around four o'clock.

CRAIG. Here?

MRS. CRAIG. So Mrs. Harold told me. Said he wanted you to get in touch with him as soon as you came in.

CRAIG. [*Rising, and crossing to the telephone*] Wonder why he didn't call the office.

MRS. CRAIG. [*Moving towards the portières*] Probably he did, and you'd gone.

CRAIG. What's Birkmire's number, do you know?

MRS. CRAIG. [*Turning at the door*] Park 840, isn't it? Unless they've changed it.

CRAIG. I think it is.

MRS. CRAIG. [*Lowering her voice*] And I'm really serious, Walter, about that woman upstairs.

CRAIG. [*Into the telephone*] Park 840. [*There is a laugh from Mrs. Frazier, at the head of the stairs.*]

MRS. CRAIG. So if I were you I wouldn't be here when she comes down. [*He silences her with a gesture; and, with a glance towards the head of the stairs, she goes out at the right.*]

MRS. FRAZIER. I used to have considerable difficulty myself, when I first started to use them.

CRAIG. Hello—Park 840?

MISS AUSTEN. [*At the head of the stairs*] Well, I think I understand it now.

CRAIG. Is Mr. Birkmire there? [*Mrs. Frazier and Miss Austen come down the stairs.*] Oh, that's too bad; I just missed him, didn't I?

MRS. FRAZIER. Well now, please don't hesitate to call me, Miss Austen, if there's anything you don't understand—

CRAIG. Yes, this is Mr. Craig speaking.

MISS AUSTEN. I will, I'll let you know.

MRS. FRAZIER. Because I haven't a solitary thing to do. [*She sees Mr. Craig at the telephone, and turns to Miss Austen, laying her finger on her lips.*]

CRAIG. Then, he'll probably be here pretty soon. [*Mrs. Frazier comes down into the room, and Miss Austen stops on the landing, looking at Mr. Craig.*] Thanks—that's fine. Thank you very much. [*He hangs up.*]

MISS AUSTEN. Hello, Walter.

CRAIG. Hello, Auntie. How are you?

MISS AUSTEN. [*Coming down from the landing*] I didn't know you were home.

CRAIG. Just got in this minute. How do you do, Mrs. Frazier?

MRS. FRAZIER. How do you do, Mr. Craig?

MISS AUSTEN. Mrs. Frazier was kind enough to come up and show me something about a new pattern that I just bought.

CRAIG. That so?

MISS AUSTEN. Mrs. Harold tells me that Harriet is home.

CRAIG. Yes, she just got in ahead of me.

MISS AUSTEN. Did she say how Mrs. Landreth was?

CRAIG. Pretty bad shape, I imagine, from what she says.

MISS AUSTEN. Where is Harriet, upstairs?

CRAIG. Yes, she's just taken her things up.

MRS. FRAZIER. Miss Austen was telling me that Mrs. Craig's sister has heart trouble.

CRAIG. Yes, she's had it a long time.

MRS. FRAZIER. Poor Woman.

MISS AUSTEN. Nearly ten years.

MRS. FRAZIER. How unfortunate. I suppose Mrs. Craig is very much upset, isn't she?

CRAIG. Yes, I suppose she is.

MRS. FRAZIER. Is she her only sister?

CRAIG. Yes, there are just the two of them.

MRS. FRAZIER. Too bad. But, that's the way it seems to go as a rule, doesn't it?

CRAIG. Yes, that's true.

MISS AUSTEN. Walter, you should see all the wonderful roses Mrs. Frazier just brought me over. [*Mrs. Frazier gives a little deprecating laugh and moves towards the piano at the left.*]

CRAIG. Oh, yes?

MISS AUSTEN. They're perfectly beautiful

MRS. FRAZIER. Not a very generous giving, I'm afraid, when there are so many of them.

[*Craig and Miss Austen, speaking together*]

CRAIG. Well, I'm sure we appreciate it very much.

MISS AUSTEN. I think it's very charming of you to remember us at all.

MRS. FRAZIER. Sometimes I think perhaps I am a bit foolish to have so many of them, because it *is* a lot of work.

MISS AUSTEN. It must be; I often say that to Walter.

MRS. FRAZIER. Yes, it is. But, you see, they were more or less of a hobby with my husband when he was alive; and I suppose I tend them out of sentiment, really, more than anything else.

MISS AUSTEN. How long has your husband been dead, Mrs. Frazier?

MRS. FRAZIER. He'll be dead ten years this coming November. Yes. Yes, he died the twenty-third of November, 1915. He was injured on the second, in an automobile accident at Pride's Crossing, Massachusetts: we were on our way back from Bar Harbor—I was telling Mr. Craig about it. And he lingered from that until the twenty-third. So, you see, the melancholy days have really a very literal significance for me.

MISS AUSTEN. I should say so, indeed.

MRS. FRAZIER. Yes, that is the one month I must get away. I don't care where I go, but I must go somewhere; I couldn't stand it here; I have too many memories. So every year, as soon as ever November comes around, I just pack up my things and go out to Dayton, Ohio. I have a married daughter living out there; her husband is connected with the National Cash Register Company. And, of course, she makes all manner of fun of my annual pilgrimages to Dayton. She says instead of being in England now that April's there, with me it's in Dayton now that November's there. [*She laughs faintly.*] We have great fun about it. But, of course, her husband's business is there. And I think sometimes perhaps I should spend more time with her; I think it would help us both. But the trouble is, when I go out there, it's so very difficult for me to get away again. She has the most adorable baby—just fifteen months old; and he thinks there's nobody in the world like his grandmother. And, of course, I think there's nobody in the world like *him*. Although, to tell the truth, I did resent him terrifically when he was born—to think that he'd made me a grandmother. But he's quite won me over; and I suppose I'm as foolish now as all the other grandmothers.

MISS AUSTEN. Is she your only daughter, Mrs. Frazier?

MRS. FRAZIER. Yes, she was my only child.

CRAIG. Then, you live alone over here, Mrs. Frazier?

MRS. FRAZIER. All alone, yes.

MISS AUSTEN. Is that so?

MRS. FRAZIER. Yes, I've lived alone now for nearly four years—ever since my daughter was married. Alone at fifty. [*She laughs lightly.*] Rather a premature desolation, isn't it? [*She laughs again, a little.*]

CRAIG. Certainly is.

MISS AUSTEN. I should say so.

MRS. FRAZIER. I remember reading a story by that name one time, a number of years ago; and I remember thinking then, how dreadful that would be—to be left alone—especially for a woman. And yet the very same thing happened to me before I was fifty.

MISS AUSTEN. Well, didn't you ever think of going out and living with your daughter, Mrs. Frazier?

MRS. FRAZIER. Well, of course, she has never given up trying to persuade me to do that; but I always say to her, "No, darling, I will live out my days in your father's house—even though he isn't there." I say, "I have my memories, at least; and nobody can take those from me." Of course, she says I'm sentimental; [*she laughs.*] but I'm not really—not the least bit. Because if I were, I should have probably married again; but I feel that—

CRAIG. I should think you would have married again, Mrs. Frazier.

MRS. FRAZIER. Well, I suppose that would have been the logical thing to do, Mr. Craig; but, I don't know—I suppose perhaps I'm one of those one-man women. There are such women, you know.

MISS AUSTEN. Yes, indeed there are.

MRS. FRAZIER. Just as there are one-woman men. And I think it's particularly unfortunate when anything happens to the attachment of a person of that kind—whether it's death, or disillusionment, or whatever it is—because the impairment is always so absolutely irreparable. A person of that type can never care very greatly again, about anything.

MISS AUSTEN. [*Looking away off*] That's very true, Mrs. Frazier.

MRS. FRAZIER. [*Falling into a mood*] Never. [*She shakes her head slowly from side to side; then starts.*] Well, I think I'd better go, or you'll be agreeing with my daughter that I'm sentimental. [*They follow her towards the door.*]

[*Miss Austen and Craig, speaking together*]

MISS AUSTEN. Oh, not at all, Mrs. Frazier; I agree with you perfectly.

CRAIG. I think a little bit of sentiment is a very nice thing sometimes.

MRS. FRAZIER. [*Turning at the door*] And I do hope you'll tell Mrs. Craig that I was inquiring about her sister.

CRAIG. I will, Mrs. Frazier, thank you very much.

MRS. FRAZIER. I hope she'll be better soon. Good afternoon, Mr. Craig. [*She goes out.*]

CRAIG. Good afternoon, Mrs. Frazier. I hope you'll come over again very soon.

MRS. FRAZIER. [*Calling back*] Thanks ever so much, I shall be delighted to.

MISS AUSTEN. [*Following her out*] And thanks again for the roses. [*Craig turns away from the door and goes up the stairs. Mrs. Craig appears between the portières, looking darkly towards the bay window at the left, where Mrs. Frazier can be seen passing across the lawn.*]

MRS. FRAZIER. Oh, don't mention it, dear child, I should have brought you twice as many.

MISS AUSTEN. And I'll let you know if there's anything I don't understand as I go along.

MRS. FRAZIER. Please do, now, Miss Austen; don't hesitate to call me.

MISS AUSTEN. I will, I'll let you know.

MRS. FRAZIER. Goodbye.

MISS AUSTEN. Goodbye, Mrs. Frazier. [*The screen door slams. Mrs. Craig moves over the mantlepiece at the right.*]

MRS. CRAIG. The silly creature. [*She stands looking in the mirror, touching her hair. Miss Austen comes in.*]

MISS AUSTEN. [*Stopping just inside the door*] Oh, Harriet, I was just going up to your room. How did you find your sister? Mrs. Harold told me a moment ago that you were back.

MRS. CRAIG. [*Without turning*] Yes, I'm back. [*Turning, with a touch of challenge in her manner*] And I think it's about time I *came* back, don't you?

MISS AUSTEN. Why, dear?

MRS. CRAIG. Why?

MISS AUSTEN. Yes, I don't understand what you mean.

MRS. CRAIG. Well, from the looks of things, if I'd stayed away much longer, I should have probably come back to find my house a thoroughfare for the entire neighborhood.

MISS AUSTEN. You mean Mrs. Frazier being here?

MRS. CRAIG. You know perfectly well what I mean, Auntie Austen; please don't try to appear so innocent. [*She moves up to the foot of the stairs, to assure herself that Mr. Craig is not within hearing distance. Miss Austen gives her a long, narrow look and moves forward at the right of the piano. There is a pause; then Mrs. Craig comes forward to the center table in a perfect fury.*] That's exactly what that woman's been trying to do ever since we've been here; and the minute you get my back turned you let her succeed—just for the sake of a lot of small talk. How did she happen to get in here?

MISS AUSTEN. Why, I asked her in, of course; you don't suppose she walked in of her own accord.

MRS. CRAIG. I wouldn't put it past her, if she knew I was away. [*Miss Austen looks at her.*] I know Mrs. Frazier's type better than you do. [*She settles the things on the table.*] What did you do; go over after her?

MISS AUSTEN. No, I did not. I was sewing on the porch there, and she brought me some roses over, which I think was very thoughtful of her.

MRS. CRAIG. Very thoughtful.

MISS AUSTEN. And I happened to mention the dress that I was making, and that the pattern that I'd bought for it wasn't quite clear to me. And she seemed to know from my description just what pattern it was, and very kindly offered to help me.

MRS. CRAIG. Of course; and you walked right into the trap.

MISS AUSTEN. [*Turning to her*] Well, why do you think she should be so anxious to get in *here*, Harriet?

MRS. CRAIG. For the same reason that a lot of other women in this neighborhood want to get in here—to satisfy their vulgar curiosity; and see what they can see.

MISS AUSTEN. And, why should you care if they do see?

MRS. CRAIG. I wouldn't gratify them—I don't want a lot of idle neighbors on visiting terms. Let them tend to their houses, and they'll have plenty to do: instead of wasting their time with a lot of silly roses. [*She crosses down to the mirror again.*] Mrs. Frazier is very likely one of those housekeepers that hides the dirt in the corners with a bunch of roses.

MISS AUSTEN. You know nothing about her house, Harriet.

MRS. CRAIG. I know what her lawn looks like—that's enough for me. [*Turning*] And you had to bring her upstairs, too, for fear she wouldn't see enough down here.

MISS AUSTEN. I don't suppose the woman knows what you've got in your house, Harriet.

MRS. CRAIG. Oh, Auntie Austen! Really, I wish you were as guileless in certain other respects as you seem to be in the matter of visiting neighbors.

MISS AUSTEN. A good neighbor is a very good thing sometimes, Harriet.

MRS. CRAIG. Well, you may have them; I don't want them running in and out to me.

MISS AUSTEN. None of them has ever run in and out to you so far that I remember.

MRS. CRAIG. One of them has just left.

MISS AUSTEN. She wasn't here to see you.

MRS. CRAIG. She was in my house, wasn't she?

MISS AUSTEN. And in your husband's house.

MRS. CRAIG. Oh—[*She gives a little laugh of mirthless amusement.*] well, she was hardly here to see my husband, was she? [*Miss Austen holds her eye for a second.*]

MISS AUSTEN. No, she was not; although I've no doubt you'd attempt such an interpretation if you thought there was any possibility of Walter's believing it. I don't think any extremity would be too great for you, Harriet, as long as it kept people out of the Temple of the Lord. This Holy of Holies. It's a great wonder to me you haven't asked us to take off our shoes, when we walk across the carpet. [*Mr. Craig coughs, somewhere upstairs, and Mrs. Craig moves suddenly to the foot of the stairs and looks up.*] Mrs. Frazier was here to see *me*, your husband's aunt. And I made her welcome; and so did he. And asked her to come back again. And I don't think you'd find him very much in accord with your attitude, if he knew about it.

MRS. CRAIG. Well, you'll probably tell him.

MISS AUSTEN. Oh, I've got a lot of things to tell him, Harriet.

MRS. CRAIG. I've no doubt you have.

MISS AUSTEN. I've had plenty of time to think about them during the past two years, up there in my room. And they've been particularly clear to me this past week that you've been away. That's why I've decided to tell Walter; [*Mrs. Craig turns sharply and looks at her.*] because I think he should be told. Only I want you to be here when I tell him, so that you won't be able to *twist* what I say.

MRS. CRAIG. [*Coming forward to the table*] You have a very good opinion of me, haven't you, Auntie Austen?

MISS AUSTEN. It isn't an opinion I have of you at all, Harriet; it's *you* that I have.

MRS. CRAIG. Well, whatever it is, I'm not at all interested in hearing about it. And I want you to know that I resent intensely your having brought Mrs. Frazier in here.

MISS AUSTEN. [*Turning away*] Oh, be honest about it, at least, Harriet!

MRS. CRAIG. What do you mean?

MISS AUSTEN. Why particularize on Mrs. Frazier?

MRS. CRAIG. Because I don't want her here.

MISS AUSTEN. You don't want anybody here.

MRS. CRAIG. I don't want *her*. [*She strikes the table with her knuckles.*]

MISS AUSTEN. [*Looking directly at her*] You don't want your husband—[*Mrs. Craig starts slightly and then stands rigid.*] only that he's necessary to the upkeep here. But if you could see how that could be managed without him, his position here wouldn't be as secure as the position of the one of those pillows there. [*She indicates the pillows on the seat at the right of the stairway.*]

MRS. CRAIG. Well, I must say, Miss Austen, that's a very nice thing for you to say to me.

MISS AUSTEN. It's the truth, whether you like to hear it or not. You want your house, Harriet, and that's all you do want. And that's all you'll have, at the finish, unless you change your way. People who live to themselves, Harriet, are generally left to themselves; for other people will not go on being made miserable indefinitely for the sake of your ridiculous idolatry of house furnishings.

MRS. CRAIG. You seem to have borne it rather successfully.

MISS AUSTEN. I did it for Walter's sake; because I knew he wanted to have me here; and I didn't want to make it difficult. But I've been practically a recluse in that room of mine upstairs ever since we've been here; just to avoid scratching that holy stairway, or leaving a footprint on one of these sacred rugs. I'm not used to that kind of stupidity. I'm accustomed to *living* in rooms; [*Mr. Craig comes quietly down the stairs and stands on the landing, looking inquiringly from one to the other. Mrs. Craig sees him out of the corner of her eye, and drifts forward to the mirror at the right.*] and I think too much of myself to consider their appearance where my comfort is concerned. So I've decided to make a change. Only I want my reasons to be made perfectly clear to Walter before I go—I think I owe it to him; for his own sake as well as mine. [*Miss Austen becomes aware of Craig's presence on the stairway and turns and looks at him. There is a dead pause. Then she turns away, and Craig comes down into the room and forward at the left of the table.*]

CRAIG. What's the matter?

MRS. CRAIG. [*Turning*] I haven't the faintest idea, I'm sure. But from what Auntie Austen has just been saying, she seems to think there are quite a few things the matter.

CRAIG. What is it, Auntie?

MRS. CRAIG. She tells me she's going to leave us. [*He looks at his wife, then at his aunt.*]

MISS AUSTEN. It's nothing very new, Walter.

CRAIG. [*To his wife*] Going to leave the house, you mean?

MRS. CRAIG. So she says. [*He looks at Auntie Austen again.*]

CRAIG. You didn't say that, did you, Auntie?

MRS. CRAIG. Haven't I just told you she said it?

MISS AUSTEN. I am leaving tomorrow, Walter.

CRAIG. But, why? What's happened?

MRS. CRAIG. She says she finds my conduct of affairs here unendurable.

MISS AUSTEN. I'll be obliged to you, Harriet, if you'll allow me to explain the reasons for my going; I know them better than you do.

MRS. CRAIG. [*Turning to the large chair in front of the fireplace and sitting down*] You haven't any reasons that I can see; except the usual jealous reasons that women have—of the wives of men they've brought up.

MISS AUSTEN. You'll have plenty of time to give your version of my leaving after I've gone.

MRS. CRAIG. Well, sit down, then, and let us hear your version of it.

MISS AUSTEN. I prefer to stand, thank you.

MRS. CRAIG. Just as you please.

MISS AUSTEN. [*Glancing at the chair at the left, below the piano*] I doubt if I'd know quite *how* to sit in one of these chairs.

CRAIG. Why, what do you mean, Auntie? I can't believe that you've had any difficulty with any one; and especially with Harriet— who thinks the world of you. [*Miss Austen smiles dryly.*] Now, you know she does, Auntie. Harriet is just as fond of you as I am. [*Turning to his wife*] Why, it's incredible, positively.

MRS. CRAIG. I'm glad you're here—to hear some of this.

CRAIG. I suppose there *are* little irritations come up around a house occasionally, just as there are in any other business; but I'm sure you're too sensible, Auntie, to allow them to affect you to the extent of making you want to leave the house. Why, what would we do around here without you? It wouldn't seem to me that we had any house at all. What was it you said to Auntie, Harriet?

MRS. CRAIG. I haven't said anything to her, of course; she's simply using her imagination.

CRAIG. Then, it isn't anything that Harriet has said to you, Auntie?

MISS AUSTEN. Oh, no—Harriet never says anything. She simply acts; and leaves you to interpret—if you're able. And it takes a long time to be able—until you find the key. And then it's all very simple—and very ridiculous, and incredibly selfish. So much so, Walter, that I rather despair of ever convincing you of my justification for leaving your house.

CRAIG. Well, what has Harriet done, Auntie?

MRS. CRAIG. I'll tell you what I did, Walter—I objected to Auntie Austen's having brought that woman across the street there in here while I was away.

CRAIG. You mean Mrs. Frazier?

MRS. CRAIG. Yes, I mean Mrs. Frazier.

CRAIG. Why, what's the matter with Mrs. Frazier?

MRS. CRAIG. She's a vulgar old busybody, that's what's the matter with her—that's been trying to get in here ever since we've been here.

CRAIG. What do you mean, she's been trying to get *in* here?

MRS. CRAIG. You wouldn't understand if I told you, Walter. It's a form of curiosity that women have about other women's houses that men can't appreciate.

MISS AUSTEN. Harriet is chiefly provoked, Walter, because she has allowed herself to be tempted off form for a moment. She would much prefer to have excluded Mrs. Frazier by the usual method—that has been employed in the exclusion of every other man and woman that has ever visited here. But since she's blundered, she must attempt to justify herself now by arraigning Mrs. Frazier as everything from a vulgarian to a busybody—and even to insinuating that her visit here this afternoon was inspired by an interest in you.

MRS. CRAIG. I insinuated nothing of the kind. I simply asked a question in answer to an insinuation of yours.

MISS AUSTEN. The details are unimportant, Harriet; I know the principle.

MRS. CRAIG. Well, tell the truth about it, at least.

MISS AUSTEN. That is exactly what I am going to do—even at the risk of Walter's disfavor.

CRAIG. I don't think you could very well incur that, Auntie.

MISS AUSTEN. You're a man, Walter; and you're in love with your wife. And I am perfectly familiar with the usual result of inter- ference under those circumstances.

CRAIG. Well, I hope I'm open to conviction, Auntie, if you have a grievance.

MISS AUSTEN. It isn't my own cause I'm about to plead; it doesn't matter about me. I shan't be here. But I don't want to be witness to the undoing of a man that was by way of becoming a very important citizen, without warning him of the danger.

CRAIG. I don't understand what you mean, Auntie.

MISS AUSTEN. That is probably the greater part of the danger, Walter— that you *don't* understand. If you did it would be scarcely neces- sary to warn you.

CRAIG. Of what? [*There is a pause; and Miss Austen looks right into his eyes.*]

MISS AUSTEN. Your wife. [*Mrs. Craig breaks into a mirthless laugh, at the absurdity of Miss Austen's implication. Craig turns and looks at her.*]

CRAIG. What are you laughing at, Harriet?

MRS. CRAIG. Why, don't you think that's very amusing?

CRAIG. I don't know that I think it's so very amusing.

MRS. CRAIG. Well, wait till you've heard the rest of it; you'll proba- bly change your mind.

MISS AUSTEN. [*Looking steadily at Mrs. Craig*] Harriet isn't really laughing, Walter.

MRS. CRAIG. What *am* I doing, crying?

MISS AUSTEN. You are whistling in the dark.

MRS. CRAIG. [*Vastly amused, and rising*] Oh, dear! [*She touches her hair before the mirror.*]

MISS AUSTEN. You're terrified that you secret has been discovered. [*Mrs. Craig turns sharply and faces her.*]

MRS. CRAIG. Really? And what *is* my secret?

MISS AUSTEN. I think it's hardly necessary to tell you that, Harriet.

MRS. CRAIG. But, I'm interested in hearing it.

MISS AUSTEN. Well, you can listen while I tell it to Walter.

MRS. CRAIG. Very well.

MISS AUSTEN. But, I want you to know before I tell him that it didn't remain for your outburst against Mrs. Frazier here a few minutes ago to reveal it to me; I knew it almost as soon as Walter's mother knew it. [*There is a pause: then Mrs. Craig moves a few steps towards her husband.*]

MRS. CRAIG. [*With a touch of mock mysteriousness*] She means that I've been trying to poison you, secretly, Walter.

MISS AUSTEN. Not so secretly, either, Harriet. [*Mrs. Craig laughs lightly.*]

MRS. CRAIG. [*Going up towards the portières*] Well, I'm sorry I must go, for I'm sure this is going to be very amusing.

MISS AUSTEN. I've asked Harriet to stay here, Walter. [*Mrs. Craig turns sharply at the portières.*]

MRS. CRAIG. Well, I don't intend to stay.

MISS AUSTEN. I didn't think you would.

CRAIG. Why not, Harriet?

MRS. CRAIG. Because I have something more important to do than listen to a lot of absurdities.

MISS AUSTEN. Then I shall have to regard your going as an admission of the truth of those absurdities.

MRS. CRAIG. Well, you may regard it as you please: only I hope when you've finished discussing me, you'll be frank in letting Walter know something of what *I've* been putting up with during the past two years. [*She goes out through the portières.*]

MISS AUSTEN. Playing the martyr as usual. [*Craig takes a step or two towards the portières, and they stand for a second looking after her. Then he turns and looks at his aunt.*] I could have almost spoken those last words *for* her, Walter; I know her so well.

CRAIG. [*Coming down to the front of the table*] I wish you'd tell me what's happened here, Auntie.

MISS AUSTEN. [*Crossing to him*] That isn't so easy to tell to a man, Walter; it requires a bit of elucidation.

CRAIG. What is it?

MISS AUSTEN. Walter—why do you suppose your mother asked you to promise her, when she was dying, that you'd take me with you when you married?

CRAIG. Why, I think that was a perfectly natural request, Auntie, considering what you'd been to both of us during her illness.

MISS AUSTEN. But, it wasn't as though I should *need* a home—for she knew I preferred to travel—that that's what I was preparing to do when she was first stricken. And I never told you, Walter, but she asked *me* to promise her that I should accept your invitation when you made it. You see, she knew her woman, Walter—the woman you were going to marry.

CRAIG. You mean that Mother didn't like Harriet?

MISS AUSTEN. Nobody could like Harriet, Walter; she doesn't want them to.

CRAIG. I like her.

MISS AUSTEN. You're blinded by a pretty face, son, as many another man has been blinded.

CRAIG. Well, what has Harriet done?

MISS AUSTEN. She's left *you* practically friendless, for one thing; because the visits of your friends imply an importance to you that is at variance with her plan: so she's made it perfectly clear to them, by a thousand little gestures, that they are not welcome in her house. Because this *is* her house, you know, Walter; it isn't yours—don't make any mistake about that. This house is what Harriet married—she didn't marry you. You simply went with the house—as a more or less regrettable necessity. And you must not obtrude; for she wants the house all to herself. So she has set about reducing you to as negligible a factor as possible in the scheme of things here.

CRAIG. You don't really believe that, Auntie, do you?

MISS AUSTEN. That is her plan concerning you, Walter, I'm telling you. That is why the visits of your friends have been discouraged.

CRAIG. I can't think that Harriet would discourage my friends, Auntie.

MISS AUSTEN. Does any of them come here?

CRAIG. Why, most of them have been here at one time or another, yes.

MISS AUSTEN. Not within the last eighteen months; and you've only been married two years.

CRAIG. Well, why shouldn't Harriet want my friends here?

MISS AUSTEN. For the same reason that she doesn't want anybody else here. Because she's a supremely selfish woman; and with the arrogance of the selfish mind, she wants to exclude the whole world—because she cannot impose her narrow little order upon it. And these four walls are the symbol of that selfish exclusion.

CRAIG. [*Turning away, and crossing towards the right*] I can't believe that, Auntie.

MISS AUSTEN. [*Extending her arms towards the front door*] Can you remember when any one has darkened that door—until here today, when Mrs. Frazier came over?—And you see the result of that. And why do you suppose that people have so suddenly *stopped* visiting you? They always visited you at home. I can hardly be that you've changed so radically in two years. And I daresay all those charming young men and women that used to have such pleasant times at home, thought that when you married your house would be quite a rendezvous. But they reckoned without their—hostess, Walter—just as they are beginning to reckon with you. [*He turns and looks at her.*] You never go out anymore.—Nobody ever asks you.—They're afraid you might bring her; and they don't want her.—Because she's made it perfectly clear to them that she doesn't want *them*. [*Craig turns away again slowly.*] And just as your friends are beginning to reckon without you in their social life, so it is only a question of time till they begin to reckon without you in their *business* life. [*He looks at her again, and she moves across towards him.*] Walter—why do you suppose your appointment as one of the directors of the local bank never materialized?

CRAIG. Why, I think Littlefield had something to do with that; he's been high-hatting me a bit lately.

MISS AUSTEN. Because Harriet insulted his wife here; I saw her do it.

CRAIG. When?

MISS AUSTEN. The week after New Year's, when Mrs. Littlefield called.

CRAIG. What did Harriet do?

MISS AUSTEN. Nothing—what Harriet always does. It was a little feline subtlety—that would sound too incredible in the ears of a man. But Mrs. Littlefield appreciated it, for all her stupidity. I *saw* her appreciate it—and you were not appointed. [*Craig looks away.*] And I want to tell you something else that I saw the other day in the city, or rather heard. I was having luncheon at the Colonnade, and two of your old Thursday night poker crowd came in, and sat at a table within hearing distance of me. And presently a man and his wife came in and sat down at another table. And the wife immediately proceeded to tell the man how he should have sat down; and how he should sit now that he *was* down, and so on. And I distinctly heard one of your friends say to the other, "Listen to Craig's wife over here." [*Craig turns his head and looks right into Miss Austen's eyes. There is a slight pause. Then he crosses in front of her, and continues over to the piano at the left. She moves towards the left also, going up above the table.*] That is a little straw, Walter, that should show you the way the wind is blowing. Your friends resent being told where they shall sit, and how; so they are avoiding the occasion of it—just as I am going to avoid it. But you cannot avoid it, so you must deal with it.

CRAIG. How? How should I deal with it?

MISS AUSTEN. [*Taking hold of the back o f the chair at the left of the table*] By impressing you wife with the realization that there is a *man* of the house here, as well as a woman; and the *you* are that man. And if you don't, Walter, you are going to go the way of every other man that has ever allowed himself to be dominated by a selfish woman.—Become a pallid little echo of her distorted opinions; believing finally that every friend you ever had before you met her was trying to lead you into perdition—and that she rescued you, and made a man of you. [*She makes a little sound of bitter amusement, and turns away towards the foot of the stairs.*] The irony of it. And yet they can do it.

CRAIG. [*Crossing back towards the right*] Harriet could never turn me against my friends.

MISS AUSTEN. [*Turning at the foot of the stairs, and speaking with level conviction*] Walter—they can make men believe that the mothers that nursed them—are their arch enemies. [*She comes forward suddenly and rests her left hand on the table.*] That's why I'm warning you. For you're fighting for the life of your manhood, Walter; and I cannot in conscience leave this house without at least turning on the light here, and letting you see what it is that you're fighting against. [*She starts for the stairs, and Craig turns suddenly and follows her.*]

CRAIG. Auntie, I can't see you leave this house!

MISS AUSTEN. [*Stopping on the second step*] But, if I'm not happy here.

CRAIG. Well, why have I been so blind that I haven't seen that you were not happy, and fixed it so that you would be!

MISS AUSTEN. [*Quietly*] Because you haven't *seen* your wife, Walter.

CRAIG. Oh, I can't be convinced that there isn't an enormous element of misunderstanding between you and Harriet. [*Miss Austen closes her eyes and shakes here head from side to side.*] Oh, I'm not disputing that she has a peculiar disposition—she may be all that you say of her—but I really can't see the necessity of your leaving the house; the thing must be susceptible of some sort of adjustment. [*Miss Austen lays her right hand on his shoulder.*]

MISS AUSTEN. No house is big enough, Walter, for two women who are interested in the same man.

CRAIG. [*Crossing over to the left*] I'll never have a minute's peace if you leave here; I'll reproach myself.

MISS AUSTEN. You have nothing to reproach yourself with, Walter; you've always been very kind and very good to me.

CRAIG. What will you do if you leave here?

MISS AUSTEN. What I've always wanted to do—travel—all over the world—far and wide: so that I shan't become—little. I have such a deadly fear of that after these past two years.

CRAIG. But, I promised Mother that you'd always have a home with me, and if you go, I'll feel somehow that I'm breaking that promise.

MISS AUSTEN. You haven't a home to offer me, Walter. [*He looks at her.*] You have a house—with furniture in it—that can only be used under highly specified conditions. I have the impression somehow or other, when I look at these rooms—that they are rooms that have died—and are laid out. [*She turns and starts up the stairs.*]

CRAIG. Well, whatever they are, they'll seem less if you leave them. I don't think I'd feel worse if it were Mother herself that were leaving. [*Miss Austen turns, with her hand on the balustrade.*]

MISS AUSTEN. Be glad that it isn't your mother, Walter; she would have left long ago. [*She goes on up the stairs, and he stands looking after her. There is a ring at the front door. He turns and looks out through the French windows, then moves to the middle of the room and looks out through the portières. The bell rings again; then Mazie comes down the stairs.*]

CRAIG. There's a little boy at the front door, Mazie.

MAZIE. Yes, sir, I heard the bell.

CRAIG. I'm expecting a gentleman, too, Mazie in a few minutes; I'll be upstairs.

MAZIE. All right, Mr. Craig, I'll call you when he comes. [*Mazie goes out to answer the bell, and Craig goes up the stairs. He stops halfway up and thinks.*]

BOY'S VOICE. [*At the front door*] Why, Christine, up at the corner, sez if you're goin' to the Society tonight, would you mind payin' her dues for her; she sez she can't go tonight. [*Craig disappears.*]

MAZIE. Oh, sure, tell her I'll be glad to.

BOY'S VOICE. She sez the card's in the envelope there with the money. [*Mrs. Harold comes in through the portières and crosses towards the door, looking out keenly.*]

MAZIE. All right, dear, tell her I'll tend to it. [*The screen door slams and Mazie comes in.*]

MRS. HAROLD. Did you answer that door, Mazie?

MAZIE. [*Crossing below the table to the mantelpiece*] Yes, it was the tailor's little boy, up at the corner, with Christine's Society money. He sez Christine can't go tonight.

MRS. HAROLD. Is tonight Society night again already?

MAZIE. [*Putting an envelope back of the center ornament on the mantelpiece*] It's the third Friday.

MRS. HAROLD. I can never keep track of that old Society.

MAZIE. Do you want me to pay your dues for you?

MRS. HAROLD. [*Moving to the foot of the stairs*] No, dear, I'm paid up to the first of July. [*Mazie turns from the mantelpiece and moves towards her.*] Where did Mr. Craig go—upstairs?

MAZIE. I guess so, unless he's out there somewhere.

MRS. HAROLD. [*Glancing towards the front porch, and taking a step or two towards Mazie*] No, he's not out there.

MAZIE. Why, what's the matter?

MRS. HAROLD. [*Laying her hand on Mazie's arm, and lowering her voice*] I think the old lady's goin' to leave. [*She tiptoes to the portières, Mazie watching her.*]

MAZIE. Miss Austen? [*Mrs. Harold nods; and then looks out through the adjoining rooms.*]

MRS. HAROLD. [*Turning to Mazie*] The lady made a row about Mrs. Frazier being here. [*She looks out again.*]

MAZIE. Did she?

MRS. HAROLD. [*Coming back*] She was furious. I knew it was coming by the face on her when she told me to take the roses out of the room. So as soon as I heard Mrs. Frazier goin', I went right up to the library; you can hear every word up there, you know, over near the radiator.

MAZIE. Yes, I know you can. Was *he* here?

MRS. HAROLD. He wasn't at first, but I think he must have come down while they were at it. I heard *her* say she didn't want her house made a thoroughfare for the neighborhood.

MAZIE. Can you imagine it—as though anybody ever came *in* here.

MRS. HAROLD. That's what *I* felt like sayin'. But Miss Austen told her.

MAZIE. Did she?

MRS. HAROLD. I should say she did. It didn't take Mrs. Craig long to get out of the room once Miss Austen got started. [*A door closes upstairs, and Mazie darts to the center table and settles the table scarf. Mrs. Harold steps to the big chair in front of the mantelpiece and feigns to be occupied in setting it straight. Mazie glances over her right shoulder up the stairs, then steps up to the foot of the stairs and glances up. Then she hurries forward to Mrs. Harold again, glancing through the portières as she goes.*]

MAZIE. What did Mrs. Craig do, walk out of the room?

MRS. HAROLD. Yes. She said she had something else to do besides listenin' to a lot of silly talk. [*Mazie raises her eyes to heaven.*] I felt like sayin' I'd like to know what it was she had to do.

MAZIE. So would I.

MRS. HAROLD. I've been here nearly a year now, and I have my first time to see her do anything—only a lot of snoopin'—after somebody else has finished.

MAZIE. It's too bad Miss Austen didn't tell her that while she was at it.

MRS. HAROLD. [*Raising her hand, with a touch of solemnity*] She told her enough. [*She goes up to the foot of the stairs and looks up.*]

MAZIE. Well, didn't *he* say anything?

MRS. HAROLD. Not very much; Miss Austen done most of the talkin'. [*She comes down to Mazie's left, confidentially.*] She told him if he didn't do something very soon, his wife 'ud make him look like an echo.

MAZIE. She will, too.

MRS. HAROLD. He said she had a peculiar disposition—and that Miss Austen didn't understand her. Well, I felt like sayin' if Miss Austen don't understand her, I do. And I'd soon tell her how well I understand her, too, only that she gives me a wide berth.

MAZIE. I feel kind of sorry for him sometimes, though.

MRS. HAROLD. Yes, it's a pity for him. [*Lowering her voice, and speaking with great conviction*] She could build a nest in his ear, and he'd never know it. [*She turns to the table and settles the various ornaments.*]

MAZIE. She certainly is the hardest woman to please that I've ever worked for.

MRS. HAROLD. Well, I don't know whether she's hard to please or not, Mazie, for I've never tried to please her. I do my work, and if she don't like it she has a tongue in her head; she can soon tell me, and I can go somewhere else. I've worked in too many houses to be out of a place very long. [*Straightening up and resting her left hand on the table*] Did I tell you about her wanting me to dust the leaves off that little tree in front of the dining room window last week?

MAZIE. Dust the leaves?

MRS. HAROLD. [*Looking to heaven for witness*] That's the honest God's fact. And me with the rheumatism at the time.

MAZIE. Can you imagine such a thing?

MRS. HAROLD. Well, you know how I done it, don't you?

MAZIE. What'd you say to her?

MRS. HAROLD. I told her right up; I said, "I'll dust no tree for nobody."

MAZIE. You done right.

MRS. HAROLD. She sez, "You mean you refuse to dust it?"—"Yes," I sez, "I refuse, and," I sez, "what's more, I'm goin' to stay refuse." "Well," she sez, "it needs dusting, whether you dust it or not." "Well," I sez, "let it need it," I sez. I sez, "A little dust won't poison it." I sez, "We'll be dust ourselves some day, unless we get drownded." [*She goes to the portières.*]

MAZIE. You done right.

MRS. HAROLD. Oh, I told her. [*She glances out through the rooms.*]

MAZIE. I think the worst kind of a woman a girl can work for is one that's crazy about her house.

MRS. HAROLD. I do, too; because I think they *are* crazy half the time. You know, you can go crazy over a house, Mazie, the same as you can over anything else.

MAZIE. Sure you can.

MRS. HAROLD. Doctor Nicholson's wife was one of them; although she wasn't as generous a woman as this one.

MAZIE. No, that's one thing you've got to say for Mrs. Craig; she's not stingy.

MRS. HAROLD. No, that's true, she isn't.

MAZIE. I don't think I've ever worked in a house where there was as good a table for the help.

MRS. HAROLD. That's right; you always get whatever they get.

MAZIE. And you never have to ask for your wages, neither. [*The doorbell rings.*]

MRS. HAROLD. No, she's very good that way.

MAZIE. [*Going to answer the door, settling her cap and apron*] I guess that's that gentleman Mr. Craig's expectin'.

MRS. HAROLD. Come out when you come in, Mazie. [*She goes out through the portières. Mr. Craig comes down the stairs.*]

BIRKMIRE. [*At the front door*] Good evening. Is Mr. Craig in?

MAZIE. Yes, sir, he's in. [*The screen door is heard to close, and Birkmire enters.*]

CRAIG. [*Coming in*] Hello, Billy, how are you?

BIRKMIRE. [*Shaking hands earnestly*] Hello, Walt. [*He looks right into Craig's eyes.*]

CRAIG. I called your house a little while ago; [*Birkmire turns to the piano with his raincoat and hat.*] there was a message here for me when I got in, saying you'd called. [*Mazie comes in and crosses towards the portières.*]

BIRKMIRE. Yes, I've been trying to get hold of you since four o'clock.

CRAIG. Let me take those things out of your way. [*Mazie stops near the portières and looks back, to see if they want her to take Birkmire's things.*]

BIRKMIRE. No, thanks, Walter, I've got to get right back to the house. [*Mazie goes out; and Craig moves down towards the table.*]

CRAIG. Your father still here?

BIRKMIRE. Yes, he'll be here for a day or two yet. [*He looks keenly out through the portières, stepping up towards the back of the room.*]

CRAIG. [*Watching him curiously*] What's the matter? [*Birkmire makes a deft gesture, signifying that Mazie may be within hearing distance.*] What is it?

BIRKMIRE. [*Stepping down close to Craig and laying his hand on his sleeve*] What about it, Walt?

CRAIG. About what?

BIRKMIRE. About Fergus and his wife. You were out there last night, weren't you?

CRAIG. Sure. That's where I talked to *you* from.

BIRKMIRE. Well, my God, what happened out there, Walter?

CRAIG. What do you mean?

BIRKMIRE. Haven't you seen the evening papers?

CRAIG. Not yet, no. Why?

BIRKMIRE. [*Smothering an exclamation, and stepping to the piano to get a newspaper out of his pocket*] Jesus, how did you miss it!

CRAIG. Why, what's happened?

BIRKMIRE. Fergus and his wife are dead.

CRAIG. What!

BIRKMIRE. Found them this morning in the library.

CRAIG. Passmore, you mean?

BIRKMIRE. [*Handing him the paper*] Here it is on the front page of the *Telegraph*.

CRAIG. [*Crossing down to the right*] What are you saying, Billy?

BIRKMIRE. [*Stepping over towards the portières and looking out*] It's in every paper in town.

CRAIG. Where is it?

BIRKMIRE. [*Coming forward at Craig's left and indicating a certain head-line*] Fergus Passmore and wife found dead in library.

CRAIG. My God!

BIRKMIRE. I happened to see it over a man's shoulder coming down in the elevator in the Land Title Building about four o'clock, and I damned near had heart failure. [*He turns away to the left and takes a cigarette from a case.*] I've been trying to get you on the phone ever since. And I saw *her* myself at the Ritz last night at twelve o'clock. I was talking to her. I took the old man over there for a bit of supper after the show, and she was there with that military gent she's been stepping it with lately. [*Suddenly laying his hand on Craig's arm*] That's my hunch on this thing, Walter. I think she's been playing this soldier fellow a little too much lately and Fergus has heard of it and probably called it when she got in last night, and busted up the show. You know, he was always jealous as hell of her. [*He takes a step or two towards the back and glances through the portières.*]

CRAIG. There must be a catch in this thing somewhere, Billy.

BIRKMIRE. [*Coming forward again*] How could there be a catch in it, Walter? Do you think they'd print that kind of stuff for a joke.

CRAIG. Well, my God, I was out there last night till twelve o'clock.

BIRKMIRE. [*Tearing the cigarette between his fingers*] Well, evidently this thing happened after you got away from there. Did she get in before you left there last night?

CRAIG. [*Looking up from the paper*] What?

BIRKMIRE. I say, did Adelaide get in last night before you left out there?

CRAIG. No, but she was there when I got out there, about nine o'clock. She was going out somewhere.

BIRKMIRE. Yes, and I know who it was she was going out *with*, too; that's the third time I've run into her with that bird lately. And I want to find out what his name is right away quick, too, for he might be in on this thing.

CRAIG. Have you been out there yet?

BIRKMIRE. Out to Fergus', you mean?

CRAIG. Yes.

BIRKMIRE. Sure, I hopped right out there as soon as I read it; but you can't get near the place.

CRAIG. I think I ought to get in touch with Police Headquarters right away, Billy.

BIRKMIRE. Well, that's why I wanted to get hold of you. It says there they're looking for a man seen leaving the house after midnight.

CRAIG. Sure, that's me.

BIRKMIRE. Well, not necessarily you, Walter.

CRAIG. That's the time I got away from there.

BIRKMIRE. That doesn't mean anything. Only I think it 'ud be a good thing to let them know right away.

CRAIG. [*Turning suddenly and going up to the telephone*] Sure, I'll call · up right away.

BIRKMIRE. [*Following him up*] Well, now, wait a minute, Walter, don't move too fast; you know a thing like this can take a thousand and one turns, and we don't want to make any false move. This kind of thing 'ud be pie for the newspapers, you know; and the fact that we were invited out there to play cards wouldn't read any too well.

CRAIG. Well, *you* weren't out there.

BIRKMIRE. I know that; but I'm not sitting back in the corner in this thing, you know, Walter. It just so happened that I *wasn't* out there. But I talked to you on the telephone out there last night, from my house, and in a thing of this kind they trace telephone calls and everything else.

CRAIG. [*Looking at the paper again*] My God, this is a terrible thing, though, isn't it, Billy.

BIRKMIRE. [*Turning away to the left, and passing his hand across his brow*] I haven't got it myself yet.

CRAIG. Terrible.

BIRKMIRE. It'll be a jar to your wife when she hears it, won't it?

CRAIG. Awful.

BIRKMIRE. She'll be very likely to see it in the paper up there in Albany.

CRAIG. She's back from Albany.

BIRKMIRE. Is she?

CRAIG. She got in a while ago.

BIRKMIRE. Well, she doesn't know anything about this yet, does she?

CRAIG. I don't think so, unless she happened to see the paper I brought home. I suppose it's in it.

BIRKMIRE. Sure, it's in all of them.

CRAIG. I just took it from the boy and put it in my pocket.

BIRKMIRE. Where is Harriet?

CRAIG. She's upstairs.

BIRKMIRE. [*Lowering his voice*] Does she know you were out there last night?

CRAIG. I don't know, I guess she does. Yes, I think I mentioned it a while ago.

BIRKMIRE. [*Stepping to Craig's side, and laying his hand on his arm*] Well, now, listen, Walter—if she doesn't happen to see the paper, what she doesn't know won't bother her. And this thing is apt to clear itself up over night. It might be cleared up now, for all we know; for I suppose the police have been working on it all day. But, I think the wise move for us is just to hop out there and try to find out what's going on; and if they haven't found anything out yet, just get in touch with Police Headquarters and let them know where we're at.

CRAIG. [*Tossing the newspaper on to the seat beside the telephone table*] Yes, let's do that. Wait till I get my hat. [*He goes through the portières.*]

BIRKMIRE. [*Crossing to the piano for his things*] I've got my car out here; we can cut across the park and be out there in ten minutes. [*He throws his raincoat across his arm, picks up his hat, and steps quickly across to get the newspaper that Craig left on the seat. He glances up the stairs and out through the portières. Then he sees Craig coming through the adjoining room, and starts for the front door.*]

CRAIG. [*Entering, wearing his hat, and carrying the newspaper he brought home*] I'll take this paper with me; keep it out of sight.

BIRKMIRE. I've got the other one here in my pocket. [*Birkmire goes out.*]

CRAIG. [*Glancing about the room as he crosses to the front door*] We take the *Globe* here in the afternoon, but I don't see it anywhere around out there. [*He goes out.*]

BIRKMIRE. [*Outside*] I've got the car right out here.

CRAIG. [*Outside*] I guess across the park will be the quickest.

BIRKMIRE. Yes, we can be over there in ten minutes. [*There is a dead pause. Then a clock somewhere out at the right strikes half-past six, with a soft gong. There is another slight pause, and then Mrs. Craig sweeps through the portières, carrying an open newspaper. She sees that no one is in the room, and rushes to the forward window to see if she can see Mr. Craig anywhere about. Then she starts for the front*] door, but changes her mind and rushes up to the landing of the stair-way.]

MRS. CRAIG. [Calling up the stairs] Walter!—Walter!—Are you up there, Walter? [She hurries down into the room again and over to the portières.] Mazie!—Mazie! [She runs across to the front door and out. Mazie comes in through the portières and looks about, then starts towards the front door. Mrs. Craig hurries in again.]

MAZIE. Were you calling me, Mrs. Craig?

MRS. CRAIG. Yes, Mazie. Have you seen anything of Mr. Craig?

MAZIE. Why, he was here a few minutes ago, Mrs. Craig, with a gen-tleman.

MRS. CRAIG. What gentleman? Who was he?

MAZIE. I don't know who he was, Mrs. Craig; I never saw him before.

Mrs. Craig. Didn't you catch his name?

MAZIE. No, Ma'm, I didn't. He came in an automobile.

MRS. CRAIG. Well, did Mr. Craig go away with him?

MAZIE. I don't know whether he did or not, Mrs. Craig. I didn't know he'd gone.

MRS. CRAIG. [Turning Mazie around quickly by the shoulder and urging her towards the portières] See if Mr. Craig's hat's on the rack out there.

MAZIE. [Hurrying out] Isn't he up in his room?

MRS. CRAIG. No, he isn't. [She turns breathlessly and looks towards the bay window at the left.] Oh, Lord! [Turning to the portières again] Is it?

MAZIE. [From somewhere out at the right] No, ma'm, it isn't.

MRS. CRAIG. Well, listen, Mazie, run over to the garage there and see if he's there! No, no, come this way, it's quicker [She waits franti-cally until Mazie rushes through the portières and across towards the front door.] And if he's there tell him to come over here immedi-ately; I want to see him.

MAZIE. Yes, ma'm. [The screen door slams after her, and she hurries past the bay window at the left.]

MRS. CRAIG. Hurry now, Mazie. Tell him I want him right away. [She *turns in the door and leans against the jamb, looking straight out, wide-eyed, and holding the newspaper against her bosom.*] Oh, my God! [*She hurries across above the center table and down to the window, forward, at the right.*] Oh, my God! [*She stands looking eagerly through the window, toward the left, as though watching Mazie running down the street.*]

THE CURTAIN DESCENDS SLOWLY

⇒ ACT II ⇐

Ten Minutes Later

Mrs. Craig is standing at the window, forward, reading the newspaper. She stops reading, glances out the window, and then moves with a kind of controlled desperation to the bay window at the left, where she looks out again eagerly. Mrs. Harold comes in from the right.

MRS. HAROLD. Is Mazie here, Mrs. Craig? [*Mrs. Craig turns nervously.*]

MRS. CRAIG. No, she isn't, Mrs. Harold; I've sent her on an errand; she'll be back in a minute.

MRS. HAROLD. [*Turning to go out again*] I told her I thought I heard you calling her. [*Telephone bell rings*]

MRS. CRAIG. See who that is, Mrs. Harold, will you, please? [*Mrs. Harold comes back and picks up the telephone.*]

MRS. HAROLD. Hello?—Hello?

MRS. CRAIG. What's the matter; don't they answer?

MRS. HAROLD. No, ma'm, they haven't answered yet. Hello!

MRS. CRAIG. [*Turning to the window again*] Never mind it, Mrs. Harold; it's probably a mistake.

MRS. HAROLD. [*Hanging up the receiver*] It does that sometimes when it's a long distance call. [*Mrs. Craig turns sharply.*]

MRS. CRAIG. They didn't say it was long distance, did they?

MRS. HAROLD. No, ma'm, they didn't say anything; nobody answered at all.

MRS. CRAIG. Well, if they want us they'll ring again.

MRS. HAROLD. Will you tell Mazie I want her when she comes in, Mrs. Craig, please?

MRS. CRAIG. Yes, I'll send her out to you as soon as she comes back. [*Mrs. Harold goes out through the portières, and Mrs. Craig crosses over and down to the window, forward, and looks out. She sees Mazie hurrying back from the garage, and steps quickly up to the door at the left. Mazie can be seen running past the bay window. The screen door slams, and Mazie rushes in.*] Isn't he over there, Mazie?

MAZIE. No, ma'm, he isn't.

MRS. CRAIG. Are you sure?

MAZIE. Yes, ma'm, I looked all around.

MRS. CRAIG. Did you go around to the back?

MAZIE. Yes, ma'm, I looked everywhere. Old Mr. Foster was standin' over there; I ast him if he'd seen anything of Mr. Craig, but he said he hadn't.

MRS. CRAIG. Is the garage locked?

MAZIE. Yes, ma'm, I tried the door.

MRS. CRAIG. Well, could you see whether or not the car was in there?

MAZIE. Yes, ma'm, they're both in there, the little one, too; I looked through the glass. [*Mrs. Craig turns away to the right, with a troubled expression, and moves down towards the mirror, and Mazie moves towards the door at the right. Mrs. Craig glances out the window, forward.*] I guess maybe he musta went away with that gentleman that was here.

MRS. CRAIG. He probably did. You say that gentleman came in a car, Mazie?

MAZIE. Yes, ma'm, I think it was his; it was standin' right in front of the house when I opened the door for him.

MRS. CRAIG. All right, Mazie. Mrs. Harold wants you for something.

MAZIE. [*Going out*] Oh, does she? [*Mrs. Craig leans against the mantelpiece and thinks hard. The telephone bell rings. She turns and looks at the telephone; it rings again. Then she moves to answer it. Mazie comes in.*]

MRS. CRAIG. I'll answer it, Mazie.

MAZIE. Oh, all right. [*She withdraws, and Mrs. Craig picks up the telephone.*]

MRS. CRAIG. [*In a subdued voice*] Mazie.

MAZIE. Yes, ma'm?

MRS. CRAIG. Come here for a minute. [*Mazie appears between the portières*] Go up and see that Miss Landreth's door is closed.

MAZIE. [*Withdrawing*] Yes, ma'm.

MRS. CRAIG. Be very quiet about it, now, Mazie, and don't disturb her if she's asleep.

MAZIE. All right. [*Telephone bell rings again*]

MRS. CRAIG. Hello?—Yes?—All right. [*She glances up the stairs and then waits.*] Hello?—Yes—[*In a louder voice*] Hello! Yes—this is *Mrs.* Craig at the telephone—Mr. Craig isn't here just now, if you wanted *Mr.* Craig. Oh—why-a- Miss Landreth is lying down just now. Who is this speaking, please?—Oh, I see. Why—not a thing in the world, Mr. Fredericks, except that she's very tired.—We've only just now gotten in from Albany, and I suggested that she go upstairs and lie down for a while. Yes—am I going to do what? No I didn't understand what you said, Mr. Fredericks. Why, yes, of course, I'd go back with her if anything unforeseen developed—otherwise she can go back herself. We're simply waiting now to hear something from her mother's physician up there.—Yes, of course I'm sure. Why, why should you put yourself to that trouble, Mr. Fredericks?—There wouldn't be anything you could do when you get here.—Well, I'd much rather not call her, if you don't mind, Mr. Fredericks; she's lying down.—Well, can't you tell me what it is you want to tell her—and I can give her the message? Well, probably it would, Mr. Fredericks—it's very nice of you to be so solicitous about her, but I don't care to disturb her just now. I'm very sorry. [*She hangs up abruptly, and glances towards the head of the stairs. Mazie appears between the portières.*]

MAZIE. The door was closed, Mrs. Craig.

MRS. CRAIG. All right, Mazie. [*Mazie withdraws, and Mrs. Craig moves forward thoughtfully. There is a tap at the front door bell. Mazie turns and crosses to answer the door. Mrs. Craig is looking sharply toward the front door.*] See what those gentlemen want, Mazie.

MAZIE. Yes, ma'm.

CATELLE. [*At the front door*] Mr. Craig in?

Mazie. No, sir, he's not in just now; he went out about twenty minutes ago.

CATELLE. What time do you expect him back?

MAZIE. Why, I couldn't say for certain; but I guess he'll be back in time for dinner, about seven o'clock.

CATELLE. Is his wife in?

MAZIE. Yes, sir, she's in.

CATELLE. I'd like to speak to her for a minute if I could. [*Mrs. Craig, who has been standing very still, listening, vanishes through the portières, looking over her shoulder apprehensively towards the front door.*]

MAZIE. Yes, sir. Will you just step in? [*The screen door closes; and immediately Mazie hurries into the room.*] If you'll just take a chair for a minute I'll call her. [*Catelle wanders in, removing his hat, followed by Harry, who also removes his hat as he enters. Catelle moves down to the center table, puts his hat down, and takes a small leather notebook from his inside pocket; and Harry comes forward and sits in the chair beside the piano. There is a pause.*]

HARRY. They didn't get this place with a pound of tea.

CATELLE. A lot of money. Phoenix Fire Insurance people. This lad's old man used to be the president of the Company. Died about twelve years ago. I guess this gent's in line for the old man's job, if he lives. [*Mrs. Craig enters through the portières. Harry rises, and Catelle turns to her.*]

MRS. CRAIG. Good evening.

HARRY. Good evening.

CATELLE. Good evening, ma'm. I called to see Mr. Craig.

MRS. CRAIG. Mr. Craig isn't in just now, I'm sorry.

CATELLE. Are you Mrs. Craig?

MRS. CRAIG. Yes.

CATELLE. Have you any idea what time Mr. Craig'll *be* in?

MRS. CRAIG. Why, I'm expecting him any minute; he was here less than a half-hour ago, when I went upstairs; so he must be right here in the neighborhood somewhere.

CATELLE. [*Consulting his watch*] I see.

MRS. CRAIG. He'll certainly be back for his dinner, at seven o'clock, if you'd care to call back.

CATELLE. Well, I've got to be over the other side of town at seven o'clock—so it may be that you could give me the information I am looking for, as well as Mr. Craig. Would you sit down for a minute?

MRS. CRAIG. Yes, certainly. [*She turns to the chair in front of the mantelpiece and sits down. Harry resumes his chair beside the piano, and Catelle sits on the small bench immediately above the center table.*]

CATELLE. I thought I'd like to speak to *Mr.* Craig first, but I don't suppose it makes a great deal of difference.

MRS. CRAIG. I thought he might be over at the garage—I wanted him myself a few minutes ago; but the maid says he isn't over there.

CATELLE. Well, I'll tell you what it is I wanted to see him about, Mrs. Craig. I suppose you've seen in the evening paper about this unfortunate affair out here on Willows Avenue?

MRS. CRAIG. You mean that shooting affair?

CATELLE. Yes, at the Passmore home.

MRS. CRAIG. Yes, isn't that a dreadful thing!—I've just been reading it here.

CATELLE. Yes, it's a very sad affair.

MRS. CRAIG. They're both dead, aren't they?

CATELLE. Yes, they're both dead.

MRS. CRAIG. Isn't that terrible. That's what I wanted to see my husband for; I wanted to ask him if he knew that man.

CATELLE. He probably did; they're pretty well known people here in town.

MRS. CRAIG. Yes, they must be, according to the paper. I haven't had a chance to read it all yet, I've just gotten in from Albany.

CATELLE. It's a rather peculiar case.

MRS. CRAIG. Was it a robbery or something?

CATELLE. No, there wasn't anything taken. Of course, it could have been a foiled *attempt* at robbery, but that 'ud hardly explain certain other circumstances.

MRS. CRAIG. Are you gentlemen working on the case?

CATELLE. Yes, ma'm, we're from Police Headquarters. But, that doesn't need to alarm *you*, Mrs. Craig; there's no particular connection between that and our visit *here*.

MRS. CRAIG. Well, I'm very glad to know that.

CATELLE. No, this Passmore affair looks to me pretty clearly a matter of jealousy motive. Of course, there are one or two attendant circumstances, as there usually are in cases of this kind, but they don't mean anything, as far as the actual shooting is concerned. There was a man seen leaving the house shortly after midnight in an automobile—one of the neighbors happened to see him; but it was too dark to establish any identification. Besides, that wouldn't account for the death of *Mrs.* Passmore; because she didn't get in until after three o'clock, and the man left there between twelve and one.

MRS. CRAIG. I see.

CATELLE. But, of course, as you understand, Mrs. Craig, it's part of our business to follow up any little outside clue that we happen to get hold of that might throw some additional light on a case.

MRS. CRAIG. Yes, of course.

CATELLE. And that's what I wanted to see Mr. Craig about.

MRS. CRAIG. You mean that you think Mr. Craig might be the man that was seen leaving there last night.

CATELLE. No, that circumstance is really not being seriously considered; a house of that description might have had any number of visitors during the evening.

MRS. CRAIG. That's very true.

CATELLE. But, we've had a report late this afternoon, Mrs. Craig, from the Lynnebrooke Telephone Exchange, where your light comes in, that there was a call made on your telephone here at five-twenty-seven this evening, asking for the address of the telephone number Levering three, one hundred; and that happens to be the number of the telephone at Mr. Passmore's home.

MRS. CRAIG. You mean that somebody called from here? [*She indicates the telephone.*]

CATELLE. On this telephone, yes, ma'm. Oakdale, six, two, three. That's the number of your telephone here, isn't it?

MRS. CRAIG. Yes, that's our number.

CATELLE. That's what I've got here.

MRS. CRAIG. But I can't imagine who it would be that called.

CATELLE. The report says it was a woman's voice.

MRS. CRAIG. Who was it that reported it, do you know?

CATELLE. I couldn't tell you that, Mrs. Craig.

MRS. CRAIG. I mean to say, would it be possible that the person who reported it could have made a mistake in the number?

CATELLE. No, they're usually pretty careful in an affair of this kind.

MRS. CRAIG. And the call was made at five o'clock this evening, you say?

CATELLE. Five-twenty-seven, my report says. The operator didn't give the address, of course; it's against the telephone company's rules. And the party rang off.

MRS. CRAIG. Well, that's extraordinary. Although it might have been one of the servants—probably saw it in the evening paper and was curious to know where it was. [*Rising*] I'll ask them.

CATELLE. Well, I could understand that curiosity if the address wasn't published; but it is; and the telephone number *isn't*. And I was interested in finding out why any one 'ud have that particular phone number today and not know the address—when it's been in all the newspapers since two o'clock this afternoon. And this call wasn't made till after five.

MRS. CRAIG. It does seem strange, doesn't it?

CATELLE. I haven't been able to figure it out.

MRS. CRAIG. But, I dare say there's some very simple explanation of it.

CATELLE. Has this telephone here been used at all, to your knowledge, Mrs. Craig, since five o'clock this afternoon?

MRS. CRAIG. Why, I *answered* a call, a few minutes ago, from Northampton, Massachusetts.

CATELLE. A long distance call, you mean?

MRS. CRAIG. Yes. It was a Mr. Fredericks, at Smith College there, calling my niece, to inquire about her mother. Her mother is ill in Albany.

CATELLE. I see.

MRS. CRAIG. That's where we've just come from.

CATELLE. You don't know whether or not anybody from the outside has been in here since five o'clock?

MRS. CRAIG. Not to my knowledge; except a neighbor from across the avenue there, Mrs. Frazier. She brought some roses over to my husband's aunt. She was here when I got in; although I scarcely think she would have used the telephone. But, I'll ask Miss Austen if you like.

CATELLE. I wish you would, please, if you don't mind.

MRS. CRAIG. [*Going to the stairway landing*] Not at all. She's up in her room I believe.

CATELLE. Would you mind asking her to step down here for a few minutes?

MRS. CRAIG. Yes, certainly. [*Calling*] Miss Austen!—Miss Austen! [*There is a sound of a door opening somewhere upstairs.*]

MISS AUSTEN. [*From upstairs*] Is someone calling me?

MRS. CRAIG. Yes—it's me, Miss Austen. Would you mind coming down here for a minute or two, Miss Austen? I'd like to speak to you.

MISS AUSTEN. All right, I'll be down in a moment. [*Mrs. Craig turns to come down.*]

MRS. CRAIG. If you will, please. She'll be right down.

CATELLE. Thank you very much.

MRS. CRAIG. [*Moving towards the portières*] I suppose I'd better call the servants too, hadn't I? They'll probably know something about it.

CATELLE. Yes, I'd like to see them for a minute.

MRS. CRAIG. [*Going through the portieres*] I'll call them right away. [*Catelle looks at his watch and rises.*]

CATELLE. [*Crossing towards the portières.*] What time have you got there, Harry? [*He watches keenly through ther portières.*]

MRS. CRAIG. Mazie!

HARRY. Just seven.

MAZIE. [*Out at the right*] Yes, ma'm?

MRS. CRAIG. Would you come here for a minute?

CATELLE. Do you mind if I use this phone here, Mrs. Craig?

MRS. CRAIG. They'll be right in. [*She enters.*]

CATELLE. Do you mind if I use this phone here for a minute?

MRS. CRAIG. [*Moving forward*] Not at all, go right ahead. I didn't hear what you said.

CATELLE. I've got a call to make at seven o'clock.

MRS. CRAIG. That's quite all right. [*He stands holding the telephone, and Mrs. Craig listens keenly.*]

CATELLE. [*Into the telephone*] Spring 4000.—Right. [*There is a stillness; then the clock strikes seven, with a soft gong. Mazie enters, on the third gong.*]

MAZIE. Did you want me, Mrs. Craig? [*Mrs. Craig motions to her to be silent; Mazie stands looking from one to the other in a state of positive bewilderment.*]

CATELLE. Thielens? Catelle.—That so?—I got away from there before six. Period? Righto, Chuck. What are you trying to do, break Harry's heart? [*He gives a rather dry little laugh.*] All right, Chuck, I'll be right over. [*He hangs up and crosses to the table for his hat.*] We'd better get right out there, Harry. [*Harry rises and moves up to the door.*] I won't have to bother you any more right now, Mrs. Craig; there's been a bit of additional information come in over at headquarters that'll hold things up temporarily.

MRS. CRAIG. [*Moving towards the center table*] Well, do you want me to have Mr. Craig get in touch with you when he comes in?

CATELLE. No, we'll get in touch with him if it's necessary.

MRS. CRAIG. And you don't want to question the rest of the people now, either? [*Harry goes out.*]

CATELLE. Not just now, Mrs. Craig, thank you very much. [*He starts for the door.*]

MRS. CRAIG. You're welcome, I'm sure. All right, Mazie. [*Mazie withdraws reluctantly, her eyes fastened upon Catelle.*]

CATELLE. I'm sorry to have had to trouble you.

MRS. CRAIG. [*Following him to the door*] That's quite all right.

CATELLE [*Turning at the door*] You can explain the circumstances to Mr. Craig, if you will.

MRS. CRAIG. Yes, I will. He'll probably know something about it.

CATELLE [*Going out*] Very likely he will.

MRS. CRAIG. And if he doesn't, I'm sure one of the others will.

CATELLE All right, thank you very much, Mrs. Craig.

MRS. CRAIG. You're very welcome, I'm sure.

CATELLE Good evening.

MRS. CRAIG. Good evening. [*The screen door closes, and Mrs. Craig turns slowly and lifts her closed hands in a quiet panic. Then she hurries forward and across to the window and watches the two detectives going down the street. Miss Austen comes down the stairs quietly, and stands on the landing, looking at her.*]

MISS AUSTEN. Did you want to see me about something, Harriet? [*Mrs. Craig starts slightly and turns.*]

MRS. CRAIG. [*Going out through the portières*] No, not now, Miss Austen; it isn't necessary. I'm sorry to have troubled you. [*Miss Austen stands for a second looking after her; then she moves forward to the window, to see what it was that had so engaged Mrs. Craig's attention. Then she moves up towards the telephone, glancing through the portières.*]

MISS AUSTEN. [*Into the telephone*] Will you give me Clearfield, six, two—six, two?—Please? [*She waits, glancing towards the portières and out the window.*] Hello? Is this the Mowers Express Office? Well, how early could I have some things taken away tomorrow morning? Six hundred and eighty Belmont Manor. Yes, just a square from the Park. Well, eight o'clock would be time enough. Miss Irene Austen. That's right. Thank you. [*She hangs up, and goes up the stairs. Mrs. Craig comes through the portières, glances towards the head of the stairs, and moves to the foot of the stairs to look up. Then she steps to the telephone table and settles everything precisely. Mazie appears between the portières.*]

MRS. CRAIG. What is it, Mazie?

MAZIE. Why, Mrs. Harold wants to know if she'll serve the dinner now, Mrs. Craig.

MRS. CRAIG. [*Moving forward, thoughtfully*] Tell her not yet for a little while, till Mr. Craig gets here; I'm expecting him any minute.

MAZIE. Yes, Ma'm. [*She goes out; and Mrs. Craig stands thinking hard for a second. The screen door closes sharply, and she wheels round with a rapid movement, crossing above the center table towards the door. Craig enters, removing his hat.*]

MRS. CRAIG. Walter! Where have you been?

CRAIG. Out with Billy Birkmire. Why?

MRS. CRAIG. [*Indicating the outer door of the glass vestibule*] Shut that door. [*He turns and shuts it, and she moves along the foot of the stairway, glancing up and out throught the portières.*]

CRAIG. [*Coming into the room again*] What's the matter? [*Mrs. Craig turns and crosses back towards him.*]

MRS. CRAIG. My God, haven't you seen the evening paper about Fergus Passmore and his wife!

CRAIG. Yes, I've seen it.

MRS. CRAIG. Well, what about it, Walter?

CRAIG. [*Putting his hat down on the piano*] I don't know any more about it than you do, Harriet.

MRS. CRAIG. My God, isn't that a terrible thing! I've been nearly out of my mind for the last half hour. I happened to see it in the paper there when I came downstairs, and I couldn't find you anywhere.

CRAIG. I went out with Birkmire.

MRS. CRAIG. Was that Birkmire that was here?

CRAIG. Yes, he wanted to see me about it.

MRS. CRAIG. I didn't even know whether you knew it or not; because you hadn't said anything about it when you came in this evening.

CRAIG. I didn't *know* it when I came in this evening.

MRS. CRAIG. [*Pointing at the paper on the table*] It's on the very front page of the paper there.

CRAIG. I didn't see the paper this evening till Birkmire showed it to me.

MRS. CRAIG. Well, why didn't you call me then, and not go rushing out of the house?

CRAIG. I didn't want to upset you.

MRS. CRAIG. [*Moving forward and across in front of the center table*] Well, I certainly couldn't have been any more upset than I have been. [*Turning to him*] Mazie said there's been a man here, and that you'd gone away with him in an automobile—so, of course, I didn't know what to think. I thought probably you'd been arrested or something. [*He looks at her sharply.*]

CRAIG. What would I be arrested for?

MRS. CRAIG. Why, in connection with this thing, of course. [*Taking a step towards him*] The police are looking for you; you know that, don't you?

CRAIG. Who says the police are looking for me?

MRS. CRAIG. Two of them have just left here, not five minutes ago.

CRAIG. Policemen?

MRS. CRAIG. They said they were from Police Headquarters; that's all I know.

CRAIG. And what are they looking for me for?

MRS. CRAIG. Well, now, why do you suppose they're looking for you, Walter?

CRAIG. I don't know.

MRS. CRAIG. Doesn't it say in the paper there that you were seen leaving Passmore's at twelve o'clock last night?

CRAIG. I doesn't say that *I* was seen leaving there.

MRS. CRAIG. It says there was a man seen leaving there, and who else could it have been but you? You were out there, weren't you?

CRAIG. Yes.

MRS. CRAIG. Well, that's enough, isn't it? [*She turns away to her left, and crosses above the table towards the portières.*]

CRAIG. But *they* don't know that.

MRS. CRAIG. Oh, don't be absurd, Walter.

CRAIG. Who saw me?

MRS. CRAIG. [*Coming back towards him*] Somebody always sees in a case of this kind.

CRAIG. Who could it have been?

MRS. CRAIG. The butler saw you, didn't he?

CRAIG. What if he did?—He didn't know me from Adam. He says so there in the paper, doesn't he?

MRS. CRAIG. He could identify your picture, couldn't he?

CRAIG. Who's going to give him my picture?

MRS. CRAIG. Don't talk so loud. [*She steps back towards the portières, to assure herself that neither of the servants is listening.*]

CRAIG. [*Moving forward at the left of the center table*] Anyway, I don't believe he'd recognize my picture if he *did* see it; he only came into the library for a couple of minutes to serve some drinks, and went right out again. And he didn't get my name, because Fergus was sitting on the lawn when I got there and took me in himself. And the butler was in bed when I left there.

MRS. CRAIG. [*Coming forward at the right of the table*] Didn't any of the other servants see you?

CRAIG. Not that I know of.

MRS. CRAIG. [*Coming very close to him and lowering her voice*] Didn't you tell me that Billy Birkmire called you on the telephone out there last night?

CRAIG. Yes, I talked to him out there.

MRS. CRAIG. Well, didn't the butler get your name then?

CRAIG. No; Fergus answered the phone himself, on the extension in the library.

MRS. CRAIG. Well, those men have been here, anyway.

CRAIG. Well, what did they want?

MRS. CRAIG. Haven't I just told you what they wanted? They wanted to see *you*.

CRAIG. Did they say they knew it was I that was out there last night?

MRS. CRAIG. I don't remember *what* they said, exactly; I was too upset. But they wanted to know where you were, and, of course, I couldn't tell them; because you were here when I left the room, and then you suddenly disappeared. [*Turning away to the right*] I was never placed in such a position in my life. I'm sure those men must have thought I was evading them.

[*Turning back to him again*] But *I* didn't know what to say to them—except that you'd probably taken a little walk around the neighborhood here; because I'd sent Mazie over to the garage to look for you as soon as I saw the paper, and she said both of the cars were in there.

CRAIG. I went out in Birkmire's car.

MRS. CRAIG. Where did you go with him?

CRAIG. Over to Fergus' house.

MRS. CRAIG. And what in heaven's name did you do a thing like that for, Walter?

CRAIG. Why not?

MRS. CRAIG. Supposing you'd run into somebody out there?

CRAIG. And what if I did?

MRS. CRAIG. Do you want your name to be dragged into this thing?

CRAIG. My name'll be dragged into it anyway, won't it?

MRS. CRAIG. Why will it?

CRAIG. You say those men have been here already.

MRS. CRAIG. And what if they have? That doesn't mean anything.

CRAIG. It means that they must have associated my name with it already, doesn't it?

MRS. CRAIG. No, it doesn't mean anything of the kind; they were simply looking for information.

CRAIG. But it was to me they *came* for that information.

MRS. CRAIG. Because you were a friend of Passmore's.

CRAIG. Exactly. And they'll very likely come back here again.

MRS. CRAIG. But, you don't have to go out looking for them, do you?

CRAIG. [*Turning away and going up towards the door at the left*] You can't be playing any game in a thing like this, Harriet.

MRS. CRAIG. [*Following him up*] No, and you don't have to go rushing out to meet a lot of scandalous publicity, either. I should think your own common sense would show you what it would mean to have your name even mentioned in a thing of this kind. [*Turning away and down towards the center table*] Why, it 'ud be in every newspaper in the country.

CRAIG. [*Coming forward at the right of the piano*] That wouldn't bother me in the least.

MRS. CRAIG. [*Aghast*] It wouldn't bother you!

CRAIG. Not the least bit.—My conscience is clear.

MRS. CRAIG. [*Stepping to his side*] Oh, don't be so absurdly romantic, Walter!

CRAIG. It isn't a question of romanticism at all.

MRS. CRAIG. No, and it isn't a question of conscience, either. It's simply a matter of discretion. If you've had nothing to do with this thing, what's the use of becoming involved?

CRAIG. What do you mean, *if* I've had nothing to do with it?

MRS. CRAIG. [*With sudden temper*] Oh, now don't start picking me up on every word! [*She turns away to the left and crosses above the center table towards the portières. Craig takes a cigarette from a case and closes the case with a snap. Mrs. Craig turns and sees that he is about to smoke.*] Now, don't smoke in this room, Walter. [*He throws the cigarette across the room to the fireplace. Mrs. Craig looks at it in astonishment, and then at him.*] Well, that's a nice place to throw it, I must say. [*She goes down to the fireplace and picks it up.*]

CRAIG. [*Sitting in the chair at the right of the piano*] Oh, what does it matter!

MRS. CRAIG. Don't you want it?

CRAIG. What good is it, if I can't smoke it?

MRS. CRAIG. [*Crossing above the table towards the front door, holding the cigarette away from her, between her thumb and finger*] There are plenty of other places in the house to smoke, if you want to smoke.

CRAIG. I don't know where they are.

MRS. CRAIG. [*Going out the door*] You can smoke in your den, can't you?

CRAIG. If I shut the door. [*He sits thinking, deeply. The screen door slams, and Mrs. Craig comes in again, looking keenly towards the portières.*] Did those men say when they'd be back here?

MRS. CRAIG. I don't remember whether they did or not—I suppose they did. They said they'd get in touch with you if it was necessary. [*Coming forward to his side, and lowering her voice*] But, if they *do* come back here, Walter, don't give them any more information than I did.

CRAIG. Well, I certainly won't deny that I was a friend of Fergus'.

MRS. CRAIG. You don't have to deny that you were a friend of his; but you certainly don't have to submit to a lot of cross-examination by detectives, either, simply because you happened to be a friend of his. [*She turns away and moves to the front of the center table.*] Let them go and cross-examine some of his other friends; you weren't the only friend he had.

CRAIG. Why did you submit to their cross-examination?

MRS. CRAIG. [*Turning to him*] Because I didn't know at the time to what extent they were justified in questioning me. I thought probably they had some information about your having been out at Passmore's last night. And I was at my wit's end, trying to keep from saying something that would imply an admission of it. I told them right away that I'd just gotten in from Albany, so I suppose they assumed that I didn't know where you'd been last night.

CRAIG. How long did they stay here?

MRS. CRAIG. About fifteen minutes, I imagine; but it seemed like a year.

CRAIG. What were they talking about all that time?

MRS. CRAIG. About you, and Fergus Passmore, and where you were, and when you'd be back, and all kinds of questions. [*She goes to the piano and picks up his hat, settling the piano scarf.*]

CRAIG. Did they say they'd been to any other of Fergus' friends?

MRS. CRAIG. I don't remember, they may have. They said something about him being very well known here socially, so they probably have. [*Craig thinks for a second, then rises abruptly and crosses below the center table and up to the telephone.*]

CRAIG. I think I'll call Birkmire up and see if they've been to see him.

MRS. CRAIG. [*With a panicky movement towards him*] Now, wait a minute, Walter! [*She puts his hat on the table as she crosses above it.*] You're not going to do anything of the kind.

CRAIG. Why not?

MRS. CRAIG. [*Taking the telephone away from him*] Now, go away from this 'phone [*She draws him forward by the arm, away from the telephone.*] Let me tell you something.

CRAIG. What's the matter?

MRS. CRAIG. Don't you realize that that telephone is being watched—and that they are probably watching Birkmire's too?

CRAIG. Who is?

MRS. CRAIG. Why, the police, of course. Haven't you any realization of your position in this affair?

CRAIG. I evidently haven't the same realization that you have.

MRS. CRAIG. Well, it's time you did have.

CRAIG. Is it?

MRS. CRAIG. Yes, it is.

CRAIG. And what realization have you of my position?

MRS. CRAIG. Never mind what realization I have; that doesn't matter now. I simply know that the very first thing the police do in a case of this kind is to watch the telephone calls to and from the house.

CRAIG. Not from this house.

MRS. CRAIG. I mean from Fergus' house.

CRAIG. I wasn't going to call Fergus' house.

MRS. CRAIG. You were going to call Billy Birkmire, weren't you?

CRAIG. At his own house, yes.

MRS. CRAIG. Well, what difference does it make, Walter. Do you think those detectives can't put two and two together? Birkmire called you last night at Passmore's, didn't he?

CRAIG. Yes.

MRS. CRAIG. And there's undoubtedly a record of the call.

CRAIG. That wouldn't involve my name, would it?

MRS. CRAIG. It would if the operator listened in.

CRAIG. And do you think she has nothing to do but listen in on calls?

MRS. CRAIG. She listened in on this one, didn't she?

CRAIG. On which one?

MRS. CRAIG. What? [*She steps back from him suddenly, and touches her hair, in an effort to appear casual.*] What did you say?

CRAIG. Which call do you say the operator listened in on?

MRS. CRAIG. I don't know which one she listened in on. But some one must have listened in on something or those men wouldn't have come here, would they?

CRAIG. Did they say the operator had reported on a call from here?

MRS. CRAIG. I don't remember what they said, distinctly. One of them kept rambling something about a telephone call, but I assumed it was the one that Birkmire made to you last night at Fergus'.

CRAIG. Didn't they say when the call was made?

MRS. CRAIG. What does it matter when it was made, Walter?

CRAIG. It matters a lot.

MRS. CRAIG. The fact remains, doesn't it, that the telephone is undoubtedly being watched now.

CRAIG. [*Whirling round and picking up the telephone again*] Well, I want to know *why* it's being watched.

MRS. CRAIG. [*Springing to his side and seizing the telephone*] Now, listen to me, Walter Craig; you *must* not use that telephone. [*She looks him straight in the eyes, then moves back several steps and looks at him defiantly.*] I will not allow you to drag my name into a notorious scandal.

CRAIG. [*Whipping the receiver off and putting it to his ear*] I've got to find out where I'm at in this thing!

MRS. CRAIG. [*Raising her voice threateningly*] If you speak over that telephone I'll leave this house! [*He takes the receiver from his ear and looks at her steadily. There is a pause.*] And you know what construction 'ud be put upon that, under the circumstances. [*He slowly hangs up and sets the telephone back onto the little table, holding her eyes steadily. Then he moves slowly towards her.*]

CRAIG. What do you mean, you'll leave this house?

MRS. CRAIG. [*Stonily*] I mean exactly what I said. Do you think I could stay in this neighborhood twenty-four hours after my name had been associated with a thing of this kind?

CRAIG. And haven't you any appreciation of the necessity of my knowing what's happening in this case?

MRS. CRAIG. I have no appreciation of any necessity except the necessity of keeping still.

CRAIG. But supposing something developed that would reveal absolutely the fact that I had been out there last night—

MRS. CRAIG. What *can* develop, if you keep still?

CRAIG. But, supposing something did? Wouldn't it be very much better for me to have been open and aboveboard from the beginning, instead of having played a waiting game, and probably create an attitude of suspicion where there are no grounds for any?

MRS. CRAIG. There *are* grounds for suspicion, Walter; don't evade the issue.

CRAIG. What are they?

MRS. CRAIG. The fact that you were out there last night.

CRAIG. That doesn't mean a thing.

MRS. CRAIG. Evidently not, to you.

CRAIG. Does it to you?

MRS. CRAIG. What does it matter what it means to me? It isn't for me to determine the degree of your guilt or innocence. I'm not interested.

CRAIG. You're not interested!

MRS. CRAIG. I'm interested only in the impression on the popular mind—and the respect of the community we've got to live in.

CRAIG. You mean you'd rather know I was involved in this thing and *keep* the respect of the community, than know I was a victim of circumstances, and lose it? [*Mrs. Harold appears between the portières. Mrs. Craig sees her over Craig's shoulder, and crosses quickly below him.*]

MRS. CRAIG. What is it, Mrs. Harold?

MRS. HAROLD. I'm sorry to bother you, Mrs. Craig, but I'm afraid the dinner'll be spoiled.

MRS. CRAIG. [*Going down to the mirror*] All right, Mrs. Harold, put it up; I'll be right out. [*Craig moves forward to the upper right hand corner of the center table.*]

MRS. HAROLD. [*Withdrawing*] All right.

CRAIG. Mrs. Harold.

MRS. HAROLD. [*Stopping*] Yes, sir? [*She comes back a few steps towards him.*]

CRAIG. Mrs. Harold, do you know if anybody has called that number that I gave you last night here, today, on this telephone?

MRS. HAROLD. You mean the number you gave me to have Mr. Birkmire call you at?

CRAIG. Yes, Levering three one hundred.

MRS. HAROLD. No, sir, I don't know that anybody has. I only gave it to Mr. Birkmire over the telephone last night when he called.

CRAIG. *You* haven't had occasion to call that number today on this telephone, have you, Mrs. Harold?

MRS. HAROLD. No, sir, I haven't, Mr. Craig.

CRAIG. All right, Mrs. Harold, thanks very much. [*She starts to go, then stops and turns again.*]

MRS. HAROLD. I never even thought about it today until Mrs. Craig asked me for it when she came in this evening. [*There is a pause. Craig shifts his eyes to his wife, who raises her arm slowly and touches her hair before the mirror.*]

CRAIG. All right, Mrs. Harold, thank you very much. [*Mrs. Harold withdraws, and Craig moves up slowly towards the portières and watches her out of hearing distance. Then he turns and looks at his wife. She stands very still. He moves a step or two slowly towards her.*] It was you that made that call. [*She turns and looks at him, with a touch of defiance.*] What were you doing, checking up on me?

MRS. CRAIG. [*Starting up towards the portières*] Don't flatter yourself, Walter.

CRAIG. That's what you were doing, wasn't it?

MRS. CRAIG. Don't flatter yourself. The man hasn't been born yet that I'd bother checking up on.

CRAIG. Why didn't you tell me the truth?

MRS. CRAIG. [*Whirling upon him*] Because I anticipated an attack of your romantic conscience.

CRAIG. You were playing safe; that was it, wasn't it?

MRS. CRAIG. Exactly!

CRAIG. And at my expense!

MRS. CRAIG. I knew the necessity of it with you!

CRAIG. [*Turning away to the left, crossing in front of the center table*] God!

MRS. CRAIG. [*Following him up*] I know if I told you I made that call, you'd be on the telephone in five minutes telling the Police.

CRAIG. [*Turning sharply*] I intended doing that anyway.

MRS. CRAIG. You silly fool!

CRAIG. That's where I went this evening, with Birkmire, when I left here—to Police Headquarters.

MRS. CRAIG. [*Aghast*] Oh!

CRAIG. And the only reason I didn't tell them then was that the man in charge of the case had gone to his dinner and wouldn't be back till eight o'clock. But he'll be told t*hen*! [*He swings up to the front door.*]

MRS. CRAIG. [*Leaning across the center table, and speaking threateningly*] Well, if you do, you'll explain my leaving you, too.

CRAIG. That wouldn't worry me in the least, Harriet.

MRS. CRAIG. Well, it might worry *them*. [*He turns sharply and looks at her, dismayed.*]

CRAIG. [*Coming back to the table*] Listen to me, Harriet. Why weren't you at least *honest* with me in this thing, and not try to make it appear the *I* was responsible for the visit of those detectives?

MRS. CRAIG. Because I knew exactly what you'd do if I told you. And that would mean an explanation of why I had called up; and the next thing would be an admission of the fact that you are the man the police are *looking for.*

CRAIG. But it's *you* those detectives are looking for.

MRS. CRAIG. Oh, you needn't try to turn it on to me! They wouldn't be looking for either of us if you'd stayed at home last night, instead of being out card playing with a lot of irregular people. [*She turns down to the mirror.*]

CRAIG. What was there irregular about Fergus Passmore?

MRS. CRAIG. [*Turning to him, in a wrath*] There must have been some irregularity, or this thing wouldn't have happened. Everybody that knew Fergus Passmore knew that he was insanely jealous of his wife; and the *you* have to go out visiting them. [*She crosses below the table to the piano.*] I felt in my bones up there in Albany that something 'ud happen while I was away; that was the reason I didn't stay up there any longer than I absolutely had to. I knew as soon as ever my back was turned you'd be out with your friends again. [*He looks at her, under his brows; and there is a pause.*]

CRAIG. And what has your back being turned got to do with my visiting my friends?

MRS. CRAIG. Never mind what it has to do with it; only you wouldn't have *been* visiting them if I'd been here.

CRAIG. How would you have stopped me?

MRS. CRAIG. I'd have stopped you all right, one way or another.

CRAIG. What would you have done—locked the door on me?

MRS. CRAIG. It wouldn't have been necessary to lock the door on you. [*Turning and looking at him directly*] You haven't *been* visiting them in the last eighteen months, have you?

CRAIG. No, I haven't.

MRS. CRAIG. And they haven't been visiting you, either?

CRAIG. No, they haven't.

MRS. CRAIG. [*Turning away*] Well—

CRAIG. [*After a slight pause*] You mean you've kept them out of here?

MRS. CRAIG. [*Turning to him again and looking him straight in the eyes*] Well, if I did the end justified the means; you at least haven't been in the shadow of the law in the last eighteen months. [*He holds her eye for a second, then moves forward to the front of the table.*]

CRAIG. You're certainly running true to form, Harriet.

MRS. CRAIG. Well, I'm glad of it if I am.

CRAIG. My aunt said here a while ago that you'd driven all my friends away from this house.

MRS. CRAIG. [*With level significance*] There are ways of getting rid of people without driving them away from the house. [*Craig makes a little sound of bitter amusement.*]

CRAIG. And I thought she was imagining things at your expense.

MRS. CRAIG. Well, you see she probably had better perception than you'd given her credit for. [*He turns and looks at her darkly.*]

CRAIG. Probably she had; for she perceived something else, Harriet, that may be equally true.

MRS. CRAIG. Is that so?

CRAIG. She said you were trying to get rid of me too—[*She darts a look at him.*] without actually driving me away from the house. [*She laughs derisively, and moves across towards the portières. He follows her up, raising his voice.*] And I believe that's true, too.

MRS. CRAIG. Keep you voice down! Do you want everybody in the house to hear you?

CRAIG. You've admitted it, by your attitude in this affair this evening.

MRS. CRAIG. [*Looking at him, and moving forward to the mantelpiece*] I don't know what you're talking about.

CRAIG. [*Coming forward and leaning on the table*] Very well, you know what I'm talking about. And you knew what my aunt was going to talk about too, here a while ago; that' the reason you left the room before she started.

MRS. CRAIG. I'm sorry I didn't stay here now.

CRAIG. No danger of your staying here, Harriet; you couldn't bear it. [*She laughs, and he moves forward to the left.*] My God, how perfectly she knows you, Harriet! She couldn't have read you any better if you'd written it out for her. And I felt rather sorry listening to her, thinking she was probably getting a little old and suspicious; particularly when she said you had excluded my friends.

MRS. CRAIG. Do you think I wanted my house turned into a tavern?

CRAIG. My friends never turned my mother's house into a tavern.

MRS. CRAIG. They didn't play poker at your mother's house till all hours of the morning.

CRAIG. Every Thursday night for ten years; till two o'clock, if they felt like it.

MRS. CRAIG. Well, evidently, your mother and I had very different ideas of a house.

CRAIG. Very different indeed, Harriet; there was more actual home in one room of my mother's house than there'd be in all of this if we lived in it a thousand years.

MRS. CRAIG. Why didn't you stay in it, then, if you found it so attractive?

CRAIG. Now you're talking, Harriet; why didn't I do *just* that. [*He turns away to the left, then turns suddenly back.*] But, don't make any mistake that I think you didn't want my friends here simply because they played cards; you wouldn't have wanted them if they'd come here to hold prayer meetings. You didn't want them because, as my aunt says, their visits implied an importance to *me* that was at variance with you little campaign—the campaign that was to reduce me to one of those wife-ridden sheep that's afraid to buy a necktie for fear his wife might not approve of it. [*He goes up towards the front door.*]

MRS. CRAIG. Oh, don't try to make yourself out a martyr; you've had your share of this bargain. [*He turns suddenly and looks at her, then comes forward again to the front of the table.*]

CRAIG. I never regarded this thing as a bargain.

MRS. CRAIG. Did you expect me to go into a thing as important as marriage with my eyes shut?

CRAIG. I wanted you to go into it honestly, as I went into it—fifty-fifty—and you've been playing it safe right form the start. [*He turns away towards the piano.*]

MRS. CRAIG. I've been going nothing of the kind.

CRAIG. Don't tell me what you've been doing; I see your game as clearly as my aunt sees it. [*He turns and comes back towards her.*] You've been *exploiting me*, consistently, in your shifty little business of personal safety. And you'd throw me right now to the suspicion of implication in this double murder—to preserve that safety. [*He goes back towards the piano again.*]

MRS. CRAIG. [*Almost crying*] I've been trying to preserve my home.

CRAIG. That's all I've heard from you since the day I married you.

MRS. CRAIG. Well, what else has a woman like me *but* her home?

CRAIG. [*Turning to her*] Hasn't she her husband?

MRS. CRAIG. She could lose her husband, couldn't she?—As many another woman has.

CRAIG. Couldn't she lose her home too?

MRS. CRAIG. She couldn't if she knew how to secure it.

CRAIG. [*Raising his finger solemnly*] That's the point in a nutshell, Harriet; if she knew how to *fix* it for herself. [*He turns away and rests his hands on the piano.*]

MRS. CRAIG. Well, what if I have fixed things for myself? You haven't lost anything by it, have you? If I've fixed them for myself I've fixed them for you too. Your home is here. And maybe if I hadn't played the game so consistently it wouldn't *be* here. And I wouldn't be the first woman that's lost her home, and her husband too, through letting the control of them get out of her hands. [*She moves up towards the back of the room, in a crying temper.*] I saw what happened to my own mother, and I made up my mind it 'ud never happen to me. [*She turns and comes forward again*] She was one of those "I will follow thee, my husband" women—that believed everything my father told her; and all the time he was mortgaging her home over her head for another woman. And when she found it out, she did the only thing that women like her *can* do, and that was to die of a broken heart—within six months; and leave the door open for the other woman to come in as stepmother over Estelle and me. [*She turns to the mantelpiece.*] And then get rid of us both as soon as Estelle was marriageable. [*Turning to him suddenly*] But the house was never mortgaged over *her* head, I'll promise you that; for she saw to it that it was put in her name before ever she took him; and she kept it there, too, right to the finish. [*She sweeps up towards the back of the room again.*]

CRAIG. Why didn't you ask me to put this house in your name?

MRS. CRAIG. [*Whirling upon him*] Because I didn't *want* it in my name!

CRAIG. It would have been more honest.

MRS. CRAIG. [*Coming forward to the right end of the table*] I haven't done anything that wasn't honest!

CRAIG. How would you know, Harriet?

MRS. CRAIG. I've simply tried to be practical; but, with your usual romanticism, you want to make me appear like a criminal for it.

CRAIG. I'm not reproaching you at all.

MRS. CRAIG. Well, you shouldn't reproach me; for there's nothing to reproach me about.

CRAIG. You simply married the wrong man, Harriet.

MRS. CRAIG. [*Witheringly*] I married a romantic fool! [*He looks at her narrowly, and she holds his eye.*] That's what I married; [*She turns away and goes up to the portières to look out.*] and I'm seeing it more every day I live. [*There is a pause. Then Craig breaks into a hard little laugh.*]

CRAIG. How well we understand each other now, Harriet.

MRS. CRAIG. [*Coming forward to the mantelpiece again*] Well, I understand you, anyway, whether you understand me or not. [*Speaking directly to him*] And you ought to thank your God that I do, for I don't know what 'ud become of you if I didn't. [*She turns to the mantelpiece, and suddenly sees the card that Mazie left back of the center ornament. She picks up the little envelope deftly, takes the card out and reads it. Craig regards her icily; and after a pause, he speaks—in a level, rather dangerous tone.*]

CRAIG. The brass of you—and the presumption. [*She looks at him.*]

MRS. CRAIG. What?

CRAIG. I'm just wondering how you *get* that way.

MRS. CRAIG. How I get what way?

CRAIG. So brazenly presumptuous, as to say such a thing to me.

MRS. CRAIG. What have I said? I don't know what you're talking about.

CRAIG. [*Moving slowly away a step or two from the piano*] What have you ever done, or a million others like you, that would warrant the assumption of such superiority over the men you're married to?

MRS. CRAIG. Nobody's assuming any superiority.

CRAIG. Doesn't your remark admit it?

MRS. CRAIG. [*Turning and moving up to the portières*] Don't get yourself into a temper.

CRAIG. That you don't know what 'ud become of me only that *you* understand me.

MRS. CRAIG. [*Glancing through the portières*] Neither I do.

CRAIG. The presumption of you.

MRS. CRAIG. What are you standing there for, Mazie?

[*Mazie and Craig, speaking together*]

MAZIE. Why, Mrs. Harold sent me in to see if you were coming to dinner.

CRAIG. That you should set yourself about to control the very destiny of a man,—

MRS. CRAIG. Yes, I'm coming right away.

[*Mrs. Craig and Craig, speaking together*]

MRS. CRAIG. But I want to see you for a minute first, Mazie.

CRAIG. As though I were some mental incompetent.

MAZIE. Yes, ma'm.

MRS. CRAIG. [*Turning and going towards Craig, lowering her voice, and trying to silence him with a gesture*] Don't make a show of yourself in front of Mazie [*Mazie comes through the portières, and Mrs. Craig turns to her.*] Mazie, what is this card here?

MAZIE. Why, it's the Society card, Mrs. Craig, of the Mutual Benevolent.

MRS. CRAIG. And what is it doing here?

MAZIE. Why, Christine sent it down about an hour ago, with the tailor's little boy, to know if I'd pay her dues for her.

MRS. CRAIG. And couldn't you find any place for it but back of that ornament?

MAZIE. Why, I was—

MRS. CRAIG. After all the times I've told you never to put anything on that mantelpiece.

MAZIE. Yes, you *have* told me, Mrs. Craig, but when I came in—

MRS. CRAIG. Then, why do you do it? Must I keep telling you the same thing indefinitely? You know perfectly well I never allow anybody even to *dust* that mantelpiece but myself. I even bought a special little brush for those ornaments, because I wouldn't trust them to anybody else. And yet the minute you get my back turned you must use them as a catchall for everything in the house.

MAZIE. Mrs. Harold asked me something when I came in, and—

MRS. CRAIG. I am not interested in what anybody asked you; that does not excuse you. [*Mazie takes a handkerchief from the pocket of her apron and touches it to her eyes.*] I have told you over and over again *never* to put anything back of those ornaments; and you deliberately disobey me. You simply will *not* do as you are told. And when a girl will not do as she is told, the best thing for her to do is to go some place where she will be *made* to do it. So I want you to get your things together tonight and leave this house tomorrow morning. [*Mazie looks at her, then turns away to leave the room.*] Here's the card. And find some place for it besides back of an ornament. [*Mazie takes the card and withdraws.*] And tell Mrs. Harold to put up the dinner, I'll be down in two minutes; [*She starts for the stairs.*] I'm going up to see what my niece wants for *her* dinner. [*She goes up the stairs haughtily. Halfway up she turns, but without stopping, and addresses Craig coldly.*] You'd better go out there and get your dinner, before it's cold. [*She disappears at the head of the stairs, and Craig stands looking at the floor. His eyes wander up the stairs after her, and then down the right side of the room. They settle upon the ornament on the mantelpiece, and he looks at it hard; then crosses slowly and picks it up. He holds it in his hand, looking at it curiously: then suddenly lifts it in the air and smashes it on the bricks in front of the mantelpiece. He stands looking at the shattered pieces for a moment; then takes a cigarette from his case and strolls back across the room towards the piano. He taps the cigarette on the case, then takes out a match and lights it, tossing the burned match on to the floor. Then he leans against the piano and smokes, thoughtfully. Mrs. Harold hurries in through the portières.*]

MRS. HAROLD. Did something get broke in her, Mr. Craig? [*He indicates the shattered ornament with a nod, and Mrs. Harold looks towards the mantelpiece. She sees the pieces of the shattered ornament, and raising her hands and eyes to Heaven, takes a step or two towards them.*] Glory be to God this day and this night, how did that happen, Mr. Craig! Did it fall off the mantelpiece?

CRAIG. [*Without moving*] No, I smashed it, Mrs. Harold.

MRS. HAROLD. [*Puzzled*] On purpose, do you mean, Mr. Craig?

CRAIG. Yes—I didn't like it.

MRS. HAROLD. I wish you'd tell Mrs. Craig it was you that done it, Mr. Craig; if she sees it she might think it was one of us that broke it.

CRAIG. I'll tell here all about it, Mrs. Harold; don't you worry about that. [*He straightens up and starts across slowly towards the big chair in front of the mantelpiece, and Mrs. Harold moves a step or two towards the portières.*]

MRS. HAROLD. [*Turning to him*] Will I get the dustpan and sweep that up, Mr. Craig?

CRAIG. No, don't bother about it now, Mrs. Harold; go out and get your dinner. [*She moves towards the portières, then stops again.*]

MRS. HAROLD. Ain't you comin' to your dinner, Mr. Craig?

CRAIG. [*Sitting down*] No, I don't want any dinner tonight, Mrs. Harold.

MRS. HAROLD. Don't you want nothing at all?

CRAIG. Not a thing. [*She withdraws; and he sits smoking and thinking.*]

MRS. CRAIG. [*From the head of the stairs*] Are you down there, Walter?

CRAIG. Yes.

MRS. CRAIG. Listen—did something *fall* down there a minute ago?

CRAIG. No.

MRS. CRAIG. Are you sure?

CRAIG. Yes, I'm sure.

MRS. CRAIG. Well, it sounded up here as though the house fell down.

CRAIG. [*After a slight pause*] Maybe it did, Harriet—I'm just sitting here wondering. [*He sits smoking. His gaze wanders up, and out, and away off.*]

THE CURTAIN DESCENDS SLOWLY

⇒ ACT III ⇐

Same as preceding act—the following morning, about eight-thirty.
Craig is still sitting in the big chair before the fireplace, asleep. After
a pause, Mrs. Harold enters through the portières, carrying a dust-
pan and hand brush. She sees Craig, looks at him curiously, and also
observes the pieces of the shattered ornament and the cigarette butts
at his feet. She turns and puts the dustpan and brush down on the
seat at the right of the stairway, and, with a glance up the stairs,
crosses and unlocks the front door and goes out. The screen door
slams after her and Craig wakes. He looks around, glances at his
watch, gets up and settles himself before the mirror. Mrs. Harold tip-
toes in, bringing the morning paper.

CRAIG. Good morning, Mrs. Harold.

MRS. HAROLD. [*Stopping above the center table*] Good morning, Mr.
    Craig.

CRAIG. I must have made a night of it sitting here.

MRS. HAROLD. Yes, I was wondering if you'd been there all night.

CRAIG. I must have fallen asleep.

MRS. HAROLD. You must feel pretty tired, don't you?

CRAIG. [*Turning to her*] No, I'm all right. Is that the morning paper
    you have there, Mrs. Harold?

MRS. HAROLD. Yes, sir, I was just bringing it in.

CRAIG. Let me see it, will you?

MRS. HAROLD. Yes, sir. [*He takes the paper; and, stepping to the window,*
    forward, reads it eagerly.] Would you like a cup of coffee, Mr. Craig?

CRAIG. Yes. I'll take a little coffee if you have it.

MRS. HAROLD. [*Starting for the portières*] It's all made—I'll just turn on the percolator for a minute. [*She goes out; and he stands reading. There is the sound of a door opening somewhere upstairs. He glances towards the head of the stairs, then crosses quickly up to the front door and out on to the porch. Mrs. Harold comes in again; and, picking up the dustpan and brush, comes forward to the mantelpiece and starts to sweep up the ornament and cigarette butts. Mrs. Craig appears on the stairway.*]

MRS. CRAIG. Mrs. Harold.

MRS. HAROLD. [*Straightening up*] Yes, ma'm?

MRS. CRAIG. Has the morning paper come yet?

MRS. HAROLD. Yes, ma'm, I just gave it to Mr. Craig; he's reading it there on the front porch.

MRS. CRAIG. [*Puzzled, and coming down the stairs*] What is *he* doing up so early?

MRS. HAROLD. I don't think he's been in bed at all, Mrs. Craig; he was sitting in this big chair here when I came in this morning, and he was sitting here last night when I locked up. [*Mrs. Craig crosses to the bay window at the left and looks out on to the porch; and Mrs. Harold resumes here sweeping. Mrs. Craig becomes aware of what Mrs. Harold is doing and turns to her.*]

MRS. CRAIG. What is that you're sweeping up there, Mrs. Harold?

MRS. HAROLD. [*Straightening up*] Why, it's that center ornament that was here, Mrs. Craig. [*Mrs. Craig crosses down in front of the center table, looking wide-eyed at the vacant place on the mantelpiece.*]

MRS. CRAIG. What!

MRS. HAROLD. It got broke last night.

MRS. CRAIG. Oh, my God, Mrs. Harold, don't tell me that that's that beautiful statuette!

MRS. HAROLD. Mr. Craig said that he broke it.

MRS. CRAIG. [*Looking at the shattered pieces in the dustpan, which Mrs. Harold is holding*] Oh, my God, look at the way it's broken!—It's smashed into a thousand pieces.

MRS. HAROLD. It must have fallen on the bricks here.

MRS. CRAIG. Oh, that never simply fell, Mrs. Harold; it's absolutely shattered—look at the size of the pieces. It's out of the question even to think of having it mended.

MRS. HAROLD. No, I don't think it could ever be mended now.

MRS. CRAIG. [*Almost crying*] That beautiful thing—that I wouldn't even allow anybody to go near, and look at it now.

MRS. HAROLD. It certainly is too bad.

MRS. CRAIG. And, of course, I might just as well throw those others away now, for they're absolutely meaningless without this one. [*She turns away, in a pang of grief, and moves a few steps towards the left, then suddenly turns again to Mrs. Harold.*] How on earth did it ever happen, Mrs. Harold?

MRS. HAROLD. I don't know, I'm sure, Mrs. Craig.

MRS. CRAIG. I suppose Mazie broke it for spite, didn't she?— Because I reprimanded her last night for putting things back of it.

MRS. HAROLD. No, she didn't break it, Mrs. Craig, for she was out there in the kitchen with me when we heard it fall.

MRS. CRAIG. [*Turning away and crossing below the center table*] Well, send here in here to me now, I want to speak to her.

MRS. HAROLD. Mr. Craig said that *he* broke it; [*Mrs. Craig turns and looks at her.*] he said he didn't like that ornament.

MRS. CRAIG. Tell Mazie I want to see her.

MRS. HAROLD. She isn't here, Mrs. Craig; she's gone.

MRS. CRAIG. You mean she's left already?

MRS. HAROLD. Yes, ma'm, she left right after she had her breakfast.

MRS. CRAIG. Of course she did, the contemptible little devil.

MRS. HAROLD. Mr. Craig said that he'd tell you all about it.

MRS. CRAIG. Where did Mazie go?

MRS. HAROLD. She said she was goin' to her married sister's for a while.

MRS. CRAIG. Did you pay her her wages?

MRS. HAROLD. Yes, ma'm, I paid her last night.

MRS. CRAIG. [*Turning away towards the front door*] All right, Mrs. Harold. [*Mrs. Harold goes out through the portières, taking the dust-*

pan and brush with her.] Walter, come in here for a minute, will you? [*She glances over her shoulder, to see that Mrs. Harold is out of earshot, then turns and waits till Craig comes in. He enters, carrying the newspaper.*] What does the paper say this morning about the Passmore thing?

CRAIG. [*Handing her the newspaper*] You're quite safe. [*He comes forward and across in front of the center table to the mirror, and straightens his tie.*]

MRS. CRAIG. [*Stepping forward to the piano and spreading the paper out eagerly*] What does it say?

CRAIG. His brother got in last night from Pittsburgh, with a letter that Fergus had written him, intimating his intentions.

MRS. CRAIG. Then, Fergus did it himself?

CRAIG. So it appears.

MRS. CRAIG. I always told you he was jealous of his wife. [*Craig turns and looks at her.*]

CRAIG. He did it because she was dishonest.

MRS. CRAIG. [*Reading*] I suppose this telegram here from his brother about Fergus' letter was the additional information that that detective spoke about here last night. [*She straightens up and speaks directly to Craig.*] He called Police Headquarters from here about seven o'clock, and then he said it wouldn't be necessary to bother us any more for a while—that there'd been some additional information come in on the case: so I suppose that's what it was; for it says here the telegram was received at Police Headquarters at six forty-five.

CRAIG. [*Moving with a wearied air towards the portières*] What does it matter now, Harriet?

MRS. CRAIG. It doesn't matter *now*, but it would have mattered—only that I kept my head last night, and didn't allow you to telephone, and make a show of us all. [*He laughs bitterly.*] You can laugh, as much as you like; but you can thank me that your name isn't in every paper in the city this morning. [*She resumes her reading.*]

CRAIG. Oh, I can thank you for more than that, Harriet.

MRS. CRAIG. Well, you can thank me for that, anyway.

CRAIG. I can thank you for having given me a new name last night—that fits me so perfectly that I've decided to continue its use. You called me a romantic fool.

MRS. CRAIG. Fergus must have known about this man that Adelaide's been going around with; for it says here he'd mentioned him once before in a letter to his brother. [*Mrs. Harold appears between the portières.*]

MRS. HAROLD. The coffee's ready, Mr. Craig.

CRAIG. [*Turning quietly towards the portières*] All right, Mrs. Harold.

MRS. CRAIG. Listen, Walter, come here for a minute. [*He turns.*]

CRAIG. What?

MRS. CRAIG. Listen. [*She glances over his shoulder after Mrs. Harold, then lowers her voice.*] Billy Birkmire 'ull very likely want you to go out there with him to Fergus' funeral; but don't you do it. And you'd better tell him not to go around there either; for one of you is apt to say something. And if that butler out there sees *you*, he might recognize you. And there's no use starting anything now, when the things all over. [*He looks at her steadily.*]

CRAIG. Is that all you wanted to tell me?

MRS. CRAIG. Well, it's the thing to do, isn't it? It certainly wouldn't help matters *now* to say anything, would it? What are you smiling at?

CRAIG. At your wanting to help matters.

MRS. CRAIG. So I *have* wanted to help them.

CRAIG. Since when?

MRS. CRAIG. [*Turning away to the center table*] Well, don't let's go into all that again. I've been wanting to help *you* principally, but you don't seem to have sense enough to appreciate it.

CRAIG. Is that all you want me for?

MRS. CRAIG. No, it isn't all I want you for. I want to know about that ornament there that was broken here last night.

CRAIG. What about it?

MRS. CRAIG. I don't know *what* about it; that's the reason I'm asking you. Mrs. Harold tells me here this morning that you told her last night that you'd broken it.

CRAIG. So I did.

MRS. CRAIG. Well, you ought to be proud of yourself.

CRAIG. I was for a moment.

MRS. CRAIG. What were you doing—leaning against the mantelpiece again as usual?

CRAIG. No, it wasn't an accident; I did it deliberately.

MRS. CRAIG. What do you mean, you did it deliberately?

CRAIG. I mean that I smashed it purposely.

MRS. CRAIG. What for?

CRAIG. I became suddenly heroic.

MRS. CRAIG. I don't believe you.

CRAIG. [*Turning away*] Very well, that's that.

MRS. CRAIG. Why would you deliberately break a beautiful, expensive ornament like that?

CRAIG. [*Turning back*] I didn't break it.

MRS. CRAIG. Well, you said you did.

CRAIG. [*Bitterly*] I said I smashed it—into a thousand little pieces, right here on these bricks here. And then I smoked one cigarette after another, till I had your sanctum sanctorum here absolutely littered with ashes and cigarette butts. I was positively a hell of a fellow around here for about an hour last night; you should have seen me.

MRS. CRAIG. What did you do, go out of your mind or something?

CRAIG. No, I was particularly clear in my mind, strange to say. You made a remark here last night, Harriet, that completely illuminated me; and illuminated you. And suddenly I saw—for the first time—everything—just as one sees an entire landscape at midnight in a flash of lightning. But, unfortunately, the lightning struck my house—and knocked it down; and I sat here all night wondering how I might build it up again.

MRS. CRAIG. What remark are you talking about?

CRAIG. You said that a woman might lose her husband but not her home, if she knew how to secure it.

MRS. CRAIG. Well, hasn't many a woman lost her husband?

CRAIG. And many a man has lost his life too, Harriet, because his wife has never made a sufficiently illuminating remark. But you did make it. And that other remark—when you said there were ways of getting rid of people without driving them away from the house. [*He smiles bitterly.*] I saw your entire plan of life, Harriet, and its relationship to me. And my instinct of self-preservation suggested the need of immediate action—the inauguration of a new régime here: so I smashed the little ornament there—as a kind of opening gun. And I was going to smash all the other little ornaments—and Gods you had set up in the temple here, and been worshipping before me. I was going to put my house in order, including my wife; and rule it with a rod of iron. [*Mrs. Craig turns away, faintly amused.*] I don't wonder that amuses you; it amused me; particularly when I suddenly remembered the truth of what you called me last night; and in view of that, the absurdity of my trying to sustain such a role indefinitely. It made me laugh—but I'm rather sorry you couldn't have seen me, anyway; I think you would at least have appreciated the sincerity of my *attempt* to continue here as your husband. [*He turns slowly and moves towards the portières.*]

MRS. CRAIG. What do you mean, your attempt to continue here as my husband?

CRAIG. The role is not *for* me, Harriet; I can only play a romantic part. [*She turns her head quietly and looks at him; and he holds her eye for a second, then goes out through the portières; and she stands looking after him. Then she moves slowly to the portières and stands, thinking. The doorbell rings, but evidently she doesn't hear it. She moves forward slowly, still thinking narrowly. Mrs. Howard comes through the portières hurriedly.*]

MRS. CRAIG. There's someone at the door, Mrs. Harold. [*The doorbell rings again.*]

MRS. HAROLD. [*Hurrying across to answer the door*] I guess maybe it's the man for Miss Austen's things.

MRS. CRAIG. Is Miss Austen leaving already?

MRS. HAROLD. [*Stopping near the door*] I think so; she said last night she was going first thing in the morning.

MRS. CRAIG. Is she up?

MRS. HAROLD. Yes, ma'm, she asked me to call her at seven. [*She goes out, and Mrs. Craig crosses after her.*]

MRS. CRAIG. Well, if that's the man for her things, Mrs. Harold, have him go round to the side door and bring her things down the back stairway; I don't want him dragging trunks down these front stairs. [*She steps to the bay window at the left and looks out at the expressman.*]

EXPRESSMAN. Trunks ready?

MRS. HAROLD. Yes, they're ready. Would you mind going around to the side door; you can bring them down the back way.

EXPRESSMAN. Around this way?

MRS. HAROLD. Yes, up the steps; I'll open it for you. [*The screen door slams, and she hurries in again, crossing towards the portières.*]

MRS. CRAIG. Are Miss Austen's things ready, Mrs. Harold?

MRS. HAROLD. Yes, ma'm, I helped her pack last night.

MRS. CRAIG. Did she say where she was going?

MRS. HAROLD. [*Stopping*] Yes, ma'm; she sez she's going to the Ritz-Carlton Hotel now, but after that she sez she's going to travel. [*Continuing to the portières*] I must open the door for that man. [*She goes out, and Mrs. Craig stands looking after her, thinking. She moves across towards the portières and stops again, looking out through the portières. Ethel hurries down the stairs, with her hat and coat on.*]

MRS. CRAIG. Ethel, dear child, what are you doing up so early?

ETHEL. I haven't been asleep all night. I've been waiting to hear some one else up.

MRS. CRAIG. You're not ill, are you dear?

ETHEL. No, but I must go home immediately, Aunt Harriet; I'm too troubled in my mind to stay here any longer.

MRS. CRAIG. But you can't go immediately, dear.

ETHEL. I must go, Aunt Harriet.

MRS. CRAIG. But there's no train, dear, until the nine-seventeen.

ETHEL. Well, that's nearly now, isn't it? [*Mrs. Craig looks at her watch.*]

MRS. CRAIG. It isn't a quarter of nine yet.

ETHEL. Well, it'll take that time to get to the station, won't it?

MRS. CRAIG. It doesn't take ten minutes, dear, in a taxicab; and I can have one here in five minutes.

ETHEL. [*Putting her bag on the table and crossing down to the mirror*] Well, will you call one, please?

MRS. CRAIG. Certainly, dear; but there's no use calling it already, you'd only have to wait around the station there.

ETHEL. I'm so worried, Aunt Harriet.

MRS. CRAIG. I know, dear child; but I'm sure you're upsetting yourself unnecessarily; we certainly would have heard something if anything had happened.

ETHEL. [*Turning to Mrs. Craig*] I really should call Mr. Fredericks on the long distance, Aunt Harriet; he'll be wondering what on earth is the matter. Because I rushed away as soon as ever I got Dr. Wood's wire, and simply left a note that Mother was very ill. And he's probably called me up at home by this time and found that I'm down here; and he won't know what to think of it.

MRS. CRAIG. Well, I wouldn't worry myself too much about what he'll think, dear.

ETHEL. But he'll think it's funny that I should be down here if Mother's so ill. [*There is a sound upstairs of a trunk being moved.*]

MRS. CRAIG. [*Dashing towards the stairs and up on to the landing*] He probably hasn't given it a thought.

ETHEL. [*Moving across above the table and looking out the bay window*] Oh, don't say that, Aunt Harriet, I know he has. [*Mrs. Craig claps her hands briskly, to attract the expressman's attention.*]

MRS. CRAIG. Please be careful of that floor there, Mr. Expressman, will you?

EXPRESSMAN. This baby got away from me. I thought it was lighter than it is.

MRS. CRAIG. Well, please try to keep it away from that wall there; I don't want that wall all scratched up; I only had it painted in April. [*There is a sound of the trunk being dragged along the hallway to the back stairs, and then a heavy thud. Mrs. Craig closes her eyes in an agony of suffering and leans heavily upon the banister to keep from fainting. Then she turns and comes down into the room again.*] Mr. Craig's aunt is sending some luggage away to be mended; and those expressman are so careless they don't care if they tear down the house.

ETHEL. I haven't had a chance to speak to Miss Austen yet.

MRS. CRAIG. I suppose she's getting dressed.

ETHEL. I haven't seen Uncle Walter yet, either.

MRS. CRAIG. He's out there having some coffee, I believe. Don't you want to come out and have some too, dear?

ETHEL. I don't think I could touch a thing, Aunt Harriet.

MRS. CRAIG. You could take a sip of coffee.

ETHEL. I don't want Uncle Walter to see me looking so terrible.

MRS. CRAIG. What does it matter, darling; he understands the circumstances. And you really shouldn't start on that trip back home without something. And when you do go back, Ethel, I want you to consider seriously what I've been saying to you about Mr. Fredericks. You're not married to him yet; and if there's anything to be done, it's now that it must be done. You can't come back and undo a thing like marriage.

ETHEL. Oh, I don't know what to do, Aunt Harriet.

MRS. CRAIG. Well, there's no hurry about doing anything just now. And don't let him hurry you. Just think it over—for his sake as well as for your own. You don't want to be a burden to him, do you?

ETHEL. Certainly not.

MRS. CRAIG. Well, what else would you be to him, dear—unless you used your own money? And that isn't conducive to respect for a man. And, in any case, you'd find in time that he'd come to resent your independence of him.

MISS AUSTEN. [*At the head of the stairs*] Yes, I have it here in my bag, Mrs. Harold.

MRS. CRAIG. [*Drawing Ethel towards the portières*] So just think it over. And come on out to the breakfast room and let me get you something. [*They go out through the portières. Miss Austen comes down the stairs, dressed for the street. She glances through the portières and picks up the telephone.*]

MISS AUSTEN. [*Into the telephone*] Will you give me Market, three, three, three, three, please? Please. [*Mrs. Harold comes down the stairs, dressed for the street and carrying a suit case and a smaller bag.*] I think you might as well take those right out on to the porch, Mrs. Harold.

MRS. HAROLD. [*Going out*] Yes, ma'm.

MISS AUSTEN. Have them ready when the cab comes. [*Into the telephone*] Hello.—Will you please send a taxicab to six hundred and eighty Belmont Manor, right away, please? Yes. [*She sets the telephone down and Mrs. Harold comes in.*] It'll be here in a few minutes, Mrs. Harold. Are you all ready?

MRS. HAROLD. Yes, ma'm, I'm ready.

MISS AUSTEN. Hadn't you better speak to Mrs. Craig about your keys, Mrs. Harold?

MRS. HAROLD. I left them with yours up on her dressing table.

MISS AUSTEN. I think you'd better tell her, Mrs. Harold.

MRS. HAROLD. Do you want me to tell them *you're* going?

MISS AUSTEN. [*Going towards the door*] No, it isn't necessary, Mrs. Harold; I'll write to Mr. Craig. But, I think you'd better tell them that *you're* going.

MRS. HAROLD. I did tell Mr. Craig I was going; I told him this morning.

MISS AUSTEN. Well, I think you'd better tell Mrs. Craig, also.

MRS. HAROLD. Yes, ma'm.

MISS AUSTEN. There might be something she'd want to ask you.

MRS. HAROLD. All right, I'll tell her.

MISS AUSTEN. I'll sit here on the porch till the taxi comes. [*She goes out, and Mrs. Harold goes to the mirror and straightens her funny hat.*]

MRS. CRAIG. [*Coming through the adjoining room*] Are you in there, Mrs. Harold? [*Mrs. Harold moves up to the foot of the stairs and stands facing the portières. Mrs. Craig comes in.*] Oh, I've been looking for you out there, Mrs. Harold; I wanted you to give my niece a little breakfast.

MRS. HAROLD. I've left everything ready out there, Mrs. Craig.

MRS. CRAIG. Where are you going, Mrs. Harold?

MRS. HAROLD. Why, I'm going with Miss Austen, Mrs. Craig.

MRS. CRAIG. Indeed?

MRS. HAROLD. She was tellin' me last night she was goin' to leave here, and I said I thought I'd be leaving pretty soon myself; so she said if I was goin' anyway soon, she'd like very much to have me go with her.

MRS. CRAIG. And where are you going with her?

MRS. HAROLD. Why, we are goin' to the Ritz-Carlton first, and after that she sez she's goin' to travel for a few years.

MRS. CRAIG. Well, that ought to be a very good experience for you.

MRS. HAROLD. Yes, I've never been many places outside of here and Long Branch, and I thought I'd better take the chance while I had it.

MRS. CRAIG. And do you think it's very considerate of you, Mrs. Harold, to walk away this way without giving me any notice?

MRS. HAROLD. You didn't give Mazie much notice last night, Mrs. Craig.

MRS. CRAIG. Mazie didn't deserve any notice; she was a very disobedient girl. She absolutely refused to do what I told her.

MRS. HAROLD. Well, I haven't always done exactly what you told me to do, either, Mrs. Craig—so maybe I deserve to go as well as Mazie.

MRS. CRAIG. Well, of course, you can suit yourself about going, Mrs. Harold, but you understand I shall have to tell Miss Hewlitt about your leaving without notice.

MRS. HAROLD. Miss Hewlitt knows all about my leaving, Mrs. Craig; she's surprised that I didn't leave a long time ago, to tell you the truth.

MRS. CRAIG. And why didn't you leave?

MRS. HAROLD. Well—there were no children—and it's near church. But Miss Hewlitt told me when I came here that if I stayed a month I'd be the first out of seven that did.

MRS. CRAIG. Miss Hewlitt has sent some very unsatisfactory women here.

MRS. HAROLD. A lot of them have worked in some pretty fine places.

MRS. CRAIG. [*Turning away, and moving down to the mirror*] Well, of course, that depends upon what a person's idea of a fine place is. And I suppose the next *batch* she sends me won't be any more satisfactory than the rest.

MRS. HAROLD. I think you're very foolish to have her send any more, Mrs. Craig, if you ask me.

MRS. CRAIG. One person can't do everything.

MRS. HAROLD. I've heard you say yourself more than once that you had to do over again everything that any woman that ever worked for you did—so why not save the money? [*Mrs. Craig turns from the mirror and comes towards her.*]

MRS. CRAIG. What about the keys?

MRS. HAROLD. I left them all on your dressin' table upstairs; and Miss Austen's too.

MRS. CRAIG. Wasn't there anything else to be left?

MRS. HAROLD. Yes, ma'm. I left the money that I had over with the week's list in an envelope with the keys.

MRS. CRAIG. [*Turning towards the portières*] All right—I hope you enjoy your world tour.

MRS. HAROLD. [*Going towards the front door*] It'll be a change, anyway. [*Mrs. Craig turns at the portières.*]

MRS. CRAIG. And I hope when you come back, you'll be able to find a place that'll be as easy as this one has been.

MRS. HAROLD. [*Stopping at the door and turning*] Don't worry about me, Mrs. Craig; nobody belongin' to me ever died in the poorhouse. [*She goes out on to the porch, and Mrs. Craig looks after her stonily. The front doorbell rings incisively, and Mrs. Craig steps forward at the right and looks keenly towards the front door.*]

FREDERICKS. [*At the front door*] How do you do?

MRS. HAROLD. How do you do?

FREDERICKS. I should like to see Miss Landreth, if I could. My name is Fredericks. [*Mrs. Craig makes a rapid movement of consternation, then looks at the portières. Ethel comes through the portières.*]

[*Ethel and Mrs. Harold, speaking together*]

ETHEL. I think I'd better get my things, Aunt Harriet; it must be nearly nine o'clock.

MRS. HAROLD. Oh, come in, please. I think Miss Landreth is just having her breakfast. [*The screen door slams.*]

[*Ethel and Fredericks, speaking together*]

ETHEL. Would you mind telephoning for a taxicab?

FREDERICKS. I suppose I am a bit early. [*Ethel hears his voice and stops at the foot of the stairs. Mrs. Craig glides out through the portières. Mrs. Harold comes in at the front door.*]

MRS. HAROLD. Oh, I was just comin' to call you, Miss Landreth; there's a Mr. Fredericks here to see you. [*He comes in.*]

FREDERICKS. Hello, Ethel. [*Mrs. Harold passes to the door, back of him, and goes out again.*]

ETHEL. Gene, there isn't anything happened to Mother?

FREDERICKS. Not a thing in the world, dear, that I know of.

ETHEL. You're sure?

FREDERICKS. 'Pon my word, Ethel. I haven't been to your house.

ETHEL. Well, why did you come away down here, then, at this hour of the morning?

FREDERICKS. [*Taking a step to her*] I wanted to see *you.* [*She begins to cry, and he takes her in his arms.*] I thought maybe you were ill or something. Don't cry, darling; I give you my word there isn't a thing wrong at home. I simply telephoned you as soon as I got your note, and they told me you'd left for here: so then I called you on the long distance. But I couldn't get any satisfaction on the long distance, and I didn't know what to think. So I just jumped on the night train and got in here at eight-twenty.

ETHEL. [*Straightening up and touching her hair*] I'm going back right away, Gene; there's a train at nine-seventeen from the station down town.

FREDERICKS. I'll go back with you.

ETHEL. I don't know why I ever came away in the first place.

FREDERICKS. [*Guiding her to the chair at the right of the piano*] Sit down here for a minute, dear; you look terribly pale. [*He puts his hat on the piano.*]

ETHEL. I haven't closed my eyes since I've been here, I've been so worried.

FREDERICKS. I've been worried about *you*, too, ever since I got your note.

ETHEL. And then I told Aunt Harriet about our engagement, and that upset me more than ever.

FREDERICKS. Why?

ETHEL. Oh, she didn't seem to approve of it exactly.

FREDERICKS. Why not?

ETHEL. [*Rising*] Oh, for several reasons, Gene—I'll tell you on the train. [*She starts for the foot of the stairs.*]

FREDERICKS. [*Taking her hand as she passes him*] I wish you'd tell me now, Ethel.

ETHEL. [*Turning to him*] There isn't time, dear.

FREDERICKS. But you make me uneasy.

ETHEL. It's nothing, Gene, particularly. She simply said she thought perhaps I hadn't considered the thing sufficiently.

FREDERICKS. What is there to consider, darling, in a thing of this kind—except that we love each other.

ETHEL. But she said a thing like marriage should be considered more practically.

FREDERICKS. I don't accept that argument, Ethel; I've seen too many carefully reasoned marriages turn out badly. It's simply a chance that one has to take, more or less. And I have a good way of getting along.

ETHEL. As a single man, yes.

FREDERICKS. And even as a married man.

ETHEL. You don't know that yet, Gene, whether you have or not.

FREDERICKS. But other fellows marry, darling, and get along, on a great deal less salary than I'm getting.

ETHEL. I know that, Gene; but, as Aunt Harriet says, their wives are not living the way I've been accustomed to living. Not that I'd mind that in the least, dear; only I wouldn't want you to feel that I was making any sacrifices. And she says you might feel that in your present circumstances.

FREDERICKS. But haven't you any faith in my ability to improve those circumstances?

ETHEL. Of course; but I wouldn't want to be a burden to you in the meantime.

FREDERICKS. But your the kind of burden I need, Ethel. You know I've had three promotions since I've known you.

ETHEL. Yes, I know you have.

FREDERICKS. Well, I attribute it to nothing but the incentive that the thought of marrying you has given me. I've worked like a dog these past two years, with just that in mind; and if it were removed—well, I just don't think beyond that, that's all. [*He turns away to the left a few steps and stands looking straight out. She crosses and lays her hand on his arm.*]

ETHEL. I hadn't thought of not marrying you, Gene; I was just thinking whether or not it would be wise to postpone it.

FREDERICKS. [*Turning to her*] It *wouldn't* be wise, Ethel; it isn't a good thing to postpone a thing like marriage—so many things happen. [*He suddenly takes her into his arms.*] And I don't want anything to happen.

ETHEL. What else have I got, Gene, if anything happened to Mother? [*She buries her face in his shoulder and cries hard.*]

FREDERICKS. Nothing's going to happen to her, sweetheart. And if it did, you wouldn't feel any worse than I'd feel if anything happened to this. [*She continues to cry for a second, then straightens up and presses her handkerchief to her eyes.*]

ETHEL. We'd better go, Gene, it must be nearly nine o'clock. [*She starts across below the table towards the mirror, and Fredericks starts across above the table towards the telephone. Craig comes in through the portières.*]

FREDERICKS. I'd better call a taxi, hadn't I?

ETHEL. Oh, Uncle Walter—this is Mr. Fredericks. [*Fredericks continues over to shake hands with Craig, and Ethel moves up to Frederick's left.*]

CRAIG. [*Shaking hands*] I'm glad to meet you, Mr. Fredericks.

FREDERICKS. How do you do, Mr. Craig?

ETHEL. Mr. Fredericks is the young man I'm engaged to be married to.

CRAIG. Well, I *am* glad to meet you.

FREDERICKS. Pretty lucky fellow, don't you think, Mr. Craig?

CRAIG. I'd say you were. And is it all set?

FREDERICKS. I hope so; although Ethel seems to feel a little nervous about it.

CRAIG. What are you nervous about, Ethel?

ETHEL. I'm not nervous—it isn't that. But I was telling Gene that I'd been discussing it with Aunt Harriet, and she seemed to think that probably I hadn't considered it enough. [*Fredericks looks at Craig.*]

CRAIG. What did she want you to consider?

ETHEL. Well, she said on account of my age she didn't think I appreciated the practical side of marriage enough.

CRAIG. That's the one side of marriage that should not be appreciated too much, Ethel; it's a lack of faith in each other.

FREDERICKS. That's what I tell Ethel.

CRAIG. The only thing I think you need to consider really seriously—is whether or not you are both absolutely honest with each other. [*Fredericks looks at Ethel, and Craig crosses below them towards the stairs.*] It doesn't seem to me that there's very much else to worry about.

ETHEL. We're going back on that nine-seventeen, Uncle Walter; do you know the number of the taxicab company?

CRAIG. You won't need a taxi, I'm going right down past the station.

ETHEL. Are you going now?

CRAIG. Right away, yes. I'll get my hat. You have plenty of time; I can get you down there in less than ten minutes.

ETHEL. Uncle Walter, will you bring my satchel down when you're coming?

CRAIG. Yes, I'll get it.

ETHEL. It's on the chair there, right inside my door. [*Picking up her bag from the table and crossing down to the mirror to fix herself*] We won't have to call a taxi. [*Fredericks glances out through the portières, then comes forward, lowering his voice.*]

FREDERICKS. Did your aunt tell you I called you last night? [*Ethel turns and looks at him.*]

ETHEL. On the long distance, you mean?

FREDERICKS. Yes, I called you from Northampton as soon as I got your note. I called you at home first, of course, and they gave me this address.

ETHEL. And you called here?

FREDERICKS. Yes, about seven o'clock. Didn't she tell you?

ETHEL. No, she didn't, Gene.

FREDERICKS. I talked to her. She said you were asleep.

ETHEL. I couldn't have been asleep, Gene.

FREDERICKS. I asked her to call you to the telephone, but she didn't seem to want to do it. She said you'd just gotten in and you were tired out.

ETHEL. Well, I *was* tired, but she could have called me; she might have known I'd want to talk to you. Because I didn't know what you'd think of my being down here, after leaving word that I was going home.

FREDERICKS. Have you seen her this morning?

ETHEL. Yes, but she didn't say anything about it. And I was talking to her here this morning about you, too. I was saying that I ought to call *you* on the long distance, that you'd be wondering what was the matter.

CRAIG. [*Hurrying down the stairs with Ethel's satchel*] I'll run over and get the car.

FREDERICKS. Can I take that, Mr. Craig?

CRAIG. I'll leave it out here on the porch. I'll be back in two minutes. You have lots of time.

FREDERICKS. [*Going to the piano for his hat*] Are you ready, Ethel?

ETHEL. Yes, I'm ready, Gene. I'd better say goodbye to Aunt Harriet.

FREDERICKS. Will I wait for you outside?

ETHEL. Don't you want to meet her, Gene?

FREDERICKS. I don't think she wants to meet me, Ethel.

ETHEL. Why not?

FREDERICKS. After what you've been telling me.

ETHEL. Oh, that's nothing, Gene.

FREDERICKS. She hung up on me last night.

ETHEL. Yes, I want to ask her about that call.

FREDERICKS. [*Going out*] I think I'd better wait for you outside. [*Ethel glances through the portières, then comes forward thoughtfully at the right. There is a slight pause. Then Mrs. Craig glides through the portières and across to the bay window to look out. Ethel watches her narrowly, then moves to the right end of the center table.*]

ETHEL. I'm just going, Aunt Harriet. [*Mrs. Craig turns, slightly startled.*]

MRS. CRAIG. Oh, I thought you'd gone. [*She comes back towards Ethel.*] I didn't hear anybody in here, and I was wondering if you'd gone without telling me.

ETHEL. No, I'm just going.

FREDERICKS. Where are Mr. Craig and Mr. Fredericks?

ETHEL. Mr. Fredericks is there on the porch. [*Mrs. Craig turns to the front door and glances out.*] Uncle Walter's gone over to get the car.

MRS. CRAIG. Oh, he's going to drive you in.

ETHEL. Yes.

MRS. CRAIG. Well, that'll be fine—you won't have to bother calling a taxi. [*Coming forward to Ethel again*] Did Mr. Fredericks have any word about your mother?

ETHEL. No, he hadn't been home.

MRS. CRAIG. Why don't you call him in, Ethel; I should like to meet him.

ETHEL. He thought probably you wouldn't care to meet him.

MRS. CRAIG. Why, how absurd. Why not?

ETHEL. I was telling him about what you said last night, when I told you I was going to marry him.

MRS. CRAIG. Well, my dear child, I was simply talking in a general way. My remarks weren't directed against Mr. Fredericks particularly. I'm sure he'd appreciate the logic of what I said himself.

ETHEL. He doesn't, Aunt Harriet; I told him what you said, and he takes quite the opposite view.

MRS. CRAIG. Well, of course, he has considerable to gain by the transaction, Ethel, you must remember that.

ETHEL. Well, Uncle Walter has nothing to gain by it, and he agrees with him.

MRS. CRAIG. Well, you remember I told you last night that Mr. Craig was extremely romantic.

ETHEL. [*Becoming very stony*] Why didn't you call me last night, Aunt Harriet, when Mr. Fredericks telephoned?

MRS. CRAIG. Because you were asleep, dear.

ETHEL. I couldn't have been asleep. I haven't closed my eyes since I've been here.

MRS. CRAIG. Well, I thought you were asleep, Ethel; I sent Mazie up to your room and she said your door was closed.

ETHEL. Well, she could have rapped.

MRS. CRAIG. Well, what was the sense of upsetting you, dear?

ETHEL. Because it was important to me.

MRS. CRAIG. I asked him if it was important, and if there was any message he wanted to leave, and he said no.

ETHEL. And you hung up on him.

MRS. CRAIG. Because he insisted upon talking to you; and you were not in any condition to be talked to. [*She turns and moves towards the bay window.*]

ETHEL. Why didn't you tell me this morning that he'd called—when I said I should call him?

MRS. CRAIG. [*Turning coldly*] Now, please, Ethel dear—I shan't answer any more questions about Mr. Fredericks. [*She goes to the bay window to look out.*] I've had quite enough to worry me this morning without thinking about Mr. Fredericks. He's going back with you, I suppose?

ETHEL. [*Crossing up to the front door*] Yes.

MRS. CRAIG. [*Turning to her*] Well, I'm glad you won't have to make the trip alone. Goodbye, dear. [*She kisses her.*] I hope you'll let me know right away how you find your mother.

ETHEL. [*Holding her hand*] Aunt Harriet—

MRS. CRAIG. What, dear?

ETHEL. [*After a pause, and holding her eye*] Aunt Harriet, is Uncle Walter *leaving* you?

MRS. CRAIG. Why, what on earth ever put that into your head, Ethel?

ETHEL. Something he was saying when I came to the head of the stairs to come down this morning.

MRS. CRAIG. And what was he saying?

ETHEL. Something about your having made a remark that made it impossible for him to continue here as your husband.

MRS. CRAIG. I'm sure I haven't the faintest idea what you're talking about, Ethel.

ETHEL. And then a while ago here, when I told him I was going to be married to Mr. Fredericks, he said the only thing we needed to consider seriously was whether or not we were absolutely honest with each other. And I was wondering if he'd found out.

MRS. CRAIG. Found out what?

ETHEL. That that you told me last night—when I said I didn't think it was honest. [*There was a movement on the front porch. The screen door slams, and Mrs. Craig turns away quickly and looks out the bay window.*]

CRAIG. [*Outside*] All set?

FREDERICKS. [*Outside*] All set. Ethel's inside.

ETHEL. [*Going out*] Goodbye, Aunt Harriet.

MRS. CRAIG. [*Turning and following her to the door*] Goodbye, dear.

ETHEL. I'll write you as soon as I get home.

MRS. CRAIG. Do, dear; let me know how your mother is.

ETHEL. Yes, I shall. [*The screen door slams.*]

CRAIG. Ready, Ethel?

ETHEL. Yes, I'm coming, Uncle Walter. [*Mrs. Craig turns nervously and moves across and down to the mantelpiece.*]

CRAIG. Your satchel's in the car. I'll be with you in a minute. [*He comes in, taking a little leather key case from his pocket, and crosses to the portières.*]

MRS. CRAIG. Are you going to the office now?

CRAIG. Yes, it's nearly nine o'clock. [*He goes through the portières, and Mrs. Craig moves up to the portières.*]

MRS. CRAIG. Mrs. Harold says you haven't been in bed all night; you won't feel much like sitting at a desk all day.

CRAIG. [*From the other room*] I'll have plenty of time to rest after a bit. [*Mrs. Craig's eyes narrow, in an attempt to fathom this remark. She comes forward again at the right, slowly and thoughtfully. Craig enters, fastening the little key case, and crosses towards the front door, picking up his hat from the table as he passes.*]

MRS. CRAIG. Did you find what you were looking for?

CRAIG. I wasn't looking for anything—I was just leaving the key to your car and the garage, with some other things I've left there for you. [*He turns at the door.*] If you should want me for anything during the next week or two, Harriet, I'll be at the Ritz. [*She turns suddenly and makes a rapid movement to the center table.*]

MRS. CRAIG. Now, listen to me, Walter Craig, you're surely not serious about leaving this house.

CRAIG. Why, I should think that decision would please you very much.

MRS. CRAIG. Well, it doesn't please me at all; it's absolutely ridiculous.

MR. CRAIG. But it's so absolutely practical.

MRS. CRAIG. Oh, don't try to be funny.

CRAIG. And you've been deploring my lack of practicality so long.

MRS. CRAIG. I'd like to know what's practical about a man walking out and leaving his wife and his home.

CRAIG. I have no wife to leave—for you neither loved nor honored me.

MRS. CRAIG. Well, you married me, whether I did or not.

CRAIG. I never saw you before in my life, Harriet—until last night.

MRS. CRAIG. You married me, didn't you?

CRAIG. And you married a house; and if it's agreeable to you, I'll see that you have it; and that you can go on having it, just as though I were here.

MRS. CRAIG. [*Turning away towards the mantelpiece*] You'll be here; unless I'm very much mistaken.

CRAIG. You don't know your man, Harriet.

MRS. CRAIG. I know him well enough for that, anyway.

CRAIG. Oh, you knew me pretty well, I'll grant you that; particularly when you said my mind worked very slowly.

MRS. CRAIG. It's working pretty slowly now, when you don't appreciate the absurdity of a move of this kind.

CRAIG. But you failed to reckon with the thoroughness of my mind, Harriet, when it *does* work. And it appreciates this situation so thoroughly that it has no illusions about the impossibility of my continuance here.

MRS. CRAIG. What is there so impossible about it?

CRAIG. We've shown our hands, Harriet, and the game is up.

MRS. CRAIG. What did I do last night that was so terrible?

CRAIG. You simply showed your hand, that was all.

MRS. CRAIG. I simply kept you from making a fool of yourself; that was all I did.

CRAIG. But you also showed me how I could keep from making a fool of myself in the future.

MRS. CRAIG. Well, you're certainly not beginning very auspiciously, I can tell you that.

CRAIG. But I shall be at least a self-respecting fool; and that's something I could never be if I stayed here. There's something in a man, Harriet, that I suppose is his essential manhood; and you insulted that last night. And I should be too embarrassed here, under your eye, knowing that you had no respect for that manhood. I should remember my lover's ardors and enthusiasms for our future; and you bearing with me contemptuously, for the sake of *your* future. I couldn't stand it.

MRS. CRAIG. You're not telling the truth; I always respected you; and I never had anything but respect for your plans, either.

CRAIG. Don't try to soften the blow, Harriet; I assure you it isn't necessary. [*He turns towards the door, and she makes a move towards him.*]

MRS. CRAIG. Where are you going when you leave here? [*He turns and looks at her.*]

CRAIG. That 'ud be rather interesting to know, Harriet—where a lot like me are going.—Out of fashion, possibly.

MRS. CRAIG. Well, what about your things?—Aren't you going to take anything with you?

CRAIG. You may send them to me if you like.

MRS. CRAIG. [*Turning away*] Well, I won't send them to you; for you'll very likely be back again within a week.

CRAIG. Perhaps it will be just as well if you don't send them to me, Harriet—for I'm rather sentimental about things; and I might look back, and be turned into a romantic fool.

MRS. CRAIG. Oh, I suppose you'll never forgive me for calling you that.

CRAIG. No, there isn't a thing in the world I don't forgive you for, Harriet; that's the reason it won't be necessary for me to come back here anymore; there's nothing to adjust. I guess possibly I'm just a bit of an old-fashioned man—I must be trusted—and you never trusted me.

MRS. CRAIG. I wouldn't trust any man after what I've seen.

CRAIG. I don't blame you. But I wonder that, with all your wisdom, it never occurred to you that one cannot play a dishonest game indefinitely.

MRS. CRAIG. I haven't played any dishonest game.

CRAIG. Possibly not, according to your standards; but I think you have. And I think you know you have. And that's the rock that you and I are splitting on, Harriet. If this affair at Passmore's hadn't revealed you, something else would: so my going may as well be today as tomorrow. Goodbye, Harriet. [*He goes out; she leans on the table. The screen door slams. She moves over to the bay window and watches him get into the automobile: then she comes forward to the window at the right and watches him down the street. After he has passed beyond her vision, her gaze wanders into the room again, and she becomes conscious of two tiny pieces of the broken ornament near the mantelpiece. She stoops and picks them up, flicking away with her foot any other invisible particles that may be about. Then she looks at the two remaining ornaments on the mantelpiece and tries to come to some conclusion about their arrangement. She places them equi-distant from each other and the ends of the mantel-*]

piece, and stands off to observe the effect. The front doorbell rings sharply. She turns and crosses to answer it.]

BOY'S VOICE. [*At the front door*] Telegram for Mrs. Walter Craig. [*She signs for the telegram, the screen door slams and she comes in, opening the telegram. She reads the telegram, looks straight ahead for a second, thinking—looks at the wire again, and bursts into tears—sinking into the chair at the right of the piano. She cries hard for a moment, then smooths the telegram out and reads it again. Mrs. Frazier appears in the door, dressed in gray, and carrying an armload of white roses. She comes forward inquiringly.*]

MRS. FRAZIER. Good morning, Mrs. Craig. [*Mrs. Craig doesn't hear her.*] Good morning. [*Mrs. Craig looks at her, startled, gets up nervously and moves across to the front of the center table, touching her eyes and her hair.*] I do hope you'll pardon my walking in without ringing, but I thought Miss Austen 'ud be on the front porch, and I wanted to bring her these roses. [*She hands Mrs. Craig the roses.*] I was telling her yesterday I'd bring her over some; she was saying she admired white roses so much; and I have so many of them over there just now.

MRS. CRAIG. I haven't seen her yet this morning.

MRS. FRAZIER. [*Preparing to go*] Well, if you'll just tell her I left them.

MRS. CRAIG. Yes, I shall; thanks ever so much.

MRS. FRAZIER. [*Turning back*] Oh, have you had any word about your sister this morning, Mrs. Craig? Miss Austen was telling me yesterday she was quite ill.

MRS. CRAIG. [*Starting to cry again*] She died this morning at six o'clock.

MRS. FRAZIER. Oh, dear me, how sad.

MRS. CRAIG. I just had this wire.

MRS. FRAZIER. Dear, dear, dear, isn't that too bad!

MRS. CRAIG. I had no idea she was so ill or I should never have come back.

MRS. FRAZIER. Dear, dear, dear, I'm so sorry. I shouldn't have bothered you at all.

MRS. CRAIG. That's quite all right.

MRS. FRAZIER. I'm sure you have my sympathy.

MRS. CRAIG. Thank you.

MRS. FRAZIER. I do hope you'll let me know, Mrs. Craig, if there's any way I can be of any service to you.

MRS. CRAIG. Thank you very much; I don't think there's anything anybody can do.

MRS. FRAZIER. I suppose you'll have to go right back up there again, won't you?

MRS. CRAIG. I don't know whether I shall be able to or not, to tell you the truth, Mrs. Frazier, it's been such a strain.

MRS. FRAZIER. Yes, those long illnesses are dreadful. But I hope you won't hesitate to let me know if there's anything I can do.

MRS. CRAIG. That's very kind of you. I'll give these roses to Miss Austen when I see her.

MRS. FRAZIER. If you will, please. [*She starts for the door.*] I'm terribly sorry. I'll run over again. [*She goes out; and Mrs. Craig stands very still until she hears the screen door close. Then she steps up to the door and clicks the latch. Then she turns, comes forward a few steps into the room again, and stands, holding the roses against her bosom and looking straight out. A clock out in one of the adjoining rooms strikes nine with a mournful gong. After the fourth gong her eyes wander in the direction of the clock and she moves slowly across towards the por-tières. Then she comes forward at the right, wandering, and crosses below the table to the piano. Several rose petals flutter to the floor. She stands at the piano for a moment, looking out through the bay win-dow, then retraces her steps. She looks unseeingly at the scattered petals, continues up towards the portières, looks out through the deserted rooms, and finally stops. A few more petals drift to the floor. The curtain commences to descend, very, very slowly. She turns deso-lately and wanders back towards the piano again, clutching the roses close, here eyes wide and despairing.*]

THE END

ʃELECTED ANNOTATED BIBLIOGRAPHY

BOOKS

Aherne, Brian. *A Proper Job*. Boston: Houghton Mifflin, 1969. Interesting comments on Kelly the director from the actor who played Walter Craig in the London production of *Craig's Wife*. Aherne calls Kelly "brilliant, but eccentric" and is surprised at the director's rigid control of his cast.

Bankhead, Tallulah. *Tallulah: My Autobiography*. New York: Harper and Brothers, 1952. The author, whom Kelly directed in *Reflected Glory*, is extravagant in her praise of his high professional standards as a dramatist and director.

Brown, John Mason. *Upstage: The American Theatre in Performance*. New York: Norton, 1930. Calls Kelly a "conscientious realist" who specializes in the everyday lives of people in their homes. Regrets the playwright's movement away form satire to serious drama. Describes Kelly as a moralist with the gift of laughter.

Flexner, Eleanor. *American Playwrights: 1918–1938*. New York: Simon and Schuster, 1938. Credits Kelly for his exposure of the "pettiness . . . of middle class life." Is especially impressed by Harriet Craig, whom she sees as a "moral phenomenon."

Gassner, John, ed. *Masters of Drama*. 3d rev. ed. New York: Dover, 1954. Praises Kelly for his vivid re-creation of character and dialogue but criticizes his "too commonplace world."

Hirsch, Foster. *George Kelly*. Boston: Twayne, 1975. By far the best book on Kelly and his career. Precise, intelligent analysis of each play, with a brief biography of the dramatist. One of the Twayne critical studies of major authors.

Kelly, Walter C. *Of Me I Sing: An Informal Autobiography*. New York: Dial Press, 1953. Largely anecdotal, personal and theatrical observations by George Kelly's monologist brother. Passing references to George's early career.

Krutch, Joseph Wood. *The American Drama Since 1918*. New York: Random House, 1939. Stresses Kelly's cold "Puritan nature" which causes him to despise aesthetic and moral vulgarity and to mete out "cruel justice" to it, especially in *Behold the Bridegroom* and *Maggie the Magnificent*.

Lewis, Arthur. *Those Philadelphia Kellys (With a Touch of Grace)*. New York: William Morrow, 1977. Contains a series of taped interviews, many with the Kelly family. Considerable space and speculation is given to the character and career of George.

McCallum, John. *That Kelly Family*. New York: Random House, 1957. Unreliable, sentimental look at the Kelly family, concentrating largely on John B. Kelly and his children John B., Jr., and Grace, Princess of Monaco. George appears only as a figure in John B., Sr.'s life.

McCarthy, Mary. *Mary McCarthy's Theatre Chronicles 1937–1962*. New York: Farrar, Straus and Co., 1963. Somewhat caustic criticism of Kelly's use of stage business, which she sees as a distraction from the superficiality of his later plays. Unusual assessment of conservative Kelly by a left-wing critic and author.

Mantle, Burns. *American Playwrights of Today*. New York: Dodd, Mead, 1929. Calls Kelly, Eugene O'Neill, and Sidney Howard the best of the 1920s dramatists. Notes Kelly's opposition to the strict plot formula.

Quinn, Arthur Hobson, *A History of the American Drama from the Civil War to the Present Day*. Rev. ed. New York: Appleton-Century-Crofts, 1936. A perceptive analysis of Kelly's development as a dramatist, from his vaudeville sketches to *Phillip Goes Forth*, by one of the earliest academic historians of the American stage.

Sievers, W. David. *Freud on Broadway*. New York: Hermitage House, 1955. An effort to analyze Kelly and his plays from a Freudian point of view. Calls Kelly "a behaviorist in drama rather than a psychologist."

ARTICLES

Bird, Carol. "The Men Who Write the Hits." *Theatre Magazine*, August 1924. Rare personal portrait of Kelly as he approaches the peak of his success. Good physical and psychological description of the dramatist, who discusses his approaches to writing and to direction.

Carmer, Carl. "George Kelly." *Theatre Arts Monthly*, April 1931. Urges Kelly to abandon his "pretentiously moral themes" and to concentrate on his talent at detailed observation of life. Thinks that Kelly may yet write "the American *Comedie Humaine*."

Crowther, Bosley. "Home, Sweet Home." *New York Times*, September 27, 1936. Interview, during which Kelly voices his negative feelings about the current (1930s) American theater.

Drutman, Irving. "Anybody Here Seen Kelly?" *New York Times*, December 3, 1967. Interview with Kelly a few years before his death. Kelly's essential conservatism and reticence about his private life are still very much present.

Maisel, Edward. "The Theater of George Kelly." *Theater Arts*, February 1947. Describes Kelly as "a moralist using the theater for simple moral purposes." Elaborates on the theme of personal vocation in his plays, which he finds "curiously out of date but . . . never dated."

Moses, Montrose J. "George Kelly." *Theater Guild Magazine*, July 1930. Comments on Kelly's resentment at the lack of refinement and culture in the United States. Detects a certain animosity toward the modern woman in Kelly's plays.

Van Druten, John. "Small Souls and Great Plays." *Theater Arts Monthly*, July 1927. Valuable evaluation of Kelly's dramatic technique by a fellow playwright. Sees Kelly's realism as selective rather than merely photographic. Defends his emphasis on "unimportant" people.

Wills, Arthur. "The Kelly Play." *Modern Drama*, December 1963. Presents Kelly as a conservative in dramatic technique, a nonexperimenter whose work looks back to the early days of theatrical realism. Notes his emphasis on characterization from the individual rather than social perspective, causing his plays to resemble sermons rather than social tracts.